READINGS IN
SOCIAL GEOGRAPHY

READINGS IN
SOCIAL GEOGRAPHY

edited by

EMRYS JONES

OXFORD UNIVERSITY PRESS
1975

Oxford University Press, Ely House, London W. 1

GLASGOW NEW YORK TORONTO MELBOURNE WELLINGTON
CAPE TOWN IBADAN NAIROBI DAR ES SALAAM LUSAKA ADDIS ABABA
DELHI BOMBAY CALCUTTA MADRAS KARACHI LAHORE DACCA
KUALA LUMPUR SINGAPORE HONG KONG TOKYO

CASEBOUND ISBN 0 19 874016 6
PAPERBACK ISBN 0 19 874060 3

© *Oxford University Press 1975*

*Typesetting by Campbell Graphics Ltd
Newcastle upon Tyne
Printed in Great Britain by*

*William Clowes & Sons, Limited
London, Beccles and Colchester*

CONTENTS

NOTE   The cover design represents the socio-economic characteristics of census
data zones in the Belfast urban area. It is reproduced from F. W. Boal's
paper 'Social Space in the Belfast Urban Area' in *Irish Geographical Studies*,
edited by Stephens and Glasscock (1970).

INTRODUCTION

A subject dealing with so wide a topic as the spatial component of human behaviour is not easy to define. If they are not too facile to be useful, definitions will always be a reflection of the time, the outlook or the philosophy of the investigator, the state of empirical knowledge of the field, the scale of investigation. Rarely do all these strands come together to satisfy a large number of people and to identify easily an academic discipline.

Geography as a whole has only recently undergone a revolution of thought which has called for a reappraisal of many of its accepted premisses.[1] The limitations of the chorographical approach and the inadequacies of the simpler explanatory models, have become only too clear following the extensive application of new analytical techniques, the borrowing of models from other fields, and, in particular, the attempt to make geography a 'scientific' study[2] —albeit one of the social sciences. Exploration of new dimensions and extensions of topics have demanded new concepts within the whole range of human geography.

On the whole the theoretical framework of social geography in the past—when it was at all apparent—was slender indeed, and totally inadequate to accommodate the spate of empirical work which has been produced over the last two decades and which is still increasing. New subject-matter has been tentatively explored and new techniques quite extensively used, even though this has often been a case of applying methods and testing models developed in other social sciences, e.g. urban ecology. The link with sociology has been particularly strong; there are several cases in Britain of academics changing their roles and their titles! But this in itself may have been an indication of how slow social geographers have been in attempting to build a coherent theory. To quote one author, social geography is still 'a field created and cultivated by a number of scholars rather than an academic discipline'. Elsewhere the same author refers to the fact that social geography has 'neither a unified concept nor even an agreed content'.[3]

The Holistic Approach

Some scholars have equated social geography with the whole of human geography. For example, Fitzgerald wrote in 1946, 'If it were possible to replace our nomenclature *ab initio*, I feel certain that I would recommend replacing "human geography" with "social geography".'[4] Harrison said that social geography was 'not a systematic treatment of society in relation to its environment, but a genetic description of social differences as they related to other factors and to differences in areas of the earth's surface'.[5] (We shall see later that this is still a fair description of much of what is being produced as social geography, probably with justification when dealing with data not previously considered.) A similar holistic approach is found in Gilbert and Steel,[6] who divided the entire field into four branches of study; population distribution, rural settlement form and distribution, urban settlement, and the distribution of social groups.

The holistic approach is made very explicit by Hans Bobek, who starts out with a conceptual framework which is universal in its application.[7] To Bobek a social geographer must look for patterns of behaviour—although these will often be seen in features of the landscape which are the results of this behaviour. These patterns can be studies on two scales, *lebensformen* (patterns of social life) and *kulturgemeinschaften* (culture groups). 'Society consists of such socially and regionally determined patterns of life, and the dissection of society into these patterns is the purpose of analysis in social geography.' Within a wider concept of geography as a whole, the social (or human/cultural) is, to Bobek, one of three spheres, the other two being the 'inorganic' and the 'organic'. The key word to Bobek's approach is 'pattern', the theme is 'integration of patterns'. The habitat is a critical element in his areal sub-division of the world, but the criteria of sub-division are primarily social. Consequently, 'regional study is the study of the fabric of identifiable groups'. This is not unlike Watson's definition of social geography, as 'the identification of different regions of the earth's surface according to the associations of social phenomena related to the total environment'.[8]

Although his conceptual basis is firmly stated and argued, many would see Bobek's work less as a novel contribution to social geography than as an indication of the introduction of a humanistic approach in post-war German geography. In many ways it is strongly reminiscent of the ideas of French geographers of half a century ago: there are echoes of the 'social basis of the personality of regions', which is also expressed admirably in Britain by Fleure and Estyn Evans, and even the later systematizers of French social geography, like Georges and Sorre.

Those scholars who have, on the other hand, thought of social geography as a particular field within human geography, have been no more forthcoming with theoretical underpinnings. Fitzgerald,[9] himself complaining of a vagueness about what it was, merely stressed that social geography was concerned 'with spatial arrangements or patterns over the world of phenomena which are of social, as distinct from political or economic significance to man'.[10]

A realization of the inadequacies of a frail structure which no longer expresses the purpose or content of social geography may lead to an increase in empirical work which will eventually contribute to new structures or to exploring theory derived from other disciplines. In either case we may well range outside the traditional bounds of geography. Social geographers have already been experimenting with many new techniques and extensively borrowing models from other fields, most promisingly within the field of urban geography and using a behavioural approach. This is a far cry from world cultural regions. Social geography has become much more systematic in its approach, and is most rewarding when dealing with dynamic models rather than with static regions.

Cultural Geography

Bobek's holistic/regional approach could be identified with cultural as well as social geography. Before exploring further the relations between social geography and sociology, it may be well to try and clarify what is meant by cultural geography. Although geographers have been slow to come to terms with behavioural studies, they have contributed widely to examining the *effects* of man's behaviour, mainly in terms of the past. It is an approach which avoids the problems of contemporary behaviour, and it is more characteristic of work which has been done in the United States. There it is usually termed 'cultural geography'.[11] The enormous contribution made by Sauer and his followers to the interpretation of the cultural landscape is a good example of such an approach.[12] Students of cultural geography focus on the works of man rather than man himself. One centre of their study is the changes made to the habitat by human exploitation—a classic example being the essays published as *Man's Role in Changing the Face of the Earth*.[13] Another focus of attention is man's exploitation of the habitat: great attention has been paid to the study of settlement forms of all kind; and not a little time devoted to the non-material aspects of culture such as language and religion, though these have been dealt with as artefacts and their distribution used to explain regional differentiation. Cultural geography has made a particularly vital impact on ideas about origins and diffusions, Sauer again making a unique contribution in this field.[14] Though the central themes are easily distinguishable it is sometimes very difficult to say where cultural geography ends and social geography begins—and probably undesirable. There are overlaps in the problems which arouse interest and in the data used to analyse them. But on the whole, the social geographer rarely gets enmeshed in the palimpsest of behavioural patterns which give historical depth to the cultural landscape, although he may try to distinguish and isolate particular behaviour patterns which explain certain contributions to the landscape.[15]

Society and Environment
The social geographer is more concerned with describing and explaining spatial elements of the society in terms of the structure of that society. Holistic and regional, or fragmentary and systematic, all approaches have this in common; that they begin with social groups. Hajdu makes explicit what many geographers have implied when he states, 'any social approach to geography implies the establishment of certain sociological laws, or at least assumptions about the behaviour of individuals as members of the group':[16] hence the concern with sociological models. This has been examined by Pahl in his contribution to *Models in Geography*.[17]

Pahl sees the sociologist and geographer coming nearest together in posing a key question which is of common interest, 'Why are some societies different from others in the way they utilise their resources and distribute themselves in space and, further, given a particular pattern of activities in relation to certain resources, what leads to change?'

Pahl is concerned with sociological models, and it would be easy to assume from this key question that the geographer is restricted to a descriptive role, the explanatory one lying in the field of sociology. In fact this may seem the only alternative to a crude environmental determinism. In so far as stress is on social groups, and in particular when the focus is on change, then it is logical to look for a conceptual approach in sociological terms. But this does not necessarily shift the field of study of social geography boldly from an environmental study to one of social structure.

Pahl's definition of social geography follows closely from the key question he posed. It is 'the study of the patterns and processes involved in understanding socially defined populations in their spatial setting'.[18] Perhaps the greatest weakness of the definition lies in the reference to 'spatial' setting, as this can be construed as nothing more than a descriptive point of reference system. Much more emphasis must be given to the way in which the use and perception of this space enters as an element in the patterns and even plays a part in the processes, in addition to the way in which the 'spatial setting' has evolved. The 'spatial setting' sounds uncomfortably like the old environmental 'stage' on which history was 'acted', even though its 'environmental' elements have been nullified to a neutral 'setting'.

The social geographer has borrowed most frequently—and with most success perhaps—from human ecology as it was developed by the urban sociologists in the United States.[19] The very word 'ecology' rings a bell to most geographers and brings them back into comforting contact with the environment. De la Blache's emphasis on the functional relation between man and the environment has been a basis of much geographical thinking. Barrow saw the whole of geography as being human ecology.[20] Much later, Max Sorre wrote, 'There is a place for an explanation drawn from the relations of a being to its environment (even though this may range from a mere concomitance to a causal relationship) and this explanation is basically ecological.'[21] This is not the place to discuss the many kinds of interpretation of the word 'ecological', even less its more recent linking with a systems approach to make an eco-system. It is interesting to speculate that such a close involvement of man with the whole of nature—in fact his acceptance as no more than another member of the animal kingdom—is a relatively recent viewpoint in the history of human thought. It is post-Darwinian, and replaces the concept of man as being different in kind, subject to moral, not scientific, laws, and whose relationships with the world of creatures were certainly not based on equality, but rather resembled more the role of 'estate manager'. The emphasis has now changed to man as the protector, preserver, and, more than anything, as the manipulator of the environment. The application of a strictly ecological explanation of human behaviour leads to a crude determinism now outmoded as a causal model; but it still leaves the environmental relationship to be explained. A functional and systems approach, avoiding the causal model, allows the introduction of diverse elements in the external environment. Alternatively, one can envisage a whole range of involvement. At one extreme the external environment is nothing more than a way of selecting points of reference to describe human activity: secondly, as we have already seen in Bobek's work, it can be the 'material sub-stratum of social reality': thirdly, factors in the environment can play a part similar to those in society influencing behaviour: fourthly, they can become more deterministic when they enter into a recognized set of relationships with a given order of social values.

Social Space

The argument shifts, however, when we appraise the environment in terms of the social values of any group of persons, when the space within which activities occur ceases to be no more than the material external objective environment.[22] Buttimer sees this as a possible central theme around which social geographical studies can revolve, and examines the concept of 'social space' in some detail.[23] This does bring us back to the geographer's prime concern with 'place', but not necessarily accepting the definition of place purely in terms of the physical habitat. Earlier works had certainly been aware that social activity bestowed characteristics on a place which were the distinguishing features of a real differentiation. As Watson said, the significant thing is not the social phenomena themselves, but the way in which they provide distinctive character to the space they fill.[24] But here we are still dealing with a given, objective space, which is then filled, so to speak, with social or behavioural characteristics. For Buttimer social space is that defined by a social order as distinct from other orders of activity in space. Much depends on how the social order perceives this space, although it is stressed that social space is a combination of perceived and real space. The subjective components of social space are supplied by the social groups themselves: the objective (real) components are themselves only socially significant elements of the whole environment.

Social space may be studied in two ways. The first is formal, emphasizing the delimitation of social regions and analysing mosaics of such regions in terms of various sub-groups in a society. The second is functional, concerned with dynamic elements—changes, movements, nodal organization, channels of circulation and of communications. This leads logically to Buttimer's definition of social geography: 'The study of areal or spatial patterns and functional relations of social groups in the context of their social environment: the internal structure and external relationship of the nodes of social activity, and the articulation of various channels of social communication'.[25]

Macro- and Micro-Studies

Reference has already been made to the growing concern of social geographers with micro-studies. Attention has been focused on the actions and reactions of groups and even on individuals and there have been references in articles to Gestalt psychology and to the stimulus-response school.[26] The data normally at the disposal of social geographers rarely meet the needs of this kind of behavioural analysis. Geographers have been concerned on the whole with aggregative studies, and the techniques for manipulating these data have become more and more sophisticated. Census material, for example, supplies plenty of data which can be manipulated in a variety of ways, mainly to provide classes of grouped individuals. The limitations of such data are twofold. First, they provide a minimum of information which enables us to study process. The population is caught in mid-flight, as it were, at a specific moment. Although this may tell us a considerable amount about the pattern of any element which we are interested in, it is completely static. Inferring processes from these is rather like inferring the plot of a film from a few stills outside a cinema. The second limitation is, that in dealing with census material we are confined to unit data: it tells nothing about social groups. Disaggregation takes us no further down the scale than, say, an enumeration district in the city, and what these data tell us are fundamentally properties of that area. We may *infer* qualities about individuals from the data, and we may *infer* relationships between sets of data for the same areal units, but both operations are open to serious questioning. Most of the geographic work in the past has assumed that we are interested in aggregate elements (e.g. regional variations are based on counties), but aggregate elements are defined by given areal units. Collecting data for a specific population—i.e. socially defined—enables us to aggregate in a totally different way and also to analyse a process.

Wayne Davies points out that dependence on 'behavioural products rather than on behaviour *per se,* e.g. on completed migrations, means that geographers have been one step behind the reality of the situation'.[27] and that this is coupled with conceptualizing in terms of the optimizing behaviour of 'rational economic man'. Net migration changes can mask gross changes which invite very different explanations. Geography has been disproportionately influenced, at least in location theory, by the idea of rational man seeking optimal solutions, and social geographers have always been concerned about the 'irrational' element which these cannot explain. This irrationality, taken to its logical conclusion, may point to the impossibility of formulating any kind of generalization about explanations.

The problem which faces us now is whether we can integrate studies of individual and aggregate behaviour. Elsewhere I have suggested a scientific framework in which behaviour on the aggregate level is a statistical expression of the total individual behaviour of a given population.[28] This means that although individuals may act in a certain way for an almost infinite variety of reasons, many of which may seem 'irrational', on the scale of the society as a whole these acts seem to conform to a limited number of patterns which can be 'explained' 'scientifically'. For example, individual movements from a suburb to a city centre can be motivated in many ways: to a geographer these motives may be subsumed in a single 'explanation' as 'journey to work'. The apparent determinacy at the macro-level hides any indeterminacy at the micro-level. The link between the two lies in the field of probability. Other geographers also see the solution in probability analysis. Curry examines the transition from individual men making decisions to groups and does so by suggesting that we accept a model of optimizing man, much as the economists have done, or of 'summation man', that is the behaviour of individuals seen through the behaviour of the group.[29] Innumerable isolated decisions on the part of individuals usually lead to a general behaviour pattern which can be nominally seen as group behaviour.

The Time Element

The search for process involves a time element. But time has another significance which may introduce identifiable patterns in the repeated behaviour of individuals. The idea of cyclic activities, that demands of space are very different at, for example, various times of the year, has always been one theme in human geography. Transhumance, seasonal farming activities, migrant labour, the journey to work, have all attracted attention. Dovetailing with studies of space on a micro-scale, it is not surprising that space-time budgeting has now been applied on the individual level. Space-time budgets are explored by keeping diaries accurately linking activities, the time given to them and their location. To the individual location is in a state of flux, and is ultimately related to allocation of time. The patterns of time-space allocation reflect identifiable norms in society because they are subject to certain constraints: in a town, for example, shopping will be limited to shopping hours. Although the use of time-budgets is by no means new, their appreciation as a means of analysing an important dimension in social geography is comparatively recent. Perhaps the most significant work in this field has been done in Sweden, where Hägerstrand[31] and his colleagues are examining the relationship between space and time in terms of constraints.

Geography and Social Problems

Recently in social geography there has been an increasing awareness of the new problems of human society and the need for geographers to apply their discipline to some aspects of these problems.[32] In Pahl's article on sociological models in geography, one of his concerns is to emphasize the need to recognize frameworks of values within which we interpret social facts. This is particularly pertinent when one goes beyond describing a static situation and tries to deal with conditions of change. He refers particularly to the social scientist who is viewing the problem, and there is a growing awareness that the social scientist, unlike the physical scientist, cannot operate in a value-neutral way. This is a plea that the values involved are made explicit, not that they imply a particular political doctrine. Recent years have certainly seen an immense growth of awareness and involvement of geographers in social problems. This has been seen by some as an emerging 'radical geography' which calls for involvement in social issues such as poverty and hunger. Clark University produced a new periodical in 1969 called *Antipode: a Radical Journal of Geography*, and its articles are an indication of the depth of involvement of the writers.[33] It would be a mistake to suppose that geographers have previously been unaware of social problems. Countless contributions concerning practical problems of society have been ranging from mortality and disease to crime and segregation. But throughout these there is an attempt to view such patterns dispassionately, and a reluctance to go beyond description to explanation and particularly to the analysis of change and to policy-making, avoiding the kind of involvement which is now advocated by some geographers. There may be a danger that the answers to some problems are 'known' before the problems have been analysed and 'the hallmark of genuine, original research questions is that you cannot foretell in advance how or when they are going to be answered'.[34] It is not easy to resolve, but undoubtedly we shall be seeing much more telling analyses of social ills—riots, discrimination, poverty—and much of this is going to be reflected in teaching, and eventually brought in within a conceptual framework. Such a framework will be largely sociological.

This introduction has done no more than indicate some recent developments in ideas about social geography, and some of the problems which now concern us seem to provide pointers to future study. It is too much to expect unanimity among social geographers concerning definition, or even agreement about the field of study until the conceptual framework is much stronger. This book does not pretend to put forward a complete conceptual framework. But now seems a propitious time to take stock, accepting the emphasis on empirical work, the new exploration at micro-level of social behaviour, the novelty of techniques, and the borrowing of models within the sciences and social sciences. There is a need for students to be able to see the range of work done on many aspects, which are gradually contributing to the emergence of an academic discipline.

The several elements which I consider important in a conceptual framework for the study of social geography can be summed up in this definition: social geography involves the understanding of the patterns which arise from the use social groups make of space as they see it, and of the processes involved in making and changing such patterns.

The form of this book is closely related to this definition, its sections being concerned with (a) patterns of distribution of social groups and their behaviour; (b) concepts of space; and (c) the processes which operate in society and the environment. Within each section the limitations of space have made the task of selection an unenviable one. Valid arguments could be found for several alternative groups of papers which would be equally original and thought-provoking. Indeed, another volume—or more—would by no means exhaust the range of topics, techniques, and concepts of social geography. In some cases the choice is made easier because a specific paper is not easily available, and it was assumed that some better-known papers are easily accessible; on the other hand, no collection would be complete without one or two papers which, although easily accessible, are basic to any considerations in social geography. It is hoped that this selection gives a coherent basis for an introduction to social geography which will lead students to a wider literature.

The obvious starting-point may well be conceptually the weakest. So much of social geography must of necessity be concerned with the preliminary examination of spatial patterns of behaviour. There are many aspects in which our knowledge in this respect is still sketchy or even rudimentary. This justifies statements of distribution—some familiar and some not—as a starting-point of further study. Most of the maps in the *Atlas of London and the London Region* take us no further than the simple statement of some social and economic aspects of census data.[35] But the data are now ordered spatially, an essential preliminary for geographical analysis. In the same way, the strength of a recent book on the geography of religions lies in its analysis of distributions rather than in formulating a 'geography' of religion: at this stage the author is avowedly looking no further, and has made a major contribution to clarifying patterns of distribution.[36] But this one aspect of social geography must be seen in relation to many others before we get much nearer to an explanation of these distributions. Again, Coates and Rawstron state in the introduction of their book[37] that 'our purpose is to measure and portray some of the economic and social variables in Great Britain'. The aim is the objective portrayal of spatial relations: the book—as its title states—is more of a contribution to the concept of region than it is to social geography, but the problems of handling data and the choice of areal bases are extremely difficult in social topics, and a necessary preliminary to a fuller explanatory approach. No social geographer can afford to ignore spatial variations in unemployment, wealth, or education. The author of a recent book on the geography of social well-being[38] deals with even less tangible variables and is concerned with looking for 'territorial social indicators'. Although his approach is conceptual, the 'empirical' material is largely descriptive, for it would be 'unwise to try and explain what is as yet inadequately described'. Spatial variations may not take us very far into the theory of social geography, but at least geographers are showing an increasing interest in those activities—e.g. politics, wealth, poverty—which are likely to be important components of the behavioural environment.

The articles selected here deal with several variables within social interaction—racial differences, occupational classes, contrasts in voting behaviour, and religious identity—and also with a variety of scales, from continental U.S.A. to a city, and to a single group of people within a city. Examples of such empirical studies could be multiplied many times.[39]

It is almost a truism now that space is not merely a medium in which society moves and acts, but a variable which we can no longer ignore. Perception studies have recently received a tremendous impetus, stemming from fundamental studies like those of Lowenthal[40] and Lynch.[41] The behavioural approach is adding enormously to our understanding of spatial problems by stressing that space is not a 'constant which it is the geographer's prerogative to interpret'. To everyone but the 'geographer in the abstract' the interpretation of space is coloured by culture and shaped by value systems. Firey's paper is an early classic exposition of the need to consider 'non-rational' elements in ecological explanations: a theme he developed in his Boston study.[42] Kirk's interpretation of the role of perception was first published in 1951,[43] but the paper reproduced here was the first introduction many readers had to these views. Lowenthal's paper, which when published seemed oddly outside the main stream of current ideas, was the forerunner of many American contributions on this theme. Buttimer's concept of 'social space' has already been referred to; Boal's is one example of an empirical study embodying these concepts. The remaining essay in this section appraises society in terms of its adaptive response to the environment.[44]

The place one should give society itself in social geographical studies is difficult to assess. In one sense it is central, and in another so implicit that to isolate it is to talk in purely sociological terms. Most courses in social geography will devote some time to the study of social groups which may be defined in many ways, from statistical differentiation to vague notions of community, with its countless definitions,[45] and to culture groups.[46] Mogey deals with identifying aggregates which, through a typology, will make the study of the relationships between society and the environment more systematic; but the emphasis is on society. In another section the Gans essay suggests the nearest approach to a familiar and 'real' situation in which we recognize the 'mix' of normal urban society: the environment here is the social environment of 'other groups'. But this last essay also reminds us that there are planning implications to be considered, and that we have spanned the range from philosophical speculation to policy-making.

Over the last two decades geographers have paid increasing attention to understanding various aspects of migration, and in particular to explaining the movement of different social groups within cities. The study of migration has a long history, Ravenstein's classic study of migration in England and Wales[47] being the starting-point of generalizations on the macro-scale.[48] One specialized aspect of migration is urbanization, a process which, in the Third World, is still very much one of transference of population. McGee's essay, part of a major contribution towards more sophisticated models of the pre-industrial city, indicates aspects of this problem in South-East Asia. It should be read in conjunction with parallel studies in other countries and in the wider context of the pre-industrial city in general and also in relation to arguments about the rural-urban continuum.[49] Mabogunje appraises these problems in terms of a systems approach. So much for the macro-scale. But attention has also focused sharply on the micro-scale, and Wolpert's paper has set a pattern of investigation for very many subsequent workers in this field. Dissatisfaction with the level of explanation on the macro-scale forced Wolpert to turn to behavioural studies and to look for decision processes which lay behind migration. Yet another dimension was investigated by Hägerstrand, who introduced time as a variable in his models. Perhaps the most interesting outcome of this work is the increasing realization that movement in time is fairly consistently patterned for any group of people and complements movement in space. Moreover, it demonstrates very clearly the number of constraints within which people act. It may well be that the significance given to choice in behavioural studies has been taken too much for granted.

Detailed analyses of some aspects of residential change are dealt with by Smith and by Simmons and by Deakin and Cohen. The studies have been chosen from a vast literature dealing with the mechanics of intra-city movement, the testing of models of diffusion, assimilation, conflict, in terms of race, ethnicity, class, and culture. Many of these studies have been conveniently brought together by Johnson,[50] who also provides an exhaustive bibliography. Of particular interest to social geographers are studies on segregation and those concerned with general models of urban social differentiation.[51]

Finally, some hint of social dilemmas and the possible involvement of the academic is found in Hyland and in Deakin and Cohen. The latter, in particular, points to policy. Orientation towards contemporary social problems is implicit in many of the studies referred to in this volume, and it would be wrong to underestimate the contribution made by geographers in applying their ideas in a planning context.[52] The final goal is a better-ordered society and the elimination of what are universally regarded as social ills based on inequality; the academic goal may well be the deeper comprehension of the social processes which produce the order and disorder which are implicit in spatial form, an understanding which will be of service to society and the basis of policy.

NOTES AND REFERENCES

[1] Davies, W. K. D. (ed.), *The Conceptual Revolution in Geography*, 1972.

[2] Harvey, D., *Explanation in Geography*, 1969.

[3] Buttimer, Anne, 'Social space in interdisciplinary perspective', *Geog. Rev.* 59 (1969).

[4] Fitzgerald, W., 'Correspondence', *Geog. Journal*, 107 (1946).

[5] Harrison, T., 'Correspondence', *Geog. Journal*, 108 (1946).

[6] Gilbert, E. W., and Steel, R. N., 'Social Geography and its place in Colonial Studies', *Geog. Journal*, 105 (1945).

[7] For a discussion of Bobek's position, see Buttimer, op.cit., and J. G. Hajdu, 'Towards a Definition of Post-War German Social Geography' *Annals Assoc. of American Geogs.* 58 (1968).

[8] Watson, W. Wreford, 'The Sociological Aspects of Geography', in Taylor, G. (ed.), *Geography in the Twentieth Century*, 1953.

[9] Fitzgerald, op.cit.

[10] Id., 'The Geographer as Humanist', *Nature*, 156 (   ).

[11] Representative of this approach is Wagner, P. L. and Mikesell, M. W., *Readings in Cultural Geography*, 1962.

[12] Sauer, C. O., 'Cultural Geography', *Encyclopaedia of the Social Sciences*, 6, 1931; Leighly, J. (ed.), *Land and Life: a Selection from the Writings of Carl Ortwin Sauer*, 1963.

[13] Thomas, E. L. (ed.), *Man's Role in Changing the Face of the Earth*, 1956.

[14] Sauer, *Agricultural Origins and Dispersals*, 1952.

[15] e.g. Lowenthal, D., and Prince, H. C., 'The English Landscape', *Geog. Journal*, 54 (1964).

[16] Hajdu, op.cit.

[17] Pahl, R., 'Sociological Models in Geography', in Chorley, R. J., and Haggett, P., *Models in Geography*, 1967.

[18] Pahl, R., 'Trends in Social Geography', in Chorley, R. J., and Haggett, P., *Frontiers in Geographical Teaching*, 1965.

[19] The relationship between geography and ecology is discussed in Hawley, A. H., *Human Ecology*, 1950. The new Chicago school is expressed in McKenzie, R. D., 'The Scope of Human Ecology' in Burgess, E. W. (ed.), *The Urban Community*, 1925, and Park, R. E., 'Human Ecology', *Am. Journal of Sociology*, 42 (1936).

[20] Barrow, H. H., 'Geography as Human Ecology', *Annals Assoc. Am. Geogs.* 11 (1923).

[21] Sorre, M., *Les Fondements de la géographie humaine* 1947.

[22] Firey, W., 'Sentiments and Symbolism as Sociological Variables', *Am. Soc. Rev.* 10 (1945).

[23] Buttimer, op.cit.

[24] Watson, op.cit.

[25] Buttimer, op.cit.

[26] Koroscil, P. M., 'The Behavioural Environmental Approach', *Area*, 13. 2 (1971).

[27] Davies, W. D., 'Geography and Behaviour', in Davies, W. K. D. (ed.), *The Conceptual Revolution in Geography*, 1972, p. 332.

[28] Jones, E., 'Cause and Effect in Human Geography', *Annals Assoc. Am. Geogs.* 46 (1956). This and other probabilistic approaches are discussed in Chapter 8 of Sprout, H. and Sprout, M., *The Ecological Perspectives on Human Affairs*, 1965.

[29] Curry, L., 'Chance and Landscape', *Northern Geographical Essays in Honour of G. Daysh*, 1967.

[30] Anderson, J., *Space Time Budgets, Potentialities and Limitations*, L.S.E. Graduate School of Geography Discussion Papers No. 40, 1970.

[31] Hagerstrand. T., 'What about People in Regional Science?', *Regional Science Assoc. Papers*, 1969.

[32] Prince, H. C., 'Questions of Social Relevance', *Area*, 3. 3 (1971). Smith, D. M., 'Radical Geography–the Next Revolution?', *Area*, 3. 3 (1971); Berry, B. T. L., 'More on Relevance and Policy Analysis', *Area*, 4. 2 (1972).

[33] See also Rees, R. (ed.), *Geographical Perspectives on American Poverty*, 1972. Social values are most explicitly discussed in Harvey, D., *Social Justice and the City*, 1973.

[34] Prince, H. C., 'Editorial', *Area*, 3. 3 (1971).

[35] Jones, E., and Sinclair, D. J., *Atlas of London and the London Region*, 1968/70.

[36] Gay, D. G., *Geography of Religion in England*, 1972.

[37] Coates. B. E., and Rawstron, E. M., *Regional Variations in Britain*, 1972.

[38] Smith, D. M., *The Geography of Social Wellbeing*, 1973.

[39]Other examples which the student will find useful and which cover a range of social activities are: Clark, B. D., and Gleave, M. B. (eds.), *Social Patterns in Cities*, Inst. Brit. Geogs. Special Publication, 1973; Collinson, P., and Mogey, J., 'Residence and Class in Oxford', *Am. Journal Sociology*, 64 (1959); Gansted, F. S., *Historical Atlas of Religion in the U.S.A.*, 1962; Giggs, J. A., 'Socially disorganised Areas in Barry: a Multivariate Approach', in Carter, H., and Davies, W. K. D., *Urban Essays: Studies in the Geography of Wales*, 1970; Howe, G. M., *National Atlas of Disease Mortality in the United Kingdom*, 1970; Jones, E., and Griffiths, I. L., 'A Linguistic Map of Wales, 1961', *Geog. Journal*, 129 (1963); Jones, E., 'Distribution and Segregation of Roman Catholics in Belfast', *Soc. Review*, 4 (1956); Melamid, A., 'The Geographical Distribution of Communities in Cyprus', *Geog. Rev.* 45 (1956); Smith, D. M., op.cit.; Zelinsky, W., 'An Approach to the Religious Geography of the United States: Patterns of Church Membership in 1952', *Annals Assoc. Am. Geogs.* 51 (1961).

[40]Lowenthal, D., 'Geography, Experience and Imagination: towards a Geographical Epistemology', *Annals Assoc. Am. Geogs.* 51 (1961).

[41]Lynch, K., *The Image of the City*, 1960.

[42]Firey, W., *Land Use in Central Boston*, 1947.

[43]Kirk, W., 'Historical Geography and the Concept of the Behavioural Environment', *Indian Geog. Journal, Silver Jubilee Vol. 1951* (1951).

[44]The implications of the behavioural environment are cogently set out by Brookfield, H. C., 'On the Environment as Perceived', *Progress in Geography*, 1(1969), and discussed by Sonnenfeld, J., 'Personality and Behaviour in Environment', *Proc. Assoc. Am. Geogs.* 1 (1969). Goodey, B., *Perception of the Environment*, Univ. of Birmingham Centre for Urban and Regional Studies Occasional Papers. No. 17, 1971, has an extended bibliography. Briefer reviews are those of Downs, P. M., 'Geographical Space Perception: Past Approaches and Future Prospects', *Progress in Geography*, 2 (1970), and Wood, J. L., 'Perception Studies in Geography', *Trans. Inst. Brit. Geogs.* 50 (1970). An early exploration of the territory was Wright, J. K., 'Terrace Incognitae: the Place of Imagination in Geography', *Annals Assoc. Am. Geogs.* 37 (1947). There are many empirical studies of which these are examples; Gould, P. R., and White, R. R., 'The Mental Maps of British School Leavers', *Regional Studies*, 2 (1968); Rushton, G., 'Analysis of Spatial Behaviour by Revealed Space Preference', *Annals Assoc. Am. Geogs.* 59 (1969); Sieverts, T., 'Perceptual Images of the City of Berlin', *Urban Core and Inner City*, 1967.

[45]Minar, D. W., and Greer, S., *The Concept of Community: Readings with Interpretations*, 1969.

[46]The study of specific social groups and communities in their environmental context has given rise to an extensive literature. On the pre-literate level introductory material can be found in Wolf, E. R., *Peasants*, 1966, in a book of readings, Shanin, T., *Peasants and Peasant Societies*, 1971, and in the classic Redfield, R., *Peasant Society and Culture*, 1956. Community studies in Britain are critically assessed by Frankenburg, R., *Communities in Britain*, 1966, but it is worth reading Rees, A. D., *Life in a Welsh Countryside*, 1950; Williams, W. M., *A West Country Village: Alsworthy*, 1963, and Young, M., and Willmott, P., *Family and Kinship in East London*, 1957. Other relevant urban studies include Dennis, N., 'The Popularity of the Neighbourhood Community Idea', in Pahl, R. E. (ed.), *Readings in Urban Sociology*, 1968, Gans, A. J., 'Urbanism and Suburbanism as Ways of Life; a Revaluation of Definitions', in Rose, A. M. (ed.), *Human Behaviour and Social Process*, 1962; Gans, A. J., *The Urban Villagers*, 1962; Ward, D., 'The Emergence of Central Immigrant Ghettoes in American Cities, 1840–1920', *Annals Assoc. Am. Geogs.* 58 (1968); Wirth, L., 'Urbanism as a Way of Life', *Am. Journal Soc.* 44 (1938).

[47]Ravenstein, E. C., 'The Laws of Migration', *Journal Royal Stat. Soc.* 48 (1885) and 52 (1889).

[48]A wide range of studies on the social aspects of migration is found in Jansen, C. J., *Readings in the Sociology of Migration* 1970.

[49]The most useful collection of essays is Breese, G., *The City in newly developing Countries* 1969: but see also a useful summary in Breese, G., *Urbanisation in newly developing Countries*, 1966. A more conceptual approach is Sjoberg, G., *The Pre-industrial City, Past and Present*, 1960. More specific are, Mabogunje A. L., *Urbanisation in Nigeria*, 1968, McGee, T. G., *The Urbanisation Process in the Third World*, 1971, Hauser, P. M., *Urbanisation in Latin America*, 1961. The effects of urbanization are given in Jones, E., 'Aspects of Urbanisation in Venezuela', *Ekistics*, 18 (1964), Maugin, W., 'Latin American Squatter Settlements: a Problem and a Solution', *Latin American Research Review*, 2 (1967); Peattie, L. R., 'Social Issues in Housing', in Frieden, B. J., and Nash, W. M. (eds.), *Shaping an Urban Future*, 1969; Turner, J. C., 'Suva's

Barriados and Corralones: Suburbs v. Slums', *Ekistics*, 19 (1965). Urbanization as a social process also brings us to the debate on the rural urban continuum, succinctly discussed by Dewey, R., 'The Rural-Urban Continuum', *Am Hournal Soc.* 66 (1960), and Pahl, R., 'The Rural-Urban Continuum', in Pahl, R. (ed.), *Readings in Urban Sociology*, 1968.

[50] Johnson, R. J., *Urban Residential Patterns*, 1971, also has a very extensive bibliography which covers most aspects of this field of research.

[51] The following will introduce the student to the basic problems: Clark, B. D., and Gleave, M. B., 'Social Patterns', *I.B.G.*, 1973. Collinson, P., and Mogey, J., 'Residence and Class in Oxford', *A. J. Soc.* 64 (1959). Morrill, R. C., 'The Negro Ghetto: Problems and Alternatives', *G.R.* 55 (1965). Shewky, E., and Bell, W., *Social Area Analysis*, 1955. Jaeuber, K. E., and Jaeuber, A. F., *Negroes in Cities: Residential Segregation and Neighbourhood Change*, 1965. Timms, D. W. C., *The Urban Mosaic*, 1971. Ward, D., Spatial Structure of Immigrant Residential Districts in the Nineteenth Century, *G. Analysis*, 1 (1969).

[52] House, J., 'Geographers, Decision-takers and Policy-makers', in Chisholm, M., and Redgers, B. (eds.) *Studies in Human Geography*, 1973. This essay has an impressive list of references to works by geographers which has direct policy implications.

PART ONE:

PATTERNS

1. GEOGRAPHICAL PERSPECTIVES ON THE HISTORY OF BLACK AMERICA

R. L. Morrill and O. F. Donaldson

Before it became wealthy, before it became powerful, before it became the United States, America was black and white. The first non-Indian permanent settlers in America may have been blacks, slaves who fled from a Spanish colony near the Pedee (now Peedee) River, South Carolina, in 1526 [1, p. 163]. As the British began to dominate the profitable trade established by the Spanish and Portuguese—the purchase of black from black—more and more slaves were imported, mainly into the Southern colonies and states. And as the number of slaves increased, so of course did the number of rebellions, some culminating in arson, violence, or death. The Thirteenth, Fourteenth, and Fifteenth Amendments, passed after the Civil War, acknowledged the American black as a free human being, an enfranchised citizen of the country he had helped to shape. The amendments did not suggest to him the way to free himself of ignorance, poverty, and laws created by whites to protect their supremacy, or the irrational fears of human prejudices.

As headlines and newscasts make clear every week, the relationship of black and white in the multi-racial United States is still evolving; so great is the concern that most Americans believe blacks represent much more than 11 per cent of the American population. Still, that 11 per cent, 23 million citizens, most inescapably distinguished by colour, is a very significant and obvious minority, particularly when it is highly concentrated in specific cities and in certain areas of the country (Table 1).

America has a dual society—a white majority which regards itself as superior and which traditionally has enjoyed almost total economic, social, and political power, and a black minority which was early proclaimed inferior and which has suffered centuries of subjugation, discrimination, and weakness. The inferiority-superiority relationship has been manifested spatially by separate institutions and facilities for blacks and whites, and by segregation of living space enforced either by law or by community pressure and custom. Competition for jobs and for living space leads to overt conflict and to violence. Since the mid-1950s, the Civil Rights movement has not only heightened the amount and intensity of conflict, but also moved black and white closer to equality than anything else in the previous three centuries. For a time the ideal of integration led to attempts to desegregate housing as well as schools, jobs, and public accommodations; but white resistance, and the black's realistic fear of diluting his culture and power, have produced a counter-movement, spatial separatism as one basis for black power.

A distinction of colour need not, in theory, be of such overwhelming concern, but the realities of history and of human prejudice and behaviour have made it so. The American dilemma, which Myrdal [28] explored so well, is how to ensure to black Americans the full fruits of citizenship. But inequality has so long been an institution, first in the extreme of legal slavery and later in a complex of

From *Economic Geography*, 48.1 (1972), 1–23. Reprinted by permission of its authors and the editor of the journal.

SOCIAL GEOGRAPHY : PATTERNS

TABLE 1
Regional Summary of the Development of the
Black Population

Date	South	North-East	North Central*	West	U.S.
PROPORTION OF BLACK POPULATION BY REGION					
1790	91	9			
1850	97	2	1		
1910	89	5	6		
1940	77	11	11	1	
1960	60	16	18	6	
1970	53	19	20	8	
PERCENTAGE OF REGIONAL POPULATION BLACK					
1790	32	6			19
1850	39	2	1		16
1910	30	2	2	1	11
1940	24	4	4	1	10
1960	21	7	7	4	11
1970	19	9	8	5	11
PERCENTAGE OF BLACK POPULATION URBAN					
1910	21	85	72	80	27
1940	35	90	87	85	48
1960	59	95	96	93	78
TOTAL BLACK POPULATION (000s)					
1790	700	67			767
1850	3534	149	44	11	3639
1910	8749	489	543	51	9828
1940	9905	1370	1420	171	12866
1960	11308	3029	3445	1071	18850
1970	12064	4342	4572	1695	22678

Source: United States Censuses, 1790 to 1970.
*Excludes Missouri 1790 and 1850.

discriminatory laws and customs, that a deep-seated fear and distrust continues to exist between black and white.

The purpose of this paper is to examine a number of geographic aspects of black America as they have developed through time; these include: the changing distribution of the black population from the period of slavery on Southern plantations, to the recent period of migration to the cities and concentration in the ghettos; regional variations in the conditions, treatment, and revolts of black people; and finally the development of ghettos and other forms of segregation.

The Colonial Period, 1500–1790

The Slave Trade. During the sixteenth century, many Portuguese, Spanish, and later British plantations in the New World became short of labour. Disease, enslavement, and overwork had so decimated the Amerindian population that the importing of slaves from Africa to the colonies came rather early (they had been imported earlier to Portugal and Spain) [23, p. 25]. From European trading posts in Senegal, Gold Coast, Ivory Coast, and Slave Coast (mainly Nigeria), Portuguese, and in the seventeenth century, British and Dutch companies began to purchase slaves from local rulers, generally in exchange for European manufactured goods (especially clothing, metal goods, spirits, and weapons). These slaves were sometimes criminals or debtors but usually captives taken during conflicts among the West African states. Most went to Cuba and Brazil, but some were taken to Florida in the late sixteenth century.

Under Portuguese and Spanish rule, slaves were treated according to Roman law, with the right to purchase their freedom, and to own property [23, p. 26]. Black men often were on the Portuguese and Spanish trips of exploration, and travelled to many areas on the North American continent before 1619 [3, p. 360]. The first non-Indian permanent settlers in America may have been blacks, slaves who revolted and fled from a Spanish colony near the Peedee River, South Carolina, in 1526. Blacks helped build the city of St. Augustine, in 1565, and Cortes brought 300 blacks with him to the California coast in 1737. In the sixteenth century, Estevanico, an African explorer with the Spanish expeditions, explored parts of Florida, New Mexico, and Arizona. The purpose of his last journey was to find 'Cibola, or the Seven Cities of Gold'.

Black Settlement. Continuous black settlement in America began with the landing of nineteen indentured black servants in Jamestown, Virginia in 1619. At first, restrictive laws were few, and some purchased their freedom. By the end of the century, however, the traffic in slaves had increased. The number entering New York, New Jersey, and New England was small in comparison with the number entering Virginia to work on tobacco plantations, and the Carolinas to work on tobacco, indigo, and rice plantations [23, pp. 36—40]. Most of the plantations were very close to tidewater. Particularly productive were the Sea Islands along the Carolina coast. As more slaves were imported, the form of slavery soon became more restrictive. Under English law, slaves were mere property and had no human rights themselves.

After 1700, the demand for plantation products increased rapidly, as did the opening of new lands, and consequently the rate of slave importation. But the largest numbers of black slaves were still being taken to Brazil and Cuba and other islands of the Caribbean. In Senegal and particularly the Slave Coast and Guinea, the increasing demand for slaves soon led to cruel and destructive inter-tribal and inter-kingdom warfare, by which whole villages were sold into slavery and the countryside depopulated.

The British soon came to dominate the profitable slave trade. A kind of triangular pattern was common. British goods purchased the slaves, British ships transported them to New World plantations; and the plantation products, including sugar for the rum which became a major commodity in trading for slaves, moved back to Britain.

By 1750 there were at least 236,000 slaves in the American colonies (including French Louisiana), still predominantly in Virginia and Maryland. The proportion of blacks in the total population reached its apex (21 per cent) during this period. Settlement and slavery were moving slowly westward from the coast, but slavery never gained a major foothold in the Piedmont or mountain areas, owing mainly to the small size of farms. The plantation system with its prodigious labour demands slowly spread down the coast into Carolina and Georgia.

Between 1750 and 1800 some 500,000 to 1,000,000 slaves came to this country [the U.S.A.]. New England shippers began to share in the fortunes to be made from the slave trade. Still, in the North slaves were rarely more than 5 per cent of the population. In the South, however, the slave proportion was increasing, owing to the predominantly large-scale plantation agriculture, orientation to growing commercial exports, and only moderate white immigration [23, pp. 39–40].

By 1770 exploitative agriculture in more accessible but marginal lands near the Virginia coast had already worn out the land; new slave shipments were now destined for the Carolinas and Georgia. About 1780, a new and valuable crop, cotton, was introduced, greatly increasing the demand both for land, especially in more southerly, warmer areas, and for slaves to clear the land and farm it. At first, because of its high-humidity requirements, cotton was grown mainly along the coast, from Virginia to Georgia; plant disease, land erosion, demand for more cotton varieties, and the invention of the cotton gin in 1793, led to a fairly rapid shift south and west after 1800.

Black Resistance. From the beginning of slavery in the colonies, black resistance occurred. In fact, the first slave revolt took place in the Pedee River colony in South Carolina. Slave revolts were not only forms of resistance to bondage. There was the day-to-day resistance of destroyed tools and crops, and work slowdowns. Attempts to kill masters and set fires also appear to have been common. In some slave states so many fires were set that some insurance companies refused to insure homes [18, p. 100]. Slaves pretended to be lame, sick, blind, or insane in order to interrupt the work of the plantation; running away was common. Thousands escaped to cities, the North, Canada, Mexico, Indian areas, and wilderness areas. Maroon colonies grew up in forested mountains or swampy areas of the Carolinas, Virginia, Louisiana, Florida, Georgia, Mississippi, and Alabama. Evidence of at least 50 such communities in various places and at various times from 1672 to 1864 have been found] [1, p. 167].

The Ante-Bellum Period: Plantation and Slavery, 1790 to 1865

The Slavery System. By 1790 the economy of the South was based firmly on export agriculture, which in turn depended on slave farm labour for its low cost. The majority of farmers may not have been slaveholders, but their farms usually were small, occupied less desirable land, and were essentially subsistent [23, p. 56]. Economic and political powers were a function of the amount of land owned, and rested in the hands of large plantation owners. In the North, however, plantations were never really successful, farming practices being transferred fairly directly from practices in the mother country. Many northern farmers, nevertheless, did employ immigrant indentured servants. Further white immigration was not encouraged by the plantation owners of the South.

In 1820 slavery was as much a part of the few urban places in the South as it was of rural farms and plantations. During the ante-bellum period the residences of blacks and whites in Southern cities usually were not spatially segregated; this was, of course, not intended to promote integration but to prevent the growth of a cohesive black community. There were, however, segregated black residential areas; and by 1860 housing segregation was increasing. The segregated black areas were usually near markets, docks, alleys, and the peripheries of the cities and towns. Town slaves, while at times restricted to the owner's compound, tended to be much better off than slaves on the plantations. Many worked at building and other trades. Not much contact or aggregation of slaves was permitted; loyalty was aided by the terrible threat of being sold off to a plantation.

Although commercial export made the South as rich or richer than the North at this time, a comparable system of towns and cities failed to develop. Direct export relations with Europe were often carried out from many small river and estuary

TABLE 2
Population*and Cotton, 1790 to 1910

States	Black Population				Slave Shift 1820 to 1860	Black Shift 1860 to 1910	Percentage of Cotton Production			
	1790	1820	1850	1910			1810	1830	1850	1910
Virginia Maryland Delaware	430	636	727	1092	−230	−200	10	3		
North and South Carolina	214	485	710	1534	−160	−131	60	26	15	15
Georgia Florida Tennessee Kentucky	56	389	891	2221	0	−100	25	40	30	22
Alabama Louisiana Mississippi	30	154	918	2631	+180	−108	5	31	50	28
Arkansas Texas Oklahoma		22	107	1428	+150	+210			5	35

Source: United States Censuses of Population and Agriculture. U.S. Department of Agriculture Cotton Statistics, various years.
* (000s)

ports, of which only a few (Charleston, S.C., Mobile, Alabama, New Orleans, Louisiana, and Norfolk) became very large. Based on the slave labour of many, exports permitted the owners of large plantations a relatively aristocratic income and the luxury of importing needed goods from England. So long as profits were high, there was little incentive to consider alternatives to slave labour.

Gradually, however, in the areas of early settlement, mainly coastal Virginia, Maryland, and North Carolina, the land deteriorated from misuse and overuse, and owners found it more and more costly to maintain large slaveholdings. Fortunately for these declining plantation areas, the rapid expansion of settlement into the richer lowlands of Georgia, Alabama, Mississippi, Louisiana, and Tennessee after 1800, and the emergence of cotton as the most profitable export crop created a huge demand for slaves, just as the slave trade was becoming more difficult.

Migration of Slaves. From 1790 to 1810 the slave trade continued high, with the origins shifting east and south to Nigeria, the Congo, and even Angola, where the Portuguese engaged in direct kidnapping raids. Some slaves were brought from Cuba to be sold in the United States. Meanwhile the American market for slaves shifted south and west to Alabama (Mobile) and the Mississippi Delta (through New Orleans). The British Parliament outlawed the slave trade in 1808, and although American ships ran the British blockades, the volume of trade began to fall drastically.

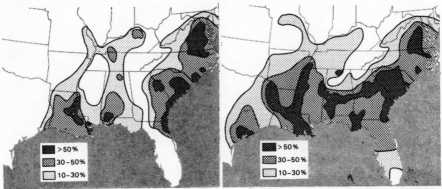

Fig. 1. Proportion of the population black in 1820.

Fig. 2. Proportion of the population black in 1850.

In the older settled areas, especially in Virginia, the black population had grown rather in excess of local needs, simply through years of natural increase. Instead of being feared, the 'surplus' was desired, for the owners in declining farming areas found it most profitable to specialize in the breeding and raising of slaves for sale and shipment to the South-West [3, pp. 83–84; 23, p.51]. The local slave markets, such as Alexandria, blatantly advertised the fecundity of female slaves, and owners gave privileges to women who bore many children. Slaves were thought of as a capital investment, earning between 5 and 15 per cent per year.

From 1810 to 1865, then, a large and profitable internal trade in slaves occurred from the 'old' to the 'new' South. In the early part of the century, before 1830, blacks went mainly from Virginia and Maryland to Kentucky, Tennessee, Georgia, and Alabama; after 1830, the Carolinas, and even Georgia and Kentucky, began to export slaves to Mississippi, Arkansas, Louisiana, and Texas. Table 2 summarizes the relation between the shifting black population and the expansion of cotton. The trade routes ran along the coast, down the Piedmont, along the Appalachian Corridor, and down the Mississippi and Ohio rivers. Since most slaves had to walk in chains, it is not surprising that many did not make it.

Population Redistribution. As a consequence of the decline of agriculture on the coastal plain, and the rapid expansion in the South-west, the distribution of slaves changed raidcally between 1790 and 1860. Although Virginia remained the leading slave state, its slave population had increased rather slowly; Maryland dropped from second to tenth in number of slaves. The proportion of blacks had fallen in both. From 1790 to 1850, Tennessee, Alabama, Mississippi, and Louisiana grew the most. By 1850 South Carolina (59 per cent), Mississippi, and Louisiana (each 51 per cent) had slave majorities. By 1850 the centre of the black population had shifted from Virginia to South Carolina, and by 1865 west into Georgia (Figures 1 and 2).

Health on the Plantation. The health care of blacks on the plantation must be understood in relation to the general environment, medical practices, and social climate of the time. The frontier conditions, inadequate medical facilities, isolated settlements, undrained lowlands and swamps, coupled with a mild climate, difficulty of preserving food, and ignorance of health practices all contributed to make the population, white and black, vulnerable to epidemic and endemic diseases. But the provision of health care was the responsibility of the dominant white society which, as it often continues to do, treated blacks as 'out-patients' at best, or not at all. Under the conditions of plantation society, the food, shelter, clothing, and medical care of the slave were subject to the control and whim of the master.

Black Mortality. It was generally true throughout the South that slaves had higher death rates and shorter life expectancies than whites [36, p. 158; 33, p. 318; 35, p. 573]. There were two to three times as many black as white deaths in South Carolina from 1853 to 1859. The infant death rate differential between white and black was greater than that of the general mortality rate. On a sugar plantation in Louisiana 21 per cent of the black babies born from 1834 to 1857 died; on a North Carolina plantation during the 1850s, 67 per cent of the black infants died; in an 11-year span in Charleston 48 per cent of the black babies died before they were four years old [33, p. 320].

The size, type and location of the plantation seem to have made a difference in the quality of slave life. In general it seems that housing, food, clothing, and health care were better on small farms than on large plantations [3, p. 72]. The health problems were most acute in the swampy coastal areas of South Carolina and Georgia and in the river bottom plantations of Alabama, Mississippi, Louisiana, and Arkansas. Most unhealthy of all were the rice plantations [19, p. 141; 33, p. 297].

There was also an abnormally high death rate among blacks in the cities [7, p. 227]. Even though Wade [39, p. 134] has indicated that slaves were treated better in the city than in the countryside, black mortality rates in the ante-bellum city were at least twice those of whites [15, p. 42].

Black Rebellion. From the beginnings of slavery in America, the strategy of whites was to make the slave forget his African culture and accept the slave identity and permanent inferiority of his status as property.

Blacks from different tribes were mixed, so that communication was difficult; talk was often forbidden and learning to read and write English was proscribed, so that 'ignorance' became self-fulfilling. Even 'good' masters acted as though slaves had no rights, often selling members of families separately; 'good' plantations offered incredibly bad living conditions, and only the economic value of slaves as workers kept the death and maiming rate from alarming levels.

As a result of injustice, cruelty, and inhuman conditions, the slave was naturally discontented, and often driven to rebellion. The layout and security measures taken within the plantation and the distance of one plantation from another made successful large-scale revolt impossible. Organization for revolt within the plantation was made difficult by a system of favouritism and informing.

But the difficulties imposed upon black communication and organization did not ensure peace for the whites. Guerrilla raids, carried out by bands of escaped slaves living in the extensive swamps or forests, were common from the seventeenth century until the Civil War. No one is certain how many 'revolts' occurred, partly because the definitions of 'revolt' do not coincide. Kilson [20], defining 'revolt' as an attempt by a group of slaves to achieve freedom, has identified 65 cases. Aptheker [2, p. 16] has recorded approximately 250 revolts and conspiracies, not including those outbreaks and plots that occurred aboard slave traders; he requires a 'revolt' to involve at least ten slaves, to have the aim of freedom, and to have contemporary references labelling the event in terms equivalent to revolt. If revolt was defined as it was in Texas in 1858, as a group of three or more slaves with arms who intend to obtain freedom by force, Aptheker asserts that several hundred slave insurrections could be counted.

Slave revolts were not evenly distributed among the states but were concentrated in Virginia, South Carolina, and Louisiana. Within these states, the revolts were clustered in only a few counties. In Virginia, for example, revolts tended to occur in the coastal, tobacco counties. In South Carolina most took place in Charleston County. And in Louisiana most revolts occurred along the Mississippi River north and west of Baton Rouge.

The more successful revolts tended to be where the slaves were better treated, especially near cities such as Richmond and Charleston where the chance to go to black churches made it easier for slaves to organize their revolts. (In the North, too, riots broke out in the cities—in Cincinnati in 1820, Providence in 1824 and 1834, Philadelphia in 1834, and in New York in 1834 and 1836 [23, p. 71, 97]. In the South-West, where plantations were larger, conditions for the slaves harsher, and discipline more severe, revolts were rarer, although discontent was undoubtedly greater.

The Underground Railroad. Escape of the individual slave to freedom in the North was a more practical alternative to armed rebellion, but his chances of success were not high, considering the great distances and his ignorance of the geography beyond his immediate area. Nevertheless, hundreds of thousands of attempts resulted in some many thousand successful escapes. The underground railroad was the clandestine network of anti-slavery individuals, including many escaped slaves, by which an escaped slave could be guided into a haven in the North [6, 34]. So perilous was the journey within the South that little is known about the routes or the mechanisms; within the North the 'railway' was more organized but still secret, since the national Anti-Fugitive Slave Laws of 1850 required northern states to return escaped slaves and permitted owners' representatives to go north and capture them. There remains a controversy over whether or not the underground railroad was a systematized network or rather a restricted number of blacks and whites organized to move slaves in certain localities [23, p. 112].

Depending on time and place, the black slave had a number of options in terms of places to which to escape. These options included Mexico, Canada, free states, Southern cities, maroon colonies, or Indian tribes such as Creeks, Cherokees, and Seminoles. In the early nineteenth century, a movement developed, among white abolitionists and some blacks, for emigration of blacks to colonies in Africa. The Liberian colony was established in 1821, but only about 15,000 emigrated over a fifty-year period [3, p. 131; 23, pp. 121, 128]. At different times certain border cities were seen by blacks as entry points or gateways to freedom. During the 1700s Pittsburgh was used by slaves escaping to the Northwest Territory. By the turn of the century, Cleveland also served this function; it was touted as the 'negroe's paradise' [30].

Many sought the relative security of the small, free black communities of northern cities, such as New York, Chicago, Rochester, Philadelphia, and Boston, where many joined the growing abolitionist forces in the North [3, chap. 6]. Their accounts of the hideousness of life in the South were hardly believed at first, and abolitionist white sentiment began largely on ethical and religious grounds among the Quakers and Congregationalists. By 1783 slavery had been abolished in Massachusetts, and by 1805 in most of the North. In the 1850s too, Massachusetts was not zealous in enforcing the Anti-Fugitive Slave Laws. On the other hand, after about 1815, New England industrialists entered the market for cheap cotton, and defended slavery—at a distance.

Escapes before the Civil War (about 90,000 went north on the underground railroad) and movement north during and just after the Civil War added up to a sizeable migration of blacks. Before 1850 most movement was to Baltimore,

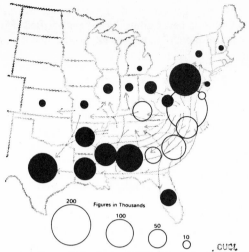

Fig. 3. Lifetime migration of blacks to 1870. Shaded circles represent net gains.

Philadelphia, Cincinnati, and other cities close to the South. After the Anti-Fugitive Slave Laws of 1850, migrants had to reach Canada to be safe (see Figure 3).

Expansion of 'Slave' and 'Free' Territories. In 1787 the Northwest Ordinance forbade slavery in the territory that was to become Illinois, Indiana, Michigan, Ohio, and Wisconsin; but many of these areas restricted the entry of blacks. In 1820 the South, with its congressional majority, obtained the Missouri Compromise which would admit states to the west and south as slave states. Nevertheless, Oregon and California were admitted free, as were the territories of the South-West, won from Mexico, which abolished slavery in 1829. The South won a temporary victory with the Kansas-Nebraska Act of 1854, but the feverish efforts of anti-slavery forces barely managed to keep Kansas free. By 1860, northern Republicans achieved a majority, Lincoln was elected, and Congress passed liberalized immigration, the Homestead Act, and protective tariffs for industry, all of which the South feared and opposed. In 1861 seven Southern states seceded to form the Confederacy. The border slave states of Kentucky, Maryland, Delaware, and Missouri, with a low proportion of slaves, had pro-union majorities and did not secede.

The Civil War. Sentiment in the North would not tolerate secession. For a time the war was between whites in the North and the South, and the issue was preservation of the Union, not abolition. As the war dragged on, attitudes hardened. Both North and South began to utilize blacks—some 300,000 in the North [18, p. 213]. The majority were limited to menial service activities, but some black combat forces were organized in liberated areas of the South and in New England. In 1863 Lincoln's Emancipation Proclamation freed the slaves in the occupied areas.

Immediately after the war, in spite of the Thirteenth Amendment abolishing slavery, the situation for blacks was little better, since Southern governments enacted 'Black Codes' which forced blacks into slavelike service for their former masters. However, northern 'radical' Republicans soon had the power to force military government and Reconstruction regimes on the South. The Reconstruction governments quickly ratified the Fourteenth and Fifteenth Amendments, which

restricted state powers and bestowed the right to vote on blacks [3, chap. 8].
Ironically, these amendments never could have been ratified if it had not been for
the Reconstruction governments, since several northern states, particularly in the
Midwest, did not ratify them.

Betrayal, Lynching, and Migration, 1865–1940

The freeing of the slaves, the enfranchisement of the blacks, and in a few areas of
more 'radical' military administration the allocation of some land to the former
slaves, brought about a period of hope. For a few years after 1866, under military
protection, many blacks were elected to Congress and to state legislatures and state
offices in the South; they never in fact gained even temporary control of any state,
but had enough influence at least to see a system of public education set up
throughout most of the South. The blacks had little preparation for legal intrigue.
As memories of the war receded, sentiment in the North ceased to support military
intervention. Most people in the North, while opposed to slavery, also viewed
blacks as inferiors, not to be given power. Thus, in the disputed election of 1876,
Hayes became president on a promise to end Reconstruction and remove the
northern 'carpetbaggers'. It took almost no time for Southern whites to
disenfranchise most blacks through the imposition of literacy tests and other
devices, including sheer terror. In the early 1890s a hopeful alliance of poor whites
and poor blacks under the banner of Populism emerged, but this alliance was short
lived.

Under slavery, social distance was automatic and institutionalized; spatial
separation was needed less to maintain superiority of whites. After the Civil War,
physical separation became legislated through a set of Jim Crow laws, forbidding
miscegenation, providing for separate institutions and facilities, and depriving
blacks of legal rights such as the right to be empanelled on a jury [3, chap. 9].
These laws became increasingly severe throughout the late nineteenth and early
twentieth centuries.

Sharecropping Serfdom. Most former slaves remained on their former
plantations. Even where they held title to the land, blacks depended on the
plantation owners to market their cotton. In most cases, however, no ownership
changed; black farmers were essentially landless peasants. A kind of serfdom
emerged—the former slaves leased land, usually very little, from the plantation
owner for a rent of from one-third to one-half of the crop. Very quickly, most
sharecroppers became permanently indebted to the owner, and were then legally
forbidden to move from the owner's holding. Not only was the sharecropper kept
in abject poverty, but the system of agriculture was so inefficient (i.e. too many
minute holdings, lack of uniform variety, inadequate care of land) that production
fell, and landowners, too, were much worse off than before the war [23, p. 140].

The plantation was rearranged: the sharecroppers were now scattered about on
small holdings throughout the former plantation. Gradually, too, many blacks
drifted back into the direct employ of the plantation owner, a life materially not
much better than slavery, but psychologically preferred, because the labourer was
free to leave providing he was free of indebtedness.

Condition of Black People. Since the blacks were still overwhelmingly rural,
perhaps even more scattered than before, scarcely educated or often illiterate, and
extremely poor, organized resistance to the new forms of subjugation was difficult.
The white community, both through grossly unfair local police power and through
the terrifyingly effective tool of lynching, could keep the black man 'in his place'.

Terrorist organizations like the Ku Klux Klan were effective in maintaining 'correct' attitudes among whites as well as in terrorizing the black population. Lynchings, and other violent and arbitrary treatment of blacks, were most intense around 1905, especially in Mississippi and Georgia [12].

For evidence of the general condition of the black population in 1910, illiteracy statistics are useful. In the North and West, white illiteracy varied between 1 and 3 per cent, black illiteracy from 12 per cent (New England) to 25 per cent (West North Central, mainly Missouri). In the South, 35 years after the Civil War, white illiteracy was 12 per cent and black illiteracy was 48 per cent—casting doubt on the adequacy of the rigidly segregated school system operated for blacks, and reflecting the difficulty of regular or long attendance.

The situation had improved by 1930, but was still extremely discriminatory. In the South, white illiteracy varied from 1 to 6 per cent, and black from 11 to 27 per cent. The low level of educational achievement of blacks, while being used to support the white view of innate black inferiority, was mainly a function of discrimination in school expenditures per pupil. Despite the alleged 'separate but equal' facilities accepted by the Supreme Court in Plessy v. Ferguson in 1896, in the Deep South in 1931 expenditure for a black pupil was less than one-third that for a white pupil. In Mississippi and South Carolina, it was only one-sixth ($5 per pupil per year).

Naturally, the notion of leaving such a precarious life occurred to many. Proposals for a separate state were made, but to think that whites were going to make land available for such a venture was folly. Many blacks did attempt to establish colonies in the new territories of the West. In 1879, some 40,000 migrated to Kansas, in a partly successful venture [6, chap. 5]. In the South itself, some all-black communities were founded in isolated, marginal land not needed by whites. Other blacks revived the idea of migration to Africa, such as to the Liberian colony established originally in 1821. This proposal was encouraged by many whites, friendly and unfriendly; not many blacks, however, wanted to return to a continent whose culture they in fact no longer shared. Some blacks gradually drifted north, but they were unwelcome in the countryside, and were subjected to rough and discriminatory treatment by the city immigrants who feared the competition for jobs. Race riots were not uncommon.

More than 5,000 black cowboys went up the cow trails from Texas after the Civil War. Black men such as James Beckworth, Jacob Dodson, Saunders Jackson, 'Pap' Singleton, and George W. Bush participated in the exploration and settlement of the West [11, 18]. Thousands of free blacks were among the 'forty-niners' who flocked to the California gold-fields. The western campaigns of the U.S. Army included four black units, the Ninth and Tenth Cavalries and the Twenty-fourth and Twenty-fifth Infantries. But whether as cowboys, cavalrymen, or settlers, blacks faced the same kind of discrimination and oppression in the West as they faced in the South and East. Black cowboys, for example, found race hatred stronger in Montana and Idaho than in other parts of the cattlemen's West [11, p. 140]. The black troops were discriminated against in terms of supplies, equipment, and assignments [37, p. 5]. Black settlers found discriminatory laws and restrictions in areas like Iowa, Illinois, and the Oregon Territory.

Population Redistribution (to 1910). During the period from 1850 to 1910, although the blacks remained almost totally rural and Southern (see Table 1 and Figure 4), there was a continuous shift of black farmers and farm labourers towards the south-west. The number of blacks continued to grow moderately, especially in

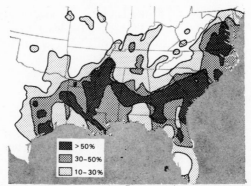

Fig. 4. Proportion of the population black in 1900.

North Carolina and Georgia, but expanded rapidly in Mississippi, Texas, and Louisiana. In 1880, the black population reached its maximum proportion of about 45 per cent of the population of the South (but only 13 per cent of the nation, owing to massive European immigration into the North).

Blacks were a majority in Louisiana (51 per cent), Mississippi (57 per cent), and South Carolina (60 per cent) and closely approached half of the population in Alabama (47 per cent), Georgia (47 per cent), and Florida (47 per cent). By 1910, although the proportion of blacks had fallen slightly, the absolute size of the black population reached a maximum in Georgia, Kentucky, and South Carolina. In 1850, Virginia and South Carolina had the largest black populations; by 1880, Virginia had the third-largest black population, below Georgia and Mississippi. By 1910 the dominance of the Deep South was clear: Georgia, Mississippi, Alabama, South Carolina, and Louisiana had the largest black populations, absolutely and relatively. The South still had 89 per cent of the black population, and 80 per cent of that was rural. In the North, where 11 per cent of the blacks lived, only 5 per cent of the population was black; these were already 80 per cent urban in 1910.

Migration (to 1910). Considering the large size of the black population in 1910 (10,000,000), the amount of lifetime migration revealed in Figure 5 does not show great mobility. Nevertheless, the out-migration from the South Atlantic states was large; the majority of people did not move too far to the north-east (especially to Baltimore, Philadelphia, and New York). There was a smaller net migration from the east south central states, about half of whom went across the Mississippi to Texas and Louisiana and about half to the North and West, especially St. Louis, Chicago, Cincinnati, and Indianapolis.

A Slow Awakening, 1910–1950 The terrible conditions at the end of the century led on one hand to a prevailing black reaction of 'accommodation', as enunciated by Booker T. Washington in 1895, and on the other to a strong current of bitterness and protest, led by W. E. B. Du Bois and others [3, 23]. Washington stressed gradual economic improvement through education and self-help; Du Bois stressed the denial of fundamental rights of blacks. After the NAACP was founded in 1910 and the Urban League in 1911, a more activist approach was accepted. The NAACP stressed legal challenges, and gains through the courts date from 1911. The Urban League worked to improve job opportunities and community relations—a difficult task.

As before, war led to an improvement in the position of the blacks [3, pp. 289–95]. The slowing of European immigration, particularly after 1914, and the

Fig. 5. Lifetime migration of blacks to 1910.

increased demand for labour in shipyards and other war industries, for the first time opened up better industrial jobs to blacks. Many were actively recruited from the rural South, and went north, especially to Chicago, Detroit, Philadelphia, and to other industrial cities. Not surprisingly, when the war bubble burst, blacks were first to be fired. Unemployment increased and a period of severe race riots ensued, becoming worst in the Red Summer of 1919, when there were severe riots in Washington, Chicago, East St. Louis, Omaha, and Knoxville.

During the early 1920s, Garvey revived the idea of colonization, but few were interested [6 chap. 13]. Conditions for blacks in the cities slowly improved in the prosperous 1920s. Blacks, concentrated in large ghettos, such as New York and Chicago, had become so numerous that the idea of black separatism and black businesses became popular. Chicago elected the first black Congressman in 1928.

The Great Depression destroyed the hopes of equality gained within 'Black Metropolis'. Again blacks were first to be fired, but since most blacks were desperately poor already, some side effects of the Depression eventually proved beneficial.

New Deal legislation, such as the minimum wage, social security, unemployment insurance, and the various work and training programmes, while perhaps instituted for the benefit of white workers, greatly aided blacks as well [23, pp. 212–13]. Perhaps the agricultural programmes were most significant. Designed to modernize and mechanize agriculture, especially in the South, the programmes forced hundreds of thousands of black sharecroppers off the land. The tiny shareholdings were hopelessly inefficient, the sharecroppers unbelievably poor, terrorized by white vigilantes, and weakened by dispersal. Forced to migrate to the northern cities, they found adjustment hard, and life in the slum ghetto far from pleasant; but a move to a northern city was the only realistic means of improving income, obtaining an education, and gaining political power.

World War II, like World War I, greatly aided blacks by opening up far more industrial jobs than ever before, for example in the steel and automobile industries. And the military itself provided valuable education and training for many blacks, although in World War II segregated units were still required. Indeed, as of 1945, in

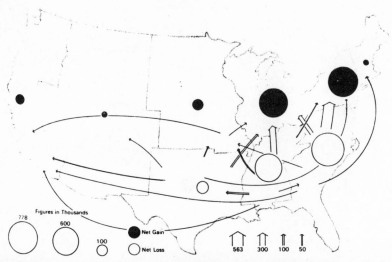

Fig. 6. Lifetime migration of blacks, 1910 to 1940.

the North as well as the South, most institutions and accommodations were still segregated.

Migration and Urban Growth, 1910–1970

Population Redistribution and Migration, 1910–1940. The 'Great Migration' of 1915 marked the beginning of a significant shift in the distribution of black people from the rural South to the urban North (Figure 6) [6, 16]. In the North an increasing need for unskilled labour accompanied by a halt in European immigration opened the labour market. As a consequence, agents were sent south to recruit black labour for northern industry. In the South, the ravages of the boll weevil and floods reduced the income of the planters, thus cutting the income, supplies, and credit of the tenants. And many people wanted to escape the legal and educational systems and terrorism. From 1910 to 1940 the proportion of the black population in the South fell from 89 to 77 per cent and the black proportion of the South fell from 30 to 24 per cent, while it increased in the North from 2 to 4 per cent. The proportion of black people in cities rose from 27 to 48 per cent (35 per cent in the South, 88 per cent in the North). For the first time a northern State, New York, was a leader in total black population. After 1910, growth of the black population ceased in the east south central states, and slowed markedly in the South Atlantic and west south central but increased greatly in the North-East, exceeding 2 million by 1940. The rate and volume of black migration out of the South increased dramatically after 1910, so that by 1940 the North-East had 1·3 million blacks (60 per cent of its total black population) who had been born in the South. The some 1·5 million blacks who left the South represented 10–15 per cent of its black population. States with largest in-migration were New York (308,000), Illinois (230,000), Pennsylvania (217,000), and Ohio (170,000); those with the largest net out-migration were Georgia (358,000), South Carolina (323,000), Mississippi (255,000), and Virginia (234,000). The pattern of migration followed the major rail corridors—up the Atlantic coast from the South Atlantic states, up the Mississippi and Ohio to the Great Lakes states, and from Arkansas, Louisiana, and Texas to the West Coast.

The Growth of Black Communities in Cities. By 1900 the black population in 14 cities, 10 of them in the South, had passed 25,000 (Table 3). The largest were those in or quite near the South: Washington (87,000), Baltimore (79,000), New Orleans (78,000), and Philadelphia (63,000). But in the next 20 years growth was rapid in the North and only moderate in the South; in 1920, of 24 cities having a black population over 25,000, 10 were in the North, although the largest populations, except for New York (169,000), were still in or near the South—Philadelphia (134,000), Washington (110,000), New Orleans and Baltimore (101,000).

From 1920 to 1940 growth was marked in the South, but more so in the North and especially rapid in Chicago, New York, Detroit, and Cleveland, indicating a shift of emphasis to longer moves, and in the direction of the Great Lakes. New York's black communities comprised more than half a million, and those of Chicago and Philadelphia 250,000; there were more than 100,000 in New Orleans, Memphis, Birmingham, Atlanta, and Washington. In the cities of the South, the proportion of blacks was often about 25 per cent; in the North, it was more than 10 per cent only in St. Louis, Philadelphia, and Detroit.

Development of the Ghetto. Up to 1900, part of the black population of cities was scattered, housed in the servants' quarters of the wealthy. From colonial times on, however, there have also been areas of towns and cities, both North and South, that have been designated by whites as black parts of town [8, 31]. In the South, poor blacks often were found in semi-rural slums on the outskirts of town, and in large cities in shacktowns along the railroad. In the North around 1900, linear black communities began to develop in old rundown houses, or shacktowns, mainly along the industrial railways near the centre of the city where no one else wanted to live (Figure 7). With growth and after 1910, conflicts between poor whites and poor blacks for poor living space were inevitable. Resistance to expansion of the ghetto forced greater and greater overcrowding and deterioration of existing housing; the black community had to grow, block by block, into the neighbouring white areas.

Ghetto expansion was made possible as overseas immigration slowed after 1920 and as a portion of the white population escaped the inner-city slums into newer, lower-middle-class housing a little further out. Jewish communities were easier to move into than eastern and southern European Catholic communities. Moves were sometimes 'concentric', that is, into areas of similarly old and poor housing. Often the concentric move involved a jump over intervening more resistant groups or richer areas. More commonly, growth was outward within the sector, along and between the railroads, and adjacent to less desirable industrial areas [10, 31]. Thus, the first to move were often middle-class blacks who could more easily afford to penetrate the somewhat better and newer housing, whose former residents again had the means to flee to the suburbs. In turn, the poorest and most recent black migrants from the South moved into the worst and oldest slums, which were to be found in the core areas of the black community.

The term ghetto is appropriate to describe black residential space, a segregated territory with boundaries enforced by both external and internal pressures. Interestingly, the black ghetto has been more rigidly defined in the North where blacks have been feared as the unknown, than in the South, where several smaller black sections were easier to control than a single large section. There were numerous external pressures against the dispersal of blacks: these included legal restrictions against housing integration, enforced by the FHA itself until 1949; refusal by the real estate industry to show or sell housing to blacks in white areas, and by banks and insurance companies to finance such sales; white and black

TABLE 3
Development of Black Population in Cities, 1880 to 1970

(1940 Rank Order) (Population in 000s)

CITY	City 1880	City 1900	City 1920	City 1940	% Black 1940	SMSA 1960	% City Black	% SMSA Black	SMSA 1970	% City Black
New York	28	68	169	504	6	1557	14	11	2368	21
Chicago	6	30	109	278	8	977	23	15	1343	33
Philadelphia	32	63	134	251	13	671	26	15	844	34
Washington	52	87	110	187	28	487	54	24	704	74
Baltimore	54	79	108	166	19	375	35	22	490	46
St. Louis	22	36	70	166	13	295	29	14	379	41
New Orleans	58	78	101	149	30	267	37	31	324	45
Detroit	3	4	41	149	9	559	29	15	751	44
Memphis	15	50	61	121	42	224	37	36	265	39
Birmingham		17	70	109	41	219	40	35	218	42
Atlanta	16	36	63	105	35	231	38	23	311	51
Houston	6	5	34	86	22	250	23	20	384	26
Cleveland	2	6	35	85	10	258	29	14	333	39
Los Angeles		2	16	64	4	465	14	7	763	18
Jacksonville	4	16	42	62	36	105	41	23	118	22
Pittsburgh	4	20	38	62	9	161	16	7	170	20
Richmond	28	32		61	32	103	42	26	130	42
Cincinnati	8	15	30	56	12	127	21	12	155	28
Indianapolis	7	16	35	51	13	100	21	14	137	18
Dallas	2	9	24	50	17	159	19	15	241	25
Nashville	16	30	36	47	35	78	37	19	96	20
Norfolk	10	6	43	46	32	149	26	26	168	28
Louisville	21	39	41	47	15	83	18	12	101	24
Savannah	16	28	39	43	40	67	35	34	64	44
Kansas City	8	18	31	42	10	116	23	11	151	22
Miami			9	37	21	137	22	15	190	23
Columbus (Ohio)	3	8	22	36	12	89	16	12	106	19
Shreveport	5	9	17	36	35	96	34	34	97	34
Montgomery	10	17	20	35	40	64	35	38	70	14
Charleston	27	25	32	32	40	78	51	37	95	45
Boston	6	12	16	24	3	88	9	3	127	16
Charlotte	3	7	15	31	28	61	28	35	95	30
Mobile	12	17	24	29	35	101	32	32	113	35
Fort Worth	1	4	16	25	14	61	16	11	83	20
Augusta	10	18	23	27	40	66	45	30	70	50
San Francisco	2	2	2	5	1	239	10	9	330	35
Tampa, St. P.		4	12	23	22	89	16	11	109	18
Columbus, Ga.	5	7	9	17	32	63	27	29	68	26
Baton Rouge	4	7	9	12	34	72	29	32	81	28
Jackson	3	4	10	24	39	75	35	40	96	40
Buffalo	1	2	5	18	23	83	13	7	109	20
Dayton	1	3	9	20	10	70	21	10	94	30
Columbus, S.C.	6	10	15	22	35	75	30	29	85	30
Beaumont		3	13	19	32	62	29	21	68	31
Milwaukee		1	2	9	1	63	9	6	107	15
Chattanooga	5	13	19	36	28	49	33	18	50	36
Macon	7	12	23	26	45	56	44	31	60	37
Winston Salem		5	21	36	45	45	37	24	118	34

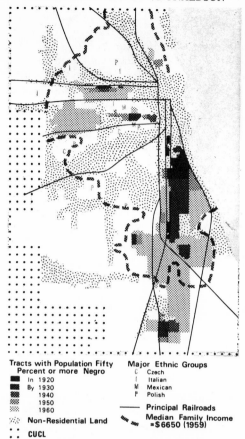

Tracts with Population Fifty   Major Ethnic Groups
Percent or more Negro   C   Czech
■   In 1920   I   Italian
■   By 1930   M   Mexican
▓   1940   P   Polish
▒   1950
▒   1960   —— Principal Railroads
⠂⠄ Non-Residential Land   ⟿ ₃₀₀ Median Family Income
⠂⠄ CUCL   =$6650 (1959)

Fig. 7. Extension of the Chicago ghetto.

mutual fear of being alone within the others' territory; lack of information about opportunities; building freeways and renewal projects, which serve as barriers to expansion; white protective organizations and violence perpetrated against blacks who attempt to enter white areas; and, the sheer poverty and political and legal weakness of blacks [27].

Internal pressures included, as they still do, the advantages of mutual protection within the ghetto, the convenience and preference for black churches, clubs, businesses, and especially friends and relatives, and the possibility of political power through spatial concentration. By 1928, the black ghetto in Chicago was large enough to elect the first black congressman since Reconstruction. In the larger New York ghettos, geographic separation and gerrymandering prevented black representation until 1940. Still, the solidarity of the ghetto has proved to be an important basis for growth of political power and activism in the more recent past.

The ghetto is mainly the product of social forces. It is true that the majority of the ghetto residents may be poor, but by no means all are. The ghetto contains all classes of blacks from the poorest slum dweller to the upper-class professional. Social distinction by colour is stronger than the usual economic determination of residential location. But the black ghetto is also an economic colony: the majority of residents rent from absentee landlords, and the majority of jobs and businesses are white-controlled. Understandably, the pattern provides the continuing potential for violent reaction.

Population Redistribution and Migration, 1940–1970. After 1940, the growth of the black population of the North-East continued to accelerate, slowing only slightly in the Middle Atlantic states after 1960, and in the east north central states after 1965. By 1960, the latter, with somewhat better job opportunities, had a larger black population than the Middle Atlantic states. By 1960 both regions passed the east south central region, whose black population had been declining absolutely, and the west south central, whose black population was growing only moderately. The black population of the North-East passed 6 million by 1963, its proportion of the total black population rising from 22 per cent in 1940 to 40 per cent by 1968. After 1940 the black population of California grew rapidly, reaching one million by 1960. The West's proportion rose from 1 per cent to 8 per cent while that in the South fell from 77 to 53 per cent. The South will probably be the residence of less than half of the black population by 1972. At the same time, the black proportion of the total Southern population fell from 24 to 19 per cent, while it increased in the North-East from 4 to 8·5 per cent and in the West from 1 to 5 per cent. The proportion of the black population living in urban areas reached 95 per cent outside of the South and even 60 per cent in the South by 1968 (up from 35 per cent in 1940).

In 1940, only one of the eleven states with high black populations was to be found outside of the South and that was ninth ranked New York. By 1960, New York had become the leading state. Illinois now ranked sixth, California ninth, and Pennsylvania eleventh. Within the South, a relative shift out of the Deep South (Mississippi, Alabama, Georgia, S. Carolina) to Florida, Louisiana, and especially Texas occurred. By 1970, the three highest states were all located outside of the South: New York, California, and Illinois.

The distribution of the black population in 1960. The black proportion of the population gives an initial impression that the black population is almost entirely Southern (Figure 8). As the less familiar map (Figure 9) of the absolute black population shows, this is not so. Figure 8 illustrates that in the South the relative number of blacks remains moderately high in rural, small-town, and city areas, from south Maryland through east Texas; and the proportion even exceeds 50 per cent in some of the early settled areas of coastal Virginia and the Carolinas, and also in the rich cotton areas of the Mississippi delta and the 'black belts' of Mississippi, Alabama, and Georgia. Figure 9 reveals that in absolute terms, the industrial states of the North and California are as important as the leading Southern states, but the black population is concentrated in a few metropolitan areas. The rural black population was still a majority (in 1960) only in North and South Carolina, Mississippi, and Arkansas. Both maps reveal the virtual absence of black population in the northern plains, the mountain states, and the Pacific north-west.

Between 1940 and 1960 the black population at least tripled in most major Northern cities and doubled in most Southern cities (see Table 3). The gradual trend towards convergence, or similar proportions of blacks in the North and South, is revealed by Figure 10.

Migration, 1940–1970. Figure 11, lifetime migration of blacks to 1960, illustrates the great increase in movement after 1940, and the relative shift to the Great Lakes region and California. About three-fourths of the 1·2 million blacks leaving the South Atlantic states moved north to the Middle Atlantic and New England states and about one-fourth to the east north central states. From the east

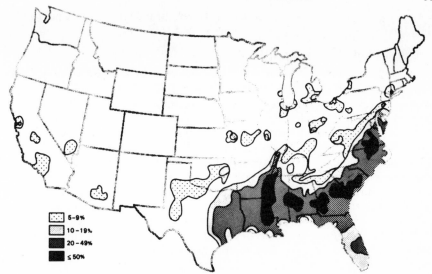

Fig. 8. Proportion of the population black in 1960.

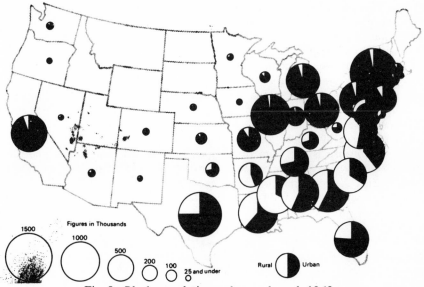

Fig. 9. Black population, urban and rural, 1960.

south central states, about 70 per cent of the 1·25 million moved up into the north
central states, 12 per cent to other parts of the South, 10 per cent to the
North-East, and 8 per cent to the West; 643,000 blacks moved from the west south
central states, 60 per cent to the West, and 40 per cent into the north central. These
paths strongly reflect the perception of the nearest opportunities from the various
regions as well as previous migrations of friends and relatives. By 1960 the leading
destination had changed to the east north central states. The rapid pace of
northward migration continued to 1965. Since then, it has greatly slowed as blacks
are finding increasing opportunities in Southern cities; the physical insecurity of

northern ghettos now may exceed that of the South; and young blacks now wish to fight the battle for equality on their home ground.

Civil Rights and Black Power, 1950–1970

The Civil Rights Movement. The 20 years from 1950–1970 might be described as a period of social revolution. A symbolic beginning was Truman's integration of the Armed Forces in 1949, his reversal of FHA housing segregation policy, and his demand for Civil Rights legislation. The latter was not acted upon until the period from 1964–1969, when persistent and increasingly strong black anger and protest made such action necessary. Many of the veterans returning from World War II and Korea were no longer easily intimidated. A number of more radical black groups and leaders emerged in the early 1950s. The crucial school desegregation of the Supreme Court in 1954, outlawing the 'Separate but Equal' doctrine, and especially the Montgomery bus boycott in 1955-6 unleashed a flood of demonstrations, protests, and conflicts, without which no change would have been possible.

The dual system of public accommodations has been substantially eliminated, and that of schools partially broken. Blacks have become far more mobile. Since 1965, after some years of improving education and after the catalyst of severe riots, job opportunities in better industrial and white-collar occupations have finally begun to open. Blacks have been able to participate in the growth of industry in the South only since 1966. This, in turn, has led to a slowdown of the migration of blacks to the North, since many prefer to remain in their home region. The occupational shift has also led to the first real improvement in the income of blacks in relation to whites. The median income of blacks, which had hovered around one-half that of whites from 1940 to 1964, increased to 63 per cent by 1969 (about 75 per cent in the North, 50 per cent in the South). The continuing reduction in employment in the lowest-paying farm-labour and domestic-service categories is being offset by movement into other services and the hitherto almost closed clerical and professional categories (Table 4).

But resistance by unions and small businesses to integration is great, and the battle for equality is far from over. Open housing bills and equal-opportunity employment laws have been passed, but often are unenforced or unenforceable. Anyone using the conditions of slavery as his base line might say that progress has been made; but to do so would be inadequate. The basic issue is not the progress of

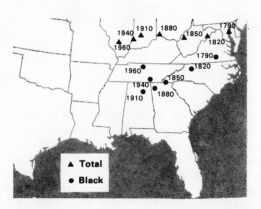

Fig. 10. Centres of the total population and the black population, 1790 to 1960.

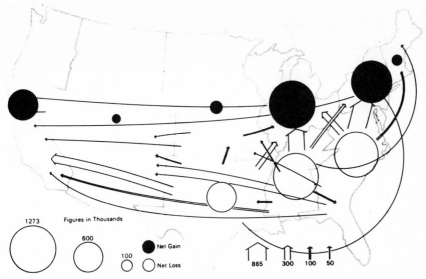

Fig. 11. Lifetime migration of blacks to 1960.

the black measured in terms of his conditions one hundred, or ten, or two years ago. Ours is a multi-racial society. The basic issue is, as it has always been when the black man is compared to the white, whether the changes have been of such a magnitude as to alter the socio-economic relationship between blacks as a group and whites as a group? In recent years, the rate of growth of income for blacks was rapid; however, the actual dollar increase of the white income was greater. Contrasted to the level of prosperity reached by much of the white population, the progress of the black seems less impressive [14, 26, 32].

Discrimination, Housing, and the Ghetto. The symbolic, legal, and rhetorical evidence of progress convince many that black progress is effectual. But there remains discrimination against blacks in virtually all American communities. Voting districts are gerrymandered to decrease the power of the black voter. School districts are so organized as to produce 'white' and 'black' schools. Health and welfare policies are used against the black family. And in many cities, services and facilities are not located where they would be readily available to the black population. Most hospitals, clinics, and physicians in Detroit [24], Chicago [9], and Los Angeles [17], for example, are located in or restricted to middle- and upper-class areas. This provides the poor, especially blacks, with inferior and infrequent care, with longer trips and longer waits, and consequently aggravates an already high incidence of disease and mortality.

Land use zoning has been used against blacks in Miami, Atlanta, and Philadelphia [38, 5, 4]. Physical barriers, whether natural or socially contrived, are also used to maintain the racial and spatial *status quo*. The Harlem, Cuyahoga, and Anacostia rivers, for example, have separated black and white residential areas in New York City, Cleveland, and Washington, respectively. Streets and railroads have been used to define and confine black areas in Durham, Detroit, Chicago, New Haven, Atlanta, and San Francisco.

Urban renewal and public housing have consistently fostered segregation, with the sanction or insistence of local governmental bodies. Research findings indicate,

TABLE 4

Changing Occupational Structure of the Black Population
(Percentage Employed in Occupations)

Occupation	1910 Black	1910 White	1950 Black	1950 White	1968 Black	1968 White	Occupation
Farmers	17	17·5	8	7	1·2	2·7	Farmers
Farm Labourers	38	15	11	4	3·7	1·8	Farm labourers
Mining		1·7	5	14	8	14	Craftsmen
Manufacturing	11	31	19	21	24	18	Operatives
Transport	4·8	6·7	14	5	11	4	Labourers
Trade	2	11	38	39	42	35·5	BLUE COLLAR
Professional	1·3*	5·6	3	8	8	14	Professionals
			2·5	12	2·8	11	Managers
Clerical	·3	6·6	3·5	14	12	17·5	Clerical
			1·2	7	2	6·6	Sales
			10	40	24	49·5	WHITE COLLAR
Professional serv.	·4	1·3	16	7	19	9	General serv.
Domestic serv.	22	6·6	18	1·5	9·5	1·4	Domestic serv.
			34	8·5	28	10·4	SERVICES

*Mainly clergy and teachers. Occupational categories not comparable 1910 and later years.
Source: United States Census of Population, and Current Population Statistics.

for example, that there have been political and social pressures to contain public housing within existing racial and poverty concentrations in Chicago, Cleveland, Detroit, Atlanta, New Orleans, Dade County (Florida), and Montgomery [22, 13, 21]. The National Commission on Urban Problems [29] found that in six of the twelve case histories it studied, the policy was to locate public housing projects in such a manner as to identify with the existing racial pattern of the cities.

Besides government policy there are a variety of apparently 'neutral' activities to maintain strictly white residential areas. These include building code decisions and inspection standards, location standards, location of water and sewer facilities, and zoning policies. Glendale, California, and Deerfield, Illinois are examples of places in which building permits and inspections have been used to keep the community white. Dearborn, Michigan, on the other hand, tried to evict black families by terminating such public facilities as gas and garbage collection. Oklahoma City unsuccessfully attempted to exclude blacks from the city by redrawing the city boundaries [25].

Not only have Federal and local governments sanctioned or forced the segregation of public housing, they have condoned the inferior quality of that housing. Wright Patman of the House Banking Committee has charged that the FHA has approved substandard housing as eligible for federal programmes. Under these programmes the government subsidizes interest payments on 'safe, sanitary and decent' housing. The Southern Regional Council found that the welfare departments of the states of Virginia, Florida, North Carolina, and South Carolina are collectively the largest slumlords in the South.

Even the elimination of many legal and financial barriers to residential integration has not resulted in any diminution in the solidity of the ghetto. Some inter-racial housing developments have been built; integrated housing does exist in many cities and in certain professional, upper-middle-class areas. But white resistance and fear remain strong, so that when an area becomes partially black, the remaining white residents find reasons to move to the suburbs for newer housing.

An indirect benefit of the white flight to the suburbs and increased general affluence has been the dramatic extension of the ghetto into areas of better-quality middle-class housing. Another benefit is that many central cities are heading towards a black voting majority—Gary by 1970, Detroit, Philadelphia, Cleveland, St. Louis, Baltimore, Atlanta, and New Orleans by 1980. This is a fascinating geographic result of minority concentration: from a pattern of dispersed share-croppers, without political strength in 1900, to one possessing the political balance of power in major cities by 1980. Cities have tried to bring middle-class whites back into the city through urban renewal, but this has so far failed to stem the tide of white outflow.

At the same time, the emergence of a strong sense of black community and culture since 1964, and the development of the black power movement have increased the internal pressures for remaining spatially separate. This has paid off in the form of increased political power, even in the South, since 1965. For example, there are now twelve black members of Congress (New York City 2; Chicago 2; Detroit 2; and Cleveland, Los Angeles, St. Louis, Oakland, Baltimore, and Philadelphia 1 each), more and more representatives in legislatures, in the South as well as the North, and even a few county sheriffs—holders of real power in the South.

Blacks recognize advantages in integration—particularly access to better schools, housing, and jobs; but they fear the dilution of power, the very real possibility of permanent subjugation as a dispersed minority. Logically, the white national majority of 89 per cent should avidly seek full integration, since they could successfully prevent the emergence of black separatism and black power; but irrationally and emotionally, the majority of whites still fear blacks socially and psychologically more than they do the prospect of a yet more racially divided and violent society.

Conclusion

In the century since Reconstruction, the majority of black Americans have abandoned a life confined to share-crop farming in the South, where they were numerically in the majority in many areas, but totally subjugated economically, socially, and politically. For many of those blacks who have remained in the South, the total subjugation remains. Out-migration has reduced the black population of the South, but black people are again becoming a majority, this time by concentrating in the ghettos of major cities, North and South. The long-term trend is towards an equalization of the black proportion of the population in the highly urban parts of the country, but in non-Southern rural, small-town, and small-city areas the black population probably will remain small. The geographic concentration in urban ghettos has undesirable aspects for both blacks and whites. In the foreseeable future, this does not seem reversible, both because of the possible political advantages it offers blacks in terms of solidarity, and because of the abiding inability of whites and blacks to overcome deep-seated fears and prejudices. Evidently not until political, economic, and social equality is achieved, and perhaps not even then, will black and white no longer be the basis for this dominant geographic separation of peoples in America.

REFERENCES

1. Aptheker, H. 'Maroons Within the Present Limits of the United States', *Journal of Negro History*, 24 (April 1939), 167–84.
2. Aptheker, H. *American Negro Slave Revolts*. New York: International Publishers, 1963.
3. Bennett, L., Jr. *Before the Mayflower*. Rev.ed. Baltimore: Penguin, 1964.
4. Blumberg, L. and M. Lalli. 'Little Ghettos: A Study of Negroes in the Suburbs', *Phylon*, 27 (Summer 1966), 117–31.
5. Blumberg, L. 'Segregated Housing, Marginal Location, and the Crisis of Confidence', *Phylon*, 25 (Winter 1964), 321–30.
6. Bontemps, A. and J. Conroy. *Anyplace But Here*. New York: Hill and Wang, 1968.
7. Brandt, L. 'Negroes of St. Louis', *Journal of the American Statistical Association*, 8 (March 1903), 203–68.
8. Clark, K. *Dark Ghetto*. New York: Harper and Row, 1965.
9. de Vise, P. *et al. Slum Medicine: Chicago's Apartheid Health System*. Chicago: University of Chicago Community and Family Study, 1969.
10. Drake, St. Clair and H. R. Cayton. *Black Metropolis*. New York: Harper and Row, 1962.
11. Durham, P. and E. L. Jones. *The Negro Cowboys*, New York: Dodd, Mead and Co., 1965.
12. Ginzburg, R. *100 Years of Lynchings*. New York: Lancer Books, 1969.
13. Glazer, N. and D. McEntire, eds. *Studies in Housing and Minority Groups*. Berkeley: University of California Press, 1960.
14. Good, P. *The American Serfs*. New York: Ballantine Books, 1968.
15. Green, C. M. *The Secret City*. Princeton: Princeton University Press, 1967.
16. Hart, J. F. 'The Changing Distribution of the American Negro', *Annals of the Association of American Geographers*, 50 (September 1960), 242–66.
17. Jacobs, P. *Prelude to Riot*. New York: Random House, 1966.
18. Katz, W. L. *Eyewitness: The Negro in American History*. New York: Pitman, 1967.
19. Kamble, F. A. *Journal of a Residence on a Georgia Plantation in 1838–1839*. Edited by J. A. Scott. New York: Alfred A. Knopf, 1961.
20. Kilson, D. 'Towards Freedom: An Analysis of Slave Revolts in the United States', *Phylon*, 25 (Summer 1964), 175–87.
21. Lowi, T. J. 'Apartheid U.S.A.', *Transaction*, 7 (February 1970), 32–9.
22. McEntire, D. *Residence and Race*. Berkeley: University of California Press, 1960.
23. Meier, A. and E. M. Radwick. *From Plantation to Ghetto*. New York: Hill and Wang, 1966.
24. Milio, N. *9226 Kercheval*. Ann Arbor: University of Muchigan Press, 1970.
25. Million, E. M. 'Racial Restrictive Covenants Revisited', *Open Occupancy vs. Forced Housing Under the Fourteenth Amendment: Symposium*. Edited by A. Avins. New York: Bookmailer, 1963.
26. Moore, W., Jr. *The Vertical Ghetto*. New York: Random House, 1969.
27. Morrill, R. L. 'The Negro Ghetto: Problems and Alternatives', *The Geographical Review*, 55 (July 1965), 339–61.
28. Myrdal, G. *An American Dilemma*. New York: McGraw-Hill, 1964.
29. The National Commission on Urban Problems. *More Than Shelter: Social Needs in Low and Moderate-Income Housing*. Research Report No. 8, Washington, D.C.: Government Printing Office, 1968.
30. Peskin, A., ed. *North Into Freedom: The Autobiography of John Malvin, Free Negro, 1795–1880*. Cleveland: Western Reserve University Press, 1966.
31. Rose, H. M. 'Social Processes in the City: Race and Urban Residential Choice'. Commission on College Geography Resource Paper No. 6. Washington, D.C.: Association of American Geographers, 1969.
32. Sloane, M. E. 'The Housing Act of 1968: Best Yet But is it Enough?', *Civil Rights Digest*, 1 (Fall 1968), 1–9.
33. Stampp, K. M. *The Peculiar Institution*. New York: Vintage Books, 1956.
34. Still, W. *The Underground Railroad*. Philadelphia: People's Publishing Co., 1871.
35. Sydnor, C. S. 'Life Span of Mississippi Slaves', *American Historical Review*, 35 (April 1930), 566–74.
36. Taylor, O. W. *Negro Slavery in Arkansas*. Durham: Duke University Press, 1958.
37. Utley, R. W. 'Pecos Bill on the Texas Frontier', *The American West*, 6 (January 1969), 4–13, 61-2.
38. Virrick, E. L. 'New Housing for Negroes in Dade County, Florida', *Studies in Housing and Minority Groups*. Edited by N. Glazer and D. McEntire. Berkeley: University of California Press, 1960.
39. Wade, R. C. *Slavery in the Cities; The South 1820–1860*. New York: Oxford University Press, 1964.

2. THE SPATIAL VARIATIONS IN URBAN LEFT-WING VOTING IN ENGLAND AND WALES IN 1951[1]

M. C. Roberts and K. W. Rumage

Characteristically, political geographers have oriented their research efforts towards such topics as international waterways, capital cities, and boundaries. In centring attention on such topics they have largely ignored significant geographic aspects of voting and voting behaviour. The lack of uniformity in the number of votes cast in favour of or in opposition to particular issues or candidates is indicative of spatial differences in voting. This lack of uniformity is of special interest to the geographer and should be as much an integral part of political geography as are the distributional aspects of other political phenomena.

The quality of any geographic analysis that attempts to explain the areal variation of voting patterns is in part influenced by the availability of pertinent data. Such data have been made available by Moser and Scott[2] in their studies of the urban structure of England, Scotland, and Wales for the years 1951 and 1955. Furthermore, in 1951, there occurred both a General Election[3] and a national census, thereby affording the political geographer an opportunity to use a variety of political and other socio-economic data comparable in terms of time. The Labour Party was selected as the focal point of this study because it is the political group that normally attracts the largest number of votes in urban areas.

In both England and Wales, spatial variations in the strength of the two major political parties pose problems of interest to the political geographer. Support for the Labour Party is concentrated in urban and industrial districts, whereas that of the Conservative Party originates in rural towns and farming areas. This study is concerned with the place-to-place variation of the Left-wing vote in the largest towns of England and Wales (Fig. 1). It utilizes quantitative techniques in an effort to add precision to the inferences drawn from the data analysed.

The dependent or criterion variable to be analysed is here defined as the vote cast for the Left-wing in the 1951 General Election[4] (Fig. 2). This vote includes not only that for the Labour Party, but also that of the other Left groups such as the British Communist Party and the Independent Labour Party.[5] The two latter parties make up such a small portion of the total Left vote, that the terms Left-wing and Labour Party may be used synonymously.

The study universe is composed of 157 towns (Fig. 1), classified in the following way: eighty county boroughs, sixty-four municipal boroughs, twelve urban districts, and the administrative county of London.[6] Each of these towns had a population of 50,000 or more in 1951. All towns specifically mentioned in the text are identified in Figure 3.

The Variables

The independent or predictor variables used in this research are those which are assumed to be functionally and areally related to the voting behaviour of individuals. The methodological framework within which this investigation is cast has been established for the United States,[7] and it is with a sense of

From *Annals of the Association of American Geographers*, 55 (1965), 161–78. Reprinted by permission of the authors and the Association.

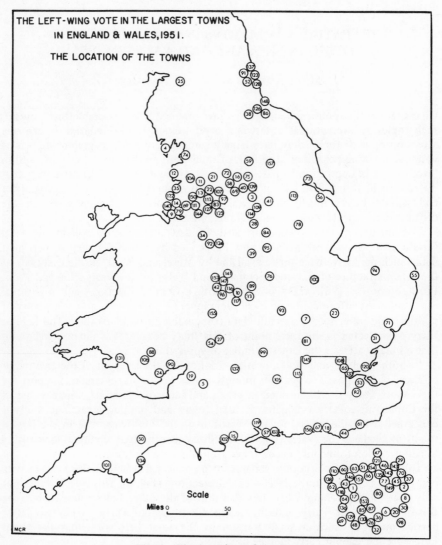

Fig. 1. The location of the towns.

experimentation that this framework is now applied to the British milieu. Writings of political scientists[8] concerned with voting behaviour help to provide a basis for the choice of predictor variables.

Hypothesized as being variables that are areally associated with the Left-wing vote in 1951 are:

(1) population aged 65 and over (X_4),

(2) females per 1,000 males (X_6),

(3) persons living in non-private households (X_{16}),

(4) overcrowded private households (X_{21}),

(5) per cent of local authority houses (X_{30}).

(6) per cent of the population working in the area in manufacture, agriculture, and mining (X_{33}),

(7) persons in Social Classes I and II (X_{41}),
(8) persons in Social Classes IV and V (X_{42}),
(9) persons who finish their formal education at age 15 (X_{56}).
(10) per cent of the population aged 15–24 in full-time attendance at an educational establishment (X_{57}),
(11) distance to the centre of the nearest coalfield (X_{60}).[9]

It will be noted that two demographic variables, age (X_4) and sex (X_6), are employed in this analsysis.[10] The recognition of sex and age as determinants in voting preference between the Labour and Conservative parties is well established in the literature.[11] An example of the influence of age is illustrated by the Bristol North East constituency (Table 1). Jennings, writing on the age factor in British politics, notes that, '. . . on the average, people get more Conservative as they grow older.'[12] The data for the 157 towns reveal a correlation between the number of people over sixty-five and the Left-wing vote of–0·579. In one sense, this is a rather surprising result, because the Labour government (1945–1951) increased pensions and social welfare benefits for the older people. The answer to this quandary has been suggested by Jennings,[13] who maintains that there are three factors associated with the preference for the older voter to support the Conservative Party. He found that the middle class has a greater life expectancy than the working class, hence the influence of the middle-class Conservative voter as it obtains to this age group is greater than has been expected. Secondly, he points out that the Labour Party is a novelty in that it is a relative latecomer as a political force in British politics. Thirdly, the fact that women with their greater longevity make up the major proportion of the over sixty-five age group.

TABLE 1
Sex and Party Vote for the Bristol N.E. Constituency, 1955

Per cent voting	Aged 21–49		Aged 50 and over	
	Men	Women	Men	Women
Conservative	44	47	50	53
Labour	50	44	36	38
Liberal	6	9	14	9
	100	100	100	100

Source: Jennings, 1960, see footnote 8.

A further extension of this last statement by Jennings is incorporated in variable (X_6). It has been found that the female voter in England and Wales, as in most other West European countries, is much more likely to vote for a Right-wing party than her male counterpart,[14] with the result that her vote is highly associated with that of the Conservative Party. This bent to the Conservative Party happens even in industrial towns although it is most clearly seen in the urbanized coastal areas. Such a situation arises because a great number of retired people live in coastal resort towns, where women outnumber men. From data collected in Bristol, Table 1 was constructed to illustrate the differences between the sexes as to voting. It will be noted that the statistics for this table are for the General Election of 1955, but the trend shown by this particular constituency also applies earlier. For the 157 towns comprising the universe the simple correlation between the number of females per 1,000 males and the Left-wing vote is –0·780, admirably corroborating the data of Table 1.

1 Acton
2 Barking
3 Barnsley
4 Barrow-in-Furness
5 Bath
6 Beckenham
7 Bedford
8 Bexley
9 Birkenhead
10 Birmingham
11 Blackburn
12 Blackpool
13 Bolton
14 Bootle
15 Bournemouth
16 Bradford
17 Brentford and
   Chiswick
18 Brighton
19 Bristol
20 Bromley
21 Burnley
22 Bury
23 Cambridge
24 Cardiff
25 Carlisle
26 Carshalton
27 Cheltenham
28 Chesterfield
29 Chigwell
30 Chislehurst and
   Sidcup
31 Colchester
32 Coulsdon and Purley
33 Coventry
34 Crewe
35 Crosby
36 Croydon
37 Dagenham
38 Darlington
39 Derby
40 Dewsbury
41 Doncaster
42 Dudley
43 Ealing
44 Eastbourne
45 East Ham
46 Edmonton
47 Enfield
48 Epsom and Ewell
49 Esher
50 Exeter
51 Finchley
52 Gateshead

53 Gillingham
54 Gloucester
55 Great Yarmouth
56 Grimsby
57 Gosport
58 Halifax
59 Harrogate
60 Harrow
61 Hastings
62 Hayes and
   Harlington
63 Hendon
64 Heston and
   Isleworth
65 Hornchurch
66 Hornsey
67 Hove
68 Huddersfield
69 Huyton with Roby
70 Ilford
71 Ipswich
72 Keighley
73 Kingston-upon-Hull
74 Lancaster
75 Leeds
76 Leicester
77 Leyton
78 Lincoln
79 Liverpool
80 London A.C.
81 Luton
82 Maidstone
83 Manchester
84 Mansfield
85 Merton and Morden
86 Middlesbrough
87 Mitcham
88 Merthyr Tydful
89 Nuneaton
90 Newport
91 Newcastle upon Tyne
92 Newcastle-under-
   Lyme
93 Northampton
94 Norwich
95 Nottingham
96 Oldbury
97 Oldham
98 Orpington
99 Oxford
100 Peterborough
101 Plymouth
102 Poole
103 Portsmouth

104 Preston
105 Reading
106 Rhondda
107 Rochdale
108 Romford
109 Rotherham
110 Ruislip-Northwood
111 St. Helens
112 Salford
113 Scunthorpe
114 Sheffield
115 Slough
116 Smethwick
117 Solihull
118 Southall
119 Southampton
120 Southend-on-Sea
121 Southgate
122 Southport
123 South Shields
124 Stoke-on-Trent
125 Stockport
126 Stockton-on-Tees
127 Stretford
128 Sunderland
129 Surbiton
130 Sutton and Cheam
131 Swansea
132 Swindon
133 Thurrock
134 Torquay
135 Tottenham
136 Twickenham
137 Tynemouth
138 Uxbridge
139 Wakefield
140 Wallasey
141 Walsall
142 Walthamstow
143 Wanstead and
   Woodford
144 Warrington
145 Watford
146 Wembley
147 West Bromwich
148 West Hartlepool
149 West Ham
150 Wigan
151 Willesden
152 Wimbledon
153 Wolverhampton
154 Wood Green
155 Worcester
156 Worthing
157 York

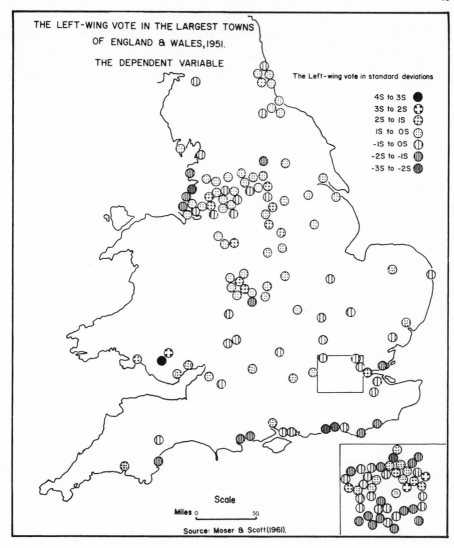

Fig. 2. The dependent variable.

Housing characteristics give the best available approximation for distinguishing between the residential areas of the different social classes within a city. Hence, housing characteristics are useful in a prediction framework for estimating the Left-wing vote. Not only are there intra-city differences but there are inter-city variations in housing as well. It is generally conceded that whereas the industrial cities have a higher proportion of overcrowded conditions, older houses, and houses lacking amenities, the predominantly suburban towns have better-quality housing with less overcrowding. Therefore it can be hypothesized that the towns with the greater proportion of better housing will favour the Conservative Party whereas the industrial towns with their poorer housing conditions will support the Labour Party.[15]

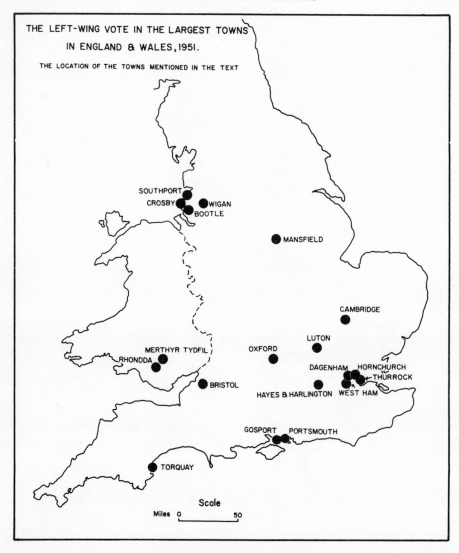

THE LEFT-WING VOTE IN THE LARGEST TOWNS
IN ENGLAND & WALES, 1951.

THE LOCATION OF THE TOWNS MENTIONED IN THE TEXT

Fig. 3. The location of the towns mentioned in the text.

Three variables related to housing are employed in this study. Variable $(X_{16})^{16}$ is included on the grounds that it takes care of people living in hotels, large boarding houses, educational establishments, military bases, and hospitals. The hypothesis that the larger number of retired persons who live in hotels and those who work in the universities vote Conservative is substantiated by the low but nevertheless significant correlation of 0·356. The second variable (X_{21}),[17] which measures overcrowding in British towns, reflects one of the results of bomb damage to residential areas during the Second World War.[18] The building rates, in the immediate postwar years, were not high enough to make any substantial impression on the amount of overcrowding. The Labour Party is an ardent supporter of the extension and increase in the number of local authority houses, and this policy, it is hypothesized, makes it attractive to the voter living in overcrowded conditions. The correlation between overcrowding and the Labour vote is 0·491.

The final housing variable (X_{30})[19] is the percentage of local authority houses built between 1945 and 1958 in a town. As previously mentioned, the Labour Party gives support to the building of local-authority houses. These houses are more or less the equivalent of the low-cost federal housing in the United States, built from standardized plans and erected in large housing estates. The exact design and rental cost vary from one locality to another. Such houses are found in their greatest numbers in the industrial towns where the manual workers do not have the capital for buying privately built houses. The latter are more prevalent in the suburban areas where the middle class predominates. The correlation coefficient between this variable and the Labour vote is a positive 0·687.

The most direct measure of the working population is provided by variable (X_{33}),[20] which may be expected to have a high correlation with the Labour vote. Harrison[21] provides a detailed study of the relationship between the unions and the Labour Party, and his discussion is invaluable in illustrating the inclination of the industrial worker to the Left-wing. The correlation of this predictor variable and the Labour vote is 0·627.

It can be said with some justification that one of the most widely held generalizations of voting behaviour in England and Wales is the relationship between class and party preference.[22] In collecting data for the British census the Registrar-General makes a grouping of occupations; these groupings, called Social Classes, are employed, with some modification, in this study. The classes are defined as: Class I, professional occupations; Class II, intermediate occupations; Class III, skilled occupations; Class IV, partly skilled occupations; and Class V, unskilled occupations. The modification consists of combining Social Classes I and II, and IV and V. Social Class III is eliminated because it exhibits a uniform spatial distribution.

The upper and middle classes, on the whole, give their vote to the Conservative Party,[23] and so it is hypothesized that variable (X_{41})[24] has a strong negative correlation with the Labour vote. It turns out to be −0·838.

The other Social Class variable (X_{42})[25] in contrast with the previous variate, has a positive correlation of 0·754. Recent research suggests that these strict class divisions in voting may be breaking down, just as the traditional industrial areas are declining and the Axial Belt[26] is gaining in importance. When people leave older areas, as they have been doing for the last three decades, the previously held social norms are often broken and new attitudes are adopted. One of the new attitudes is some degree of working-class support for the Conservative Party. Hoggart and Williams, in a paper concerned with this apparent trend, write:

... some of the more striking instances of working-class political solidarity seem to have occurred not only in the larger and unmistakably working-class industries but also to have gained from a sense of continuing local—using this now to mean quite a large area—traditions, loyalties, consciousness.

Today people are moving around more; many of the old areas are being split up; new industries and new forms of industry are recruiting people from all over, offering good wages and a more fluid range of opportunities.[27]

The growth of new industrial areas and the mobility of labour may cause widespread shifts in voting behaviour, although the simple correlation above does not lend much support for this contention as regards the 1951 General Election.

Educational characteristics are introduced in an attempt to bring another dimension to the socio-economic facets of voting behaviour. The first variable (X_{56})[28] indicates those who left school early and are mainly employed in the unskilled and semi-skilled jobs. Benney, et al., from their investigation into the voting preferences of persons in Greenwich, a constituency in south-east London, found that '... those with only elementary education are more likely to vote Labour and less likely to vote Conservative than those with a higher education'.[29]

The second variable (X_{57})[30] considers those in attendance at a place of higher education, and this factor, it is hypothesized, is a good measure of the size of the middle class in a voting community. It is the middle class that has the highest relative proportion in full-time education beyond the school-leaving age of 15. The correlation coefficient with the Labour vote is -0.754.

The final variable (X_{60})[31] considers a distance factor in relation to the Left-wing vote. In essence, it is employed as a spatial variable to measure the propensity of the Labour vote to decrease the further one gets from the centre of a traditional industrial area. The centre of a traditional industrial district (traditional, in the sense, that it is located on a coalfield, and attained its greatest importance in the late nineteenth and early twentieth centuries) is defined as the oldest coal-producing area on the coalfield,[32] and from this point distances to the individual towns are measured. In a simple correlation framework it is hypothesized that the shorter the distance between a town and the centre of the nearest coalfield, the greater the Labour vote. The coefficient turns out to be -0.393, which is statistically significant, and illustrates the value of a spatial variate in a geographic evaluation of voting patterns.

This measure of distance is introduced into the investigation to add another dimension to the geographic notion of areal association. A previous study that examines the effect of distance is that by McCarty[33] on the spatial distribution of the 1952 McCarthy vote in Wisconsin. Unlike McCarty, who introduced distance into the problem at the stage of hypothesis reformulation, the current study incorporates it from the beginning on *a priori* grounds.

TABLE 2

Simple Regressions between the Left-wing Vote for 1951,
and the Predictor Variables

	r	r^2		r	r^2
X_{47} with X_4	-0.579*	0.335	X_{47} with X_{41}	-0.838*	0.704
X_{47} with X_6	-0.780*	0.608	X_{47} with X_{42}	0.754*	0.568
X_{47} with X_{16}	0.355*	0.126	X_{47} with X_{56}	0.694*	0.482
X_{47} with X_{21}	0.491*	0.241	X_{47} with X_{57}	-0.754*	0.569
X_{47} with X_{30}	0.687*	0.472	X_{47} with X_{60}	-0.393*	0.154
X_{47} with X_{33}	0.630*	0.397			

*Significant at the 99 per cent level.
Source: Calculated by authors.

The Analysis

The analysis and explanation of the spatial distribution of the Left-wing vote in England and Wales may be approached by means of a series of regression models. It is possible, based on the knowledge of the relationships between the Labour vote and the selected socio-economic factors (Table 2), to test the degree of association between the criterion and the predictor variables by using multiple regression.

TABLE 3

The Multiple Regression Equations for Model I:
Population Characteristics

	R	R^2
$X_{47} = 75 \cdot 711 - 2 \cdot 082 X_4 - 0 \cdot 261 X_{60}$	$0 \cdot 620*$	$0 \cdot 384$
$X_{47} = 169 \cdot 804 - 0 \cdot 113 X_6 - 0 \cdot 081 X_{60}$	$0 \cdot 783*$	$0 \cdot 613$

*Significant at the 99 per cent level.
Source: Calculated by authors.

The variables may be grouped in terms of their intrinsic differences. These groupings can then be used in the analysis to provide the basis for the erection of a series of prediction models. Once these basic models are established it is possible to erect a model containing the combination of the most crucial variables.

Residual maps can be constructed in order to portray graphically the spatial variation of the amount of explanation given by a particular model. Further, these residual maps can be the basis for the formulation of new hypotheses. The maps are not in the usual $Y - Yc/Syc$ form,[34] but in the $Yc - Y/Syc$ arrangement. This latter type of residual is used in order to reduce the time spent changing the output of the computer. In following this procedure the positive values are those which are underpredicted, whereas the negative values are overpredicted.

A discussion of the models and the accompanying residual maps is now in order.

Model I: Population Characteristics

The two multiple regressions (Table 3) reveal that variable (X_6) is the most efficient of the two population characteristics since it explains $61 \cdot 3$ per cent of the variation as against $38 \cdot 4$ per cent with variate (X_4). The residuals are computed from the equation containing variables (X_6) and (X_{60}).

In Figure 4, and for each of the following maps, the equation giving the highest amount of explanation for a particular model is the one retained. The towns standing out as being inadequately explained by the model are Merthyr Tydfil, Rhondda, Dagenham, West Ham, and Wigan. Except for Dagenham, each is in an old-established industrial area where, as suggested by Hoggart and Williams,[35] class solidarity is very high and those who in some places would normally vote Conservative follow the community preference. The rationale for this situation, it may be assumed, is related to the notion that female voters more closely follow the psephologic preference established by the males. Such a situation reflects the solidarity of the different neighbourhoods making up these old-established industrial towns. However, it should be noted, that Dagenham differs from these urban places in that it is not an old-established working-class town. Its growth since the 1930s is closely linked to the fortunes of the Ford Motor Company plant located in the area. The extremely militant nature of the trade unionism[36] at the plant, combined with the almost total lack of middle-class residents in the city, may account for the unpredicted swing to the Labour Party.

Although the towns that are well predicted have a scatter through both countries, there are, nevertheless, two distinguishable areal groupings. One group, comprising the textile towns in the counties of Lancashire and Yorkshire, is slightly overpredicted, whereas the second group, containing the towns of the London conurbation and the south coast, is mainly underpredicted.

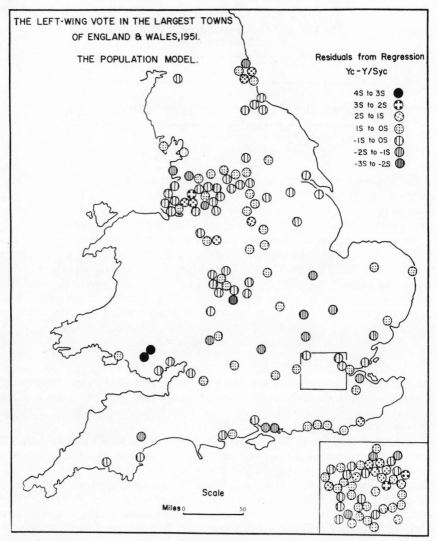

Fig. 4. The population model.

Model II: Housing Characteristics

In England and Wales, as in most West European countries, a good index of the standard of living and the industrial nature of a particular area is provided by the housing statistics. The simple correlations between the Left-wing vote and the housing factors are shown in Table 2. The two multiple correlation models, in Table 4 differ very little, but since the addition of (X_{60}) makes a difference, this equation is the one that has been mapped.

As with the previous one, this map (Fig. 5) clearly shows the underprediction of the heavy Labour vote in the industrial towns of West Ham, Dagenham, Merthyr Tydfil, and Rhondda. In this model four other towns are clearly underpredicted, Hayes and Harlington, Hornchurch, Mansfield, and Thurrock. The last is not only located close to Dagenham, but has very similar characteristics. The flat marshland

TABLE 4
The Multiple Regression Equations for Model II:
Housing Characteristics

	R	R^2
$X_{47} = -43 \cdot 063 + 0 \cdot 638 X_{16} +$ $0 \cdot 664 X_{21} + 0 \cdot 378 X_{30}$	$0 \cdot 7361*$	$0 \cdot 542$
$X_{47} = -44 \cdot 601 + 0 \cdot 647 X_{16} +$ $0 \cdot 673 X_{21} + 0 \cdot 383 X_{30} + 0 \cdot 020 X_{60}$	$0 \cdot 7362*$	$0 \cdot 543$

*Significant at the 99 per cent level.
Source: Calculated by the authors.

along the floodplain of the Thames river has become ideal building land for large industrial plants producing such products as margarine, cement, and refined oil. The residential housing is recent, and of quite a high standard compared to many working-class areas in the north of England. Many of the persons living in these Thurrock housing estates have moved in from the heavily bombed East End of London, an area which was and is a strong Labour area. Many people moving from this area have retained their political beliefs. Hayes and Harlington, and Hornchurch, although on opposite sides of London, are towns with recent residential deelopments and new manufacturing industries. Finally, Mansfield, with considerable recent specialization in boot and shoe manufacture,[37] is another of the towns that has had a marked local authority housing expansion since World War II.

At the other end of the scale are the overpredicted towns of Crosby and Southport, both located on the Lancashire coast north of Liverpool. They are residential towns with many retired persons and commuters to the Merseyside conurbation. In relation to the British average very few of the residents of Crosby and Southport are employed in manufacturing.[38] On the other hand, these towns rank first and ninth, respectively, in terms of numbers employed in the retail and service trades. The large number in these industries helps to explain the overprediction. Studies of voting behaviour of people employed in such occupations[39] show that although they are technically of the working class their motivations tend towards the middle class. The result is a working-class vote for the Conservatives. In these circumstances, the housing factors are not adequate in explaining the overprediction of the Labour vote in these two Lancashire towns.

TABLE 5
The Multiple Regression Equations for Model III:
Social Class Indices

	R	R^2
$X_{47} = 61 \cdot 510 - 1 \cdot 024 X_{41} + 0 \cdot 253 X_{42}$	$0 \cdot 843*$	$0 \cdot 711$
$X_{47} = 59 \cdot 492 - 1 \cdot 036 X_{41} +$ $0 \cdot 297 X_{42} + 0 \cdot 074 X_{60}$	$0 \cdot 845*$	$0 \cdot 714$

*Significant at the 99 per cent level.
Source: Calculated by authors.

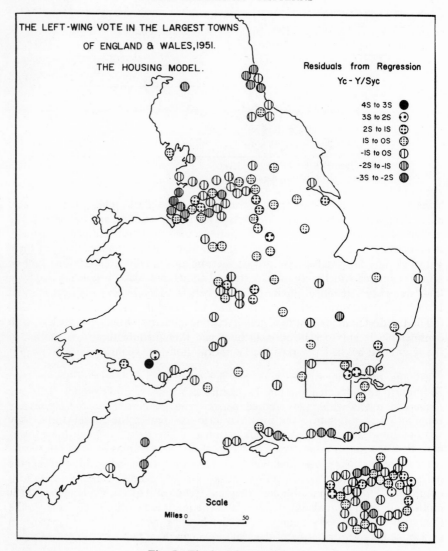

Fig. 5. The housing model.

Model III: Social Class Indices

The Registrar-General's definition of class leaves much to be desired in that it is based solely on occupation[40] and ignores other pertinent aspects of class distinction. Nevertheless, even with these apparent shortcomings the amount of 'explanation' gained by this model 71·4 per cent (Table 5), is high compared to the previous ones.

Even though this model is fairly successful in terms of explanation it still leaves us with several towns that are inadequately predicted (Fig. 6). The extreme cases of over- and underprediction are worthy of further examination. Torquay, Gosport, and Portsmouth, the towns with the greatest values of overprediction, are all located along the south coast. Torquay is a seaside resort in Devon with many

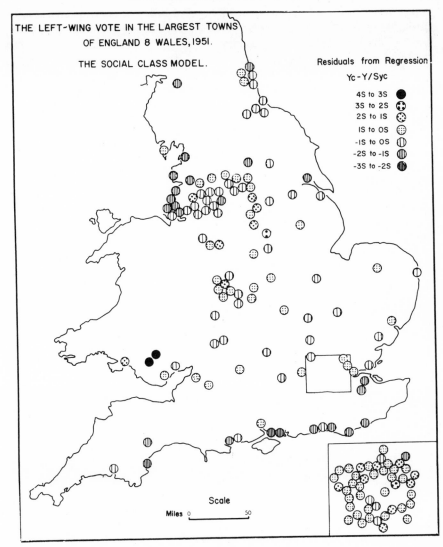

Fig. 6. The social class model.

retired people. Apparently, that part of Torquay's population that works in hotel and service industries do not, as might be expected, vote for the Labour Party. Union membership among these workers is not usually very high and a Left-wing inclination in voting preference is not a normal characteristic.[41]

Portsmouth and Gosport are anomalies for which the formulation of a suitable rationale is rather difficult. It is probable that any model employed to predict these two towns in a satisfactory manner must incorporate a more meaningful measure of the military vote (Portsmouth is a naval base) and a greater consideration of the service industries. In other words, caution must be practised in handling social class variables in the political geography of electoral behaviour in England and Wales. A similar note of caution is applicable to the towns of Merthyr Tydfil, Rhondda, Mansfield, and West Ham which are notably underpredicted.

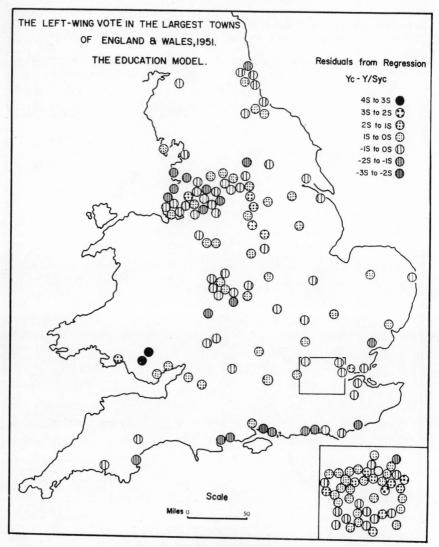

Fig. 7. The education model.

The London conurbation (Insert, Fig. 6) is the one urbanized region which shows a relative uniformity in terms of prediction. The towns comprising this conurbation are nearly all underpredicted by the Social Class model; a suitable explanation for this situation awaits future research.

Model IV: Educational Characteristics

Although at the outset it was realized that any predictive model based on educational characteristics is one that is closely linked, in terms of 'explanation', to Models II and III, these characteristics were included to add a further dimension to the spatial variation of the socio-economic factors in relation to the Left-wing vote (Table 6).

An examination of Figure 7 reveals a fourfold regional breakdown based on

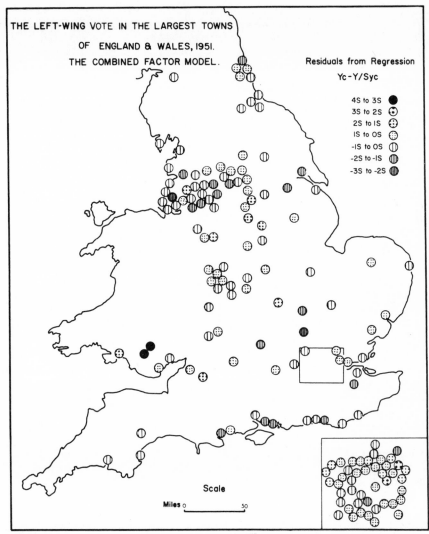

Fig. 8. The combined factor model.

residual values: (1) the south coast towns, (2) the London conurbation, (3) the Midlands, and (4) the northern textile towns. Generally, the towns in both 'regions' 2 and 3 are satisfactorily predicted. However, in 'regions' 1 and 4 the situation is reversed; the towns are poorly predicted.

On an intuitive basis it was considered that the university towns would, with their greater numbers in higher education, be distinguished on the residual map by having a uniform pattern. This assumption is verified in that university towns are nearly all well predicted. However, the question arises as to why these towns are so well predicted. In part, the explanation lies in the increasingly industrial nature of these towns. For example, Oxford is the home of the Morris automobile plant, whereas Cambridge is the location of a large electronics firm. Hence the situation arises where the vote to the Left-wing, given by the industrial workers, is apparently balanced by the predominantly Right-wing vote of the university members.[42]

TABLE 6

The Multiple Regression Equations for Model IV:
Educational Characteristics

	R	R^2
$X_{47} = 5.606 + 0.675X_{56} - 0.064X_{60}$	0.696*	0.484
$X_{47} = 63.425 + 0.076X_{56} -$		
$1.949X_{57} - 0.068X_{60}$	0.758*	0.575

*Significant at the 99 per cent level.
Source: Calculated by authors.

Model V: The Combined Factors

The previous models are very informative at the exploratory level for which they were designed. However, any combined model that attempts to use selected predictor variables has to consider the problem of collinearity. It is obvious that many of the variables used so far in this study measure very similar attributes. Thus, the problem arises of erecting a model that not only gives the greatest amount of 'explanation' but avoids much of the collinearity.

A technique helpful in solving this dilemma is referred to as multiple regression with elimination. The procedure behind the elimination process is based on two factors, (1) the standard partial regression coefficients are tested for significance and the nonsignificant coefficients are deleted from the regression, and (2) the R^2 of the regressions before and after deletion are tested for significant difference. The programme[43] terminates if either of the following two situations occurs, when by deletion the remaining variables have significant standard partial regression coefficients, or the values of R^2 differ significantly between the deleted and nondeleted regression equations.

The initial multiple regression equation is composed of all the predictor variables that have been used previously. The deletion process removes four variables, population aged 65 or over (X_4), overcrowded private households (X_{21}), percentage of local-authority houses (X_{30}), and persons who finished their formal education at age 15 (X_{56}). Hence, the variables retained are: females per 1,000 males (X_6), persons living in non-private households (X_{16}), per cent of the population working in the area in manufacture, mining, and agriculture (X_{33}), persons in Social Classes I and II (X_{41}), persons in Social Classes IV and V (X_{42}), per cent of the population age 15–24 in full-time attendance at an educational establishment (X_{57}), and distance to the centre of the nearest coalfield (X_{60}). The

TABLE 7

The Multiple Regression Equation for Model V:
The Combined Factors

	R	R^2
$X_{47} = 40.413 - 0.039X_6 + 0.415X_{16} +$		
$0.123X_{33} - 0.933X_{41} + 0.410X_{42} +$		
$0.0853X_{57} + 0.195X_{60}$	0.898*	0.807

*Significant at the 99 per cent level.
Source: Calculated by authors.

R for the initial regression (eleven variables) is 0·903, whereas the R for the deleted regression (seven variables) is 0·898 (Table 7). Hence, we have increased the efficiency of the final model while the amount of 'explanation' has declined an insignificant amount.

Reflecting the final R of 0·898 are the large number of well-predicted towns illustrated by Figure 8. However, several regional groupings can be distinguished. Overpredicted are most of the towns of the Lancashire and Manchester textile area as are all but one of the towns of the south coast.

The towns of the North-east, Yorkshire, and Midlands' industrial areas are on the whole well predicted. There exists in these areas a degree of variation such that over- and underprediction occurs in a fairly random point distribution as regards the scatter of the towns. The residual pattern for the London conurbation is not as uniform as it was for the previous models. The eastern half of the conurbation is underpredicted, whereas the south-west quadrant is overpredicted. Finally, the four most deviant cases, those that are least 'explained' by the present model, are Merthyr Tydfil, Rhondda, Luton, and Bootle. The first two are underpredicted and the last two overpredicted.

Conclusion

In this study a number of variables were initially hypothesized as having an important part to play in accounting for the distribution of the Left-wing vote in England and Wales. As the work progressed, it became evident that some of these variables were measuring the same factor, if only in a slightly different way. The recognition of this duplication, or collinearity as the statisticians call it, led to the employment of a technique that may be referred to as multiple regression with elimination. Using this technique those variables not playing a pertinent part in the analysis were automatically dropped. The collinearity of apparently two different variates is clearly illustrated by the example of the number of local-authority houses (X_{30}) and the per cent of the population engaged in manufacturing (X_{33}). Where the number of industrial workers is high, the number of local-authority houses is also high; hence, two variables measure the same attribute. Through the process of elimination four of the eleven initially hypothesized variables were deleted. The seven variables retained in the combined factor model (see discussion of Model V for the listing of these variables) yield a coefficient of determination of 81 per cent. This high degree of statistical explanation is welcomed, because it illustrates the value of using socio-economic variables in a multivariate framework for the analysis of voting patterns.

Many of the previous qualitative generalizations concerning voting behaviour in England and Wales are substantiated and expanded by the results of this study. Factors such as education, social class, occupation, and housing are key elements in explaining the distribution of the Left-wing vote. More precisely, we may conclude that the Labour vote:

(1) Is positively associated with the voters in industrialized towns lying on or near the coalfields, with workers in mining and manufacture, and with those classified as occupying the lower echelons of the social class hierarchy.

(2) Is negatively associated with the upper and middle strata of the social class hierarchy, with those who have attained higher levels of education, and with female voters.

The correspondence of the above conclusions with respect to geographic reality is shown by the residual maps (Figs. 4–7) which indicate how well the generalizations apply in the 157 towns.

In other countries, where data may be collected in a somewhat different fashion, or where cultural values differ from those in England and Wales, there will be the necessity for operationalizing new socio-economic variables. However, the variables selected in this study may well provide the starting-point for other geographic studies in voting behaviour.

NOTES AND REFERENCES

[1] The computational costs of this study were defrayed by the University of Iowa Computer Center (Project 150–0026). The writers wish to acknowledge the help of Clyde F. Kohn, Professor of Geography, the State University of Iowa, for his pertinent comments and criticism.

[2] The book by C. A. Moser and W. Scott, *British Towns: A Statistical Study of Their Social and Economic Differences* (London: Centre for Urban Studies, Report No. 2, 1961), is a fruitful source of data dealing with British cities and provides most of the basic data employed in this study.

[3] Among the major studies of General Elections in England and Wales are those by M. Benney, A. P. Gray, R. H. Pear, *How People Vote: A Study of Electoral Behaviour in Greenwich* (London: Routledge and Kegan Paul, 1956); J. Bonham, *The Middle Class Vote* (London: Faber and Faber, 1954); H. G. Nicholas, *The British General Election of 1950* (London: Macmillan and Co. Ltd., 1951).

[4] The dependent variable (X_{47}) is defined as 'The percentage of votes cast for Labour or other Left-wing candidates in the 1951 General Election', *The Times Guide to the House of Commons 1951* (London: The Times, 1951).

[5] J. K. Pollack, *British Election Studies, 1950* (Ann Arbor: The George Wahr Publishing Co., 1951); D. E. Butler, *The British General Election of 1951* (London: Macmillan and Co. Ltd., 1952).

[6] Moser and Sott, op. cit., note 2, pp. 3–6.

[7] H. F. Gosnell and N. N. Gill, 'An Analysis of the 1932 Presidential Vote in Chicago', *American Political Science Review*, 29 (1935), 967–84; H. F. Gosnell and M. Schmidt, 'Factorial and Correlation Analysis of the 1934 Vote in Chicago', *American Statistical Association Journal*, 31 (1936), 507–18; P. F. Lazarsfeld, B. Berelson, and H. Gaudet, *The Peoples' Choice* (New York: Columbia University Press, 1948); S. A. Rice, *Quantitative Methods in Politics* (New York: Alfred A. Knopf, 1928).

[8] Gosnell and Schmidt, op. cit., note 7, p. 511; W. George, 'Social Conditions and the Labour Vote in the County Boroughs of England and Wales', *British Journal of Sociology*, 2 (1951), 225–9; Sir Ivor Jennings, *Party Politics, Volume 1, Appeal to the People* (Cambridge: Cambridge University Press, 1960), pp. 228–48.

[9] The numbering of these variables $(X_4–X_{57})$ is that adopted by Moser and Scott, op. cit., note 2, p. 112. Variable (X_{60}) was developed specially for this study.

[10] Variable (X_4) is defined as 'The percentage of the population aged 65 and over, 1951', General Register Office, Census 1951, England and Wales, *County Reports* (London, H.M.S.O.). Variable (X_6) is defined as 'The number of females per 1,000 males, age-group 25–44, 1951', ibid.

[11] Benney, Gray, and Pear, op. cit., note 3, pp. 105–6 and 134–5. Jennings, op. cit., note 8, pp. 296–303.

[12] Jennings, op. cit., note 8, p. 298.

[13] Jennings, op. cit., note 8, pp. 298–9.

[14] Jennings, op. cit., note 8, p. 299; S. M. Lipset, *Political Man: The Social Bases of Politics* (New York: Doubleday, 1963), pp. 156 and 166.

[15] Benney, Gray, and Pear, op. cit., note 3, pp. 147–54.

[16] Variable (X_{16}) is defined as 'The percentage of persons living in dwellings occupied by non-private households, 1951', Census 1951, op. cit., note 10.

[17] Variable (X_{21}) is defined as 'The percentage of private households in overcrowded condition, 1951', Census 1951, op. cit., note 10. See Moser and Scott, op. cit., note 2, p. 100 for a discussion of this definition.

[18]George, op. cit., note 8, p. 255.

[19]Variable (X_{30}) is identified as 'New houses built by local authorities between 1/4/1945 and 30/6/1958 as a percentage of total new houses built in this period', *Housing Return for England and Wales* (London: Ministry of Housing and Local Government, 1958).

[20]Variable (X_{33}) is defined as 'The percentage of the population working in the area, in manufacturing, agriculture and mining, 1951' (Standard Industrial Classification Groups I–XVI), *Industry Tables* (London: General Register Office, Census 1951, 1962).

[21]M. Harrison, *Trade Unions and the Labour Party Since 1945* (Detroit: Wayne State University, 1960).

[22]Jennings, op. cit., note 8, pp. 228–57 and 296–303; R. R. Alford, *Party and Society: The Anglo-American Democracies* (Chicago: Rand McNally, 1963), pp. 130–4; Bonham, op. cit., note 3, pp. 179–81.

[23]Jennings, op. cit., note 8, pp. 288–9; Benney, Gray, and Pear, op. cit., note 3, pp. 120–1.

[24]Variable (X_{41}) is defined as 'The percentage of occupied and retired males in Social Classes I and II, 1951', General Register Office, Census 1951, England and Wales, *County Reports* (London: H.M.S.O.).

[25]Variable (X_{42}) is defined as 'The percentage of occupied and retired males in Social Classes IV and V, 1951', ibid.

[26]J. N. L. Baker and E. W. Gilbert, 'The Doctrine of an Axial Belt of Industry in England', *Geographical Journal*, 103 (1944), 49–72; A. C. Hobson, 'The Great Industrial Belt', *Economic Journal*, 61 (1951), 562–76.

[27]R. Hoggart and R. Williams, 'Working Class Attitudes', *New Left Review*, 1 (1960), 26–30, quotation from p. 28.

[28]Variable (X_{56}) is defined as 'The percentage of the occupied population aged 20–24 whose terminal age was under 15, 1951', Census 1951, op. cit., note 10.

[29]Benney, Gray, and Pear, op. cit., note 3, p. 110.

[30]Variable (X_{57}) is defined as 'The percentage cf the population aged 15–24 attending full-time at an educational establishment, 1951', Census 1951, op. cit., note 10.

[31]Variable (X_{60}) is a measure, developed for this study, of the distance from a town to the centre of the nearest coalfield. The measure was operationally defined in centimetres. See also J. W. Watson, 'Geography–A Discipline in Distance', *Scottish Geographical Magazine*, 71 (1951), 1–13.

[32]Handbooks of the Regional Geology of Great Britain: *Northern England* (1953); *East Yorkshire and Lincolnshire* (1948); *South Wales* (1948) (London: The Geological Survey and Museum).

[33]H. H. McCarty, 'McCarty on McCarthy: The Spatial Distribution of the McCarthy Vote', 1952 (unpublished manuscript, Iowa City: Department of Geography, State University of Iowa, no date). Quoted by E. N. Thomas, pp. 42–7, see following note.

[34]E. N. Thomas, *Maps of Residuals from Regression: Their Characteristics and Uses in Geographic Research* (Iowa City: Department of Geography, Monograph Series No. 2, State University of Iowa, 1960), pp. 22–4.

[35]Hoggart and Williams, op. cit., note 27, pp. 27–8.

[36]G. Turner, *The Carmakers: Ford* (London: The Observer, 27 October 1963), p. 28.

[37]W. Smith, *An Economic Geography of Great Britain* (London: Methuen and Co., 1953), p. 540; L. Dudley Stamp and S. H. Beaver, *The British Isles: A Geographic and Economic Survey* (London: Longmans, Green and Co., 1954), p. 524.

[38]Moser and Scott, op. cit., note 2, pp. 127 and 129.

[39]Benney, Gray, and Pear, op. cit., note 3, pp. 118–19.

[40]J. Blondel, *Voters, Parties, and Leaders: The Social Fabric of British Politics* (Baltimore: Penguin Books Inc., 1963), pp. 21–48.

[41]Bonham, op. cit., note 3, p. 108 and pp. 147–8.

[42]Jennings, op. cit., note 8, pp. 179–85.

[43]We are indebted to Dr. H. P. Bechtoldt, Psychology Department, State University of Iowa, for providing this particular multiple regression programme with elimination. Further, we wish to acknowledge his generous co-operation and interest in this research.

3. RESIDENTIAL LOCATION BY OCCUPATIONAL STATUS

J. O. Wheeler

Few researchers have investigated occupational distributions by residence in metropolitan areas, despite increasing availability of detailed areal data from census and transportation surveys. The traditional emphasis on land use analysis and classes of residential structure has perhaps diverted attention from spatial studies dealing specifically with occupational groups.[1] Another reason for the neglect may be the multivariate approaches of social area analysis which have emphasized the inter-relationships of several socio-economic variables, including occupation, income, and educational level.[2] While a multivariate approach is valuable in providing useful generalizations of social rank differentials of individuals, families, and neighbourhoods, it is also fruitful to isolate a particular variable to examine its spatial structure and associations.

This lack of spatial research on the distribution of occupations within cities is revealed in a recent textbook in urban geography, which, although devoting a chapter to the three familiar concepts of city structure (the concentric zone, the sector, and the multiple nuclei patterns), makes no specific statement regarding occupational structure within cities.[3] One is forced to turn largely to the literature of sociology for urban studies of occupational distributions.

Even here the studies are remarkably few, in spite of the concern of sociologists with correlates of status, occupational mobility, and differential migration and movement of urban residents. Several studies have compared the central city with suburban areas in socio-economic status.[4] The results show suburbanization at first attracted primarily high-status occupations but that suburban areas have become increasingly heterogeneous, although status differentials continue to exist between central cities and suburbs. Other studies have focused around one or more of the three traditional concepts of generalized urban structure.[5]

The Duncans' study of Chicago remains the major empirical description of residential areas by occupational status.[6] Their ecological analysis yields 'a close relationship between spatial and social distance ...', although their 'spatial distance' does not include an analysis of particular parts of the metropolitan area. Neither does it take up the social and economic forces underlying residential location. These forces have more recently been reviewed by Anderson, who in addition to the factors of population concentration and competition for land focuses on 'social interaction preferences'.[7] These preferences, manifest in social rivalries and hostilities among groups, supplement economic theory in accounting for residential location by socio- economic status.

Kain, drawing on work by Alonso, Wingo, and others, shows how residential location by status can be expressed as a function of income, space preference, and economic rent.[8] Assuming a declining surface of economic rent away from the city centre, a household with a given preference for space will attempt to maximize the utility of its income by locating where the marginal cost of transport intersects marginal savings in location rent. This trade-off function between transport costs

From *Urban Studies*, 5 . 1 (1968), 24–35. Reprinted by permission of the author and editor of the journal.

and economic rent is related to the nature of urban population densities, land use zonation, and the spatial composition of socio-economic groups. Rigorous verification of the theory has been hampered by problems of empirical definition of the cost components of the model.[9]

Purpose

It is the purpose of this study to examine the general occupational structure of residential areas in the Pittsburgh metropolitan area. Based on existing theory and limited empirical findings, it is hypothesized that groups of similar occupational status will have similar patterns of residential location; and, as the status level widens, location of residence will become increasingly dissimilar. This hypothesis is not stated to test a specific theory, but rather is intended as a framework for empirical evaluation. Occupational status levels should have relatively distinct residential locations, which in turn will be associated with a pattern of employment locations.

Method of Investigation

There are problems of measurement associated with testing the hypothesis. The problem of categorizing workers into eight occupational groups may result in certain groups representing broader ranges of status than others. In addition, the size of the areal units may modify the results, since too large a unit would not properly differentiate among status groups and too small a unit would create an artificial difference. Data used in this study are provided by the Pittsburgh Area Transportation Study (PATS); occupational classifications are taken as given, and seventy-four metropolitan zones are used for analysis.[10] Although the zones are of unequal size, their increasing size away from the city centre is inversely related to their population total.

A separate problem involves the ranking of occupations by status. Basically, the classical Edwards's grouping is used here.[11] (See Table 1.) However, Edwards combined sales and clerical workers and labourers and service workers. Another frequently used prestige rating of occupations, the North-Hatt grouping, separates governmental officials into the highest-ranking category.[12] Public administrators in this study are included as managers. The North-Hatt rating also does not differentiate between sales and clerical workers. Other studies have shown clerical workers to be similar to sales and managerial workers in education and prestige but below craftsmen-foreman in income.[13] The groupings here are those provided by the PATS and closely follow the categories of the U.S. Bureau of the Census. Private household workers are combined with service workers, and sales workers are ranked ahead of clerical workers.

To measure residential differentiation by occupational status, locational indices and correlation techniques are employed. Specifically, location quotients are determined for each zone to indicate how far above or below average a particular occupation falls in residential concentrations among Pittsburgh zones, a value of 100 being average.[14] These locational indices for eight occupations are inter-correlated to show the degree of similarity or dissimilarity among the groups, and the indices are also correlated with distance from the central business district (CBD). The index of dissimilarity is used to show the degree to which an occupation differs residentially from another occupation.[15] The coefficient of geographic association shows how one occupation is different from all other occupations, a low value indicating a large deviation.[16]

Findings for Pittsburgh

One commonly used indication of the physical structure of a metropolitan area is the way in which some variable relates to distance from the CBD. Coefficients of simple correlation were computed relating the residential location quotients by zone with distance from the heart of Pittsburgh's Golden Triangle. (See Table 1.) All occupations except professionals, sales workers, and operatives show a significant relationship to distance, although none is strong. Labourers, service, and clerical workers have significant inverse correlations with distance, since these occupations are most concentrated near the CBD. Clerical workers, of whom nearly 40 per cent work in the CBD, also reside in large proportion in the central city, in contrast to other high-status groups. The only significant positive correlations are for managers and craftsmen-foremen, groups with dissimilar occupational status. Therefore, although correlations are found between the relative concentrations of certain occupational groups and distance from the CBD, the coefficients are weak and do not suggest a simple relationship between residential location and occupational status, as implied by the Burgess concept of city structure.

Coefficients of variation are used with the residential location quotients to show the degree of variation among zones by occupation.[17] A high coefficient of

TABLE 1
Residential Location Quotient and Distance

Occupation	Coefficient of Correlation
Professionals	0·04
Managers	0·43*
Sales workers	0·22
Clerical workers	−0·34*
Craftsmen-foremen	0·34*
Operatives	−0·11
Service workers	−0·49*
Labourers	−0·33*

*Significant at the 99 per cent level.
Source: Computed from PATS data, 1958.

variation, for example, would indicate that the occupational group is either well above or below the metropolitan average. Low coefficients reflect a more uniform distribution of an occupation among zones. The residential pattern of those occupations at the lowest and highest ends of the socio-economic scale is the most segregated. (See Table 2.) Service workers and labourers are the most segregated occupations residentially, and these groups consist of 26 and 20 per cent Negro, respectively. Operatives, craftsmen-foremen, and especially clerical workers show a strong tendency to occupy residential zones in which there is a high degree of occupational mixture.

Another measure of residential segregation of occupational groups is the coefficient of geographic association, which shows the degree to which each occupational group is spatially similar to all other occupations. This coefficient, also shown in Table 2, reveals that occupations occupying intermediate status positions are least segregated and are found most commonly in all residential areas.

The only exception to a consistent status/segregation relationship is the reversal of craftsmen-foremen and operatives. Clearly the two highest- and lowest-status occupations reside in the most segregated patterns.

TABLE 2
Measures of Segregation

Occupations	Coefficients of Variation of Location Quotient by Zone	Coefficient of Geographic Association
Professionals	54	0·761
Managers	52	0·812
Sales workers	48	0·836
Clerical workers	30	0·881
Craftsmen-foremen	38	0·834
Operatives	40	0·842
Service workers	75	0·772
Labourers	71	0·731

Source: Computed from PATS data, 1958.

Coefficients of correlation were computed between residential indices for the eight occupations. Examination of Table 3 discloses a degree of regularity and occupational patterning in the Pittsburgh metropolitan area. Nineteen of the 28 intercorrelation coefficients (excluding the diagonal) are significant at either 95 or 99 per cent confidence level, 16 of the 19 at the latter level.

TABLE 3
Intercorrelation of Location Quotients by Zones

	Professionals	Managers	Sales workers	Clerical workers	Craftsmen-foremen	Operatives	Service workers	Labourers
Professionals	1	0·65†	0·20	0·04	−0·26*	−0·58†	−0·49†	−0·62†
Managers		1	0·45†	−0·05	−0·25*	−0·50†	−0·54†	0·60†
Sales workers			1	−0·09	−0·11	−0·38†	−0·35†	−0·36†
Clerical workers				1	−0·17	−0·13	−0·27*	−0·36†
Craftsmen-foremen					1	0·32†	−0·34†	−0·12
Operatives						1	0·05	0·24*
Service workers							1	0·71†
Labourers								1

*Significant at the 95 per cent level.
†Significant at the 99 per cent level.
Source: Computed from PATS data, 1958.

Looking first at the four highest-status groups, one notes that among the highest correlations in the matrix is the one between the residential index values of professionals and managers. However, no other occupation shows a statistically similar distribution to professionals, but sales workers have a residential pattern somewhat similar to managers. Clerical workers are not similar in residential structure to any other white-collar group but are significantly different from labourers and to a lesser extent from service workers, but not from craftsmen-foremen or operatives. On the other hand, each of the four lowest-status occupations is significantly different from the residential pattern of professionals and managers. And the degree of this inverse relationship tends to increase as the occupational status decreases. Sales workers are different residentially from all the four lowest-status groups, except the craftsmen-foremen, but these inverse correlations are not as high for sales workers as for professional and managerial workers. White-collar occupations thus tend to be similar in their residential index and generally different from the lower-status groups.

While craftsmen-foremen are significantly different residentially from only professionals and managers of the high-status group, they are also dissimilar to service workers and show no meaningful correlation with labourers. Operatives, however, have a significantly similar residential grouping to craftsmen-foremen, a barely significant correlation with labourers, but no correlation with service workers. The pattern for operatives is dissimilar to those for high-status workers—professional, managerial, and sales workers—and is increasingly dissimilar as status rises. Service workers and labourers have either a positive or a negative correlation residentially with all groups except operatives and craftsmen-foremen, respectively. The correlations are mostly negative for both service workers and labourers with all the white-collar groups, and in addition different from craftsmen-foremen for the service workers. The highest correlations between the residential indices of one occupation and another is between service workers and labourers.

The index of dissimilarity is another measure of differences in residential location among occupations. The proportion of each occupation residing in each zone is computed, and the percentage difference between two occupations for each zone is summed and divided by two. Specifically, the index measures the percentage of an occupational group that would have to change residential zones to be identical with some other group. For example Table 4 shows that only 14 per cent of professionals would have to move to be consistent with residential locations

TABLE 4
Index of Dissimilarity

	Profes-sionals	Man-agers	Sales workers	Clerical workers	Craftsmen-foremen	Opera-tives	Service workers	Labourers
Profes-sionals	—	14	20	22	28	31	35	43
Managers		—	15	17	25	28	33	39
Sales workers			—	16	20	27	32	35
Clerical workers				—	19	17	22	30
Craftsmen-foremen					—	15	27	26
Operatives						—	18	22
Service workers							—	20
Labourers								—

Source: Computed from PATS data, 1958.

by zone of managers; but 43 per cent of professionals would have to change zones to be identical to labourers. These two examples represent the smallest and largest displacement within Table 4.

If the hypothesis of this study holds, index values should increase away from the diagonal. Thus occupations with similar socio-economic ranks will have similar residential distributions, and as one increases the socio-economic separation, the residential dissimilarities will increase. This relationship obtains with only two exceptions. Clerical workers are somewhat less closely related to craftsmen-foremen than expected (or more closely related to operatives), and craftsmen-foremen are not as similar residentially to service workers as hypothesized (or are more similar to labourers). In general the four highest-status groups are more similar residentially among themselves than are the four lowest-status occupations.

Conclusion

The intercorrelation matrix derived from location quotients reflects a somewhat different approach to residential location by status from the matrix of dissimilarity indices. Both provide only partial solutions to the problem. The dissimilarity index suggests a strong and consistent relationship between status and residential location, while the correlation coefficients show a weaker association. The significant negative coefficient of correlation between craftsmen-foremen and service workers is consistent with the dissimilarity index; likewise, the greater difference than expected in dissimilarity index between clerical workers and craftsmen-foremen is noted by a weak negative correlation coefficient.

The findings here corroborate the Duncans' classical Chicago study and provide a firmer foundation for describing socio-economic variation within metropolitan areas. A complementary investigation might focus on the residential location of Negroes by occupational status. Much of the value in this approach lies in relating the findings to occupational employment indices and to the pattern of work-trips. Although such is beyond the purpose of this paper, a number of journey-to-work studies have isolated occupation as an important variable in determining work-trip length.[18] Moreover, an investigation of urban social circulation is a needed and logical extension of these findings.

NOTES AND REFERENCES

[1] Recent studies reflecting this traditional emphasis include: J. Tait Davis, 'Middle Class Housing in the Central City', *Economic Geography*, 41 (July 1965), 238–51; T. L. C. Griffin, 'The Evolution and Duplication of a Pattern of Urban Growth', *Economic Geography*, 41 (April 1965), 133–56; and Richard E. Preston, 'The Zone in Transition: A Study of Urban Land Use Patterns', *Economic Geography*, 42 (July 1966), 236–60.

[2] Maurice D. Van Arsdol, Jr., Santo Camilleri, and Calvin F. Schmid, 'The Generality of Urban Social Area Indexes', *American Sociological Review*, 23 (June 1958), 277–84; Eshref Shevky and Wendell Bell, *Social Area Analysis* (Stanford University Press, 1955); Calvin F. Schmid, Earle H. MacCannell, and Maurice D. Van Arsdol, Jr., 'The Ecology of the American City: Further Comparison and Validation of Generalizations', *American Sociological Review*, 23 (August 1958), 392–401; and J. Richard Udry, 'Increasing Scale and Social Differentiation: New Tests of Two Theories, of Shevky and Bell', *Social Forces* 42 (May 1964), 403–13.

[3] Raymond E. Murphy, *The American City: An Urban Geography* (New York: McGraw-Hill, 1966).

[4] Beverly Duncan, George Sabagh, and Maurice D. Van Arsdol, Jr., 'Patterns of City Growth', *American Journal of Sociology*, 67 (January 1962), 418–29; Sidney Goldstein and Kurt B. Mayer, 'Demographic Correlates of Status Differences in a Metropolitan Population',

Urban Studies, 2 (May 1965), 67–84; Bernard Lazerivitz, 'Metropolitan Community Residential Belts, 1950 and 1960', *American Sociological Review*, 25 (April 1960), 245–52; Leo F. Schnore, 'The Socio-Economic Status of Cities and Suburbs', *American Sociological Review*, 28 (February 1963), 76–85.

[5]Homer Hoyt, 'Where the Rich and the Poor People Live', *Technical Bulletin*, 55 (Washington, D.C.: Urban Land Institute, April 1966); P. J. Smith, 'Calgary: A Study in Urban Pattern', *Economic Geography*, 38 (October 1962), 315–29; B. T. Robson, 'An Ecological Analysis of the Evolution of Residential Areas in Sunderland', *Urban Studies*, 3 (June 1966), 120–39.

[6]Otis D. Duncan and Beverly Duncan, 'Residential Distribution and Occupational Stratification', *American Journal of Sociology*, 60 (March 1955), 493–503.

[7]Theodore R. Anderson, 'Social and Economic Factors Affecting the Locations of Residential Neighbourhoods', *Papers and Proceedings of the Regional Science Association*, 9 (1962), 161–70.

[8]John F. Kain, 'The Journey-to-Work as a Determinant of Residential Locations', *Papers and Proceedings of the Regional Science Association*, 9 (1962), 137–60; William Alonso, 'A Theory of the Urban Land Market', *Papers and Proceedings of the Regional Science Association*, 6 (1960), 149–57; William Alonso, *Location and Land Use* (Cambridge, Mass.: Harvard University Press, 1964); John D. Herbert and Benjamin H. Stevens, 'A Model for the Distribution of Residential Activity in Urban Areas', *Journal of Regional Science*, 2 (Fall 1960), 21–36; and Lowdon Wingo, Jr., *Transportation and Urban Land* (Washington, D.C.: Resources for the Future, 1961).

[9]See Leslie J. King, 'Approaches to Locational Analysis: An Overview', *The East Lakes Geographer*, 2 (August 1966), 7: 'There has been little ... vigorous testing of ... urban rent-models.'

[10]These data are based on a 4 per cent sample of households in the 420 square mile Pittsburgh metropolitan area and represent 92 per cent of the population of Allegheny County (about 1·5 million persons). Data were made available on some 14,000 IBM punch cards, each card representing a residential location of a member of the work force.

[11]Alba M. Edwards, 'Socio-Economic Groups of the United States', *Journal of the American Statistical Association*, 15 (June 1917), 643–61.

[12]Cecil C. North and Paul K. Hatt, 'Occupational Status and Prestige', *Opinion News* 9 (September 1947), 3–13.

[13]Duncan and Duncan, op. cit., pp. 502–3; and Beverly Duncan, 'Factors in Work-Residence Separation: Wage and Salary Workers, Chicago 1951', *American Sociological Review*, 21 (February 1956), 48–56.

[14]Location quotients are computed by:

$$\frac{X_i / \Sigma X_i}{N_i / \Sigma N_i} \cdot 100$$

where X_i equals the number in occupation X residing in zone i and N represents the total members of all occupations residing in zone i.

[15]The index of dissimilarity is computed by:

$$\sum_{i=1}^{n} \frac{|(X_i / \Sigma X_i) - (Y_i / \Sigma Y_i)|}{2} \cdot 100$$

where X_i represents one occupation and Y_i represents another occupation residing in zone i.

[16]The coefficient of geographic association is computed by:

$$1 - \sum_{i=1}^{n} \frac{|(X_i / \Sigma X_i) - (N_i / \Sigma N_i)|}{2}$$

where X_i and N_i are defined in reference 14. The coefficient has a range from zero to one.

[17]The coefficient of variation is a measure of relative deviation, obtained by dividing the mean into the standard deviation.

[18]Sidney Goldstein and Kurt Mayer, 'Migration and Social Status Differentials in the Journey-to-Work', *Rural Sociology*, 29 (September 1964), 278–87; Louis K. Loewenstein, *Residences and Work Places in Urban Areas* (New York: The Scarecrow Press, 1965); James O. Wheeler, 'Occupational Status and Work-Trips: A Minimum Distance Approach', *Social Forces*, 45 (June 1967), 508–15.

4.   SOCIAL TOPOGRAPHY
OF A LONDON CONGREGATION

THE BAYSWATER SYNAGOGUE 1863–1963

V. D. Lipman

Trollope in *The Small House at Alington*, in a chapter published in November 1863, describes the area for whose Jewish residents the Bayswater Synagogue had been opened a few months earlier.

A residence had been taken for the couple in a very fashionable row of buildings abutting on the Bayswater Road. . . . The house was quite new, and the street being unfinished had about it a strong smell of mortar . . . but nevertheless it was acknowledged to be a quite correct locality. From one end of the crescent a corner of Hyde Park could be seen, and the other abutted on a very handsome terrace indeed in which lived an ambassador—from South America—a few bankers' senior clerks, and a peer of the realm.

The history of the Bayswater Synagogue provides an interesting example of the influence of topography on the development of a congregation. To appreciate this, it is necessary to relate the spread of London Jewry to the building up of this part of London and to analyse the places of residence of members of the congregation at different periods, which can be done from the printed membership lists.

Until about 1820 most of London Jewry lived in the City, the Whitechapel area to the east, and the area around the Strand to the west. By 1840, however, the wealthier members had largely moved into the West Central area, extending to the New or Marylebone Road in the north and to the Edgware Road and Hyde Park in the west. The Central Synagogue in Great Portland Street, which it was decided to found in 1849, served this area, as did the branch of the Spanish and Portuguese Congregation opened in Wigmore Street in 1853, and the Reform Synagogue, transferred from Burton Street to Margaret Street, Cavendish Square, in 1849. But fashionable Jewry continued to move westwards and by the 1860s had already crossed the Edgware Road into what was then known as Tyburnia.

The area north of Hyde Park had, in fact, begun to develop somewhat earlier, although as late as 1820 there was still only the isolated village of Paddington, nestling around its green on the rural road to Harrow. In 1825 the gallows at Tyburn (Marble Arch) was removed and from 1827 began the process of laying out the elegant squares and crescents of Tyburnia, in the angle between the Edgware and Bayswater Roads. This was followed by a similar development of the Lancaster Gate area from 1850 onwards; the planned development of Ladbroke Grove was somewhat earlier, about 1840. However, in the early 1860s building intensified and the still vacant spaces between the earlier squares and crescents filled up, as Trollope described. With the influx of people with businesses in the City, communication was provided by the first underground railway, with its western

From *Jewish Journal of Sociology*, 6 . 1 (1964), 69–74. Reprinted by permission of the author and the editor of the journal.

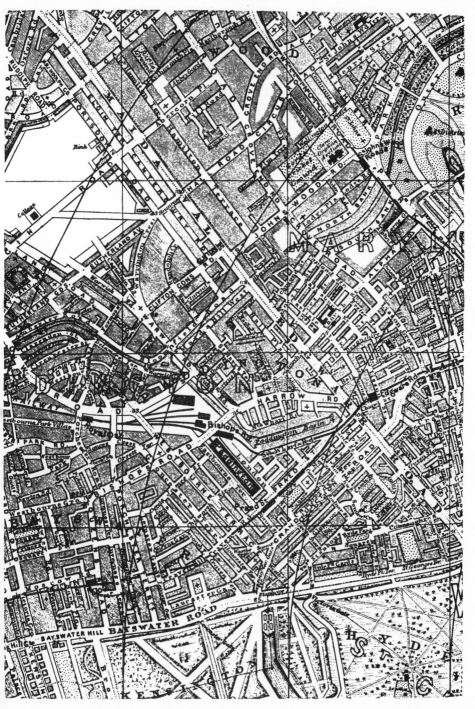

Fig. 1. The Bayswater area in 1885 (the Synagogue is just north of Royal Oak Station, at left-centre of the map).

terminus at Bishop's Bridge Road, opened in 1864, the same year as the Bayswater Synagogue.

It is said that Bayswater had taken 'a whole congregation' from Great Portland Street; but, if so, they had already moved their homes first. Out of the 224 original members in 1863, 110, or practically half, lived in the area north of the Park and Kensington Gardens, but south of the Harrow Road (equivalent to the present W.2 and the adjacent part of W.11 postal districts). The main axis of the congregation lay along Westbourne Terrace, but a considerable number lived in the most fashionable area of all, to the east of Leinster Square and Cleveland Square. Very few, about 5 per cent, still lived in the central area around Great Portland Street. This area was ceasing to be the height of fashion, as Trollope mockingly wrote in the passage already quoted: 'We know how vile is the sound of Baker Street and how absolutely foul to the polite ear is the name of Fitzroy Square [although] the houses in those purlieus are substantial, warm and of good size.'

As to the area of Maida Vale (roughly equivalent to the W.9 postal district), which can be defined as a triangle between the Maida Vale Road, the Harrow Road, and Walterton and Cambridge Roads, this had relatively few Jewish residents in 1863; about 55 members of Bayswater, a quarter of the membership, lived there. Only the southern parts of Maida Vale, such as Blomfield Road and Warwick Avenue, were then built up, although building had begun about 1830.

Why the founders of the congregation chose Chichester Place is not yet clear. One would have expected them to find a site further south, in the midst of the Bayswater area proper between Harrow Road and the Park, where the greatest number of original members lived. It may have been that they were influenced by the proximity to Paddington Green, the traditional administrative and ecclesiastical focus of the whole area; or they may have foreseen the future growth of Maida Vale. In the next twenty years two major developments occurred which altered the whole character of the congregation. First, in spite of extensions soon after the Synagogue was opened, it was not large enough for the potential membership. A group of members living in the Park area, led by Samuel Montagu and his brother-in-law Ellis Franklin, obtained a decision to build a Synagogue near the Park but further west, and this was opened as the New West End Synagogue in 1879. Second, the area in Maida Vale north of the canal was further built up: Portsdown Road (now Randolph Avenue), Warrington Crescent, Randolph Crescent, Clifton Road, and Clifton Gardens were completed by about 1870, although there was still some open land north of Sutherland Avenue; and Elgin Avenue and Lauderdale Road were not filled with more modern, smaller non-basement houses and blocks of flats till about 1900. The Maida Vale area attracted a considerable middle-class Jewish settlement. As a result of these two factors the membership in 1890 showed a very different pattern of distribution from that of 1863. By far the largest group—250 out of 438, or more than half—now lived in Maida Vale; only 102, a smaller number than in 1863 and less than a quarter of the total membership, now lived in the Park area. The attraction of members from this area to the New West End Synagogue, and the growth of Maida Vale, had thus turned the congregation into one predominantly serving Maida Vale rather than Bayswater proper: one can see this symbolized by the fact that Dr. Adler, Minister till 1891, lived in Queensborough Terrace, by the Park; his successor, Sir Herman Gollancz, lived in Clifton Gardens in Maida Vale.

This change in the area of residence of members in the 1880s had important social connotations. Novelists of the period have described, or purported to describe, the life of the Jews of Bayswater and Maida Vale in the 1880s. Their accounts are distorted, but that these were two separate areas, clearly distinguishable to contemporary eyes, is evident. Amy Levy makes a snobbish contrast between the 'mean houses' of Maida Vale (which she unfairly typifies as Walterton Road) and the splendours of Lancaster Gate. She refers to the Maida Vale family to whose 'eminently provincial minds' their Bayswater relations 'were very great people indeed, and they derived no little prestige in Maida Vale from their connections with so distinguished a family'; and she refers to Whiteley's as the 'neutral territory where Bayswater nodded to Maida Vale and South Kensington took Bayswater by the hand' (the quotations are from *Reuben Sachs*, published in 1889). The novel by Julia Frankau ('Frank Danby') *Dr. Phillips; A Maida Vale Idyll*, also published in 1889, deals exclusively with the Maida Vale community. The criticism of the Jewish community is so overdone that, although the author claims to speak from local knowledge, one cannot rely on the factual accuracy of the description: the central character, who lives in Portsdown Road, and his neighbours are scarcely recognizable as people like our predecessors. However, one can see the extent to which this had become a Jewish area: 'that new Jerusalem which they have appropriated, with their slow and characteristic walk ... congregating in Clifton Road, in the gardens of Sutherland Avenue, in Warrington Crescent', with their card parties followed by suppers of smoked beef and cucumber, and their devotions at the Bayswater Synagogue. They must have been concentrated because their numbers, to judge from Synagogue membership, would have been over 1,000, possibly 2,000, in an area with (according to the breakdown of population in the Booth Survey of London Life and Labour) about 10,000 total population. The Booth Survey map shows most of this Maida Vale area in 1888 as 'middle class—well to do', with only Sutherland Avenue, Warrington Crescent, Randolph Crescent, Clifton Gardens, and part of the Maida Vale Road as 'upper middle-class or upper-class—wealthy'. On the other hand, nearly all of the Park area is shown as 'upper middle-class or upper-class wealthy' and relatively little of it as plain 'middle-class'.

From 1890 onwards there were two new factors, which to some extent counteracted. First, Maida Vale was one of the earliest places to see substantial building of flats (Cunningham Mansions, 1892; Aberdeen and Blomfield Courts, 1903; Biddulph Mansions, 1907; Delaware Mansions, 1908, etc.). These flats tended to keep in the area older people no longer needing a large house, who might have moved elsewhere, and later attracted newcomers into the area. The other development was the trend to move into St. John's Wood and into the newer areas of Hampstead, Kilburn, and Brondesbury. In 1863 only seven out of 224 members lived in St. John's Wood and five in Hampstead. In 1890 out of 438 members, there were 16 in St. John's Wood and 17 in Hampstead, Brondesbury, and Kilburn. By 1914, however, there were 47 in St. John's Wood and 58 in the other north-west districts. As a result of this movement to the north-west, while the total membership in 1914 remained about the same at 456, and the number in the Park area still remained about a quarter at 115, the number living in Maida Vale had begun to decline and at 187 was less than 40 per cent of the total membership.

The decline in the proportion of members living in Maida Vale continued between 1914 and 1939, as conditions in the Maida Vale area became less attractive. In 1939 only 91 of the total membership which had fallen to 386 lived in Maida Vale—about 25 per cent. The number of members living near the Park fell to 73, or less than 20 per cent. On the other hand, residents of St. John's Wood were now 35, or nearly 10 per cent; and 66 (or 20 per cent) lived in the north-western suburbs. Thus the number of those living in the vicinity of the Synagogue, whether in Maida Vale, the Park area, or St. John's Wood, was little over 200—or not much more than half the membership.

Recent years have, however, seen more changes. Membership rose well into the 500s during the 1950s, and while it had fallen again to 514 in 1962, this was well above the 1939 level, and even above that of 1914. The proportion living near the Park, about a fifth, was not dissimilar from that of the previous seventy or eighty years. With some rebuilding and rehabilitation in Maida Vale and the general trend for those who could to move back into inner London, the number of residents of Maida Vale had increased to 226 or 40 per cent of the total. Ten per cent of the members lived in the north-west suburbs and another 10 per cent—50—in St. John's Wood. This also reveals a curious fact. Whereas only 50 residents of St. John's Wood are members of Bayswater, the St. John's Wood Synagogue membership includes about 130 residents in Maida Vale. Thus for every three Jewish residents of Maida Vale who are members of Bayswater, there are two who are members of St. John's Wood. Presumably distance and the character of the immediate surroundings of the Bayswater Synagogue have had some influence on this choice. In any case, the increase in Maida Vale membership has not been proportionately reflected in regular Synagogue attendance, and there would be a long way to go to restore the intensely traditional Jewish atmosphere of Maida Vale between 1880 and 1914.

To sum up, the development of the Bayswater congregation has been greatly influenced by its original location, between the Park and the Maida Vale areas, and by the subsequent foundation of the New West End and St. John's Wood Synagogues. What the future holds in store is beyond the scope of this study, but it is hoped that it has shown that useful material for Anglo-Jewish history can be drawn from the analysis of membership lists, and the relation of a congregation to its topographical setting.

Analysis of Membership Lists
(including Lady Members in their own right)

Year	Park Area (W.2, W.11)	Maida Vale (W.9)	St. John's Wood (N.W.8, N.W.1)	North-west (N.W.2, 3, 6, 8, 10, 11)	Elsewhere	Total
1863	110	55	8	5	46	224
1890	102	249	16	17	54	438
1914	115	187	47	58	49	456
1939	73	91	35	66	121*	386
1962	113	226	49	51	75	514

*Includes 17 in W.1, 28 in other W. districts, and 25 outside London.

BIBLIOGRAPHICAL NOTE

The main source used has been the collection of membership lists in the offices of the United Synagogue, Woburn House, London and the writer is indebted to Mr. A. Silverman (Secretary) and Mr. J. Julius (Membership Officer) for their help in connection with them.

For the general development of London Jewry, reference may be made to the writer's *Social History of the Jews in England 1850–1950* (London, 1954). For the topographical background, use has been made principally of N. Pevsner's *London* volume in his *Buildings of England* series and H. P. Clunn, *The Face of London* (5th edn., 1934).

5. SOME ASPECTS OF THE CHANGING DISTRIBUTION OF COLOURED IMMIGRANTS IN BIRMINGHAM, 1961–66

P. N. Jones

Both from a theoretical and applied point of view, the distribution of coloured immigrants in British cities must rank as a major field of research in urban geography. The dominant features of the distribution pattern of the immigrants in England and Wales have been demonstrated on a variety of levels (P. Collison, 1967; R. B. Davison, 1963; R. Glass, 1960, 1965; G. C. K. Peach, 1966A, 1968) but there still exists a need for further research into the distribution of coloured immigrants *within* these urban areas.

Many problems in the fields of social administration and urban planning have been linked with the influx of coloured Commonwealth immigrants. The most acute area of conflict between resident city and immigrant populations undoubtedly centres on housing availability and utilization, as J. Rex and R. Moore (1967) have so graphically described in the case of Birmingham. In this area of conflict we can witness the merging of urban sociological and ecological theory, and practical administrative action in the series of decisions and regulations which control entry into the various branches of the urban housing market. Similarly, the emergence of 'enclaves' or 'colonies' of immigrants within our cities has been the subject of much comment and indeed speculation, being associated with severe if localized pressures on education and other social services, and also with what K. Little (1967) has termed 'colour-shock'. Undertones of 'ghetto-formation', with its suggested implications of violent stress, are present in many spheres. Against this background the changes which occurred in the distribution of coloured immigrants between 1961 and 1966 are obviously significant, particularly in the light they may shed upon the underlying trends at work in these five years.

Coloured Immigration and Urban Ecological Concepts

It is important that coloured immigration into British cities be measured against the more important concepts which have been put forward as explanations of the spatial patterns of social groups, so that trends can be evaluated in the context of an established body of ideas. In terms of urban ecological concepts, immigration is but one facet of a constant but gradual process of residential invasion and succession, by which residential areas change in social and demographic character with age. The underlying mechanism is the constant centrifugal movement of the city population as the demand for better housing and space standards is met by new house construction on the periphery of the city. All levels of urban society are affected to a greater or lesser extent, so that neighbourhoods pass through a cycle of residential succession, beginning in youthful prime and ageing into physical obsolescence; at the same time as the original population moves away to newer and better areas, it is replaced by poorer populations. The rate of 'turnover' of the population is not a constant one spatially, but varies considerably in response to the

From *Transactions of the Institute of British Geographers*, 50 (1970), 199–218. Reprinted by permission of The Institute of British Geographers.

different social and physical character of the initial development. Thus the North American land economist, H. Hoyt (1939), responsible for many seminal investigations in this field, suggested that the most rapid turnover and obsolescence rate was associated with those districts built initially for the richer elements of urban society. E. W. Burgess (1925), in his classic work in Chicago, demonstrated a strong connection between the areas of immigration and what he termed the 'transition zone', an area of maximum physical obsolescence and high population turnover.

Also associated with urban ecological theory has been the process of segregation, the expression of a strong tendency for a spatial organization of urban social groups in terms of homogeneous units, which has also embraced segregation of groups identified by ethnic, national, or racial characteristics. Because of the operation of stronger pressures to adopt the social and economic *mores* of the city, the process of outward movement of population has usually led to the dispersal and dissipation of such segregated enclaves after a varying length of time, although segregation in terms of income or social status remains as strong as ever. However, with Negro immigration in the cities of the northern U.S.A., the distinguishing feature from the outset has been the very sharpness of segregation. All other forms of segregation have been blurred and less intense, yet even in the 1920s Burgess (1925) was forced to insert a 'Negro Belt' for this reason, which does not accord with his general concentric construct. Again, Hoyt (1939) was one of the first to suggest that the ecological processes of residential invasion and succession appeared to accelerate whenever Negroes were involved, so confirming that colour had assumed a special status in the development of spatial groupings in the North American city. Further work since 1945 in the United States has shown how the dispersal of Negro immigrants from initial clusters or colonies has been slower than could be expected if 'normal' ecological forces were at work. Thus R. Novak (1956) has demonstrated that the Puerto Rican immigrants in New York City had achieved a far wider dispersal since 1945 than the Negroes since about 1900. In other words, Negro immigration in North American cities has been notable for the completeness and persistency of segregation, in which the normal diffusion of immigrants from initial nuclei appears to have been thwarted (R. Morrill, 1965).

The establishment of immigrant 'colonies' would appear to be an essential part of the initial settlement of any immigrant population in an urban area (Rex and Moore, 1967). D. Ward (1968) has recently published evidence of strong ethnic and national colonies in North American Atlantic Seabord cities from the 1880s onward. But in all cases, a subsequent dispersal phase has been a natural ecological development as the aspirations of the immigrants rise above the 'zone of transition' in which they have usually settled. To date, what has distinguished the British situation from its North American counterpart, apart from obvious cultural and numerical differences, has been the less 'exclusive' composition of population in those parts of our cities which could be classed as areas of immigration. As Glass has stated in relation to London: 'The boroughs with the highest percentage of (coloured) immigrants were all areas of high population turnover, with a high incidence of furnished and shared accommodation. But while those boroughs housed newcomers and transients of all kinds, none of them was predominantly a place of immigrant settlement' (R. Glass and J. Westergaard, 1965). In North American cities, with a relatively open market, strong pressures have been created to contain Negro populations in restricted sectors, often uniting groups of the urban population who would otherwise have little in common. In British cities the structure of the housing market is more complex, particularly in the existence of a powerful public housing sector, so that more flexible alternatives exist to modify ecological processes should this be considered necessary.

Problems of Data Comparability: 1961 and 1966

Any study of the distributional changes in the coloured immigrant population of British cities must reconcile itself to basic deficiencies in the census data sources, in so far as these are studied at an enumeration district scale essential for detailed work. Perhaps the most obvious deficiency is that the data collection for 1961 is ostensibly a complete enumeration, although both Rex and Moore (1967) and Peach (1966B) have demonstrated evidence of considerable under-enumeration among coloured immigrants—as much as 20 per cent for West Indians according to Peach; whereas the comparable tabulations for 1966 were conducted on a 10 per cent sample basis. Consequently, because of the wide range of population estimates obtained at an individual enumeration district level when the standard error of estimate is incorporated, the enumeration district data have been used in their simplest form, and subjected to processes of cartographic generalization by which it is hoped the essential points of the analysis can be stated while minimizing the inherent weaknesses of the data. No attempt at a ratio level of measurement has been made at an individual enumeration district level for 1966, but only where data have been aggregated for groups of enumeration districts covering considerable areas, so reducing the error factor proportionately.

Other deficiencies impose limitations on the flexibility of the data. Only birthplace tabulations are available for both years, so that children born in the U.K. to coloured immigrants cannot be distinguished. It is therefore implicit in the paper that coloured immigrants are being discussed, and not the coloured 'population'. Furthermore, 'birth-place' cannot be completely equated with colour, especially among those born in the former Indian Empire. Comparisons of citizenship and birthplace tables for the 1961 census have put the possible white proportion of immigrants born in India, Ceylon, and Pakistan as high as one-quarter, so this factor must be borne in mind. Nevertheless, in the absence of specific evidence concerning the distribution of white and non-white elements one can do little except assume that, for the major part, the population represented by those born in India, Ceylon, Pakistan, and the West Indies is coloured.

The 1961 census also distinguished between immigrants born in the former Indian Empire and those born in the former British Caribbean territories. A broad breakdown on these lines was essential in a country such as Britain where the composition of coloured immigration is so varied (Little, 1967). Unfortunately this distinction does not appear in the 1966 tables, so that for comparative work the 1966 data must be aggregated. A further complication then arises in that immigrants born in former British East, West, and Central Africa, Malta, and Cyprus were also separately tabulated in 1961. In 1966 these categories came under one broad grouping along with the main coloured immigrant source areas of India, Pakistan, and the West Indies. The only division thus available in 1966 at the enumeration district level is between the old or 'white' Commonwealth (the former Dominions such as Australia, Canada, etc.) and the 'New' Commonwealth, to adopt the terminology of the General Register Office. Therefore the maps and tables for 1961 have been constructed using tabulations for the immigrants from countries grouped together in 1966 as the New Commonwealth. Thus besides the most important sub-groups of coloured immigrants the data include some immigrants such as Cypriots or Maltese who would not be considered as part of the *coloured* immigrant population. Some indication of the effect of these extraneous groups can be gained by an examination of the 1961 data for Birmingham, when the total number of iimmigrants from the African territories, Malta, and Cyprus amounted to only 1,647, so that on a city scale the aggregated figures for 1961 will include about 6 per cent who were not from the key source areas. This small ratio, which is unlikely to have altered materially by 1966, suggests that it would be wrong to forego the opportunity of analysing and comparing the two distributions; this is especially so in the case of Birmingham where Maltese and Cypriots were of negligible significance in 1961, when compared with the high level of immigration into Greater London. In particular, it is felt that the prime purpose of the paper, which is to identify in general terms some of the processes at work in the changing distribution of the coloured immigrants between 1961 and 1966, would not be seriously affected.

The Background

In the intercensal period 1961–6 the coloured immigrant population of Birmingham expanded rapidly. From a 1961 figure of 28,169 (including West and East Africans, Maltese, and Cypriots), the total almost doubled to 49,870.[1] In the same period the total city population fell from 1,107,187 to 1,064,220; inevitably, the proportion of coloured immigrants rose from 2·4 per cent to 4·7 per cent. In 1966 the West Midlands conurbation emerged clearly as the main focus of coloured immigration outside Greater London, and approximately five-eighths of the conurbation's total immigrants were recorded in Birmingham itself.

Even the broad ward statistics in 1966 demonstrate that, as in 1961 (P. N. Jones, 1967), unevenness was still the hallmark of the coloured immigrants distribution, as Table 1 shows. It is seen that almost one-half of the coloured immigrants were enumerated in only one-eighth of the total number of wards, while the upper quartile of the wards accounted for almost three-quarters of the coloured immigrants.

The maps attempt to portray the distribution of coloured immigrants in as much detail as the data allow. The statistical basis is the enumeration district returns for 1961 and 1966, and no assumptions have been made about the distribution pattern *within* any enumeration district, except to exclude obviously non-residential areas which can be unambiguously identified from the 1:10,560 Ordnance Survey sheets. Otherwise, an even scatter of immigrants within any district has been the basis of construction.

TABLE 1
Concentration of coloured immigrants in Birmingham on a ward basis, 1966

Ward group	Total immigrants enumerated	Per cent of coloured immigrants
First-ranking 3 wards	15,340	30·6
First-ranking 5 wards	22,760	45·6
First-ranking 10 wards	36,670	73·5
Total wards = 39	49,870	100

The Distributions in 1961 and 1966 as Depicted by Dot Maps

Figure 1 illustrates the distribution of coloured immigrants in 1961 after the 'formative' phase of immigration in the 1950s. The pattern, including the spatial differences between Asian and West Indian immigrants, has been examined in some detail elsewhere by the author (Jones, 1967), so that attention here is focused on the over-all distribution of the immigrants.

The dot map demonstrates with exceptional clarity the compact and clustered distribution of immigrants within the city in 1961; vast areas of the city were quite unaffected by immigration. The pattern expressed by the dots is of a roughly concentric belt surrounding the inner core of the city; the belt is about 1·5 kilometres wide, but is not continuous. There are concentrations of immigrants in some areas, especially to the north of the city core, while some wedge- or sector-like interruptions, as at Duddeston or Edgbaston, are relatively empty. This clustering arose as a result of what Peach (1968) called 'positive' factors—low

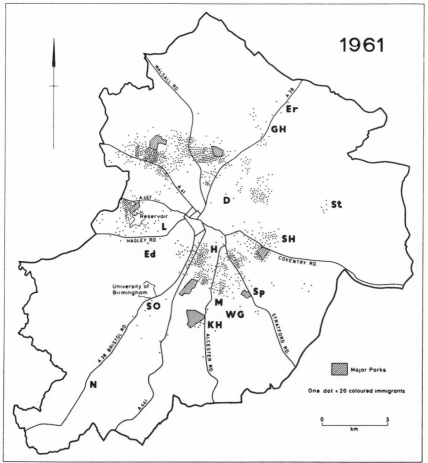

Fig. 1. The distribution of coloured immigrants in 1961. Districts are denoted by letters: Er—Erdington; GH—Gravelly Hill; D—Duddeston; St—Stechford; L—Ladywood; Ed—Edgbaston; H—Highgate; SO—Selly Oak; M—Moseley; Sp—Sparkhill; SH—Small Heath; KH—Kings Heath; WG—Wake Green; N—Northfield.

income, poor housing status, a desire to live close to compatriots, and so on. The
dots are less evenly distributed to the south of the city core, and in the sector
between the Bristol and Coventry Roads the pattern is fragmented compared with
the sector north of the city core. Only in the Calthorpe Park area to the west of
Highgate is there a large and dense concentration. The Sparkbrook area, to the
south-east of Highgate, does not appear to be noticeably significant in terms of
over-all distribution. Outliers of isolated concentration appear at Summerfield Park,
in West Birmingham, and at Saltley to the east of Duddeston. Saltley is physically
isolated by pronounced railway and industrial zones to the north, west, and south.
The more complex isolating factors in operation in the case of Summerfield Park
stem partly from the rapid transition in house types as the junction of low-density
Edgbaston and high-density All Saints; partly from the industrialized line of the
former London and North-Western Railway and Birmingham to Wolverhampton
Canal in the north; and partly from the presence of the large Rotton Park reservoir.

Those parts of the city where relatively few immigrants were recorded are the
inner core, which includes many non-residential uses such as the central area and
major industrial zones such as the Jewellery Quarter together with a good
proportion of sub-standard clearance property; and the outer suburban areas,
essentially developed after 1920 but in some cases containing considerable pockets
of pre-1914 housing (M. B. Stedman, 1958). The writer has shown elsewhere that a
causal link between zones of immigration and the poorest, cheapest housing within
the city cannot be substantiated, although ecological theory would point to the
central area transition zone as the likely zone of concentration (Jones, 1967). The
basic reason is the greater complexity of the urban housing market in British as
opposed to North American cities, because a high proportion of the inner
'transition zone' property has been vested in municipal ownership since the early
post-war period, and a gradual programme of voluntary purchase is absorbing the
remainder. This housing is thus not freely available to any immigrant regardless of
origin, but has to be used prior to clearance in assisting with the general housing
problems of the city. The zone of immigration in 1961 was thus pushed out further
into the later Victorian and Edwardian parts of the city, immediately beyond the
'captive' inner core. The process of 'invasion' was not a simple one, however, as the
discontinuities in the dot map illustrate, and density and related property
differences within the broadly concentric zone have assumed considerable
significance, of which the socially exclusive Edgbaston 'wedge' forms an outstanding example. In 1961 only a handful of immigrants had settled beyond the
'zonal' limits of pre-1914 housing, to outliers such as Gravelly Hill or Stechford.

Figure 2 demonstrates the impact of five years of further immigration after
1961, and the outstanding feature is the further concentration in the main
concentric belt. Although this increase in density has occurred in all sectors, its
impact is more noticeable to the south and east of the city core, and the former
fragmented pattern has congealed into a solid belt almost as complete as that to the
north. There have also been increases in density in the outer zone, and thin scatters
appear in areas previously unaffected. Gravelly Hill, Erdington, and King's Heath
are examples of outer districts whose immigrant populations have clearly expanded.

Less obvious perhaps, but equally important, are indications of areal spread
within the main concentration. The sector to the north of Hagley Road is a good
instance, and also the southward development in the Sparkhill and Moseley
districts; but other smaller extensions, together with the general increase in density,
leave a much clearer image of 'concentricity' in 1966. Infilling and spill-over had

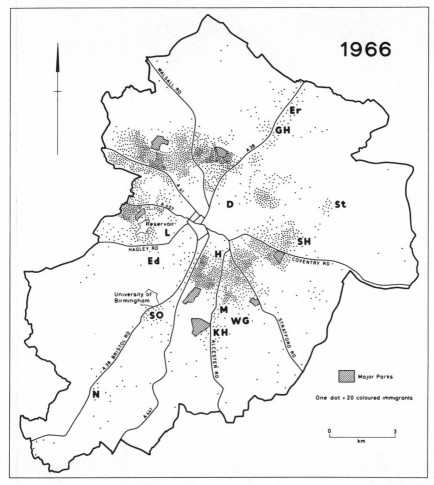

Fig. 2. The distrubution of coloured immigrants in 1966. District names as on Fig. 1.

obviously made a considerable impact by 1966, and only the remarkable Edgbaston low-density wedge formed a really impressive sectoral interruption.

The dot maps of immigrant distribution at both dates indicate a clustered, non-random pattern and further analysis could be developed in terms of the dot pattern. The dot maps convey an immediate visual pattern, which because of its precision within defined limits is capable of direct comparative analysis with the morphology of residential areas; it can also be used as a basis for 'field' studies. Equally important, one can derive maps from these dot maps which represent a further stage of generalizations, namely maps of density of immigrant population expressed as 'surfaces' through the medium of isopleths. These maps are not a substitute for, but a logical development from, the essential dot maps. The density of immigrants has been measured in persons per square kilometre. The isopleth maps have been constructed using the 'floating grid' technique, similar to that outlined by C. F. Schmid and E. H. MacCannell (1955). Inevitably, much of the value and meaning of an isopleth map, in which the control points have been

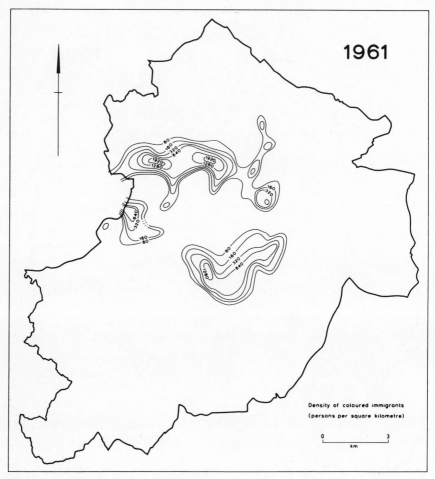

Fig. 3. The density of coloured immigrants in 1961 per km^2.

objectively measured, depends on the final choice of an appropriate isopleth interval. In order that isopleths should portray a meaningful spatial array of values, the scale of interval has been made a geometrical one, with the addition of one isopleth interval in an intermediate position at the higher end of the scale. The geometrical scale proved the only manageable method of accommodating the very large range of values from zero to a peak point of almost 4000/km^2. The identical scale has of course been used for both maps to make comparisons possible, and two density surfaces can thus be drawn which are capable of description and further measurement.

Isopleth Maps of Density of Coloured Immigrants

Isopleth maps generalize the detailed and accidented dot maps into smooth surfaces. The unit area of density chosen, the square kilometre, appears to be a satisfactory size for a study of city dimensions, being neither too large to obscure important features of the distribution; nor too small so that minor irregularities, some of which would undoubtedly be of spurious accuracy, would appear. The

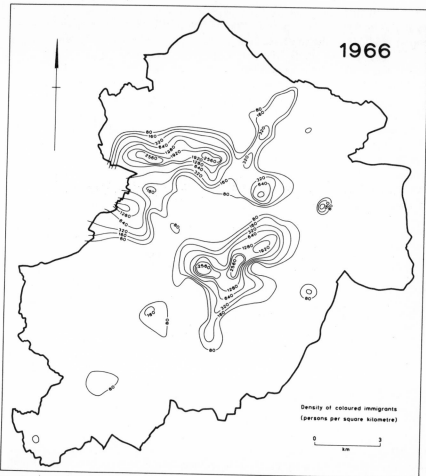

Fig. 4. The density of coloured immigrants in 1966 per km^2.

isopleths indicate in a broad way the pressure exerted by immigrant populations across the entire city.

In 1961 two major 'plateau' features are present, one being perhaps more ridge-like and sinuous than the other. To the north of the city core, an elongated ridge stretches from the city boundary across the northern 'middle ring' (Stedman, 1958) to Saltley, and extends a finger of relatively lower density northward along the line of the Rea valley to Gravelly Hill. The major section between Handsworth and Aston in the east forms a plateau at a density of 640/km^2, with two elevations in Handsworth and Aston where the density exceeds 1920/km^2 by far the highest densities reached anywhere in the city, and so representing the twin 'peaks' of intense concentration and pressure. The Saltley extremity of the ridge only reaches 640/km^2 in its core, and the same is true of the Summerfield Park area. In the latter area it will be seen that the isopleths run across the city boundary into the Smethwick section of Warley County Borough. To the south of the city core is a broad V-shaped plateau which achieves a peak continuous density of 640/km^2. A small area in Calthorpe exceeds 1280/km^2, and represents the peak of the surface.

Density gradients as revealed by the isopleth spacings are obviously more gradual
and gentle in this southern plateau than in the north, or in Summerfield Park. The
steepest gradient in the south is along the south-west edge where 'resistant' features
such as Cannon Hill Park and the contiguous exclusive residential districts of
Moseley occur. Overall, the isopleth pattern is rather straightforward, only one
extension and some small breaks disturbing a basically symmetrical pattern around
the city core, but in which the northern rim achieves higher densities over larger
areas than the southern rim.

In 1966 the greater complexity of the isopleth patterns is very evident. The two
extensive plateaux to the north and south of the city core are still dominant, but
their shape and intensity have been evidently modified. To the north, the plateau of
high density has greatly increased in intensity everywhere, but especially in the
main section between and including Handsworth and Aston. This section, which in
1961 was defined by the '640' isopleth, is now delimited by the '1280' isopleth,
while the two 'peaks' at Handsworth and Aston exceed 2560. A narrow ridge
connects these peaks at a density of $1920/km^2$. The edges of the northern plateau
have been pushed out to north and south, so that it has become continuous at a
lower density with Summerfield Park. The latter has changed from a rather small
outlier to a substantial high-density feature with a peak density in the core of over
$1920/km^2$. The finger-like extension in the Rea valley has increased in density and
pushed further outward to Erdington, while small localized peaks exceed $320/km^2$.
Two 'breaks' in the total surface separate the northern plateau from the southern
plateau, at Saltley and in Edgbaston.

The southern plateau has clearly altered in shape quite considerably, mainly as a
result of throwing out three lobes in southerly and easterly directions to King's
Heath, Sparkhill, and Small Heath. Together with a general increase in density in
the area as a whole, this has had the effect of emphasizing the importance of sharp
townscape barriers such as the Small Heath-Tyseley industrial belt along the former
Great Western Railway (London) line, and the Cannon Hill Park belt. Three
separate peaks of density have emerged in the former V-shaped plateau, defined by
the '1920' isopleth. Cannon Hill-Calthorpe and Sparkbrook peaks exceed
$2560/km^2$ while continuity of the belt to include the third peak in Small Heath is
achieved at $1280/km^2$.

A further significant feature of Figure 4 is the emergence of outliers defined by a
minimum density of $80/km^2$, but in most cases rising to 160. The most important
are at Acocks Green, Stechford, Selly Oak, and Northfield. This incipient suburban
movement is still, however, confined to considerable morphological outliers of
pre-1914 housing, although the general environmental quality is far superior to the
major parts of the *zonal* middle ring areas, and this is reflected in house prices.

Density gradients are steep in most areas, but exceptions are found in actively
extending margins, such as in the southern margins of the southern 'plateau', or
where the Summerfield Park concentration is extending towards the Hagley Road.

Two processes have been operating since 1961 in controlling the distribution of
immigrants—outward spread, and intensification of existing density. An isopleth
map of density change between 1961 and 1966 has been drawn to illustrate these
processes, along with selected profiles across the city.

Figure 5 demonstrates the obvious importance of increase in density within areas
already significant in 1961; this process dominates the spatial aspect of change in
the density of coloured immigrants. The peaks of density increase are found in the
northern and southern plateau-like concentrations, where the '640' isopleth defines

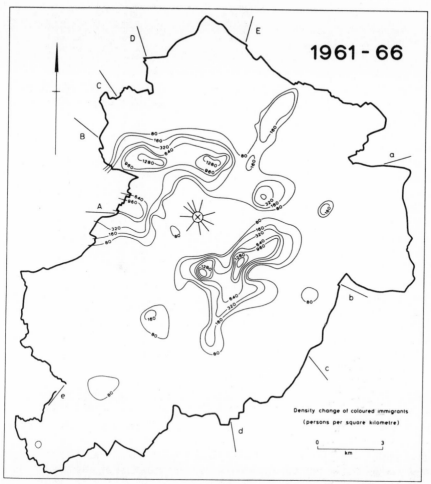

Fig. 5. Density change of coloured immigrants per km², 1961—66. Also shown are the outer edges of the profiles Aa, Bb, etc., used in the construction of Fig. 6.

large continuous areas. In both major areas, smaller peaks of density change are present—exceeding 1280/km² increase in Handsworth and Aston in the north— while the two peaks of intensive increase in density in the southern area, at Sparkbrook and Cannon Hill-Calthorpe, are separated by a lower 'col' in the Highgate district. The density increase in the southern peaks, in excess of 1920/km² is higher than that in the north, and the actual peak city increase was over 2200/km² in the Cannon Hill district. Even in the Summerfield Park district the increase at the core has been of the order of 960/km².

The most significant density increases are concentrically arranged around the inner city core, and the outer extensions are of lesser significance, because of their much lower densities compared with the main concentric zone. The extensions from the major areas are the most important, particularly those to Erdington, King's Heath, and Sparkhill.

The contrast between 'outward movement' and 'intensification' can be further demonstrated by constructing a series of density profiles across the city. The

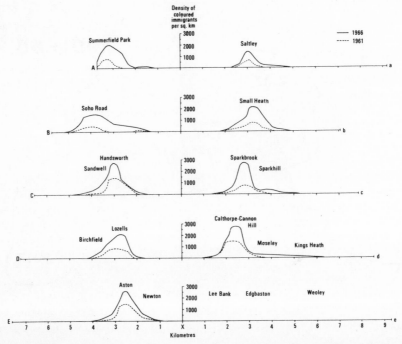

Fig. 6. Density profiles across the city in 1961 and 1966. The origins of the profile lines are shown on Fig. 5.

profiles which comprise Figure 6 were selected from thirty randomly chosen traverses which pass through a common origin in the city central area. The selection has been based on the position of the traverses in relation to the 1966 isopleth map, with a view to illustrating radial variations in immigrant densities. The traverses were applied to both the 1961 and 1966 isopleth maps, so that the changes in density could also be plotted. The traverse lines are shown on Figure 5.

Perhaps the chief feature of all the profiles is the caldera-like feature they demonstrate at both dates—a depression corresponding to the inner city core, with its central area proper and its integuments of poor-quality housing mixed with various types of commercial and industrial land uses. The 'empty' core of the city is about 4 kilometres across, and the peak density of the surrounding rim tends to occur at about 2·5—3·0 kilometres from the city centre in all directions. Nowhere is the width of the 'rim', at a density of over 640/km², greater than about 2 kilometres. This is relatively limited in relation to the total profile lengths of between 6 and 9 kilometres generally. This fact is inevitably reflected in the very steepness of the density profiles as a whole.

The profiles also draw attention to the changes which occurred between 1961 and 1966. In all, the remarkable increase in density at the peak zone in 1961 is the outstanding factor, which further substantiates previous observations. In most cases the areal increases recorded have been clearly in an outward direction, although in all cases the densities have been at a relatively low level, 320/km² and less. The main exception occurs in Summerfield Park (Aa) whose outer edge abuts on Smethwick, and whose only avenue for expansion is eastward and southward. This outward movement is best seen in profiles Cc and Dd, especially the southern sections. Nevertheless, these outward movements are in the final analysis overshadowed by the increases in the density of immigrants in existing concentrations. This 'intensification' process has clearly been the dominant ecological process of the years 1961—6, and its effects must reveal themselves in related spheres, such as a tendency for over-concentration of immigrants in certain schools to increase.

Absolute Population Changes 1961—66 and Their Relationship with Segregation

One of the major issues surrounding coloured immigration is the existence, or supposed existence, of 'enclaves' or 'colonies' of coloured immigrant populations within our major cities. Such enclaves would have immediate repercussions on educational and other highly localized social services, and perhaps damaging longer-term effects in creating a mood of resentment at 'second-class' citizenship.

The dominant factor to emerge from the analysis of the cartographic evidence is that coloured immigrants have increased most markedly in areas where they were most highly concentrated in 1961. A detailed analysis of the 1961 enumeration district data by the author revealed the existence of reasonably well-defined 'clusters' of coloured immigrants (Jones, 1967). The clusters were established on the basis of an objective assessment of coloured immigrants as a proportion of the total population in each enumeration district, those enumeration districts falling in the upper quartile of the distribution being recognized as part of an immigrant cluster. Ten clusters of various sizes were recognized, and these were all located within the concentric zone of peak coloured immigrant density of 1961, as shown in Figure 3. These clusters represented polarization points rather than exclusive ghettos, since in no instance did coloured immigrants form even one-third of the total population. Broadly similar findings for Greater London were published by Ruth Glass and her co-researchers (Glass and Westergaard, 1965). Yet the evidence of the paper so far would suggest that some change must have occurred in the intervening years 1961—66.

The clusters in 1961 were obviously identified in terms of 1961 enumeration district boundaries, and these can only be approximately equated with the pattern of the 1966 enumeration districts, which generally consist of amalgamations of three or sometimes four 1961 districts. In certain instances 1961 districts have been dismembered, but fortunately these are not very numerous in the areas which comprise the main immigrant concentrations. In the few cases where this has occurred an arbitrary allocation of total and coloured immigrant populations has been made on a *pro rata* basis. In order to make the areal basis for the comparison of populations within the immigrant clusters completely consistent, it has been necessary to regroup the 1961 enumeration districts in terms of the larger 1966 enumeration districts as a first step. This was done for the inner and middle ring wards of the city previously used (Jones, 1967), again omitting the CBD enumeration districts to give a total of 214 districts. The percentage of immigrants in each of these districts in 1961 was calculated, the distribution being highly skewed, with 137 districts having a ratio of less than 4 per cent, and only 29 having ratios of over 10 per cent. Therefore, as before, the clusters were constituted by a ranking procedure in which the upper quartile of the districts was identified and mapped, giving a very distinctive pattern illustrated in Figure 7. A comparison with the original scheme established with the much finer areal mesh of the 1961 districts reveals the consistency of the method, allowing for the greater degree of

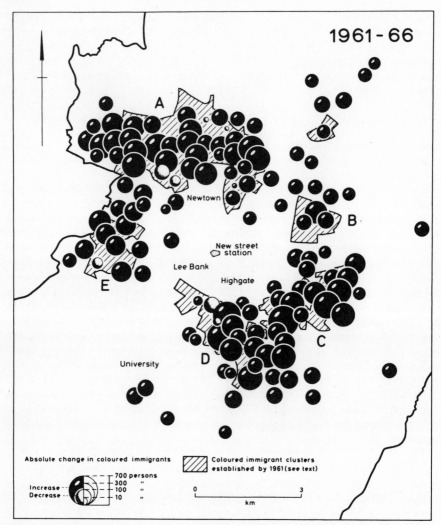

Fig. 7. Absolute changes in the coloured immigrant population, 1961–66. The clusters are as follows: A–North Birmingham; B–Saltley; C–Small Heath and Sparkbrook; D–Calthorpe and Balsall Heath; E–Summerfield Park.

generalization in the 1966 districts. The upper quartile value emerged as 6·60 per cent. With directly comparable 'reconstituted' immigrant clusters, we are now in a position to comment in more detail on the internal changes which occurred in these critical areas of coloured immigration in the city. Two problems in particular stand out—the possible increase in segregation and 'exclusiveness' of the existing clusters, and the importance of the clusters to the total immigrant population distribution.

   The pattern revealed by Table 2, even allowing for the data problems, is an interesting one. In the clusters as a whole the total population fell from 134,000 to between 118,000 and 127,000; yet the numbers of coloured immigrants increased very considerably to between 26,000 and 30,000. Inevitably the coloured immigrant proportion of the total has also increased from just over 12 per cent in

1961 to between 20 and 26 per cent. Within some clusters this proportion is higher. First in rank in both 1961 and 1966 was Calthorpe-Balsall Heath, which in 1966 recorded an immigrant ratio of between 26 and 34 per cent, while in the largest cluster in area and population, the elongated North Birmingham belt, the proportion of coloured immigrants had reached the 20–24 per cent range. In Small Heath and Sparkbrook also the coloured immigrant ratio had exceeded 20 per cent by 1966, a level also exceeded in Saltley and Summerfield Park.

A pronounced build-up of coloured immigrant populations between 1961 and 1966 is thus indicated for those parts of the city which can be objectively identified as already the critical areas of coloured immigration in 1961. Yet, although the polarization and increasing exclusiveness trends had continued, the pattern was still not one of complete segregation even within the clusters. In all clusters, coloured immigrants remained very much a minority group, albeit a large and noticeable minority. On this evidence, therefore, ghetto-like conditions are a long way off, but two further points need to be considered.

The first, and most difficult to evaluate, is that no useful or precise comment upon the segregation of the total coloured population, which is the crucial social geographical index, can be made. All that can be said without detailed field analysis is that, without exception, the percentage ranges quoted for 1966 are under-estimates of the coloured population, and that probably predominantly West Indian areas would need to be adjusted upward rather more than the more 'male' Indian and Pakistani areas. But even with very generous additions for coloured U.K.-born children, it is difficult to see any cluster except possibly that of Calthorpe-Balsall Heath having a coloured majority in 1966. Precise breakdowns of immigrant household size within various areas are needed to advance any firm conclusions.

The second point relates to the different trends in the coloured immigrant and 'other populations' within the clusters; most of the latter group will of course be white, although an increasing proportion will be coloured children. Table 2 shows that the downward movement of the 'other population' is a necessary accompaniment of the build-up of the coloured immigrant population, since the actual total population is declining. The forces making for an increasingly segregated pattern of distribution were thus in full swing, reflecting both the inward pressure of continued immigration and an accelerating outward movement of the resident white population from districts which were already static or declining in population before the onset of coloured immigration.

The rate of increase of the coloured immigrants in the clusters has been within the range 54·39–80·11 per cent, which is very high for a five-year interval. But in the same period it can be seen that the over-all city increase was rather higher, being in the 61·19–92·86 per cent range. Thus there is reason to believe that, although the build-up of coloured immigrants in the clusters was rapid, it was probably less rapid than elsewhere in the city, so that an important role must be allotted to increases outside the established clusters. That these increases were essentially peripheral to the clusters can be deduced from previous cartographic evidence, but it has nevertheless had the important consequence of reducing the degree of segregation which might otherwise have been attained in the main clusters.

The over-all importance of these established immigrant clusters to the total coloured immigrant population can now be assessed. In 1961 they accounted for 60 per cent of the latter, as compared with only 12 per cent of the total city population. In 1966 the clusters still accounted for about 11 per cent of the total population, but the possible proportion of the total coloured population fell to

SOCIAL GEOGRAPHY : PATTERNS

TABLE 2

Population of coloured immigrant clusters, 1961–66

Cluster	1961 population			1966 population*		
	Total	Coloured immigrants Number	Per cent	Total	Coloured immigrants Number	Per cent
North Birmingham†	70,044	9,073	12·95	65,860	14,230	20·58
				69,140	15,790	23·97
Summerfield Park	13,609	1,583	11·63	11,600	2,340	18·00
				13,000	2,980	25·69
Small Heath and Sparkbrook	22,777	2,174	9·54	18,660	4,190	20·52
				20,420	5,070	27·17
Calthorpe–Balsall Heath	18,955	3,084	16·27	14,660	4,190	25·90
				16,180	5,030	34·30
Saltley	9,046	923	10·20	7,510	1,150	13·33
				8,630	1,630	21·70
Total	134,431	16,837	12·52	118,290	26,100	20·49
				127,370	30,500	25·78

*Two figures are quoted for both total and coloured immigrant populations for each cluster, representing the range of population estimates obtained at a 95 per cent probability level. The percentage column for 1966 indicates the minimum and maximum range.
†Includes the isolated district at Gravelly Hill.

between 48 and 67 per cent. In view of the wide range of percentage values at the later date, all one can state is that the clusters have not shown any marked tendency to abstract a much greater proportion of the total coloured immigrant population than in 1961. We know that the dominant process has been intensification, so there must have been a considerable 'overspill' of immigrant populations from the clusters to other districts within the middle ring zone of immigrant concentration.

Figure 7 illustrates the pattern of absolute increases between 1961 and 1966. Only those 1966 enumeration districts with over 100 coloured immigrants have been considered for the sake of clarity. The outlines of the clusters are shown.

The clusters stand out in an imposing manner, suggesting that a considerable proportion of the immigrants are diffused in enumeration districts where they numbered less than 100 in 1966, and thus do not appear on the diagram. But more important is the fact that the main areas of increase outside the clusters are in adjacent districts, so that 'gaps' in the concentric arrangement of the clusters have absorbed most of the increases. This is especially seen in the north and west, and along the south-east of the clusters. It is noticeable how little expansion has taken place on the inner margins of the clusters. The outward extensions along the line of the Rea valley and Lichfield Road stand out clearly. Evidence of decline resulting from urban redevelopment is seen in the Calthorpe area.

Some Conclusions

Despite its apparent simplicity, the morphological factor is the dominant large-scale control in the distribution of coloured immigrants in 1966, as in 1961. Whereas in 1961 the initial nuclei or 'colonies' of immigrants owed their origin to complex factors in detail (and probably randomly controlled in a spatial sense), the ecological processes of immigrant reception ensured that the colonies, once established, would grow in a relatively restricted radius. Evidence of the operation of these ecologically controlled processes is afforded by the 1961 census data, in the pronounced degree of internal segregation shown by Asian and West Indian immigrant groups (Jones, 1967). By 1966 the evidence suggests that virtually the entire middle ring of the city had become important for the reception of coloured immigrants, reflected in a tremendous increase in the density of coloured immigrants in this zone between 1961 and 1966.

Intensification has remained the dominant spatial process rather than a hoped-for dispersal and suburbanization. Movement to areas of post-1920 housing, whether private or municipal, is clearly not large enough to make any significant impact in comparison with the concentration of the middle ring of the city.

Fears of 'ghetto-formation' are still not supported on the evidence of 1966 data, although this relates to immigrants only and not the total coloured population. But we must be aware of the potential position, since in all the large clusters the immigrant proportion alone almost certainly exceeded 20 per cent and this must be adjusted upward to allow for U.K.-born coloured children. Immigration has of course continued since 1966, while the dominant demographic tendency which is built into the system of immigration control since 1962 is for family units to be completed, and a better male-female ratio to be achieved among the immigrant populations. Table 3, based on the statistics for national immigration control, clearly illustrates the strong 'weighting' in favour of women and children in the years 1965 and 1966 for the primary sources of coloured immigration.

TABLE 3
Net migration balances from the major source regions for 1965 and 1966

Area of origin	1966			1965		
	Men	Women	Children	Men	Women	Children
West Indies	−344	1,816	8,158	1,215	3,862	8,323
India	4,537	5,475	8,390	5,510	5,873	7,432
Pakistan	−914	2,707	6,215	1,046	2,485	3,896
Total	3,279	9,998	23,763	7,871	12,220	19,651

Source: Home Office, Commonwealth Immigrants Act 1962, Control of Immigration Statistics 1966 (Cmd. 3258, 1967); 1965 (Cmd. 2979, 1966)

It is thus not inconceivable that, if trends continue even in a modified form, the proportion of total coloured population in many of the clusters could at least *approach* a majority position in a relatively limited time span. It is this possibility which must be recognized and appropriate action taken to avoid the establishment of such a degree of segregation.

ACKNOWLEDGEMENTS

The author thanks Mr. K. Scurr, Technician in the Department of Geography Drawing Office, University of Hull, for drawing the maps and diagrams which illustrate the paper. He is grateful to the University of Hull for a grant towards the cost of illustrations.

NOTE

[1] Strictly, persons enumerated in the sample census multiplied by ten. See R. Neale and G. Haine, *City of Birmingham Statistical Yearbook, 1968*. This convention is used throughout in the conversion of the 1966 data on a city scale, but in considering sub-regions of the city the standard error of estimate at a 95 per cent level has been incorporated in all cases.

REFERENCES

Burgess, E. W. (1925) 'The growth of the city', Chapter II in *The City* by R. E. Park, E. W. Burgess, and R. D. McKenzie (Chicago).

Collison, P. (1967) 'Immigrants and residence', *Sociology*, 1. 277–92.

Davison, R. B. (1963) 'The distribution of immigrant groups in London', *Race*, 5. 56–70.

Glass, R. (1960) *Newcomers: the West Indians in London.*

Glass, R. and J. Westergaard (1965) *London's housing needs.*

Hoyt, H. (1939) 'The structure and growth of residential neighbourhoods in American cities', *Federal Housing Admin.*, pp. 96–122.

Jones, P. N. (1967) *The segregation of immigrant communities in the City of Birmingham 1961* (Hull).

Little, K. (1967) 'Colour, class and culture in Britain', *Daedalus*, Spring 1967, pp. 512–26.

Morrill, R. (1965) 'The negro ghetto–problems and alternatives', *Geogrl Rev.* 55. 342–60.

Novak, R. (1956) 'The distribution of Puerto Ricans in Manhattan Island', *Geogrl Rev.* 46. 182–6.

Peach, G. C. K. (1966a) 'Factors affecting the distribution of West Indians in Great Britain', *Trans. Inst. Br. Geogr.* 38. 151–63.

Peach, G. C. K. (1966b) 'Under-enumeration of West Indians in the 1961 Census', *Sociol, Rev.* 14. 73–80.

Peach, G. C. K. (1968) *West Indian migration to Britain–a social geography.*

Rex, J. and R. Moore (1967) *Race, community and conflict.*

Schmid, C. F. and E. H. MacCannell (1955) 'Basic problems, techniques and theory of isopleth mapping', *J. Am. Statist. Ass.* 50. 220–39.

Stedman, M. B. (1958) 'The townscapes of Birmingham in 1956', *Trans. Inst. Br. Geogr.* 25. 225–38.

Ward, D. (1968) 'The emergence of central immigrant ghettoes in American cities: 1840–1920', *Ann. Ass. Am. Geogr.* 68. 343–59.

PART TWO:

CONCEPTS OF SPACE

6. PROBLEMS OF GEOGRAPHY

W. Kirk

If everything occurred at the same time there could be no *development*. If everything existed in the same place there could be no *particularity*. Only space makes possible the particular, which then unfolds in time. Only because we are not equally near to everything; only because everything does not rush in upon us at once; only because our world is restricted for every individual, for his people and for mankind as a whole can we in our finiteness endure at all. . . . Particularity is the price of our existence. . . . The mighty elements of spatial discipline tend to preserve geographical and cultural roots in spite of freedom.

August Losch[1]

Kant, in his doctrine of our knowledge of the external world, taught that the categories through which we saw it were identical for all sentient beings, permanent and unalterable; indeed this was what made our world one, communication possible. But some of those who thought about history, morals, aesthetics, saw change and difference; that what differed was not so much the empirical content of what these successive civilizations saw or heard or thought, as also the patterns in which they perceived them, the models in terms of which they conceived them, the category spectacles through which they saw them.

Isaiah Berlin[2]

In attempting to solve the methodological problems posed by the apparent heterogeneity of geography, and in trying to define, for ourselves or others, its role in the total field of intellectual endeavour, it behoves us to remember that we are creatures of a particular culture or intellectual environment in which great importance has been attached to the empirical study of objects in our external environment. One of the great strengths of the West European scientific revolution in which we are still living has been its insistence on the division of intellectual labour by material categories—the specialization of thought and the development of analytical techniques in association with particular phenomena. Indeed so great have been the achievements of this approach, so deeply has it been impressed on our educational system and modes of thought, that we now find it difficult to conceive of an intellectual discipline that does not have a unitary object of study.

During our early years at school, when mental horizons were extended simultaneously in many directions, and knowledge of the external world was organized teacher-wise rather than subject-wise we were not conscious of such distinctions. The adventure into reality was sufficiently exciting in itself.[3] Later however, as our interests were channelled into particular academic pursuits, discrete subjects began to emerge and our view of reality fragmented and narrowed. Our perceptions of the world were disciplined into an accepted academic mould and we became concerned with the material objects of different courses and segments of knowledge. The content of 'Geography' was seen to be different from the content of, say, 'Chemistry' or 'History' and from the confident heights of the Upper School it was possible to look across this academic landscape and clearly discern the material boundaries between subjects. By this time, however, we were also aware of

From *Geography*, 48 (1963), 357–71. Reprinted by permission of the author and The Geographical Association.

divisions within the field of geography dependent on the type of phenomena studied, and upon entering university we came to realize that such divisions were more numerous than we had imagined, and that much of the teaching, examination, and research was organized on this basis. At one moment we wrestled with the trigonometrical complexities of map projections, at the next with the functions of C.B.D.s. We trod the prehistoric ridgeways of the Pays de Galles in search of Celtic saints or enjoyed the vicarious pleasures of bullock-cart days and Irrawaddy nights. We sought out knick-points on Wealden streams, and as first-year virgins trimmed the seven lamps of Mackinder. If ever we found the time to sit back and consider the subject as a whole we realized that the sharp external boundaries of the field of geography had become vague frontier zones shading off into the spheres of other disciplines, and that in the process internal boundaries had become more definitive. If we were worried by the apparent lack of unity within our subject and sought authoritative guidance we found that the authorities[4] spoke with many tongues; and if we examined what professional geographers did rather than what they said they did similar discrepancies stood revealed. It appeared that if we wanted unity within our subject— and not all authorities were agreed that this was either necessary or desirable—then what we had to do was build bridges, synthesize, integrate—and most of us to a greater or lesser degree have been trying to integrate ever since.

The difficulties of achieving a unified discipline from a conceptual framework such as that illustrated in Fig. 1 are at once apparent. If one claims that geography is a description—even an explanatory description—of the earth as a whole, and that consequently *all* earth-bound facts are geographical facts, then in materialist terms this is tantamount to saying that no facts are geographical facts, since many such facts or phenomena lie within the fields of other systematic sciences and thus cannot be claimed as exclusively geographical. If, on the other hand, one restricts the term 'geographical' to a particular category of earthly facts, fellow geographers may rightly object that phenomena of geographical significance are thereby excluded and that geography is being too closely identified with the material of a particular systematic science. Research workers in the systematic branches of geography are constantly exposed to this danger. By concentrating on a specific category of materials they often find it necessary to master the science—or at least sections of the science—within whose special provenance the material lies, otherwise they find it difficult to evaluate its findings in relation to their own study.

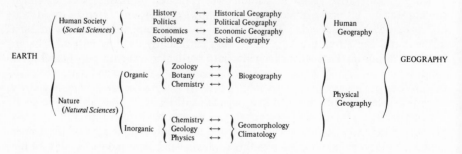

Fig. 1.

In so doing they frequently become involved in the problems as well as the materials of the associated discipline, or find that their study of the material has become an end in itself, and that they have much more in common with workers bound to the same materials than they have with geographers studying other materials. Thus physical geographers find themselves drawn into the orbit of those sciences studying the physical, chemical, and biological nature of the earth and its atmosphere, and human geographers find themselves in the company of social scientists working on problems such as population structures and trends, forces influencing migration, occupational structures of urban communities, economic underdevelopment, land tenure and agrarian reform, industrial growth, and the like.[5] Of course it is true that geographers can often make substantial contributions to such problems—and indeed should be encouraged to do so. The danger lies in mistaking the part for the whole—in creating a kind of fissiparous geography that is entirely aimed at trying to solve other men's problems and grows by consuming unwanted scraps from other men's tables. Modern geography was created by scholars trained in other disciplines asking themselves geographical questions and moving inwards in a community of problems; it could die by a reversal of this process whereby trained geographers move outwards in a fragmentation of interests seeking solutions to non-geographical problems.*

This dilemma of material-orientated study is of course not confined to geography. It is an issue that sooner or later most sciences must face. But it is particularly apparent in geography as a result of the multiple origins of our subject, and reactions to it have played an important part in modern developments within our discipline.

There are those for example who, arguing on materialistic grounds, would maintain that there never can be a unified discipline of geography—that as long as we continue to study man and nature two disciplines at least must be involved.[6] This is the *dualist* position, which has had most powerful advocacy recently in criticisms levelled by Zakharov, Kalesnik, and other Leningrad geographers at a monograph, *Theoretical Problems of Geography* by V. A. Anuchin, published in Moscow in 1960.[7] In it Anuchin argues that geography can be regarded as a single integrated science—a point of view apparently supported by his colleagues at Moscow University but bitterly opposed by the dualists of Leningrad. In terms which would have done credit to the slanging matches of Victorian scientific conferences they condemn Anuchin's thesis of a unified (*monist*) geography as a 'thick theoretical fog', a 'labyrinthine display of scholastics rather than science', an example of 'bourgeois environmentalism', anti-Marx, and, worst of all, American. They argue that not only are the materials of human geography ('economic geography' in the U.S.S.R.) completely different from those of physical geography, but since social processes are unlike natural processes, the laws governing the one cannot be applied to the other:

In contrast to the majority of foreign geographers, Soviet geographers do not combine physical and economic geography as a science for a very simple reason; these two disciplines lack a common study object that could be investigated according to specific laws applying equally well to actual social and natural phenomena.[8]

The practical, administrative development of this dualist position appears in a suggestion by Pomazanov[9] that economic (human) geography should be handed

---

*The recency of geography as a university discipline in this country is indicated by the fact that the present generation of professors of geography is the first to have been trained as geographers. The modern founders of our discipline were drawn from a considerable variety of academic backgrounds.

over entirely to economics faculties and be housed in separate economics institutes, where human geographers could work in close contact with other social scientists.

Of course as long as one continues to think in nineteenth-century materialist terms the dualist position is a perfectly valid argument—and not so rare among 'western bourgeois monists' as the Leningrad geographers appear to think. There are a number of schools of geography that would maintain in principle the concept of a unified discipline but in practice behave as though it was a mere complex of object-orientated geographical sciences. To avoid this dilemma various courses are open to us.

We can maintain, for example, as many have done, that although the normal categories of phenomena have their appropriate systematic sciences there are certain complexes of materials to which geography can establish exclusive claims: hence the claims put forward from time to time that geography is 'the study of landscape', 'the science of spatial distributions', 'the study of places', 'the synthetic study of regions', or the science of 'areal differentiation'. Each concept has had in its time powerful support, and indeed much to commend it as an object of geographical study, but none has received universal recognition as *the* definitive, exclusive object. Landscape constitutes one of the most important documents and points of reference in geographical research, but no one could maintain that the study and interpretation of landscape is the exclusive preserve of the geographer, or that the landscape contains all that is geographical. The concept is factually too all-embracing or too restrictive, and in practice tends to break down into the old dichotomy of cultural landscape (for human geographers) and physical landscape (for physical geographers), or, under the influence of the mystic Germanic usage of *landschaft*, dissolves into the concept of area.[10] Geography as the science of distributions is open to similar objections. Again, spatial distributions of terrestrial phenomena are of great consequence in geographical work, providing another important category of empirical data for the solution of certain geographical problems, but do not in themselves provide a definitive criterion. It would be exceedingly difficult to maintain the position that all terrestrial phenomena that are spatially discrete could *ipso facto* be claimed as geographical. Probably the most popular and persistent of these concepts, however, is the idea of the region. Regions in the sense of spatial structures or *gestalten*, forged in patterns of mutual interrelationships, certainly have existence and the recognition of such unities has constantly enlivened geographical thought on areas, but whether they can be regarded as permanent, concrete *objects* of study is doubtful. Certainly in their guise as 'homogeneous areal units' or total phenomenal complexes' they have reality often only in the mind of the beholder. Homogeneous areas have a tendency to dissolve into unique *places* if they are examined in greater detail or the criterion of uniformity is changed; while the endless task of piling up more and more factual information on 'total phenomenal complexes' has brought regional geography of this type into disrepute as mere additive description and led to its abandonment in some schools of geography.[11]

In view of the difficulty of preserving the philosophical unity of geography on materialist grounds the question arises whether it is possible to attain this end by using other criteria. Can we, for example, dismiss a material base altogether and define our discipline in terms of methodology? Do we think and work geographically, rather than think and work on geographical materials?

This alternative approach appears to have much to commend it, for undoubtedly there are a number of techniques and modes of analysis commonly employed by geographers over a wide range of materials. The use of maps, for example, is so commonplace in geographical study that their significance is often overlooked in methodological discussions. In the 470 pages of Hartshorne's *Nature of Geography* only three[1][2] are devoted to the contribution of maps to the science of geography, and yet Hartshorne himself admits that a convenient rule of thumb to test the geographical character of a problem is to ask whether it can be studied fundamentally by maps, usually by a comparison of several maps. The map is not only a precise instrument for describing by recording, but a machine capable of producing more than is put into it. Raw data are fed in, the machine programmed, and patterns emerge. In combination with the study of distributions maps provide the means of thinking geographically in one important respect—namely the correlation of spatial patterns.

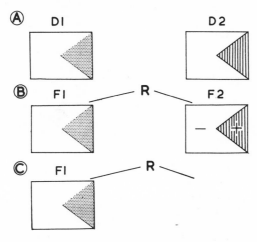

Fig. 2.

This method of geographical investigation is analysed diagrammatically in Fig. 2. Distribution maps of terrestrial phenomena are first prepared and at Stage A two are discovered to have identical patterns—D^1 and D^2. The materials recorded differ but their spatial existence is the same. At Stage B a correlation of spatial coincidence is enunciated as R, and the two distributions now become fundaments (F^1, F^2) in relational thinking. At Stage C, F^1 is discovered again and the problem arises whether, given the relationship R (the principle), F^2 can be established again in all cases. Ability to predict the occurrence of F^2 will obviously depend on the true nature of R. Is the spatial coincidence purely fortuitous or does it represent the expression of causal connections? Is one distribution pattern causally related to the other?[13] The answer to such questions cannot be deduced simply from the patterns themselves. One needs further information about the nature of the materials recorded. It is necessary to know, for example, the time relations of the two patterns—whether one pattern predates the other, and if so whether it was still extant at the time that the second pattern was formed. One also requires to know whether one is a pattern of living things, or the products of living things, and the other a pattern of non-living things—whether the living things are capable of rational behaviour, exercise a conscious choice of location, have freedom of movement, etc. One must ensure that a relationship other than spatial coincidence *can* exist between the two sets of materials recorded; and rule out the possibility that the observed coincidence may be the result of some other, unrevealed pattern influencing the occurrence of both sets of known data. In some cases it may also be necessary to determine at Stage B whether the pattern recorded in F^2 is a positive one, with strong areal attractions, rather than the resultant of negative forces elsewhere. Thus if F^1 represented a pattern of refugee camps and F^2 political areas, the negative area of F^2 may be of greater significance in establishing causal relationships than the positive area. Not until all such possibilities and variables had been examined, and the situation recorded in Stage B had been shown to occur over and over again would it be possible to predict with any degree of probability the occurrence of F^2 in Stage C.

Correlative thinking by maps, leading in certain cases to the enunciation of principles or laws of areal relationships, is a basic geographical technique. Does it define our discipline?

It is true that other disciplines use maps to record data they are analysing; it is also true that correlative thinking in time as well as space is by no means the exclusive prerogative of geographers; but a combination of the two is certainly not common. The only other discipline to make extensive use of a similar technique is archaeology, and in so far as it does, it tends to become more and more geographical in character. Fox's *Personality of Britain* was from an archaeological point of view a pioneer exercise in this field, and was hailed by material-bound archaeologists as a new growth point in their science.[14] In fact it, and many other similar contributions by British archaeologists,[15] are essentially geographical in spirit and illustrate a process that has contributed much to the development of our discipline during the last hundred years—namely a moving into geography of scholars trained in other disciplines through the application of geographical techniques. Indeed it could be argued that the logical, ultimate end of archaeology is to become geography.

Correlative thinking by maps thus appears to constitute a useful criterion for determining the external relations of our subject. In so far as it is a technique commonly employed by exponents of the various systematic branches within geography it also promotes internal unity by transcending phenomenal barriers. It is basic in both the analytical and synthetical aspects of our study, and can be applied to the study of landscape, places, distributions, areas, regions, and other terrestrial patterns. It certainly comprises much of the spirit of geography—but does it equally define the purpose of our subject?

It is doubtful whether one can ever base the unity of a subject on technique alone. By its very nature a technique cannot be an end in itself—it must be subservient to something else. It can be subservient to materials—but this path we have rejected. The only other alternative must be its subservience to *problems*. One must not forget that an older, and perhaps more fundamental, way of defining the fields of particular disciplines is to ask, not what materials they study, nor what techniques they use, but for what kind of problems in human experience have they been invented to provide the answers. The kind of answers we can give obviously depends on the techniques at our disposal at any particular time, and upon the empirical data with which we work but ultimately the position of a discipline in the total field of intellectual endeavour depends on the kind of problems it handles. Are there, then, problems of a specifically geographical kind, or for which geographers have a special responsibility?

In as much as the origins of geography, like so many disciplines, reach back to the first vague questioning of man concerning the world around him, most geographical problems have an environmental content. But whereas the systematic sciences have become exclusively concerned with specific aspects of nature, geography has throughout retained its interest in environment not as a thing apart but as a field of human action. The rise and great success of the systematic sciences since the nineteenth century have masked but not destroyed that function of geography. We have been led by an over-emphasis on material objects of study to consider man and environment as things apart, and consequently have been drawn into discussions of environmental determinism and possibilism which spring from this dichotomy, but our real responsibilities remain within the unified field of the Geographical Environment and the problems it generates. Within this field the true division of geographical labour is not between man and environment but between Phenomenal Environment (including the works of man) and Behavioural Environment as is suggested in Fig. 3.

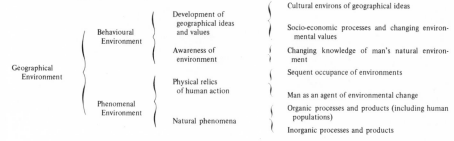

Fig. 3.

The concept of Phenomenal Environment does not require much explanation here—it is an expansion of the normal concept of environment to include not only natural phenomena but environments altered and in some cases almost entirely created by man. Since so great a proportion of the earth's population now live in environments largely of their own creation—many on great refuse heaps of past human action—and since man is both a product of and force in natural processes, it is surely illogical to reserve the term environment in the geographical sense to non-human phenomena. To a student of Geographical Environment a break of slope in the skyline of a city may be environmentally as significant as a knick-point in a river profile and equally worthy of study as a feature in the physical environment. The areal variation in the physical constitution of mankind is no less a fact of nature than the ecological complexity of equatorial rain forest.

The concept of Behavioural Environment, however, is less well known,[16] and since the true nature of Geographical Environment is dependent on the combination of this concept with that of the Phenomenal Environment it is necessary first to establish its general meaning before applying it to geographical contexts. It is a concept developed by the school of Gestalt Psychology[17] in work on perception and perhaps can best be illustrated by reference to a well-known optical illusion.

Fig. 4 is a part of a sketch by Toulouse Lautrec. In it the artist has arranged a number of physical phenomena—lines and areas, in such a way as to differentiate a figure from its background. He has produced a map of reality—in this case a female figure. The pattern which emerges is clearly more than the mere sum of the physical lines drawn by the artist—it has shape, cohesiveness, and meaning added to it by the act of human perception. 'The whole is greater than the sum of the parts.' It

Fig. 4.

appears to be part of objective reality—a phenomenal structure, but to demonstrate the extent to which this spatial pattern is a subjective feature, dependent as much on the character of the perceiver as on the material perceived, it is necessary to look again at this pattern of lines. To most of us, for reasons which need not detain us here, this is a sketch of the head and shoulders of a young Parisienne, complete with neck ribbon. But if the neck-band is seen as a mouth, the, pattern changes and reconstitutes itself as the head of a hook-nosed old crone. The patterns are mutually exclusive, but can be changed at will to give the impression of movement. Yet once established each picture resists change and has a certain momentum.

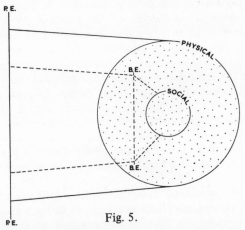

Fig. 5.

This experience can be translated into a conceptual model in which the Phenomenal Environment (P.E.) is shown to be related to human behaviour at two different levels (Fig. 5). At one level physical man is in direct contact with the

Phenomenal Environment, and physical action will lead to changes on both sides of the relationship. At a second, equally important, level however the facts of the Phenomenal Environment will enter the Behavioural Environment (B.E.) of man, but only in so far as they are perceived by human beings with motives, preferences, modes of thinking, and traditions drawn from their social, cultural context.[18] The same empirical data may arrange themselves into different patterns and have different meanings to people of different cultures, or at different stages in the history of a particular culture, just as a landscape may differ in the eyes of different observers. The Behavioural Environment is thus a psycho-physical field in which phenomenal facts are arranged into patterns of structures (*Gestalten*) and acquire values in cultural contexts. It is the environment in which rational human behaviour begins and decisions are taken which may or may not be translated into overt action in the Phenomenal Environment. An alternative way of presenting the same idea is depicted in Fig. 6 where the social and physical facts of the Phenomenal Environment are shown to constitute parts of the Behavioural Environment of a decision-taker (D) only after they have penetrated a highly selective cultural filter of values.

The importance of this concept to geographical reasoning is at once apparent. Facts which exist in the Phenomenal Environment but do not enter the Behavioural Environment of a society have no relevance to rational, spatial behaviour and consequently do not enter into problems of the Geographical Environment. The Coal Measures of the concealed coalfields of Britain have existed for millions of years in the Phenomenal Environment but did not become geographically significant until geological discovery, improvements of mining techniques, and demand for power brought them into the Behavioural Environment of British

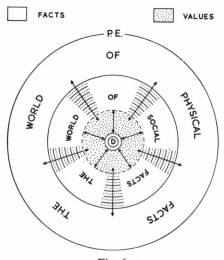

Fig. 6.

entrepreneurs. To attempt to correlate the distribution of the Bronze Age Beakers with areas of concealed coalfields is thus palpably absurd—as absurd as trying to explain the routes of early seafarers in terms of a round world and Great Circles. These are extreme cases, and easily avoided, but in less clear-cut instances how often do we fall into the trap of attempting to explain the actions of one community in terms of the values and Behavioural Environment of another, different culture. The classic case of this is recorded by Herodotus in the opinion expressed by Megabazus, a General of the Persian empire, concerning the location of Chalcedon on the eastern bank of the Bosphorus:

This same Megabazus once made a remark for which the people along the Hellespont have never forgiven him; he was in Byzantium and on hearing that Chalcedon was settled seventeen years earlier than that city he said 'The men of Chalcedon must have been blind at that time or they never would have chosen the inferior site when such a superior one [Byzantium] was available.'[19]

This assessment of the behaviour of the men of Chalcedon was of course quite unjustified. When Chalcedon was founded agricultural values were uppermost in the Behavioural Environment of the settlers and in this respect their decision was correct since Chalcedon was superior agriculturally to the site of Byzantium. Indeed it was agricultural *failure* which led the Byzantine Greeks to turn to commerce and realize the hitherto neglected values of the harbour of the Golden Horn.

Value-transference of the Megabazus type is by no means uncommon in more recent geographical work—historical geographers and western geographers interpreting Oriental landscapes are particularly exposed to such pitfalls—and when geographers grapple with problems by 'experimenting' in the great laboratory of the past or seek to analyse alien environments it is clear that they must recreate not only Phenomenal Environments as they were or are but also the Behavioural Environments of the communities whose spatial actions they are trying to interpret. Only thus will the Geographical Environment and its problems achieve reality and be capable of rational interpretations.

The Geographical Environment so delineated is capable of analysis by the traditional geographical techniques described above, and the concepts of location, distribution, areal differentiation, etc. all have a place within it. An understanding of it indeed requires the application of many techniques and concepts. It is not a concrete object of study in the sense we have described at the outset of this paper. Rather can it be regarded as a problem-producing situation in which human communities are perpetually confronted by problems concerning their particular environments and obliged to take decisions which have spatial, environmental consequences. It is a gigantic decision-taking model of a special, geographical type.

One set of problems[20] generated by this model, for example, is that illustrated in Fig. 7. Here the theme is the cultural-spatial diversification of mankind via a series of decision-taking situations similar to the learning situations experienced in the life of an individual. Achievement is plotted against time.

At the outset certain communities A, B, and C have attained a measure of equilibrium in their Geographical Environments, with stresses in their Behavioural Environments reduced to a minimum. Then change occurs in the structure. This may arise in a variety of ways. It may arise from an increase in population without concomitant expansion of the resource base. It may spring from social or technical innovation leading to a revaluation of environment, or from an exhaustion of certain traditional resources. It may be the result of climatic or vegetational change. In most cases such changes will lead to factual modifications of the Phenomenal Environment, but unless these give rise to alterations in and the development of stress in the Behavioural Environments of the respective communities no decision-taking situation will arise. Three reactions to such a Time of Decision are illustrated in the model (Fig.7). Group A does not realize that it is facing an environmental problem. No stresses develop in its Behavioural Environment and no decisions are taken at a conscious, rational level. The community continues to behave as though no structural change had occurred in its Geographical Environment and remains at the same level of achievement. If change does occur it does so at a Phenomenal Environment level, with chance playing a large part and usually working against the long-term survival of the group. Group B on the other hand recognizes the problem and is involved in a decision-taking situation. However, in environmental terms, it gives the wrong answer, does not raise its level of achievement, and finds that the new environmental structure is working against it. In this particular case the group is shown as surviving until it is given a second chance of redeeming its fortunes at a later time of decision, but it is not difficult to imagine situations in which a wrong decision would result in Group B declining at a more rapid rate and reaching an earlier demise than Group A. In the case of Group C, however, the community not only perceives the problem but finds an appropriate geographical solution. The structure of its newly created Geographical Environment works to its advantage and it enters a period of rapid progress. In time, however, progress arising from the initial decision slows down and the community attains a new equilibrium on a higher plateau of achievement. It could remain indefinitely on this plateau, but historical evidence indicates that communities which have moved through one learning situation successfully will probably be confronted with further times of decision and environmental problems which would not have been conceivable at all had they remained at their earlier level of attainment. Indeed, both in the life of a community and an individual, experience teaches that the more problems that are solved the more arise—or, in Parkinsonian terms, problems expand and multiply to fill the capacity for their solution. 'To him that hath shall be given. . . .'

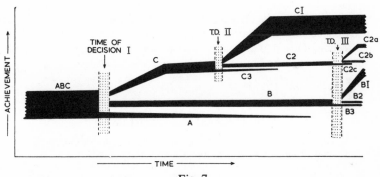

Fig. 7.

All models of reality suffer from the weakness of over-simplification and of course this is no exception. It disregards for example the powerful influence of cultural diffusion in human affairs—the ability of a community at a low level of achievement to learn by contact with a community at a higher level, or to have times of decision thrust upon them by such external societies. It also disregards situations in which one community is absorbed by another, and omits cases in which a community stumbles by pure chance into an advantageous environmental structure. But it at least has the merit of revealing one of the geographical processes that has contributed to the diversification of mankind. The end-product of the model combines spatial and cultural diversification. 'Space makes possible the particular which then unfolds in time.'

The model also focuses attention on one of the most important categories of problems implicit in the nature of the Geographical Environment—namely decision taking. Obviously not all decisions are geographical, only those that take place within the context of the Geographical Environment; but in the last analysis it will be seen that a great number of geographical problems resolve into the study of decision-taking situations. The problems of town and industrial location are examples. How often do we mistake factors of growth for factors of location when examining the position of particular industrial establishments or cities, forgetting that very often the locational decisions which brought them into being on particular sites were taken for very different reasons from those responsible for their later developments. Behind many of the distributions we map and study—villages, farms, fields, crops, mines, routes, artefacts—lie countless locational decisions, some well documented, others less so, but unless we are able to recreate the decision-taking situations which produced them the determinants of their spatial patterns will never be fully known. Political boundaries—expressing perhaps the most powerful form of regionalism in the world today, capital cities, naval bases, the strategic disposition of military personnel and resources in war and peace—all these too involve environmental decisions. If it is agreed that the problems of Geographical Environment are central to our discipline then it follows that the study of decision taking must rank highly in our search for solutions.

These then are some of the problems that give purpose and unity to our subject, that make it a single discipline rather than a congeries of materially orientated sciences. It was for the solution of such problems in human experience that geography was created and for which we still bear the responsibility. The search for answers is still an exciting and intellectually rewarding task. The selection of empirical data and making of maps are skilled crafts requiring long apprenticeship; but we must be constantly on guard against mistaking means for ends. Only by constant reference back to the problems themselves can we test the relevance of our data and techniques and play our particular part in the ultimate purpose of all intellectual endeavour—the heightening of human consciousness.

NOTES AND REFERENCES

[1] August Losch, *The Economics of Location*, New Haven, Conn., 1954, p. 508.

[2] Sir Isaiah Berlin, 'The Purpose of Philosophy', *Sunday Times*, 4 Nov. 1962, p. 23.

[3] And, one might add, of an essentially animistic and individualistic kind; see, for example Jean Piaget, *The Child's Conception of the World*, London, 1960, and *The Child's Construction of Reality*, London, 1955; and with Barbel Inhelder, *The Child's Conception of Space*, London 1956.

[4] The most comprehensive guide to such authorities is Richard Hartshorne's *Nature of Geography*. Assoc. Amer. Geogr., Lancaster, Pennsylvania, 1939, and his later *Perspective on the Nature of Geography*, Chicago, 1959. See also Preston E. James and Clarence F. Jones (eds.), *American Geography: Inventory and Prospect*, Syracuse, N.Y., 1954; Griffith Taylor (ed.), *Geography in the Twentieth Century*, New York, 1951; and T. W. Freeman, *A Hundred Years of Geography*, London, 1961. Each contains abundant references to a copious literature on methodological problems.

[5] Compare, for example, S. W. Wooldridge, *The Geographer as Scientist*, London, 1956, and Isaiah Bowman, *Geography in Relation to the Social Sciences*, New York, 1934; and both with Alfred Hettner, *Die Geographie, ihre Geschichte, ihr Wesen und ihre Methoden*, Breslau, 1927, and Max Sorre, *Les Fondements de la géographie humaine*, 3 vols., Paris, 1947–8.

[6] For a discussion of 'dualism' see R. Hartshorne, *Perspective on the Nature of Geography*, 1959, Chapter VII.

[7] V. A. Anuchin, *Teoreticheskiye Problemy Geografii*, Moscow, 1960. Review and criticisms by N. D. Zakharov, S. V. Kalesnik, and others appear in translation in *Soviet Geography* (published by American Geographical Society), vol. 2, Dec. 1961, and vol. 3, Sept. 1962.

[8] S. V. Kalesnik, *Soviet Geography*, 3, Sept. 1962, 7.

[9] S. I. Pomazanov, 'On theoretical problems in economic geography and regional geography', *Izvestiya A. N. SSSR, seriya geograficheskaya*, no. 3, 1961, referred to by V. A. Anuchin in *Soviet Geography*, 3, Sept. 1962, 25.

[10] See R. Hartshorne on *landschaft* and 'landscape' in *Nature of Geography*, 1939, Chapter V.

[11] For an attack on this type of regional geography see, for example, George H. T. Kimble, 'The Inadequacy of the Regional Concept', *London Essays in Geography*, Cambridge, 1961, pp. 151–74. But cf. Preston E. James, 'Toward a further understanding of the regional concept', *Annals Assoc. Amer. Geogr.* 42, 1952, 195–222.

[12] R. Hartshorne, *Nature of Geography* pp. 247–9.

[13] For a discussion of geographical causality see Emrys Jones, 'Cause and effect in human geography', *Annals Assoc. Amer. Geogr.* 46, 1956, 369–77; A. F. Martin, 'The necessity for determinism: a metaphysical problem confronting geographers', *Trans. Inst. Brit. Geogr.* 17, 1951, 1–12; H. C. Montefiore and W. W. Williams, 'Determinism and possibilism', *Geographical Studies*, 2, 1955, 1–11; and O. H. K. Spate, 'Toynbee and Huntington: a study of determinism', *Geogr. Jour.* 118, 1952, 406–28.

[14] Sir Cyril Fox, *The Personality of Britain*, 3rd edn., Cardiff, 1938: first read as a paper to the International Congress of Prehistoric and Protohistoric Sciences in London, 1932. See also his *The Archaeology of the Cambridge Region*, Cambridge, 1923.

[15] The work of J. G. D. Clark affords many illustrations of this approach—particularly his *Prehistoric Europe: the Economic Basis*, London, 1952, and *The Mesolithic Settlement of Northern Europe*, Cambridge, 1935. See also Christopher Hawkes, 'The ABC of the British Iron Age', *Antiquity*, 33, 1959, 170–82, and A. L. F. Rivet, 'The Iron Age in Northern Britain', *Antiquity*, 36, 1962, 24–31, for interesting essays in regional analysis by archaeologists.

[16] See W. Kirk, 'Historical geography and the concept of the Behavioural Environment', *Indian Geographical Journal, Silver Jubilee Vol.*, 1951, pp. 152–60. Since this volume is not easily accessible I repeat here some of the argument used therein. See also a discussion of the concept in Harold and Margaret Sprout, *Man-Milieu Relationship Hypotheses in the Context of International Politics*, Princeton, N.J., 1956.

[17] The term *gestalt* can be translated as configuration, pattern, structure, form. Gestalt theory arose from the pioneer studies of Max Wertheimer fifty years ago on the perception of stroboscopic motion. Later, in the work of his collaborators Kurt Koffka and Wolfgang Köhler, it was applied more widely to perception in learning situations. See W. Köhler, *The Place of Value in a World of Facts*, New York, 1938, and *Gestalt Psychology*, New York, 1947; K. Koffka, *Principles of Gestalt Psychology*, London, 1950; G. W. Hartmann, *Gestalt Psychology*, New York, 1935; and W. D. Ellis (ed.), *A Source Book of Gestalt Psychology*, New York, 1938. The general principles of gestalt theory have now been accommodated within studies of perception (see Floyd H. Allport, *Theories of Perception and the Concept of Structure*, London, 1955); and an increasing awareness of the importance of perception in geographical work is shown *inter alia* by David Lowenthal, 'Geography, experience and imagination', *Annals Assoc. Amer. Geogr.* 51, 1961, 241–60, and H. C. Darby, 'The problem of geographical description', *Trans. Inst. Brit. Geogr.* 30, 1962, 1–14.

[18] This point is also made by K. G. T. Clark, 'Certain underpinnings of our arguments in human geography', *Trans. Inst. Brit. Geogr.* 16, 1950, 20.

[19] Herodotus, *Histories*, Bk. IV, Chapter 144.

[20] Similar in character to the problem posed by Arnold J. Toynbee in *A Study of History*, Abridgement, vols. 1–6 by D. C. Somervell, London, 1947, pp. 48–51, but with a different purpose in mind.

7. GEOGRAPHY, EXPERIENCE, AND IMAGINATION: TOWARDS A GEOGRAPHICAL EPISTEMOLOGY[1]

D. Lowenthal

'The most fascinating *terrae incognitae* of all are those that lie within the minds and hearts of men.' With these words, John K. Wright concluded his 1946 presidential address before the Association of American Geographers. This paper considers the nature of these *terrae incognitae*, and the relation between the world outside and the pictures in our heads.[2]

The General and the Geographical World View

Neither the world nor our pictures of it are identical with geography. Some aspects of geography are recondite, others abstruse, occult, or esoteric; conversely, there are many familiar features of things that geography scarcely considers. Beyond that of any other discipline, however, the subject-matter of geography approximates the world of general discourse; the palpable present, the everyday life of man on earth, is seldom far from our professional concerns. 'There is no science whatever', wrote a future president of Harvard, a century and a half ago, 'which comes so often into use in common life.'[3] This view of geography remains a commonplace of contemporary thought. More than physics or physiology, psychology or politics, geography observes and analyses aspects of the milieu on the scale and in the categories that they are usually apprehended in everyday life. Whatever methodologists think geography ought to be, the temperament of its practitioners makes it catholic and many-sided. In their range of interests and capacities—concrete and abstract, academic and practical, analytic and synthetic, indoor and outdoor, historical and contemporary, physical and social—geographers reflect man generally. 'This treating of cabbages and kings, cathedrals and linguistics, trade in oil, or commerce in ideas', as Peattie wrote, 'makes a congress of geographers more or less a Committee on the Universe.'[4]

Geographical curiosity is, to be sure, more narrowly focused than mankind's; it is also more conscious, orderly, objective, consistent, universal, and theoretical than are ordinary queries about the nature of things. Like geography, however, the wider universe of discourse centres on knowledge and ideas about man and milieu; anyone who inspects the world around him is in some measure a geographer.

As with specifically geographical concepts, the more comprehensive world of ideas that we share concerns the variable forms and contents of the earth's surface, past, present, and potential—'a torrent of discourse about tables, people, molecules, light rays, retinas, air-waves, prime numbers, infinite classes, joy and sorrow, good and evil'.[5] It comprises truth and error, concrete facts and abstruse relationships, self-evident laws and tenuous hypotheses, data drawn from natural and social science, from history, from common sense, from intuition and mystical experience. Certain things appear to be grouped spatially, seriated temporally, or related causally: the hierarchy of urban places, the annual march of temperature, the location of industry. Other features of our shared universe seem unique,

From *Annals of the Association of American Geographers*, 51 (1961), 241–60. Reprinted by permission of the author and the Association.

amorphous, or chaotic: the population of a country, the precise character of a region, the shape of a mountain.[6]

Universally Accepted Aspects of the World View

However multifarious its make-up, there is general agreement about the character of the world and the way it is ordered. Explanations of particular phenomena differ from one person to another, but without basic concurrence as to the nature of things, there would be neither science nor common sense, agreement nor argument. The most extreme heretic cannot reject the essence of the prevailing view. 'Even the sharpest dissent still operates by partial submission to an existing consensus,' reasons Polanyi, 'for the revolutionary must speak in terms that people can understand.'[7]

Most public knowledge can in theory be verified. I know little about the geography of Sweden, but others are better informed; if I studied long and hard enough I could learn approximately what they know. I cannot read the characters in Chinese newspapers, but hardly doubt that they convey information to the Chinese; assuming that there is a world in common, other peoples' ways of symbolizing knowledge must be meaningful and learnable.

The universe of geographical discourse, in particular, is not confined to geographers; it is shared by billions of amateurs all over the globe. Some isolated primitives are still ignorant of the outside world; many more know little beyond their own countries and ways of life; but most of the earth's inhabitants possess at least rudiments of the shared world picture. Even peoples innocent of science are privy to elements of our geography, both innate and learned: the normal relations between figure and ground; the distinctive setting of objects on the face of the earth; the usual texture, weight, appearance, and physical state of land, air, and water; the regular transition from day to night; the partition of areas by individual, family, or group.

Beyond such universals, the geographical consensus tends to be additive, scientific, and cumulative. Schools teach increasing numbers that the world is a sphere with certain continents, oceans, countries, peoples, and ways of living and making a living; the size, shape, and general features of the earth are known by more and more people. The general horizon of geography has expanded rapidly. 'Until five centuries ago a primal or regional sense of space dominated human settlements everywhere'; today, most of us share the conception of a world common to all experients.[8]

The General Consensus Never Completely Accepted

The whole of mankind may in time progress, as Whittlesey suggests, to 'the sense of space current at or near the most advanced frontier of thought'. But no one, however inclined to pioneer, visits that frontier often, or has surveyed more than a short traverse of it. 'Primitive man', according to Boulding, 'lives in a world which has a spatial unknown, a dread frontier populated by the heated imagination. For modern man the world is a closed and completely explored surface. This is a radical change in spatial viewpoint.'[9] But the innovation is superficial; we are still parochial. 'Even in lands where geography is part of a compulsory school curriculum, and among people who possess considerable information about the earth,' Whittlesey points out, 'the world horizon is accepted in theory and rejected in practice.'[10]

The 'dread unknowns' are still with us. Indeed, 'the more the island of knowledge expands in the sea of ignorance, the larger its boundary to the unknown.'[11] Primitive world views were simple and consistent enough for every participant to share most of their substance. Within Western scientific society, no one really grasps more than a small fraction of the public, theoretically communicable world view. The amount of information an individual can acquire in an instant or in a lifetime is finite, and minuscule compared with what the milieu presents; many questions are too complex to describe, let alone solve, in a practicable length of time. The horizons of knowledge are expanding faster than any person can keep up with. The proliferation of new sciences extends our powers of sense and thought, but their rigorous techniques and technical languages hamper communication; the common field of knowledge becomes a diminishing fraction of the total store.[12]

On the other hand, we tend to assume things are common knowledge which may not be; what seems to me the general outlook might be mine alone. The most devoted adherents to a consensus often mistake their own beliefs for universal ones. For a large part of our world view, we take on faith much of what we are told by science. But we may have got it wrong; as Chisholm points out, 'we are all quite capable of believing falsely at any time that a given proposition is accepted by the scientists of our culture circle.'[13] In our impressions of the shared world view we all resemble the fond mother who watched her clumsy son parade, and concluded happily, 'Everyone was out of step but my Johnnie.'

The World View Not Shared by Some

The most fundamental attributes of our shared view of the world are confined, moreover, to sane, hale, sentient adults. Idiots cannot suitably conceive space, time, or causality. Psychotics distinguish poorly between themselves and the outside world. Mystics, claustrophobics, and those haunted by fear of open space (agoraphobia) tend to project their own body spaces as extensions of the outside world; they are often unable to delimit themselves from the rest of nature. Schizophrenics often underestimate size and overestimate distance. After a brain injury, invalids fail to organize their environments or may forget familiar locations and symbols. Impairments like aphasia, apraxia, and agnosia blind their victims to spatial relations and logical connections self-evident to most. Other hallucinatory sufferers may identify forms but regularly alter the number, size, and shape of objects (polyopia, dysmegalopsia, dysmorphopsia), see them always in motion (oscillopsia), or locate everything at the same indefinite distance (porrhopsia).[14]

A fair measure of sensate function is also prerequisite to the general view of the common world. No object looks quite the way it feels; at first sight, those born blind not only fail to recognize visual shapes but see no forms at all, save for a spinning mass of coloured light. They may have known objects by touch, but had nothing like the common conception of a space with objects in it. A purely visual world would also be an unreal abstraction; a concrete and stable sense of the milieu depends on synesthesia, sight combined with sound and touch.[15]

To see the world more or less as others see it, one must above all grow up; the very young, like the very ill, are unable to discern adequately what is themselves and what is not. An infant is not only the centre of his universe, he *is* the universe. To the young child, everything in the world is alive, created by and for man, and endowed with will: the sun follows him, his parents built the mountains, trees exist because they were planted. As Piaget puts it, everything seems intentional; 'the child behaves as if nature were charged with purpose', and therefore conscious. The clouds know what they are doing, because they have a goal. 'It is not because the child believes things to be alive that he regarded them as obedient, but it is because he believes them to be obedient that he regards them as alive.' Asked what something is, the young child often says it is *for* something—'a mountain is for climbing'—which implies that it has been *made* for that purpose.[16]

Unable to organize objects in space, to envisage places out of sight, or to generalize from perceptual experience, young children are especially poor geographers. To learn that there are other people, who perceive the world from different points of view, and that a stable, communicable view of things cannot be obtained from one perspective alone, takes many years. Animism and artificialism give way only gradually to mechanistic outlooks and explanations. 'No direct experience can prove to a mind inclined towards animism that the sun and the clouds are neither alive nor conscious'; the child must first realize that his parents are not all-powerful beings who made a universe centred on himself. Piaget traces the development in children of perceptual and conceptual objectivity, on which even the most primitive and parochial geographies depend.[17] Again in old age, however, progressive loss of hearing, deficiencies of vision, and other infirmities tend to isolate one from reality and to create literally a second geographical childhood.[18]

Different as they are from our own, the perceived milieus, say, of most children of the same age (or of many schizophrenics; or of some drug addicts) may closely resemble one another. But there is little communication or mutual understanding of a conceptual character among children. No matter how many features their pictures of the world may have in common, they lack any *shared* view of the nature of things.

Mutability of the General Consensus

The shared world view is also transient: it is neither the world our parents knew nor the one our children will know. Not only is the earth itself in constant flux, but every generation finds new facts and invents new concepts to deal with them. 'You cannot step twice into the same river,' Heraclitus observed, 'for fresh waters are ever flowing in upon you.' Nor does anyone look at the river again in the same way: 'The vision of the world geographers construct must be created anew each generation, not only because reality changes but also because human pre-occupations vary.'[19]

Because we cherish the past as a collective guide to behaviour, the general consensus alters very slowly. Scientists as well as laymen ignore evidence incompatible with their preconceptions. New theories which fail to fit established views are resisted, in the hope that they will prove false or irrelevant; old ones yield to convenience rather than to evidence. In Eiseley's phrase, 'a world view does not dissolve overnight. Rather, like ... mountain ranges, it erodes through long centuries.'[20] The solvent need not be truth. For example, in the seventeenth century many scholars believed that the earth—the 'Mundane Egg'—was originally 'smooth, regular, and uniform; without Mountains, and without a Sea'; to chastise man for his sins, at or before the Deluge, God crumpled this fair landscape into continents and ocean deeps, with unsightly crags and chasms; modern man thus looked out on 'the Ruins of a broken World'. This version of earth history was overthrown, not by geological evidence, but principally by a new aesthetic standard: to eighteenth-century observers, mountains seemed majestic and sublime, rather than hideous and corrupt.[21]

Anthropocentric Character of the World View

Mankind's best conceivable world view is at most a partial picture of the world—a picture centred on man. We inevitably see the universe from a human point of view and communicate in terms shaped by the exigencies of human life. ' "Significance" in geography is measured, consciously or unconsciously,' says Hartshorne, 'in terms of significance to man'; but it is not in geography alone that man is the measure. 'Our choice of time scale for climatology', according to Hare, 'is conditioned more by the length of our life span than by logic'; the physics of the grasshopper, Köhler points out, would be a different physics from ours.[22] 'All aspects of the environment', as Cantril puts it, 'exist for us only in so far as they are related to our purposes. If you leave out human significance, you leave out all constancy, all repeatability, all form.'[23]

Purpose apart, physical and biological circumstances restrict human perception. Our native range of sensation is limited; other creatures experience other worlds than ours. The human visual world is richly differentiated, compared with that of most species, but others see better in the dark, perceive ultraviolet rays as colours, distinguish finer detail, or see near and distant scenes together in better focus. To many creatures the milieu is more audible and more fragrant than to us. For every sensation, moreover, the human perceptual world varies within strict limits; how bright the lightning looks, how loud the thunder sounds, how wet the rain feels at any given moment of a storm depends on fixed formulae, whose constants, at least, are unique to man.[24]

The instruments of science do permit partial knowledge of other milieus, real or hypothetical. Blood ordinarily appears a uniform, homogeneous red to the naked eye; seen through a microscope, it becomes yellow particles in a neutral fluid, while its atomic substructure is mostly empty space. But such insights do not show what it is actually like to see normally at a microscopic scale. 'The apparently standardized environment of flour in a bottle', Anderson surmises, 'would not seem undifferentiated to any investigator who had once been a flour beetle and who knew at first-hand the complexities of flour-beetle existence.'[25] The perceptual powers and central nervous systems of many species are qualitatively, as well as quantitatively, different from man's. We can observe, but never experience, the role of surface tension and molecular forces in the lives of small invertebrates, the ability of the octopus to discriminate tactile impressions by taste, of the butterfly to sense forms through smell, or of the jellyfish to change its size and shape.

The tempo of all varieties of experience is also specific. Time yields humans on the average eighteen separate impressions, or instants, every second; images presented more rapidly seem to fuse into continuous motion. But there are slow-motion fish that perceive separate impressions up to thirty each second, and snails to which a stick that vibrates more than four times a second appears to be at rest.[26]

As with time, so with space; we perceive one of many possible structures, more hyperbolic than Euclidean.[27] The six cardinal directions are not equivalent for us: up and down, front and back, left and right have particular values because we happen to be a special kind of bilaterally symmetrical, terrestrial animal. 'It is one contingent fact about the world that we attach very great importance to things having their tops and bottoms in the right places; it is another contingent fact [about ourselves] that we attach more importance to their having their fronts and backs in the right places than their left and right sides.'[28] Up and down are everywhere good and evil: heaven and hell, the higher and lower instincts, the heights of sublimity and the depths of degradation, even the higher and the lower latitudes have ethical spatial connotations. And left and right are scarcely less differentiated.

Other species apperceive quite differently. Even the fact that physical space seems to us three-dimensional is partly contingent on our size, on the shape of our bodies (an asymmetrical torus), and, perhaps, on our semicircular canals; the world of certain birds is effectively two-dimensional, and some creatures apprehend only one.[29]

Man's experienced world is, then, only one tree of the forest. The difference between this and the others is that man knows his tree is not the only one; and yet can imagine what the forest as a whole might be like. Technology and memory extend our images far beyond the bounds of direct sensation; consciousness of self, of time, of relationship, and of causality overcomes the separateness of individual experiences.[30] Thanks to what has been likened to 'a consummate piece of combinatorial mathematics',[31] we share the conception of a common world. Whatever the defects of the general consensus, the shared world view is essentially well founded. 'We are quite willing to admit that there may be errors of detail in this knowledge,' as Russell wrote, referring to science, 'but we believe them to be discoverable and corrigible by the methods which have given rise to our beliefs, and we do not, as practical men, entertain for a moment the hypothesis that the whole edifice may be built on insecure foundations.'[32]

Personal Geographies

Separate personal worlds of experience, learning, and imagination necessarily underlie any universe of discourse. The whole structure of the shared picture of the world is relevant to the life of every participant; and anyone who adheres to a consensus must personally have acquired some of its constituent elements. As Russell put it, 'If I believe that there is such a place as Semipalatinsk, I believe it because of things that have happened to *me*.'[33] One need not have been in Semipalatinsk; it is enough to have heard of it in some meaningful connection, or even to have imagined (rightly or wrongly) that it exists, on the basis of linguistic or other evidence. But if the place did not exist in some—and potentially in all—personal geographies, it could scarcely form part of a common world view.

Individual and Consensual Worlds Compared

The personal *terra cognita* is, however, in many ways unlike the shared realm of knowledge. It is far more localized and restricted in space and time: I know nothing about the microgeography of most of the earth's crust, much less than the sum of common knowledge about the world as a whole and larger parts, but a great deal about that tiny fraction of the globe I live in—not merely facts that might be inferred from general knowledge and verified by visitors, but aspects of things that no one, lacking my total experience, could ever grasp as I do. 'The entire earth', as Wright says, is thus 'an immense patchwork of miniature *terrae incognitae*'[34]—parts of private worlds not incorporated into the general image. Territorially, as otherwise, each personal environment is both more and less inclusive than the common realm.

Complex Nature of Personal Milieus

The private milieu is more complex and many aspects of it are less accessible to inquiry and exploration than is the world we all share.

Like the earth of a hundred years ago [writes Aldous Huxley], our mind still has its darkest Africas, its unmapped Borneos and Amazonian basins. ... A man consists of ... an Old World of personal consciousness and, beyond a dividing sea, a series of New Worlds—the not too distant Virginias and Carolinas of the personal subconscious . . . ; the Far West of the collective unconscious, with its flora of symbols, its tribes of aboriginal archetypes; and, across another, vaster ocean, at the antipodes of everyday consciousness, the world of Visionary Experience. . . . Some people never consciously discover their antipodes. Others make an occasional landing.[35]

To be sure, the general world view likewise transcends objective reality. The hopes and fears of mankind often animate its common-sense perceptions. The supposed location and features of the Garden of Eden stimulated medieval mapmakers; many useful journeys of exploration have sought elusive El Dorados. Delusion and error are no less firmly held by groups than by individuals. Metaphysical assumptions, from original sin to the perfectibility of man, not only colour but shape the shared picture of the world. But fantasy plays a more prominent role in any private milieu than in the general geography. Every aspect of the public image is conscious and communicable, whereas many of our private impressions are inchoate, diffuse, irrational and can hardly be formulated even to ourselves.

The private milieu thus includes much more varied landscapes and concepts than the shared world, imaginary places and powers as well as aspects of reality with which each individual alone is familiar. Hell and the Garden of Eden may have vanished from most of our mental maps, but imagination, distortion, and ignorance still embroider our private landscapes. The most compelling artifacts are but pale reflections of the lapidary architecture of the mind, attempts to recreate on earth the visionary images ascribed by man to God; and every marvel unattained is a Paradise Lost.[36]

In each of our personal worlds, far more than in the shared consensus, characters of fable and fiction reside and move about, some in their own lands, others sharing familiar countries with real people and places. We are all Alices in our own Wonderlands, Gullivers in Lilliput and Brobdingnag. Ghosts, mermaids, men from Mars, and the smiles of Cheshire cats confront us at home and abroad. Utopians not only make mythic men, they rearrange the forces of nature: in some worlds water flows uphill, seasons vanish, time reverses, or one- and two-dimensional creatures converse and move about. Invented worlds may even harbour logical absurdities: scientists swallowed up in the fourth dimension, conjurors imprisoned in Klein bottles, five countries each bordering on all the others.[37] Non-terrestrial geometries, topographical monsters, and abstract models of every kind in turn lend insight to views of reality. If we could not imagine the impossible, both private and public worlds would be the poorer.

Extent to Which Private Worlds Are Congruous with 'Reality'
Though personal milieus in some respects fall short of and in others transcend the more objective consensual reality, yet they at least partly resemble it. What people perceive always pertains to the shared 'real' world; even the landscapes of dreams come from actual scenes recently viewed or recalled from memory, consciously or otherwise, however, much they may be distorted or transformed. Sensing can take place without external perception (spots before the eyes; ringing in the ears), but 'so expressive a phrase as "the mind's eye" ' is current, Smythies points out, because there is 'something very like seeing about having sensory mental images.[38]

Illusions do not long delude most of us; 'we see the world the way we see it because it pays us and has paid us to see it that way.'[39] To find our way about, avoid danger, earn a living, and achieve basic human contacts, we usually have to perceive what is there. As the Sprouts express it, 'the fact that the human species has survived (so far) suggests that there must be considerable correspondence between the milieu as people conceive it to be, and as it actually is.'[40] If the picture of the world in our heads were not fairly consistent with the world outside, we should be unable to survive in any environment other than a mental hospital. And if our private milieus were not recognizably similar to one another, we could never have constructed a common world view.

Range and Limits of Personal Knowledge of the World
However, a perfect fit between the outside world and our views of it is not possible; indeed, complete fidelity would endanger survival. Whether we stay put or move about, our environment is subject to sudden and often drastic change. In consequence, we must be able to see things not only as they are, but also as they might become. Our private milieus are therefore flexible, plastic, and somewhat amorphous. We are physiologically equipped for a wide range of environments, including some of those that we create. But evolution is slow; at any point in time, some of our sensate and conceptual apparatus is bound to be vestigial, better suited to previous than to present milieus.

As individuals, we learn most rapidly about the world not by paying close attention to a single variable, but by superficially scanning a great variety of things. 'Everyday perception tends to be selective, creative, fleeting, inexact, generalized, stereotyped' just because imprecise, partly erroneous impressions about the world in general often convey more than exact details about a small segment of it.[41] The observant are not necessarily most accurate; effective observation is never unwaveringly attentive. As Vernon emphasizes, 'changing perceptions are necessary to preserve mental alertness and normal powers of thought.' Awareness is not always conductive to survival. He who fails to see a tiger and hence does not attract its attention 'may escape the destruction which his more knowing fellow invites by the very effects of his knowledge'. So, Boulding concludes, 'under some circumstances, ignorance is bliss and knowledge leads to disaster,[42]

Essential perception of the world, in short, embraces every way of looking at it: conscious and unconscious, blurred and distinct, objective and subjective, inadvertent and deliberate, literal and schematic.

Perception itself is never unalloyed: sensing, thinking, feeling, and believing are simultaneous, interdependent processes. A purely perceptual view of the world would be as lame and false as one based solely on logic, insight, or ideology. 'All fact', as Goethe said, 'is in itself theory.' The most direct and simple experience of the world is a composite of perception, memory, logic, and faith. Looking down from a window, like Descartes, we say that we see men and women, when in fact we perceive no more than parts of hats and coats. The recognition of Mt. Monadnock, Chisholm demonstrates, is a conceptual as well as a visual act:[43]

Suppose that you say to me, as we are riding through New Hampshire, 'I see that that is Mt. Monadnock behind the trees.' If I should ask, 'How do you know it's Monadnock?' you may reply by saying, 'I've been here many times before and I can *see* that it is.' . . . I may ask, 'What makes you *think* that's Monadnock that you see?' . . . An appropriate answer would be this: 'I can see that the mountain is shaped like a wave and that there is a little cabin near the top. There is no other mountain answering to that description within miles of here.' . . . What you now claim to see is, not that the mountain is Monadnock, but merely that it has a shape like a wave and that there is a cabin near the top. And this new 'perceptual statement' is coupled with a statement of independent information ('Monadnock is shaped like a wave and there is a cabin near the top; no other mountain like that is within miles of here')—information acquired prior to the present perception.

And each succeeding perceptual statement can similarly be broken down into new perceptual claims and other additional information, until 'we reach a point where we find . . . no *perceptual* claim at all'.

Uniqueness of Private Milieus

Despite their congruence with each other and with the world as it is, private milieus do diverge markedly among people in different cultures, for individuals within a social group, and for the same person as child and as adult, at various times and places, and in sundry moods. 'The life of each individual', concludes Delgado, 'constitutes an original and irreversible perceptive experience.'[44]

Each private world view is unique, to begin with, because each person inhabits a different milieu. 'The fact that no two human beings can occupy the same point at the same time and that the world is never precisely the same on successive occasions means', as Kluckhohn and Mowrer put it, that 'the physical world is idiosyncratic for each individual'. Experience is not only unique; more significantly, it is also self-centred; I am part of your milieu, but not of my own, and never see myself as the world does. It is usually one's self to which the world attends; 'we will assume that an eye looks at us, or a gun points at us', notes Gombrich, 'unless we have good evidence to the contrary.'[45]

Each private world view is also unique because everyone chooses from and reacts to the milieu in a different way. We elect to see certain aspects of the world and to avoid others. Moreover, because 'everything that we know about an object affects the way in which it appears to the eye', no object is apt to seem quite the same to any two percipients.[46] Thus 'in some respects', as Clark says, 'each man's appraisal of an identical situation is peculiarly his own.'[47]

Cultural Differences in Aspects of World Views

Appraisals are, of course, profoundly affected by society and culture. Each social system organizes the world in accordance with its particular structure and requirements; each culture screens perception of the milieu in harmony with its particular style and techniques.[48]

Consider social and cultural differences in habits of location and techniques of orientation. Eskimo maps, Stefansson reports, often show accurately the number and shape of turns in routes and rivers, but neglect lineal distances, noting only how far one can travel in a day. The Saulteaux Indians do not think of circular motion, according to Hallowell; to go counter-clockwise is to move, they say, from east to south to west to north, the birth order of the four winds in their mythology. To find their way about, some peoples utilize concrete and others abstract base points, still others edges in the landscape, or their own locations. The Chukchee of Siberia distinguish twenty-two compass directions, most of them tied to the position of the sun and varying with the seasons. The precise, asymmetrical navigation nets of Micronesian voyagers made use of constellations and islands. Tikopians, never far from the ocean, and unable to conceive of a large land mass, use *inward* and *seaward* to help locate anything: 'there is a spot of mud on your seaward cheek.'[49] In the Tuamotus, compass directions refer to winds, but places on the atolls are located by reference to their direction from the principal settlement. Westerners are more spatially egocentric than Chinese or Balinese. The religious significance of cardinal directions controls orientation indoors and out on the North China plain, and the Balinese give all directions in terms of compass points. Where we would say 'go to the left', 'towards me', or 'away from the wall', they say 'take the turn to the West', 'pull the table southward', or, in case of a wrong note on the piano, 'hit the key to the East of the one you are hitting'.[50] Disorientation is universally disagreeable; but inability to locate north quite incapacitates the Balinese. The English writer Stephen Potter was amazed to find that most Americans neither knew nor cared what watershed they were in, or which way rivers flowed—facts he maintained were second nature to Englishmen.[51]

Apperception of shape is also culturally conditioned. According to Herskovits, an electrical engineer working in Ghana complained that 'When a trench for a conduit must be dug, I run a line between the two points, and tell my workers to follow it. But at the end of the job, I invariably find that the trench has curves in it.' In their land 'circular forms predominate.... They do not live in ... a carpentered world, so that to follow a straight line marked by a cord is as difficult for them' as drawing a perfect freehand circle is for most of us.[52] Zulus tested with the Ames trapezoidal window actually saw it as a trapezoid more often than Americans, who usually see it as a rectangle; habituated to man-made rectangular forms, we are apt unconsciously to assume that *any* four-sided object is a rectangle.[53]

Territoriality—the ownership, division, and evaluation of space—also differs from group to group. In American offices, workers stake out claims around the walls and readily move to accommodate new employees; but the Japanese gravitate towards the centre of the room, and many Europeans are loathe to relinquish space once pre-empted. Eastern Mediterranean Arabs distinguish socially between right- and left-hand sides of outer offices, and value proximity to doors. In seeing and describing landscapes, Samoans emphasize the total impression, Moroccans the details. The Trukese sharply differentiate various parts of open spaces, but pay little attention to dividing lines or edges—a trait which makes land claims difficult to resolve.[54]

As with shapes, so with colours. Our most accustomed hues, such as blue and green, are not familiar in certain other cultures; whereas gradations scarcely perceptible to us may be part of their common experience. 'There is no such thing as a "natural" division of the spectrum', Ray concludes. 'Each culture has taken the spectral continuum and has divided it into units on a quite arbitrary basis.... The effects of brightness, luminosity, and saturation are often confused with hue; and the resulting systems are emotional and subjective, not scientific.'[55] Among the Hanunóo of Mindoro, Conklin shows, the most basic colour terms refer to degrees of wetness (saturation) and brightness; hue is of secondary interest.[56]

As the diverse views of colour suggest, it is not merely observed phenomena that vary with culture, but whole categories of experience. A simple percept here may be a complex abstraction there. Groupings of supreme importance in one culture may have no relevance in another. The Aleuts had no generic name for their island chain, since they did not recognize its unity. The Aruntas organize the night sky into separate, overlapping constellations, some out of bright stars, others out of faint ones. To the Trukese, fresh and salt water are unrelated substances. The gauchos of the Argentine are said to have lumped the vegetable world into four named groups: cattle fodder, bedding straw, woody material, and all other plants—including roses, herbs, and cabbages.[57] There is no natural or best way to classify anything; all categories are useful rather than true, and the landscape architect rightly prefers a morphological to a genetic taxonomy. The patterns people see in nature also vary with economic, ethical, and aesthetic values. Aesthetically neutral to Americans, colours have moral connotations to Navahos; an Indian administrator's attempt to use colours as impartial voting symbols came to grief, since the Navahos viewed blue as good and red as bad.[58]

The Significance of Linguistic Differences in Apperception of the Milieu

The very words we use incline us towards a particular view of the universe. In Whorf's now classic phrase, 'We dissect nature along lines laid down by our native languages. . . . We cut nature up, organize it into concepts, and ascribe significance as we do, largely because we are parties to an agreement to organize it in this way—an agreement that holds throughout our speech community.'[59] To be sure, language also adjusts to the world view, just as environment moulds vocabulary: within a single generation the craze for skiing has given us almost as many different words for *snow* as the Eskimos have.

Linguistic patterns do not irrevocably imprison the senses, but rather, Hoijer judges, 'direct perception and thinking into certain habitual channels'.[60] Things with names are easier to distinguish than those that lack them; the gauchos who used only four floristic terms no doubt saw more than four kinds of plants, but 'their perceptual world is impoverished by their linguistic one'.[61] Classifications into animate or inanimate, masculine, feminine, or neuter, and mass (sand, flour, grass, snow) or particular nouns (man, dog, thimble, leaf) variously affect the way different speech communities view things. We tend to think of waves, mountains, horizons, and Martinis as though they were composed of discrete entities, but conceive surf, soil, scenery, and milk as aggregates, principally because the former terms are plurals, the latter indefinite nouns.[62]

The structural aspects of language influence ways of looking at the world more than do vocabularies. Seldom consciously employed, usually slow to change, syntax pervades basic modes of thought. In Shawnee, La Barre suggests, 'I let her have one on the noggin' is grammatically analogous to 'The damned thing slipped out of my hand.'[63] Lacking transitive verbs, Greenlanders tend to see things happen without specific cause; 'I kill him', in their language, becomes 'he dies to me'. In European tongues, however, action accompanies perception, and the transitive verb animates every event with purpose and cause. The Hopis have subjectless verbs, but most Indo-European subjects have objects, which gives expression a dualistic, animistic stamp. In Piaget's illustration, to say 'the wind blows' 'perpetrates . . . the triple absurdity of suggesting that the wind can be independent of the action of blowing, that there can be a wind that does not blow, and that the wind exists apart from its outward manifestations'.[64] Important differences also occur within linguistic families. The French distinction between the imperfect tense (used for things and processes) and the perfect (used for man and his actions) contrasts the uniformity of nature with the uniqueness of man in a way that English does not ordinarily express.

That such distinctions can all be conveyed in English shows that language does not fetter thought; with sufficient care and effort, practically everything in any stem of speech can be translated. Nevertheless, a concept that comes naturally and easily in one tongue may require awkward and tedious circumlocution in another. The difference between what is customary for some but difficult for others is apt to be crucial in terms of habits of thought and, perhaps, orders of events. European scientists, whose languages lump processes with substances as nouns, took much longer to account for vitamin deficiencies than for germ diseases, partly because 'I have a germ' was a more natural locution than 'I have a lack of vitamins.' In short, as Waismann says, 'by growing up in a certain language, by thinking in its semantic and syntactical grooves, we acquire a certain more or less uniform outlook on the world. . . . Language shapes and fashions the frame in which experience is set, and different languages achieve this in different ways.'[65]

Personal Variations in Aspects of the World View

Private world views diverge from one another even within the limits set by logical necessity, human physiology, and group standards. In any society, individuals of similar cultural background, who speak the same language, still perceive and understand the world differently. 'You cannot see things until you know roughly what they are', comments C. S. Lewis, whose hero on the planet Malacandra at first perceives 'nothing but colours—colours that refused to form themselves into things.'[66] But what you think you know depends both on what is familiar to you and on your proclivities. When the well known is viewed from fresh perspectives, upside-down or through distorting lenses, form and colour are enhanced, as Helmholtz noted; the unexpected has a vivid, pictorial quality. On the other hand, prolonged observation may change red to apparent green, or shrink a figure in proportion to its surroundings.[67]

The purpose and circumstances of observation materially alter what is seen. The stage electrician cares how the lights look, not about the actual colours of the set; the oculist who tests my eyes is not interested in what the letters are, but in how they appear to me. Intent modifies the character of the world.[68]

Outside the laboratory, no two people are likely to see a colour as the same unless they similarly identify the thing that is coloured. Even then, preconceptions shape appearances, as Cornish points out: 'The exquisite colours which light and atmosphere impart to a snowy landscape are only half seen by many people owing to their opinion that "snow is really white".'[69] Such stereotypes may outweigh other physiological facts. The United States Navy was advised to switch the colour of survival gear and life jackets from yellow to fluorescent red, not so much to increase visibility as to buoy the confidence of the man lost at sea; dressed in red, he imagines, 'They can't fail to see me.'[70]

The way a landscape looks depends on all the attendant circumstances, for each sense is affected by the others. Velvet looks soft, ice sounds solid, red feels warm because experience has confirmed these impressions. The sight of gold and blond beech trees lit by sunlight made Cornish forget that he was cold; but he could not appreciate a 'frosty' blue landscape seen from a cold railway carriage. 'Quite often', notes H. M. Tomlinson, 'our first impression of a place is also our last, and it depends solely upon the weather and the food.'[71]

Circumstance apart, each person is distinctively himself. 'The individual carries with him into every perceptual situation ... his characteristic sensory abilities, intelligence, interests, and temperamental qualities', according to Vernon; and his 'responses will be coloured and to some extent determined by these inherent individual qualities.'[72] Ability to estimate vertical and horizontal correctly, for example, varies with sex and personality as well as with maturity: strong-minded men are better at telling which way is up than are women, neurotics, and children, whose kinesthetic sense reinforces visual perception less adequately.[73] The story of the Astronomer Royal, Maskeleyne, who dismissed a faithful assistant for persistently recording the passage of stars more than half a second later than he did, is often told to illustrate the inevitability of perceptual divergence under the best of circumstances.[74] Each of us warps the world in his own way and endows landscapes with his particular mirages.

People at home in the same environments, for example, habitually select different modes of orientation. There is only one published 'New Yorker's Map of the United States', but Trowbridge found a great variety of personal imaginary maps. Individual deviations of direction ranged from zero to 180 degrees off course;

some were consistent, others more distorted at Times Square than at the Battery, or accurate about Albany but not about Chicago. Still others assumed that streets always point towards cardinal directions, or imagined all distant places as lying due east or west. A few know which direction they face the moment they emerge from subways and theatres, others are uncertain, still others are invariably mistaken. Lynch characterizes structural images of the environment as positional, disjointed, flexible, and rigid, depending on whether people orient themselves principally by distant landmarks, by memories of details in the landscape, by crossings, street turns, or directions, or by maps.[75]

Subjective Elements in Private Geographies

Another reason why private world views are irreducibly unique is that all information is inspired, edited, and distorted by feeling. Coins look larger to the children of the poor,[76] the feast smells more fragrant to the hungry, the mountains loom higher to the lost. 'Had our perceptions no connection with our pleasures', wrote Santayana, 'we should soon close our eyes on this world.'[77] We seldom differentiate among people, places, or things until we have a personal interest in them. One American town is much like another to me, unless I have a good motive for telling them apart. The most exhaustive study of photographs and ethnological evidence does not enable us to distinguish among individuals of another race with the ease, speed, and certainty generated by strong feeling. All Chinese may look the same to me, but not to the man—however foreign—with a Chinese wife. Only the flea circus owner can tell you which is which among his performing fleas.[78]

Stereotypes influence how we learn and what we know about every place in the world. My notions of Australia and Alaska are compounds of more or less objective, veridical data and of the way I happen to feel about deserts, ice-fields primitive peoples, pioneers, amateur tennis, and American foreign policy. Similar evanescent images come readily to mind; to Englishmen in the 1930s, according to one writer, Kenya suggested 'gentleman farmers, the seedy aristocracy, gossip columns and Lord Castlerosse'; South Africa 'Rhodes and British Empire and an ugly building in South Parks Road and Trafalgar Square'.[79] Education and the passage of time revise but never wholly displace such stereotypes about foreign lands and people. The present consensus of teen-aged geography students in an English school is that 'South Africans break off from the Boer War to eat oranges, make fortunes from gold and diamonds, and oppress natives, under a government as merciless as the ever-present sun.'[80] Those who think of China as an abode of laundrymen, France as a place where people eat snails, and the Spanish as hot-blooded are only a trifle more myopic than anyone else; it is easier to deplore such generalizations than to replace them with more adequate and convincing images.

Because all knowledge is necessarily subjective as well as objective, delineations of the world that are purely matter-of-fact ordinarily seem too arid and lifeless to assimilate; only colour and feeling convey versimilitude. Besides unvarnished facts, we require fresh first-hand experience, individual opinions and prejudices. 'The important thing about truth is not that it should be naked, but what clothes suit it best.'[81] The memorable geographics are not compendious texts but interpretative studies embodying a strong personal slant. A master at capturing the essence of a place, Henry James did so by conveying 'less of its appearance than of its implications'.[82] In Blake's lines,[83]

> This Life's dim Windows of the Soul
> Distorts the Heavens from Pole to Pole
> And Leads you to Believe a Lie
> When you see with, not thro', the Eye.

The ideal traveller, according to one critic, ought to be 'aware not only of the immediate visual aspect of the country he visits, its history and customs, its art and people, but also of his own relation to all these, their symbolic and mythic place in his own universal map'.[84] We mistrust science as the sole vehicle of truth because we conceive of the remote, the unknown, and the different in terms of what is near, well known, and self-evident for us, and above all in terms of ourselves. What seems to us real and true depends 'on what we know about ourselves and not only on what we know about the external world. Indeed', writes Hutten, 'the two kinds of knowledge are inextricably connected.'[85]

The Role of the Individual Past in Apperception of the Milieu

Personal as well as geographical knowledge is a form of sequent occupance. Like a landscape or a living being, each private world has had a career in time, a history of its own. Since personality is formed mainly in the earliest years, 'we are determined, simultaneously, both by what we were as children and by what we are experiencing now'. In Quine's words, 'We imbibe an archaic natural philosophy with our mother's milk. In the fullness of time, what with catching up on current literature and making some supplementary observations of our own, we become clearer on things. But ... we do not break with the past, nor do we attain to standards of evidence and reality different in kind from the vague standards of children and laymen.'[86]

The earlier mode of thought continues throughout life. According to Portmann, we all remain to some extent pre-Copernican: 'The decisive early period in our contact with nature is strongly influenced by the Ptolemaic point of view, in which our inherited traits and responses find a congenial outlet. ... Nor is the Ptolemaic merely a phase to be outgrown, a kind of animal experience; it is an integral part of our total human quality.'[87]

As every personal history results in a particular private milieu, no one can ever duplicate the *terra cognita* of anyone else. An adult who learns a foreign word or custom does not start from *tabula rasa*, but tries to match concepts from his own language and culture—never with complete success. Among 'children, exposed serially to two cultures', notes Mead, '... the premises of the earlier may persist as distortions of perception into later experience, so that years later errors in syntax or reasoning may be traced to the earlier and "forgotten" cultural experience'.[88]

We are captives even of our adult histories. The image of the environment, as Boulding says, 'is built up as a result of all past experience of the possessor of the image. Part of the image is the history of the image itself'. I have touched on this in connection with colour perception: 'The color in which we have most often seen a thing is imprinted ineffaceably on our memory and becomes a fixed attribute of the remembered image,' says Hering. 'We see through the glass of remembered colors and hence often differently than we should otherwise see them.'[89] The sitter's family invariably complain that the painter has made him look too old, because they view as a composite memory the face the painter confronts only today. 'Everyone sees the world as it was in the past, reflected in the retarding mirror of his memory.'[90]

Memory need not be conscious to influence images; as Hume pointed out, aspects of our past that we fail to recall also leave their imprint on mental maps. 'The unconscious inner world', writes Money-Kyrle, 'is peopled by figures and objects from the past, as they are imagined often wrongly to have been.' Correct or not, recollections can virtually efface aspects of the actual contemporary landscape. Pratolini's *Il Quartiere* portrays inhabitants of a razed and empty section of

Florence who instinctively continued to follow the lines of the former streets, instead of cutting diagonally across the square where buildings had stood.[91]

Memory likewise moulds abstract ideas and hypotheses. Everything I know about America today is in part a memory of what I used to think about it. Having once conceived of the frontier as a cradle of democracy, it is quite another thing for me to learn that it was not than it is for someone else to learn the 'true' fact without the old error. What we accept as true or real depends not only on what we think we know about the external world but on what we have previously believed.

Shared perspectives of whole cultures similarly incorporate the past. 'Meanings may reflect not the contemporary culture but a much older one.' The landscape in general, Lynch remarks, 'serves as a vast mnemonic system for the retention of group history and ideals'.[92]

Conclusion

Every image and idea about the world is compounded, then, of personal experience, learning, imagination, and memory. The places that we live in, those we visit and travel through, the worlds we read about and see in works of art, and the realms of imagination and fantasy each contribute to our images of nature and man. All types of experience, from those most closely linked with our everyday world to those which seem furthest removed, come together to make up our individual picture of reality.[93] The surface of the earth is shaped for each person by refraction through cultural and personal lenses of custom and fancy. We are all artists and landscape architects, creating order and organizing space, time, and causality in accordance with our apperceptions and predilections. The geography of the world is unified only by human logic and optics, by the light and colour of artifice, by decorative arrangement, and by ideas of the good, the true, and the beautiful. As agreement on such subjects is never perfect nor permanent, geographers too can expect only partial and evanescent concordance. As Raleigh wrote, 'It is not truth but opinion that can travel the world without a passport.'[94]

NOTES AND REFERENCES

[1] This is an expanded version of a paper read at the XIXth International Geographical Congress, Stockholm, August 1960. For encouragement, advice, and criticism, I am grateful to George A. Cooper, Richard Hartshorne, William C. Lewis, William D. Pattison, Michael G. Smith, Philip L. Wagner, William Warntz, J. W. N. Watson, and John K. Wright. Richard F. Kuhns, Jr., has kindly read and commented on several drafts of the manuscript, and I am indebted to him for numerous suggestions and references.

[2] John K. Wright, 'Terrae Incognitae: the Place of the Imagination in Geography', *Annals Assoc. American Geographers*, 37 (1947), 1–15, on p. 15. The phrase 'The World Outside and the Pictures in Our Heads' is the name of the first chapter in Walter Lippmann, *Public Opinion* (New York: Macmillan, 1922). As my subtitle suggests, this is not a study of the meaning or methods of geography, but rather an essay in the theory of geographical knowledge. Hartshorne's methodological treatises analyse and develop logical principles of procedure for geography as a professional science, 'a form of "knowing" ', as he writes, 'that is different from the ways in which we "know" by instinct, intuition, *a priori* deduction or revelation' (Richard Hartshorne, *Perspective on the Nature of Geography* [Chicago: Rand McNally, for Association of American Geographers, 1959], p. 170). My epistemological inquiry, on the other hand, is concerned with *all* geographical thought, scientific and other: how it is acquired, transmitted, altered, and integrated into conceptual systems; and how the horizon of geography varies among individuals and groups. Specifically, it is a study in what Wright calls *geography*: 'the nature and expression of geographical ideas both past and present ... the geographical ideas, both true and false, of all manner of people—not only geographers, but farmers and fishermen,

business executives and poets, novelists and painters, Bedouins and Hottentots' ('Terrae Incognitae', p. 12). Because geographers are 'nowhere . . . more likely to be influenced by the subjective than in their discussions of what scientific geography ought to be' (ibid.), epistemology helps to explain why and how methodologies change.

[3] Jared Sparks, MS. in Sparks Collection (132, Misc. Papers, Vol. I, 1808–14), Harvard College Library; quoted in Ralph H. Brown, 'A Plea for Geography, 1813 Style', *Annals Assoc. American Geographers*, 41 (1951), 235. For similar nineteenth-century views see my 'George Perkins Marsh on the Nature and Purpose of Geography', *Geographical Journal*, 126 (1960), 413–17.

[4] Roderick Peattie, *Geography in Human Destiny* (New York: George W. Stewart, 1940), pp. 26–7. 'In the broadest sense', Richard Hartshorne notes, 'all facts of the earth surface are geographical facts' (*The Nature of Geography: a Critical Survey of Current Thought in the Light of the Past* [Lancaster, Pa.: Association of American Geographers, 1939], p. 372). On the interests and capacities of geographers, see J. Russell Whitaker, 'The Way Lies Open', *Annals Assoc. American Geographers*, 44 (1954), 242; and André Meynier, "Réflexions sur la spécialisation chez les géographes," *Norois* 7 (1960), 5–12.

Most of the physical and social sciences are, both in theory and in practice, more generalizing and formalistic than geography. The exceptions are disciplines which, like geography, are in some measure humanistic: notably anthropology and history. The subject matter of anthropology is as diversified as that of geography, and more closely mirrors the everyday concerns of man; But anthropological research still concentrates predominantly on that small and remote fraction of mankind—"primitive" or non-literate, traditional in culture, homogeneous in social organization—whose ways of life and world views are least like our own (Ronald M. Berndt, 'The Study of Man: an Appraisal of the Relationship between Social and Cultural Anthropology and Sociology', *Oceania*, 31 [1960], 85–99). More particularistic, more concerned with uniqueness of context than geography, history also comprehends more matters of common interest (especially the acts and feelings of individuals); but because the whole realm of history lies in the past, most historical data are secondary, derivative. Although 'geography cannot be strictly contemporary' (Preston E. James, 'Introduction: the Field of Geography', in *American Geography: Inventory and Prospect* [Syracuse University Press, for Association of American Geographers, 1954], p. 14), geography is usually *focused* on the present; direct observation of the world plays a major role in geography, a trifling one in history. In theory, at least, the remote in space is everywhere (on the face of the earth) personally accessible to us, the remote in time accessible only through memories and artifacts.

[5] W. V. Quine, 'The Scope and Language of Science', *British Journal for the Philosophy of Science*, 8 (1957), 1–17, on p. 1.

[6] For various combinations of geographical facts and relationships, see John K. Wright, ' "Crossbreeding" Geographical Quantities', *Geographical Review*, 45 (1955), 52–65. For the varieties of data that comprise knowledge in general, see Rudolph Carnap, 'Formal and Factual Science', in Herbert Feigl and May Brodbeck, eds., *Readings in the Philosophy of Science* (New York: Appleton-Century-Crofts, 1953), pp. 123–8; Karl R. Popper. *The Logic of Scientific Discovery* (New York: Basic Books, 1959), appendix x, pp. 420–41: Friedrich Waismann, 'Analytic-Synthetic', *Analysis*, 11 (1950–1), 52–6; J. W. N. Watkins, 'Between Analytic and Empirical', *Philosophy*, 32 (1957), 112–31.

[7] Michael Polanyi, *Personal Knowledge: Towards a Post-Critical Philosophy* (Chicago: University of Chicago Press, 1958), pp. 208–9.

[8] Derwent Whittlesey, 'The Horizon of Geography', *Annals Assoc. American Geographers*, 35 (1945), 1–36, on p. 14.

[9] Kenneth E. Boulding, *The Image* (Ann Arbor: University of Michigan Press, 1956), p. 66.

[10] Whittlesey, op. cit., pp. 2, 14.

[11] L. S. Rodberg and V. F. Weisskopf, 'Fall of Parity', *Science*, 125 (1957), 627–33; on p. 632.

[12] Polanyi, *Personal Knowledge*, p. 216; Rafael Rodriguez Delgado, 'A Possible Model for Ideas', *Philosophy of Sciences*, 24 (1957), 253–69, on p. 255. 'The organism has a definite capacity for information which is a minute fraction of the physical signals that reach the eyes, ears, and epidermis' (Colin Cherry, *On Human Communication: a Review, a Survey, and a Criticism* [New York: Wiley, 1957], p. 284). See also George A. Miller, 'The Magical Number Seven, Plus or Minus Two: Some Limits on Our Capacity for Processing Information', *Psychological Review*, 63 (1956), 81–97; Henry Quastler, 'Studies of Human Channel Capacity', in Colin Cherry, ed., *Information Theory; Papers Read at the Third London Symposium, 1955* (New York: Academic Press, 1956), pp. 361–71.

13 Roderick M. Chisholm, *Perceiving: a Philosophical Study* (Ithaca: Cornell University Press, 1957), p. 36. Personal surprise and disappointment are evidence to most of us that our private worlds are not, in fact, identical with the common world view (R. E. Money-Kyrle, 'The World of the Unconscious and the World of Commonsense', *British Journal for the Philosophy of Science*, 7[1956], 86–96, on p. 93). G. A. Birks, 'Towards a Science of Social Relations' (ibid. 7 [1956], 117–28, 206–21), shows what happens when private ideas about the world have to be adjusted to conform with the consensus.

14 For the effects of various types of illness and injury on perception and cognition of the milieu see Otto Fenichel, *The Psychoanalytic Theory of Neurosis* (New York: W. W. Norton, 1945), p. 204; C. O. de la Garza and Philip Worchel, 'Time and Space Orientation in Schizophrenics', *Journal of Abnormal and Social Psychology*, 52 (1956), 191–4; T. E. Weckowicz and D. B. Blewett, 'Size Constancy and Abstract Thinking in Schizophrenia', *Journal of Mental Science*, 105 (1959), 909–34; H. J. Eysenck, G. W. Granger, and J. C. Brengelmann, *Perceptual Processes and Mental Illness*, Institute of Psychiatry, Maudsley Monographs No. 2 (London: Chapman and Hall, 1957); G. W. Granger, 'Psychophysiology of Vision', in *International Review of Neurobiology*, 1 (1959) [New York: Academic Press], 245–98; Andrew Paterson and O. L. Zangwill, 'A Case of Topographic Disorientation Associated with a Unilateral Cerebral Lesion', *Brain*, 68 (1945), 188–212; A. R. Luria, 'Disorders of "Simultaneous Perception" in a Case of Bilateral Occipito-Parietal Brain Injury', *Brain*, 82 (1959), 437–49.

15 'From a perception of only 3 senses ... none could deduce a fourth or fifth' (William Blake, 'There Is No Natural Religion: First Series', in *Selected Poetry and Prose of William Blake* [New York: Modern Library, 1953], p. 99); the congenital deaf-mute does not know how music sounds even though he knows that tones exist. For the effects of sensory deprivation, see Felix Deutsch, 'The Sense of Reality in Persons Born Blind', *Journal of Psychology*, 10 (1940), 121–40; Kai von Fieandt, 'Toward a Unitary Theory of Perception', *Psychological Review*, 65 (1958), 315–20; Géza Révész, *Psychology and Art of the Blind* (London: Longmans, Green, 1950); J. Z. Young, *Doubt and Certainty in Science: a Biologist's Reflection on the Brain* (Oxford: Clarendon Press, 1951), pp. 61–6.

16 Jean Piaget, *The Child's Conception of the World* (Paterson, N. J.: Littlefield and Adams, 1960), pp. 248, 357.

17 *Child's Conception of the World*, pp. 384–5; *Construction of Reality in the Child* (New York: Basic Books, 1954), pp. 367–9. Piaget and his associates have worked chiefly with schoolchildren in Geneva. How far their categories and explanations apply universally or vary with culture and milieu remains to be determined. Margaret Mead ('An Investigation of the Thought of Primitive Children, with Special Reference to Animism', *Journal of the Anthropological Institute*, 62 [1932], 173–90) found that Manus children rejected animistic explanations of natural phenomena. They were more matter-of-fact than Swiss children (and Manus adults) because their language was devoid of figures of speech, because they were punished when they failed to cope effectively with the environment, because their society possessed no machines too complex for children to understand, and because they were barred from animistic rites until past puberty. In Western society, on the other hand, 'the language is richly animistic, children are given no such stern schooling in physical adjustment to a comprehensible and easily manipulated physical environment, and the traditional animistic material which is decried by modern scientific thinking is still regarded as appropriate material for child training' (p. 189). (Indeed, books written for children show clearly that adults think children *ought* to be animists.) Elsewhere, however, child animism appears to be significant and tends to decline with age and maturity (Gustav Jahoda, 'Child Animism: I. A. Critical Survey of Cross-Cultural Research', *Journal of Social Psychology*, 47 [1958], 197–212).

18 The decline of sensory perception leads the elderly to make false judgements about the environment, and often arouses feelings of isolation and apathy. See Alfred D. Weiss, 'Sensory Functions', and Harry W. Braun, 'Perceptual Process', in J. E. Birren, ed., *Handbook of Aging and the Individual: Psychological and Biological Aspects* (Chicago: University of Chicago Press, 1959), pp. 503–42 and 543–61, respectively.

19 Marcel Bélanger 'J'ai choisi de devenir géographe', *Revue Canadienne de Géographie*, 13 (1959), 70–2, on p' 70' This version of Heraclitus is in Bertrand Russell, *A History of Western Philosophy* (New York: Simon and Schuster, 1945), p. 45; a somewhat different phrasing appears in Plato's *Cratylus* (*The Dialogues of Plato*, B. Jowett, tr., 2 vols. [New York: Random House, 1937], Vol 1, p. 191).

20 Loren Eiseley, *The Firmament of Time* (New York: Atheneum, 1960), p. 38. Scientists at the French Academy in the seventh century denied evidence for the fall of ineteorites, obvious

to most observers, because they opposed the prevalent superstition that meteorites came by supernatural means. For this and other instances of how 'the most stubborn facts will be set aside if there is no place for them in the established framework of science', see Polanyi *Personal Knowledge*, pp. 138–58.

[21] Marjorie Hope Nicolson, *Mountain Gloom and Mountain Glory: The Development of the Aesthetics of the Infinite* (Ithaca: Corneli University Press, 1959); quotations (from Thomas Burnet's *Sacred Theory of the Earth* [London, 1684]) on pp. 198, 206.

[22] Hartshorne, *Perspective on the Nature of Geography*, p. 46; F. Kenneth Hare, 'The Westerlies', *Geographical Review* 50 (1960), 367; Wolfgang Köhler, *The Place of Value in a World of Facts* ([1938 ed.] New York: Meridian Books, 1959). 'There is no ultimate source for the physicist's concepts', adds Köhler, "other than the phenomenal world' (p. 374).

[23] Hadley Cantril, 'Concerning the Nature of Perception', *Proceedings of the American Philosophical Society*, 104 (1960), 467–73, on p. 470. 'The environment with which we are concerned is not the one which is measured in microns, nor that which is measured in light years, but that which is measured in millimetres or meters . . . [It] is not that of particles, atoms, molecules, or anything smaller than crystals. Nor is it that of planets, stars, galaxies, or nebulae. The world of man . . . consists of matter in the solid, liquid, or gaseous state, organized as an array of surfaces or interfaces between matter in these different states' (James J. Gibson, 'Perception as a Function of Stimulation', in Sigmund Koch, ed., *Psychology: a Study of a Science, Study I. Conceptual and Systematic: Vol. I. Sensory, Perceptual, and Physiological Foundations* [New York: McGraw-Hill, 1959], pp. 456–501, on p. 469).

[24] S. S. Stevens, 'To Honor Fechner and Repeal His Law', *Science*, 133 (1961), 80–6. For human and animal sensory and perceptual capacities see Adolf Portmann, 'The Seeing Eye', *Landscape*, 9 (1959), 14–18; Ernest Baumgardt, 'La Vision des insectes', *La Nature*, 90 (1960), 96–9; Donald R. Griffin, 'Sensory Physiology and the Orientation of Animals', *American Scientist*, 41 (1953), 208–44; M. J. Wells, 'What the Octopus Makes of It: Our World from Another Point of View', *Advancement of Science*, 17 (1961), 461–71; J. von Uexküll, *Umwelt und Innenwelt der Tiere* (Berlin: Julius Springer, 1909); Karl von Frisch, *Bees: their Vision, Chemical Senses, and Language* (Ithaca: Corneli University Press, 1950), pp. 8–12, 34–6; Donald R. Griffin, *Listening in the Dark: the Acoustic Orientation of Bats and Men* (New Haven: Yale University Press, 1958); K. von Frisch, "Über den Farbsinn der Insekten', and G. Viaud, 'La Vision chromatique chez les animaux (sauf les insectes)', in *Mechanisms of Colour Discrimination* (New York: Pergamon Press, 1960), pp. 19–40 and 41–66, respectively; Conrad G. Mueller, 'Visual Sensitivity', Irwin Pollack, 'Hearing', and Lloyd M. Beidler, 'Chemical Senses', in *Annual Review of Psychology*, 12 (1961), 311–34, 335–62, and 363–88, respectively.

[25] Edgar Anderson, 'Man as a Maker of New Plants and New Plant Communities', in William L. Thomas, Jr., ed., *Man's Role in Changing the Face of the Earth* (Chicago: University of Chicago Press, 1956), pp. 763–77, on p. 776.

[26] J. von Uexküll, *Theoretical Biology* (London: Kegan Paul, 1926), pp. 66–8; Ludwig von Bertalanffy, 'An Essay on the Relativity of Categories', *Philosophy of Science* 22 (1955), 243–63, on p. 249.

[27] Visual space is Euclidean only locally; for normal observers with binocular vision, space has a constant negative curvature corresponding with the hyperbolic geometry of Lobachevski. See Rudolph K. Luneburg, *Mathematical Analysis of Binocular Vision* (Princeton: Princeton University Press, 1947), and Albert A. Blank, 'Axiomatics of Binocular Vision. The Foundations of Metric Geometry in Relation to Space Perception', *Journal of the Optical Society of America*, 48 (1958), 328–34. But under optimal conditions, Gibson maintains, perceptual space is Euclidean ('Perception as a Function of Stimulation', pp. 479–80).

[28] Bernard Mayo, 'The Incongruity of Counterparts', *Philosophy of Science*, 25 (1958), 109–15, on p. 115; Martti Takala, *Asymmetries of Visual Space* [*Annales Academie Scientiarum Fennicae*, Ser. B., Vol. 72, No. 2] (Helsinki, 1951). Because gravity, unlike bilateral symmetry, affects everything on earth, people adapt more rapidly to distorting spectacles that invert up and down than to those that reverse left and right (Julian E. Hochberg, 'Effects of the Gestalt Revolution: the Cornell Symposium on Perception', *Psychological Review*, 64 [1957], 74–6).

[29] G. J. Whitrow, 'Why Physical Space Has Three Dimensions', *British Journal for the Philosophy of Science*, 6 (1955), 13–31; I. J. Good, 'Lattice Structure of Space-Time', ibid. 9 (1959), 317–19. On righteousness as a function of height, see Geraldine Pederson-Krag, 'The Use of Metaphor In Analytic Thinking', *Psychoanalytic Quarterly*, 25 (1956), 70. Of the opposition of right and left, Robert Hertz remarks, 'if organic asymmetry had not existed, it

would have had to be invented' (*Death and the Right Hand* [Glencoe, Ill.: Free Press, 1960], p. 98), and Rodney Needham concludes that 'in every quarter of the world it is the right hand, and not the left, which is predominant' ('The Left Hand of the Mugwe: an Analytic Note on the Structure of Meru Symbolism', *Africa*, 30 [1960], 20).

30'Il y a une différence fondamentale dans la 'facon d'être-au-monde' de l'homme et de l'animal supérieur: ce fait d'être comme englué dans l'objet, de ne pouvoir le survoler, dû . . . à l'unité que fait l'animal avec le monde . . . L'animal ne peut transcender le réel immédiat' (Jean-C. Filloux, 'La Nature de l'univers chez l'animal', *La Nature*, 85 [1957], 403–7, 438–43, 490–3, on p. 493). Analogous points are made by Boulding, *Image*, p. 29; Géza Révész, 'The Problem of Space with Particular Emphasis on Specific Sensory Spaces', *American Journal of Psychology*, 50 (1937), 434n., Ernst Cassirer, *An Essay on Man: Introduction to a Philosophy of Human Culture* (New Haven: Yale University Press, 1944 and New York: Doubleday Anchor Books, n. d.), p. 67.

31Max Born, *Natural Philosophy of Cause and Chance* (Oxford: Clarendon Press, 1949), p. 125. For a critique on the formation of the common world view, see J. P. McKinney, 'The Rational and the Real: Comment on a Paper by E. Topitsch', *Philosophy of Science*, 24 (1957), 275–80.

32Bertrand Russell, *Our Knowledge of the External World* (New York: Mentor, 1960), p. 56. The question whether the so-called real world actually exists lies beyond the scope of this paper. As Russell says (p. 57), 'universal skepticism, though logically irrefutable, is practically barren'. Sanity and survival depend on the 'sense of being a solid person surrounded by a solid world' (Money-Kyrle, op. cit. [see n. 13], p. 96).

33Bertrand Russell, *Human Knowledge: Its Scope and Limits* (New York: Simon and Schuster, 1948), p. xii. But see J. K. Feibleman, 'Knowing about Semipalatinsk', *Dialectica*, 9 (1955), 3–4.

34Wright, 'Terrae Incognitae', pp. 3–4. On the other hand, the consensual universe of discourse comprises elements from an infinite number of private worlds—not only those of existing persons, but also those that might conceivably be held. No square mile of the earth's surface has been seen from every possible perspective, but our view of the world in general is based on assumptions about such perspectives, as analogous with those that have been experienced. The Amazon basin would look different in design and detail from the top of every tree within it, but we know enough of the general character and major variations of that landscape to describe it adequately after climbing—or hovering in a helicopter over—a small fraction of its trees.

35*Heaven and Hell* (New York: Harper, 1955), pp. 1–3.

36'Man's spatialization of his world . . . never appears to be exclusively limited to the pragmatic level of action and perceptual experience. . . . Human beings in all cultures have built up a frame of spatial reference that has included the farther as well as the more proximal, the spiritual as well as the mundane, regions of their universe' (A. Irving Hallowell, *Culture and Experience* [Philadelphia: University of Pennsylvania Press, 1955], pp. 187–8). The genesis of these mental maps is explained in R. E. Money-Kyrle, *Man's Picture of His World: a Psycho-analytic Study* (London: Duckworth, 1960); see p. 171. For instances of theological location, see Erich Isaac, 'Religion, Landscape and Space', *Landscape*, 9 (1959–60), 14–18. The visionary transfiguration of the everyday world by means of gems and precious stones is a central theme in Huxley, *Heaven and Hell*.

37Edwin A. Abbott, *Flatland, a Romance of Many Dimensions* (New York: Dover, 1952 [London, 1884]), is a classic of two-dimensional life. For samples of the impossible, see Clifton Fadiman, ed., *Fantasia Mathematica* (New York: Simon and Schuster, 1958), notably Martin Gardner, 'The Island of Five Colors', pp. 196–210.

38J. R. Smythies, 'The Problems of Perception', *British Journal for the Philosophy of Science*, 11 (1960), 224–38, on p. 229; see also his *Analysis of Perception* (New York: Humanities Press, 1956), pp. 81–105. 'The widespread belief that a mirage is something unreal, a sort of trick played on the eyes, is wrong. The picture a mirage presents is real but never quite accurate' (James H. Gordon, 'Mirages', in *Smithsonian Institution, Annual Report for 1959* [Washington, D. C., 1960], pp. 327–46, on p. 328). On the form and content of landscapes in dreams, mirages, and hallucinations, and their relations with 'reality', see Charles Fisher, 'Dreams, Images and Perception: A Study of Uncoscious-Preconscious Relationships', *Journal of the American Psychoanalytic Association*, 4 (1956), 5–48; Charles Fisher and I. H. Paul, 'The Effect of Subliminal Visual Stimulation on Images and Dreams: a Validation Study', ibid. 7 (1959), 35–83; Peter Hobart Knapp, 'Sensory Impressions in Dreams', *Psychoanalytic Quarterly*, 25 (1956), 325–47; C. T. K. Chari, 'On the "Space" and "Time" of Hallucinations',

British Journal for the Philosophy of Science, 8 (1958), 302–6; Aldous Huxley, *The Doors of Perception* (London: Chatto and Windus, 1954).

³⁹Boulding, *The Image*, p. 50.

⁴⁰Harold Sprout and Margaret Sprout, *Man-Milieu Relationship Hypotheses in the Context of International Politics* (Princeton University Center of International Studies, 1956), p. 61. The essential correspondence between the perceived and the actual milieu is stressed in James J. Gibson, *The Perception of the Visual World* (Boston: Houghton Mifflin, 1950).

⁴¹Ibid., p. 10; see also Miller, 'The Magical Number Seven' [see n. 12], pp. 88–9. We can count only a few of the stars or raindrops we see, beyond which everything becomes blurred; but our vagueness could not be rectified by looking longer or more carefully: 'the blur is just as essential a feature of sense perception as other features are . . . Sense perception is inexact in a very different sense from that in which . . . a map is inexact' (Waismann, 'Analytic-Synthetic' [see n. 6], *Analysis*, 13 [1953], 76–7). Types and ranges of perception and learning are surveyed in M. D. Vernon, *A Further Study of Visual Perception* (Cambridge: Cambridge University Press, 1952); R. J. Hirst, *The Problems of Perception* (London: Allen & Unwin, 1959); James Drever, II, 'Perceptual Learning', in *Annual Review of Psychology*, 11 (1960), 131–60. For a concise theoretical review, see William Bevan, 'Perception: Development of a Concept', *Psychological Review*, 65 (1958), 34–55.

⁴²Magdalen D. Vernon, 'Perception, Attention and Consciousness', *Advancement of Science*, 16 (1959), 111–23, on p. 120; Boulding, *The Image*, p. 169. The classic story illustrating the virtues of ignorance of the geographical environment is in Kurt Koffka, *Principles of Gestalt Psychology* (New York: Harcourt-Brace, 1935), pp. 27–8.

⁴³Chisholm, *Perceiving*, pp. 55–8; for the Descartes argument, from his *Meditations*, see pp. 154–6. See also Joseph R. Royce, 'The Search for Meaning', *American Scientist*, 47 (1959), 515–35; Ernst Casirer, *The Philosophy of Symbolic Forms; Volume Three: The Phenomonology of Knowledge* (New Haven: Yale University Press, 1957), p. 25.

⁴⁴Delgado, 'A Possible Model for Ideas' [see n. 12], p. 255.

⁴⁵Clyde Kluckhohn and O. H. Mowrer, ' "Culture and Personality": a Conceptual Scheme', *American Anthropologist*, 46 (1944), 1–29, on p. 13; E. H. Gombrich, *Art and Illusion: A Study in the Psychology of Pictorial Representation* (New York: Pantheon Books, 1960 [Bollingen Series, XXXV, No. 5]), p. 276. See also Sprout, *Man-Milieu Relationship Hypotheses*, p. 18.

⁴⁶Vaughan Cornish, *Geographical Essays* (London: Sifton, Praed, [1946]), pp. 78–9.

⁴⁷K. G. T. Clark, 'Certain Underpinnings of Our Arguments in Human Geography', *Transactions of the Institute of British Geographers*, 16 (1950), 15–22, on p. 20.

⁴⁸Only exceptionally do we react in any literal sense to stimuli . . . Rather, we react to our interpretations of stimuli. These interpretations are derived in considerable part from our culture and from each person's specific experiences in that culture' (Clyde Kluckhohn, 'The Scientific Study of Values and Contemporary Civilization', *Proceedings of the American Philosophical Society*, 102 [1958], 469–76, on p. 469). The classic case study is T. T. Waterman, *Yurok Geography* (Berkeley: University of California Press, 1920); see also Erik H. Erikson, *Childhood and Society* (New York: W. W. Norton, 1950), pp. 141–60. The literature on world views is ably summarized by Clyde Kluckhohn, 'Culture and Behavior', in Gardner Lindzey, ed., *Handbook of Social Psychology*, 2 vols. (Cambridge, Mass.: Addison-Wesley, 1954), Vol. 2, pp. 921–76.

⁴⁹Raymond Firth, *We, the Tikopia: a Sociological Study of Kinship in Primitive Polynesia* (London: Allen & Unwin, 1936), p. 19. For the previous examples, see the letter from Vilhjalmur Stefannson quoted in Erwin Raisz, *General Cartography* (New York: McGraw-Hill, 1948), p. 4; Hallowell, *Culture and Experience*, p. 201; Waldemar Bogoras, *The Chukchee. II.–Religion*. The Jesup North Pacific Expedition, Vol. 7, Memoir of the American Museum of Natural History (Leiden: Brill; New York: Stechert, 1907), pp. 303–4. The cultural and environmental contexts of orientation are considered at length in Hallowell, op. cit., pp. 184–202, and Kevin Lynch, *The Image of the City* (Cambridge, Mass.: Technology Press and Harvard University Press, 1960), pp. 123–33.

⁵⁰Bengt Danielsson, *Work and Life in Raroia: an Acculturation Study from the Tuamotu Group, French Oceania* (London: Allen & Unwin, 1956), pp. 30–1; Derk Bodde, 'Types of Chinese Categorical Thinking', *Journal of the American Oriental Society*, 59 (1939), 200–19, on p. 201n., Jane Belo, 'The Balinese Temper', *Character and Personality*, 4 (1935), 120–46, on pp. 126–7. Einar Haugen, 'The Semantics of Icelandic Orientation', *Word*, 13 (1957), 447–59, shows how cardinal orientation can depend on one's location with reference to an ultimate destination; thus an Icelander heading for the southern tip of the island is going 'south'

even if his coastwise route happens to be south-west or west. For other early or 'primitive' methods of pathfinding, see B. F. Adler, *Maps of Primitive Peoples* (St. Petersburg, 1910), abridged by H. de Hutorowicz, *Bulletin of the American Geographical Society*, 43 (1911), 669–79; Waldemar Bogoras, 'Ideas of Space and Time in the Conception of Primitive Religion', *American Anthropologist*, 27 (1925), 212–15; Pierre Jaccard, *Le Sens de la direction et l'orientation lointaine chez l'homme* (Paris: Payot, 1932); Harold Gatty, *Nature Is Your Guide: How to Find Your Way on Land and Sea by Observing Nature* (New York: Dutton, 1958).

[51]'I hardly found an American who knew which watershed he was in, which left me, as an Englishman who is uneasy unless he knows which ocean will receive his urination, somewhat scandalized' (*Potter on America* [London: Hart-Davis, 1956], p. 13).

[52]Melville J. Herskovits, 'Some Further Comments on Cultural Relativism', *American Anthropologist*, 60 (1958), 266–73, on pp. 267–8.

[53]Gordon W. Allport and Thomas F. Pettigrew, 'Cultural Influence on the Perception of Movement: the Trapezoidal Illusion among Zulus', *Journal of Abnormal and Social Psychology*, 55 (1957), 104–13. Under 'optimal' visual conditions, however, the Zulus mistook the trapezoid for a rectangle almost as often as Americans do, perhaps because most of them recognized it as a model of a Western-type window (Charles W. Slack, 'Critique on the Interpretation of Cultural Differences in the Perception of Motion in Ames's Trapezoidal Window', *American Journal of Psychology*, 72 [1959], 127–31). Another aspect of spatial perception which varies with culture is surveyed in Donald N. Michael, 'Cross-Cultural Investigations of Closure', in David C. Beardslee and Michael Wertheimer, eds., *Readings in Perception* (New York: Van Nostrand, 1958), pp. 160–70.

[54]Edward T. Hall, *The Silent Language* (New York: Doubleday, 1959), pp. 197–200, and 'The Language of Space', *Landscape*, 10 (1960), 41–5; Thomas Gladwin and Seymour B. Sarason, *Truk: Man in Paradise*, Viking Fund Publications in Anthropology No. 20 (New York: Wenner-Gren, 1953), pp. 225–6, 269–70.

[55]Verne F. Ray, 'Techniques and Problems in the Study of Human Color Perception', *Southwestern Journal of Anthropology*, 8 (1952), 251–9, on pp. 258–9; see also Ray, 'Human Color Perception and Behavioral Response', *Transactions of the New York Academy of Sciences*, Ser. 2nd. 16 (1953), 98–104.

[56]Harold C. Conklin, 'Hanunóo Color Categories', *Southwestern Journal of Anthropology*, 11 (1955), 339–44.

[57]The Argentine data are cited in Karl Vossler, 'Volkssprachen und Weltsprachen', *Welt und Wort*, 1 (1946), 97–101, on p. 98, and discussed by Harold Basilius, 'Neo-Humboldtian Ethnolinguistics', *Word*, 8 (1952), 95–105, on p. 101. For the rest, see Gladwin and Sarason, *Truk*, p. 30, and Lynch, op. cit., pp. 131–2.

[58]Hall, *Silent Language*, pp. 132–3. Many landscape features exist as separate entities only in our minds. As Gombrich says (*Art and Illusion*, p. 100), 'There is a fallacy in the idea that reality contains such features as mountains and that, looking at one mountain after another, we slowly learn to generalize and form the abstract idea of mountaineity.' Owing to the nineteenth-century popularity of Alpine climbing, the English standard of mountains changed dramatically: for Gilbert White the 800-foot Sussex Downs were 'majestic mountains'; today anything below 2,000 feet is at best a 'hill' (Vaughan Cornish, *Scenery and the Sense of Sight* (Cambridge: Cambridge University Press, 1935), p. 77.

[59]'Science and Linguistics' [1940], in *Language, Thought, and Reality; Selected Writings of Benjamin Lee Whorf*, John B. Carroll, ed. (Cambridge, Mass.: Technology Press; New York: Wiley; London: Chapman and Hall, 1956), p. 213.

[60]Harry Hoijer, 'The Relation of Language to Culture', in A. L. Kroeber *et al.*, *Anthropology Today: an Encyclopedic Inventory* (Chicago: University of Chicago Press, 1953), pp. 554–73, on p. 560.

[61]Garrett Hardin, 'The Threat of Clarity', *ETC.: a Review of General Semantics*, 17 (1960), 269–78, on p. 270. Similarly, people more readily perceive and identify colours that have widely known specific names (like blue and green) than those that do not (Roger W. Brown and Eric H. Lenneberg, 'A Study in Language and Cognition', *Journal of Abnormal and Social Psychology*, 49 [1954], 454–62).

[62]'English terms, like "sky, hill, swamp", persuade us to regard some elusive aspect of nature's endless variety as a distinct THING, almost like a table or chair' (Whorf, *Language, Thought, and Reality*, p. 240; see also pp. 140–1). But Roger W. Brown (*Words and Things* [Glencoe, Ill.: Free Press, 1958], pp. 248–52) maintains that the distinction between mass and specific nouns makes perceptual sense and corresponds well with perceived reality. One can easily, as critics of Whorf have pointed out, make too much of such distinctions.

The fact that the word for *sun* is masculine in French and feminine in German, whereas that for *moon* is feminine in French and masculine in German, cannot easily be correlated with the habits of thought or *Weltanschauung* of either people. The fact that in Algonquian languages the gender class of 'animate' nouns includes such words as *raspberry*, *stomach*, and *kettle*, while 'inanimate' nouns include *strawberry*, *thigh*, and *bowl* does not imply 'that speakers of Algonquian have a shrine to the raspberry and treat it like a spirit, while the strawberry is in the sphere of the profane' (Joseph H. Greenberg, 'Concerning Inferences from Linguistic to Nonlinguistic Data', in Harry Hoijer, ed., *Language in Culture*, American Anthropological Association, Memoir No. 79 [Chicago, 1954], pp. 3–19, on pp. 15–16). In short, 'If grammar itself was once founded on an unconscious metaphysic, this linkage is now so vestigial as to have no appreciable bearing on the structure of philosophic ideas' (Lewis S. Feuer, 'Sociological Aspects of the Relation Between Language and Philosophy', *Philosophy of Science*, 20 [1953], 85–100, on p. 87). This may be true of most aspects of language, and of philosophical ideas in their broadest sense. On the other hand, the fact that English-speaking mid-Victorians clad table and piano legs in ruffs and deplored direct reference to them in mixed company was not a necessary outgrowth of prudery but depended also on the metaphorical extension of the word for human limbs to furniture–a connection not made by speakers of other languages. In this respect, language certainly altered the English–and still more the American–home landscape.

⁶³Weston La Barre, *The Human Animal* (Chicago: University of Chicago Press, 1954), p. 204. See Whorf, op. cit., p. 235.

⁶⁴Piaget, *Child's Conception of the World*, p. 249. A book has been written to tell parents how to answer a child who asks such questions as 'what does the wind do when it's not blowing?' (Ruth Purcell, 'Causality and Language Rigidity', *ETC.* 15 [1958], 175–80, on p. 179). Whorf (*Language, Thought, and Reality*) compares Hopi language and thought with that of 'Standard Average European' in several papers (e.g. pp. 57–64, 134–59, 207–19).

Unlike most psychologists and anthropologists, geographers have tended to assume, with positivistic philosophers, that we could rid ourselves of animistic and teleological kinds of explanation and ways of looking at the world by substituting other words and phrases in our language. 'Ritter's teleological views . . . though they colour every statement he makes, yet do not affect the essence', according to H. J. Mackinder; 'it is easy to re-state each proposition in the most modern evolutionary terms' (President's address, Section E, British Association for the Advancement of Science, *Report of the 65th Annual Meeting*, Ipswich, 1895 [London: Murray, 1895], pp. 738–48, on p. 743); that is, Mackinder found it easy to accommodate Ritter's brand of determinism to his own. For other views on the relation between teleological language and habits of thought, see Sprout, *Man-Milieu Relationship Hypotheses*, pp. 27–8; A. J. Bernatowicz, 'Teleology in Science Teaching', *Science*, 128 (1958), 1402–5; Ernest Nagel, 'Teleological Explanation and Teleological Systems', in Feigl and Brodbeck, eds., *Readings in the Philosophy of Science*, pp. 537–58; Karl A. Sinnhuber, 'Karl Ritter 1779–1859', *Scottish Geographical Magazine*, 75 (1959), 160.

⁶⁵Waismann, 'Analytic-Synthetic' [see n. 6], *Analysis*, 13 (1952), 2. 'The fact that an ethnologist can describe in circumlocution certain distinctions in kin that are *customarily* made by the Hopi does not alter his conclusion that the Hopi name kin and behave towards them differently from us' (Harry Hoijer, review of Roger W. Brown, *Words and Things in Language*, 35 [1959], 496–503, on p. 501). For a range of views on metalinguistics see Eric H. Lenneberg, 'Cognition in Ethnolinguistics', *Language*, 29 (1953), 463–71; Franklin Fearing, 'An Examination of the Conceptions of Benjamin Whorf in the Light of Theories of Perception and Cognition', in Hoijer, ed., *Language and Culture*, pp. 47–81; Anatol Rapoport and Arnold Horowitz, 'The Sapir-Whorf-Korzybski Hypothesis: a Report and a Reply', *ETC.* 17 (1960), 346–63.

⁶⁶*Out of the Silent Planet* (New York: Macmillan, 1952), p. 40.

⁶⁷For Helmholtz, see Cassirer, *Philosophy of Symbolic Forms*, Vol. 3, pp. 131–2. On changes in apparent colour and size, see T. N. Cornsweet et al., 'Changes in the Perceived Color of Very Bright Stimuli', *Science*, 128 (1958), 898–9; Dorothea Jameson and Leo M. Hurvich, 'Perceived Color and Its Dependence on Focal, Surrounding, and Preceding Stimulus Variables', *Journal of the Optical Society of America*, 49 (1959), 890–8; Wolfgang Köhler, *Dynamics in Psychology* (New York: Grove Press, 1960 [1940]), pp. 84–6.

⁶⁸'Without the conception of the individual and his needs, a distinction between illusion and "true" cognition cannot be made' (Horace B. English, 'Illusion as a Problem in Systematic Psychology', *Psychological Review*, 58 [1951], 52–3). The size and shape of objects seem appropriately and necessarily constant, but most of us can afford to be 'fooled' by the apparent bending of a stick half-submerged in water.

⁶⁹Cornish, *Scenery and the Sense of Sight*, p. 22. On the dissimilar impressions of identical

shapes and colours, see Karl Duncker, 'The Influence of Past Experience upon Perceptual Properties', *American Journal of Psychology*, 52 (1939), 255–65; Jerome S. Bruner and Leo Postman, 'Expectation and the Perception of Color', *American Journal of Psychology*, 64 (1951), 216–27, Arthur Kapp, 'Colour-Image Synthesis with Two Unorthodox Primaries', *Nature*, 184 (1959), 710–13; Edwin H. Land, 'Experiments in Color Vision', *Scientific American*, 200, No. 5 (May 1959), 84–99.

[70] 'Navy Research on Color Vision', *Naval Research Reviews* (October 1959), p. 19.

[71] *The Face of the Earth; with Some Hints for Those About to Travel* (Indianapolis: Bobbs-Merrill, 1951), p. 52.

[72] Vernon, *A Further Study of Visual Perception*, p. 255.

[73] H. A. Witkin et al., *Personality Through Perception: an Experimental and Clinical Study* (New York: Harper 1954); Herman A. Witkin, 'The Perception of the Upright', *Scientific American*, 200, No. 2 (February 1959), 51–6.

[74] Polanyi, *Personal Knowledge*, pp. 19–20, recounts this and similar episodes. H. J. Eysenck, 'Personality and the Perception of Time', *Perceptual and Motor Skills*, 9 (1959), 405–6, shows that introverts and extroverts clock the passage of time at systematically different rates. See also John R. Kirk and George D. Talbot, 'The Distortion of Information', *ETC.* 17 (1959), 5–27; Melvin Wallace and Albert I. Rubin, 'Temporal Experience', *Psychological Bulletin*, 57 (1960), 221–3.

[75] C. C. Trowbridge, 'On Fundamental Methods of Orientation and "Imaginary" Maps', *Science*, 38 (1913), 891–2; Lynch, *Image of the City*, pp. 88–9, 136–7. See also T. A. Ryan and M. S. Ryan, 'Geographical Orientation', *American Journal of Psychology*, 53 (1940), 204–15.

[76] Jerome S. Bruner and Cecile C. Goodman, 'Value and Need as Organizing Factors in Perception', *Journal of Abnormal and Social Psychology*, 42 (1947), 33–44. Further tests yielded significant differences in size estimation principally when coins were judged from memory (Launor F. Carter and Kermit Schooler, 'Value, Need, and Other Factors in Perception', *Psychological Review*, 56 [1949], 200–7), but the initial general hypothesis has been substantially confirmed (J. S. Bruner and George S. Klein, 'The Functions of Perceiving: New Look Retrospect', in Bernard Kaplan and Seymour Wapner, eds., *Perspectives in Psychological Theory: Essays in Honor of Heinz Werner* [New York: International Universities Press, 1960], p. 67).

[77] George Santayana, *The Sense of Beauty; Being the Outline of Aesthetic Theory* [1896] (New York: Dover Publications, 1955), p. 3. 'I cannot', writes Gardner Murphy, 'find an area where hedonistic perceptual theory cannot apply' ('Affect and Perceptual Learning', *Psychological Review*, 63 [1956], 7).

[78] Anton Ehrenzweig, *The Psycho-Analysis of Artistic Hearing and Vision: an Introduction to a Theory of Unconscious Perception* (New York: Julian Press, 1953), p. 170. See also James J. Gibson and Eleanor J. Gibson, 'Perceptual Learning: Differentiation or Enrichment?' *Psychological Review*, 62 (1955), 32–41. Science is more often apt to be accelerated 'by the passionate, and even the egocentric partisan bias of researchers in favour of their own chosen methods or theories' than by disinterested impartiality (W. B. Gallie, 'What Makes a Subject Scientific?', *British Journal for the Philosophy of Science*, 8 [1957], 118–39, on p. 127). Metaphysical doctrines which can neither be proved nor disproved 'play regulative roles in scientific thinking' because 'they express ways of seeing the world which in turn suggest ways of exploring it' (J. W. N. Watkins, 'Confirmable and Influential Metaphysics', *Mind*, 67 [1958], 344–65, on pp. 360, 356).

[79] Graham Green, 'The Analysis of a Journey', *Spectator*, 155 (1935), 459–60. 'Even if we remember as many facts about Bolivia as about Sweden, this has little relevance to the relative importance of these two countries in our psychological world' (Robert B. MacLeod, 'The Phenomenological Approach to Social Psychology', *Psychological Review*, 54 [1947], 206).

[80] John Haddon, 'A View of Foreign Lands', *Geography*, 65 (1960), 286–9, on p. 286. If their view of South Africa is recognizable, the students' impressions of America leave more to be desired: 'America is a country of remarkably developed, highly polished young women, and oddly garbed, criminally inclined young men travelling at great speed in monstrous cars along superhighways from one skyscraping city to the next; the very largest cars contain millionaires with crew-cuts; everyone is chewing gum' (p. 286). Such stereotypes die hard, even face to face with contrary realities, as one traveller noted among Americans in Russia (Richard Dettering, 'An American Tourist in the Soviet Union: Some Semantic Reflections', *ETC.* 17 [1960], 173–201).

[81] Russell Brain, *The Nature of Experience* (London: Oxford University Press, 1959), p. 3.

[82] A. Alvarez, 'Intelligence on Tour', *Kenyon Review*, 21 (1959), 23–33, on p. 29; see

Henry James, *The Art of Travel*, Morton D. Zaubel, editor, (New York: Doubleday, 1958). The virtues of the personal slant on description are discussed by Freya Stark, 'Travel Writing: Facts or Interpretation?', *Landscape*, 9 (1960), 34, and Wright, 'Terrae Incognitae' [see n. 2], p. 8.

[83] William Blake, 'The Everlasting Gospel' [c. 1818], in *Selected Poetry and Prose*, pp. 317–28, on p. 324.

[84] Peter Green, 'Novelists and Travelers', *Cornhill Magazine*, 168 (1955), 39–54, on p. 49. 'Man can discover and determine the universe inside him only by thinking it in mythical concepts and viewing it in mythical images' (Cassirer, *Philosophy of Symbolic Forms*, Vol. 2, p. 199, see also pp. 83, 101).

[85] Ernest H. Hutten, '[review of] *Sigmund Freud: Life and Work*, Vol. 3, by Ernest Jones', *British Journal for the Philosophy of Science*, 10 (1959), 81. Experience always influences the severest logic: no matter how convinced a man is that heads and tails have exactly equal prospects, he is not likely to bet on tails if heads has come up the previous fifty times (Popper, *Logic of Scientific Discovery*, pp. 408, 415; John Cohen, *Chance, Skill, and Luck: the Psychology of Guessing and Gambling* [Baltimore: Penguin Books, 1960, pp. 29, 191]). See also Ernst Topitsch, 'World Interpretation and Self-Interpretation: Some Basic Patterns', *Daedalus*, 88 (Spring 1959), 312.

[86] Hutten, op. cit., p. 79; Quine, 'Scope and Language of Science' [see n. 5], p. 2.

[87] Portmann, 'The Seeing Eye', *Landscape*, 9 (1959), 18. See also D. O. Hebb, *The Organization of Behavior; a Neuropsychological Theory* (New York: Wiley, 1949), p. 109; Felix Deutsch, 'Body, Mind, and Art', in *The Visual Arts Today*, special issue of *Daedalus*, 89 (Winter 1960), 34–45, on p. 38; Edward S. Tauber and Maurice R. Green, *Prelogical Experience: an Inquiry into Dreams and Other Creative Processes* (New York: Basic Books, 1959), p. 33.

[88] Magorah Maruyama, 'Communicable and Incommunicable Realities', *British Journal for the Philosophy of Science*, 10 (1959), 50–4; Margaret Mead, 'The Implications of Culture Change for Personality Development'. *American Journal of Orthopsychiatry*, 17 (1947), 633–46, on p. 639.

[89] Boulding, *The Images*, p. 6; Ewald Hering, *Grundzüge der Lehre vom Lichisinn* (Berlin: Springer, 1920), pp. 6 ff.; quoted in Cassirer, *Philosophy of Symbolic Forms*, Vol. 3, pp. 132–3. See also J. S. Bruner and Leo Postman, 'On the Perception of Incongruity: a Paradigm', in Beardslee and Wertheimer, *Readings in Psychology*, pp. 662–3; Bruner and Klein, 'Functions of Perceiving' [see n. 78], p. 63.

[90] Maurice Grosser, *The Painter's Eye* (New York: Rinehart, 1951), p. 232.

[91] David Hume, *A Treatise of Human Nature* [1739], Book I, part iv, sec. vi; Money-Kyrle, *Man's Picture of His World*, p. 107; Vasco Pratolini, *The Nakes Streets* (New York: A. A. Wyn, 1952), p. 204.

[92] Kluckhohn, 'Culture and Behavior' [see n. 48], p. 939; Lynch, *Image of the City*, p. 126.

[93] As natives of places we acquire and assimilate information differently than we do as travellers; and personal observation, whether sustained or casual, yields impressions different in quality and impact from those we build out of lectures, books, pictures, or wholly imaginary visions. The climates of each of these modes of geographical experience, and the kind of information they tend to yield about the world, will be considered in a series of essays to which this one is meant to be introductory.

[94] Quoted in C. V. Wedgwood, *Truth and Opinion: Historical Essays* (London: Collins, 1960), p. 11.

8.   SOCIAL SPACE IN INTERDISCIPLINARY PERSPECTIVE

A. Buttimer

Dramatic and exciting challenges confront geographers today. Revolutionary changes in empirical social patterns have spelled obsolescence for many traditional analytical procedures; radical transformations in the scholastic world have raised questions concerning the philosophical basis of social-science procedures. Behaviourists and existentialists pose the fundamental question: can science continue to serve a useful function by measuring and explaining the objective face and underlying mechanics of social reality, or must it also penetrate and incorporate its subjective dimensions?[1] As Edward T. Hall[2] so convincingly poses it: does time talk, does space speak? How does the silent language of time and space influence mankind's cultural variations? Geographers ask themselves: should we be satisfied with drafting an opaque, objective map of social patterns in space, or must we supplement this with the subjective or inside view?[3]

This problem is certainly not new. Jules Sion's 1908 study of Normandy showed how differences in the mentality of Norman and Picard peasants reflected and reinforced the contrasts between two physically similar regions.[4] Pierre Gourou's cleverly applied notion of *civilization* proved how attitudes and skills influenced the evolution of landscape in the Far East.[5] Walter Firey's well-known Boston study[6] demonstrated how cultural variations and traditions have influenced land values in an urban area, and Renée Rochefort's Sicilian study[7] left little doubt concerning the predominant influence in social life on that island: the Mafia! In principle, and in practice, then, substantive work demonstrates the need for a penetrating analysis of this subjective component in geographical study. A recent article by Paul Claval[8] even suggests that the geographer's unique contribution might well be in comparative cross-cultural studies of group mentality. Few scholars, however, have given concrete and applicable research leads to this kind of analytical endeavour. Among those who have introduced some creative precedents along these lines are two French scholars, Maximilien Sorre and Paul-Henri Chombart de Lauwe, who developed the notion of social space. The present paper is an attempt to sketch certain dimensions of the social-space concept that developed through the dialogue between geographer and sociologist in France, and to discuss its application in urban research today.

Sorre, a traditional geographer with an eye to many new horizons, and Chombart de Lauwe, a sociologist-ethnologist with an equally ecumenical horizon, have many characteristics in common. Both can be considered, in a sense, as prophets unacceptable in their own country. French geographers have paid little overt tribute to Sorre: they have tended to regard him as unorthodox, verbose, and perhaps inclined to confuse science and philosophy. Sociologists of the Sorbonne vintage have sometimes dismissed Chombart de Lauwe's work as superficial, value-laden, and marginal to the mainstream. However, if the French echo is faint, the international one is not; Sorre's ideas have claimed a wide audience in

From *Geographical Review*, 59 (1969), 417–26. Copyrights © 1969 by the American Geographical Society of New York. Reprinted by permission of the author and the Society.

disciplines outside geography, and the precedents laid down by Chombart de Lauwe have been welcomed by many schools of sociology and regional planning.

Among Sorre's many contributions to geography are the liaisons that he forged with other disciplines, particularly with biology and sociology. Volume 1 of his *chef d'oeuvre, Les Fondements de la géographie humaine,*[9] is permeated with an ecological theme, as its subtitle 'Les fondements biologiques de la géographie humaine' indicates. Volume 2 has a more sociological, and sometimes psychological, theme—social groupings were placed within the context of their environment and treated as 'techniques of social life'—and Volume 3 deals with settlement patterns as the visible inscription of group activity, attitude, and cultural tradition in the rural landscape. It was in the third volume of Sorre's *Fondements* that Chombart de Lauwe found inspiration for his now famous study of Paris,[10] in which he applied and extended the notion of 'social space', loosely defined by Sorre.

From his younger colleague's research Sorre then drew conclusions and wrote during the 1950s on further applications of his social-space concept.[11] At the same time Chombart de Lauwe and his colleagues were advancing along new fronts, leaning more towards urban problems and related spatial planning.

The Concept of Social Space

The concept of social space was first articulated and applied in the 1890s by Émile Durkheim, whose approach to the study of social differentiation was somewhat innovative. Durkheim objected to the environmentalism of Friedrich Ratzel's *Anthropogeographie*, to the evolutionism implicit in Herbert Spencer's *Principles of Sociology*, and to the formalism of Georg Simmel's *Soziale Differenzierung.*[12] Durkheim saw social differentiation in purely social terms: sociology consisted of social morphology, which is the study of the *substrat social* (distribution of social forms), and of social physiology, which is the study of the segmentation, interaction, and 'moral density' of society.[13] His definition of the *substrat social* was the social environment, or group framework, independent of the physical setting. Sorre considered Durkheim's definition of environment too narrow and cited many instances where physical conditions influenced social differentiation.[14] He believed the *substrat social* should incorporate both the physical and social environments, and for this twofold *substrat* he used Durkheim's term 'social space', qualifying the original meaning to include the physical environment.

In the analysis of social space, the geographer's basic contribution would seem to consist primarily of mapping the distribution of various social groups (Durkheim's 'social morphology'). However, the regional monographs of the Vidalian School also contributed to social physiology, showing, for example, the creative role of human groups in transforming their environment (*substrat*).[15] To place the concept of social space within Sorre's over-all framework for human geography, we must recall a few general points laid out in the *Fondements*. For Sorre, social life was an integral unity, and thus patterns of organization—from family and kinship groups to nation states and political blocs—were 'techniques' of social life.[16] Consequently, he considered political space (the *Lebensraum* of a particular nation) or economic space (functional regions surrounding the *pôles de croissance*) to be constituent dimensions of social space. When he discussed the spaces of a more purely social nature (for example, religious, ethnic, or linguistic space), his language became confused and somewhat ambiguous.

On a global scale, then, Sorre envisioned social space as a mosaic of areas, each homogeneous in terms of the space perceptions of its inhabitants. Within each of the areas a network of points and lines radiating from certain *points privilégié* (theatres, schools, churches, and other foci of social movement) could be identified. Each group tended to have its own specific social space, which reflected its particular values, preferences, and aspirations. The density of social space reflected the complementarity, and consequently the degree of interaction, between groups.[17] This sounded unorthodox to Sorre's fellow geographers, but it inspired Chombart de Lauwe in sociology, who applied Sorre's ideas in empirical urban studies. Let us now examine some of these applications.

Perception of Habitat and Urban Social Space

Chombart de Lauwe's famous 1952 team study of Paris illustrated new dimensions of the social-space concept. A distinction appeared, for example, between the objective and the subjective components of social space.[18] Objective social space was defined as 'the spatial framework in which groups live; groups whose social structure and organization have been conditioned by ecological and cultural factors'. Subjective social space was defined as 'space as perceived by members of particular human groups',[19] Practically, then, urban spatial patterns were studied on two levels: each *arrondissement, quartier,* and *secteur* was described first in objective terms—that is, the spatial setting with its physical boundaries and communications network—and then in terms of the perceived dimensions and characteristics of that segment as these were subjectively identified by the occupants. In many cases objective and subjective 'spaces' failed to coincide— subjective space reflecting values, aspirations, and cultural traditions that consciously or unconsciously distorted the objective dimensions of the environment.

The habitat-perception theme (*conceptions de l'habitation*) well illustrates the continuity between Sorre's original formula for social space and Chombart de Lauwe's subsequent research.[20] In Volume 3 of the *Fondements*, Sorre suggested that every life style (*genre de vie*) tended to inscribe itself in a typical habitat form. In the case of rural habitat, for example, he showed how work rhythms, agricultural regimes, social structure, and economic activities were related to house types and village patterns. He wrote at length on the 'ecology of rural life', on the harmonious nexus binding society, economy, and geographical environment into a cohesive whole, which was reflected in a region's habitat forms. But in the urban context Sorre's ecological formula failed to explain or describe the habitat in functional terms. Like Vidal de la Blache, Sorre was a ruralite at heart, and though he paid homage to urbanization as a tremendous social feat, he consistently deplored the debilitating influence of smog, pollution, racial disharmony, and the rupture of his beloved 'habitat ecology'. It was Chombart de Lauwe who really explored the ecology of urban habitat.[21] Two cardinal concepts that permeate his work are social space on the one hand and social milieu on the other.

Social Space

For Chombart de Lauwe, urban social space connotes a hierarchy of spaces, within which groups live, move, and interact.[22] First there is 'familial space', or the network of relationships characteristic of the domestic level of social interaction; then 'neighbourhood space', or the network that encompasses daily and local movement; 'economic space', which embraces certain employment centres; and finally the 'urban sector', or 'urban regional' social space. The progressively larger and overlapping dimensions of these spatial horizons reflect daily, weekly, and occasional orbits of group social activity and constitute the normal spatial framework within which groups feel at ease.

Chombart de Lauwe has calculated thresholds in space beyond which certain groups cannot travel without experiencing frustrations, tensions, and feelings of *anomie*; such thresholds provide useful references for the urban planner and constitute critical indexes of what a satisfactory housing or neighbourhood unit might be.[23] An interesting complication arises, however, in that socio-professional groups differ significantly from one another in their perceptions of space. For each socio-professional group a general characteristic pyramid or hierarchy of spaces could be discerned, and numerous combinations of these hierarchies could be found within an urban region.[24] Viewed horizontally, then, social space comprises a network of roughly concentric bands or sectors that circumscribe the orbits of daily, weekly, and occasional circulation.[25]

Chombart de Lauwe has also explored the vertical dimension of social space. How many square feet per person constitute a desirable residential density? Few objective indices of satisfactory levels of residential density exist, though various density thresholds have been proposed for animals.[20] The effects of crowding and stress have been studied,[27] and the United States Office of Civil and Defense Mobilization has made specific recommendations concerning adequate space per person in shelters.[28] These indices, however, pertain to abnormal circumstances and provide tolerance thresholds under duress rather than optimal levels under normal conditions. When Chombart de Lauwe analysed residential conditions among working-class families in Paris, he discovered that a density of 10–13 square metres of space per person per dwelling unit was optimal.[29] Where the density was less than 8–10 square metres per person, crime rates, *anomie*, and tension increased, probably because of overcrowding. Where the density was more than 14 square metres, other social and psychological problems arose, stemming from the patterns of parent-child relationships characteristic of an upwardly mobile socio-economic class.[30] As a result, a specific, objective index of residential density desirable for one socio-economic class was derived.

In retrospect, then, whereas Soree's criteria for the delimitation of areas within social space were based on macroscopic and universal categories such as language and ethnic groups, nation states, and *genres de vie*, Chombart de Lauwe's criteria were microscopic and more sociological (for example, socio-economic and special-interest groups). The contrast between them is not only in the approach, but also in the scale: one applies to the world in general and to rural settlement in particular; the other is strictly oriented to the urban environment.

Social Milieu

In the urban context also, a complementary notion occurs in Chombart de Lauwe's work, namely the concept of social milieu. What is meant by social milieu? Every schoolboy knows that life in the Quartier Latin is not the same as life on Montmartre, nor is Montparnasse comparable to the XXe arrondissement, but what definition or formula could specify the actual ingredients that make up the social milieu of these places? Chombart de Lauwe identified three distinct levels: *milieu géographique*, or time-space framework; *milieu technique* or level of technological equipment; and *milieu culturel*, or the traditional atmosphere perceived by the inhabitants or ascribed by others.[31] All three levels, in vital combination, constitute the effective social milieu, in the context of which all social behaviour should be placed.

But how are these three levels to be separated for systematic analysis, while simultaneously maintaining a holistic conception of social milieu? Chombart de Lauwe criticizes the factor-analytic approach evident in American sociology; he refuses to employ such terms as 'factors' and 'elements', or to use other concepts that imply a unidirectional pattern of relationships. He regards it as more important to decipher the intricate and complex fibre that holds a milieu together than to deal with the actual mechanics of specific parts. Thus he speaks of variables that pattern themselves around certain recognizable ensembles. In practice, however, his own methodological procedure could be regarded as simply a carefully designed factor analysis of five major groups of phenomena: (1) population patterns within a time-space framework; (2) economic-activity patterns; (3) social groupings, relationships, behaviour, and attitudes; (4) communications and cultural and spiritual life; and (5) educational level.[32] Each of these ensembles, then, constitutes a system, or organic whole, vitally linked with other ensembles by the value system, attitudes, and needs of its component groups. We see again the relationship between social milieu and the emergence of social-space hierarchies for particular groups. It is in fact the combined contrasts of social-milieu and social-space hierarchies that constitute the basic differences between eastern, western, and central Paris.[33]

Sorre's Resume: Avenues for Co-operative Research

By the late 1950s Sorre could recapitulate his original ideas and could modify, contradict, and refine some of his original suggestions. He no doubt rejoiced to see empirical evidence that space assumed different meanings in the life patterns of different groups and that these differences influenced the geography of Paris. But did this apparent success also threaten obsolescence? Were these findings proof that physical 'geographical' space was of little significance in urban study? On the contrary, Sorre cautioned that the problem for an urban geographer was not so much one of slicing up social space into a series of component 'spaces', as of examining how these were harmonized in the concrete life situations of particular urban regions.[34] From the Paris study, there was some evidence, for example, that when a group's aspirations transcended their attainable horizons, or when spatially juxtaposed groups held widely contrasting ideas about space, tensions arose, which influenced spatial movements, thus affecting the geography of that sector of the city.

The Paris findings reinforced some of Sorre's original hunches (for example, that the social rift which persisted in the dormitory village of Petit-Clamart was entirely due to differences of *genre de vie*)[35] and dispelled others (for example, the necessary relationship between habitation form and *genre de vie* in the urban context). Ecological principles governing rural habitat could not be applied in the urban context where functional relations between work and home were entirely different, and there was no obvious harmony of social structure, life style, and settlement type such as that found in the Breton hamlet or in the Lorraine village.

One of the most valuable conclusions Sorre drew was that geographer and sociologist could co-operate in the study of such complex questions as social mobility and migrations.[36] Only through such collaboration could one discover how social mobility relates to spatial mobility or unravel the psychological ties that make certain settlement forms forces that stabilize and others forces that stimulate migration of rural and urban groups. Resistance to change—for instance, the inertia of the *vignoble* in Bas-Languedoc, of the mining communities of Lorraine, of the textile workers of Lancashire—provided suitable subjects for interdisciplinary work. Thus throughout the late 1950s—and especially in his *nunc dimittis* volume, *L'Homme sur la terre*—Sorre repeatedly advocated collaboration between geographers and sociologists.[37]

Chombart de Lauwe and Spatial Preferences

Since the early 1960s Chombart de Lauwe and his team have advanced along many new fronts.[38] *L'Intégration du citadin à sa ville et à son quartier*,[39] for example, approached the study of social space on three levels: on the behavioural level (where and how people live and move), on the level of knowledge (where people know that alternative opportunities are available), and on the aspirational level (where people would like to go if they had the opportunity). The whole tone of their research has thus taken on a behavioural orientation, which again affords a potential link with current research in geography, the *géographie volontaire*,[40] so popular among French scholars at the present time.

Three questions, then, are posed. Where do Parisians live? Where would they like to live? And what prevents them from living where they wish? Parisians evidently would like to live outside the metropolitan area, and would migrate if their employer would move. But there are marked differences in the attitudes of socio-economic groups regarding a choice of locale. Working-class families on the whole, if their housing conditions are reasonably good, do not want to leave Paris; but most other groups believe that the ideal place to live would be 'en province'. The three major poles of attraction are the Alps, the Midi, and Brittany, and the optimum size of the receiving town is in the neighbourhood of 100,000 to 400,000 population.

Analysis of the internal spatial preferences yield more clear-cut differences among socio-professional groups.[41] (1) The flight to the suburbs is made primarily by the liberal professionals and the more wealthy executives. If industrial workers' families move at all, it is to the 'inner suburbs', where they still have access to public transportation facilities. Persons employed in service activities tend to remain near the centre, close to their clientele. (2) For most occupational groups the ideal place to live is in a neighbourhood that has some kind of identity. This identity can be defined by clear-cut physical boundaries, by a traditional reputation, by a commercial atmosphere, or by other special earmarks that people attach to that environment. (3) Tendencies towards spatial segregation for social reasons are most marked among the clerks and office workers, are less marked among industrial workers, and are scarcely evident at all among the service-occupation group. Residential segregation and spatial mobility go hand in hand in most cases. (4) Among the most highly prized characteristics of an ideal place to live are privacy, space, and the freedom to choose either participation or no involvement in local life.

These generalizations offer interesting points of comparison with patterns evident in other countries. The evolving spatial order of metropolitan suburbs in the United States follows less definite lines, but also reveals a response to socially held values and attitudes. Recent literature suggests an increasing social consciousness in the design and selection of residential areas, and a correlative decline in the importance of economic forces.[42] Thus whatever the social or political context, we find a widespread acceptance of planning for social preferences rather than individual responses to the laws of a market economy, as a major determinant of spatial form today.

Practical Applications

On the basis of these French precedents one may speculate on the practical utility of the social-space concept in urban analysis today. On the whole, its primary value perhaps is in the connections postulated between the internal subjective order (attitudes, traditions, and aspirations) and the external spatial order, within an urban milieu. Research on these connections parallels recent work in other fields.

Notions akin to social space (for example, ethnic domain, biotope, and so on) can be found in anthropology, but for the most part they are approached from an ecological or psychological point of view. A biotope is defined in social psychology as the 'habitat or locale to which an organism is attracted through some combination of learning, imprinting, and instinct'.[43] An ecological approach to the study of such biotopes is demonstrated in Barth's study of ethnic communities in North Pakistan,[44] and Hall's 'science of proxemics' applies similar concepts to urban analysis.[45] Chombart de Lauwe's work would suggest, in these terms, that every biotope has an internal hierarchial structure composed of personal, familial, neighbourhood, and regional spaces, and second, that this structure varies from one socio-economic group to another. This raises the question of whether individuals within particular professional groups have a consistent pattern of biotope preferences with respect to housing design and location, to recreational needs, and to the propensity to move. Is there, for instance, any consistent relationship between workaday ('proximate') space facilities—for example, in office, classroom or factory—and the weekend recreational preferences? Is there a relationship between the lack of sensory stimulation in routine urban occupations and the quest for sensory stimulation in outdoor recreational activities during vacations? Again, how is adjustment to biotope (defined in ecological and psychological terms) related to turnover rates in suburban housing developments? The spatial order of metropolitan fringe areas provides a fascinating field of research when viewed from this perspective.

Another possibility for the co-operative work between geographer and sociologist suggested by Sorre lies in the realm of mobility and migrations. It is a cliché that spatial mobility is closely associated with social mobility among middle-class Americans; however, the class differentials in propensity to move within metropolitan suburbs are less well defined than was previously imagined.[46] Chombart de Lauwe has unravelled some of the motivations behind changes of residence in the Parisian context and has shown that failure to attain the ideal leads to psychotic disorders and social tensions.[47] The notion of social space has thus served as a heuristic and seminal concept, producing a number of distinct research orientations, each of which could be analysed more incisively by specialists in different disciplines. It may serve in the future as a co-ordinating framework for interdisciplinary research on the subjective dimensions of human behaviour in space. Like so many other rich ideas in the history of social science, the distintegration and demise of social space as a single unified analytical concept is simply the necessary prelude to a new harvest of research endeavours.

Sorre and Chombart de Lauwe in Perspective

Despite their common philosophical and methodological ideas, Sorre and Chombart de Lauwe differed radically in one respect: Sorre could never reconcile himself to the idea of planning, whereas Chombart de Lauwe's work is almost entirely directed towards practical goals. This perhaps reflects a difference of generation, Sorre representing the prewar bourgeois 'knowledge for knowledge's sake' tradition, and Chombart de Lauwe the postwar *avant-garde* style of non-academic applied knowledge. Because of their fundamental difference in outlook, their writings must be evaluated from a different perspective. Sorre's work is essentially a kind of armchair conceptualization, which can serve as a preamble to, and an organizational framework for, empirical research. Chombart de Lauwe, on the other hand, seemingly so anxious to arrive at quick solutions to urgent social problems, often appears to slide too rapidly through the analytical part to arrive at readily applicable results.

In retrospect, what these two scholars have given us is a set of conceptual guidelines rather than readily usable research formulas. Sorre, the great humanist, has bequeathed excellent textbooks for teaching social geography, but he did not establish a research school; he had few students who, overtly at least, followed up his proposed leads. Chombart de Lauwe could in many ways be considered as the first great internationalist among French sociologists since the time of Marcel Mauss and Maurice Halbwachs. He has simplified and integrated many conceptual lines developed in American, German, and British schools of social science, and thus has helped to stimulate dialogue among the various traditions as well as among the specialists within particular schools. He calls for a common language that will enable sociologists to communicate with architects and engineers and that will permit citizens and planners to collaborate in the creation of the new social environment.

NOTES AND REFERENCES

[1] Martin G. Plattel: *Social Philosophy* (Pittsburgh, 1965); A. C. de Waehlens: *L'Existentialisme de Merleau-Ponty* (Brussels, 1963).

[2] Edward T. Hall: *The Silent Language* (Premier Books; New York, 1965). See also id. *The Hidden Dimension* (Garden City, N. Y., 1966).

[3] Paul Claval: 'Géographie et psychologie des peuples', *Rev. de Psychologie des Peuples*, 21 (1966), 386–401; id.: *Essai sur l'évolution de la géographie humaine* (Paris, 1964). See also R. W. Kates and J. F. Wohlwill, eds.: 'Man's Response to the Physical Environment', *Journ. of Social Issues*, 22, No. 4 (1966).

[4] Jules Sion: *Les Paysans de la Normandie orientale: Pays de Caux, Bray, Vexin Normand, Vallée de la Seine/ Étude géographique* (Paris, 1909). See also the review of this work by Paul Vidal de la Blache in the *Annales de Géographie* 18 (1909), 177–81?

[5] Pierre Gourou: 'Étude du tropical.', *L'Annuaire du collège de France*, 63 (1962–3), 261–75; id.: 'Changes in Civilization and Their Influence on Landscape', *Impact*, 14 (1964), 57–71.

[6] Walter Firey: *Land Use in Central Boston* (Cambridge, Mass., 1947).

[7] Renée Rochefort: *Le Travail en Sicile*, (Paris, 1961).

[8] 'Géographie et psychologie des peuples' [see note 3 above].

[9] Maximilien Sorre: *Les Fondements de la géographie humaine* (3 vols.; Paris, 1943–52). For a summary of Sorre's publications, see Françoise Grivot: 'Bibliographie des oeuvres de Max. Sorre, *Annales de Géographie*, 72 (1963), 186–91.

[10] See the introductory statement by Chombart de Lauwe in *Paris et l'agglomération parisienne* (by P.-H. Chombart de Lauwe and others; 2 vols.; Paris, 1952), Vol. 1, pp. 19–26.

[11] Maximilien Sorre: *Les Migrations des peuples: Essai sur la mobilité géographique* (Paris, 1955): *Rencontres de la géographie et de la sociologie* (Paris, 1957); and 'La Géographie psychologique: L'adaptation au milieu climatique et biosocial', in *Traité de psychologie appliquée* (Paris, 1958), Vol. 6, chap. 3. pp. 1343–93.

[12] Émile Durkheim: *De la division du travail social* (Paris, 1893; 5th ed., 1926). See also id: *Les Règles de la méthode sociologique* (Paris, 1895); Friedrich Ratzel: *Anthropogeographie* (2

vols.; Stuttgart, 1882 and 1891); Herbert Spencer: *Principles of Sociology* (London, 1876); and Georg Simmel: *Soziale Differenzierung* (Berlin, 1890).

[13] *De la division du travail social* [see note 12 above].

[14] Sorre, *Rencontres de la géographie et de la sociologie* [see note 11 above], chap. 1.

[15] Ibid.

[16] Maximilien Sorre: *L'Homme sur la terre* (Paris, 1961).

[17] Maximilien Sorre: 'L'Espace du géographe et due sociologue', in *Rencontres de la géographie et de la sociologie* [see note 11 above], pp. 87–114.

[18] Chombart de Lauwe and others, op. cit. [see note 10 above]. See also Paul-Henri Chombart de Lauwe: *Paris: Essais de sociologie* (Paris, 1966).

[19] Chombart de Lauwe and others, *Paris et l'agglomération parisienne* [see note 10 above], and Chombart de Lauwe, *Essais de sociologie* [see note 18 above], pp. 96–101.

[20] Paul-Henri Chombart de Lauwe: *Famille et habitation*: Vol. 1: *La Vie quotidienne des familles ouvrières* (Paris, 1956), and Vol. 2: *Science humaines et conceptions de l'habitation* (Paris, 1959).

[21] Chombart de Lauwe's ecological and integrative tone is best illustrated in his lectures and articles; for example, in his lecture on 'Sociologie, sciences humaines et transformations sociales', delivered at Louvain in November 1966, and published in *Revue de l'Enseignement Supérieur*, 1–2 (1965), 11–19. See also his *'Des hommes et des villes'* (Paris, 1965).

[22] Paul-Henri Chombart de Lauwe: 'L'Évolution des besoins et la conception dynamique de la famille', *Rev. Francaise de Sociologie*, 1 (1960), 403–25; and id.: 'Le Milieu social et l'étude sociologique des cas individuels', *Information Sociales*, 2 (February 1959), 41–55.

[23] *Famille et habitation* [see note 20 above], Vol. 1; *Des hommes et des villes* [see note 21 above]. For the pathological consequences of unattained horizons, see Paul-Henri Chombart de Lauwe: 'Hypotheses pour une psychosociologie de la fatigue', *Rev. de Medecine Psychosomatique et de Psychologie Medicale*, 3 (1966), 275–86.

[24] Chombart de Lauwe, *Des hommes et des villes* [see note 21 above].

[25] Chombart de Lauwe and others, *Paris et l'agglomration parisienne* [see note 10 above].

[26] Neal M. Burns, R. M. Chambers, and E. Hendler: *Unusual Environments and Human Behavior* (New York, 1963).

[27] John B. Calhoun: 'Population Density and Social Pathology', *Scientific American*, 206, No. 2 (1962), 139–48; W. Craig: 'Why Do Animals Fight?', *Internat'l. Journ. of Ethics*, 31 (1921), 264–78.

[28] 'Guide for Executives' (Office of Civil and Defense Mobilization, Battle Creek, Mich., 1959 [OCDM NP-10-1]); 'Guide for Architects and Engineers' (ibid., 1960 [OCDM NP-10-2]). See also 'Procedures for Managing Large Fallout Shelters' (Dunlap and Associates, Stanford, Calif., 1959).

[29] Chombart de Lauwe, *Famille et habitation* [see note 20 above], Vol. 2.

[30] Hall, *The Hidden Dimension* [see note 2 above], pp. 161–2.

[31] This is emphasized particularly in 'Le Rôle de l'obsérvation en sociologie' *(Rev. de l'Institut de Sociologie* [Université Libre de Bruxelles], 1, No. 1 (1960), 27–43).

[32] Ibid. See also 'Le Milieu social et l'étude sociologique des cas individuels' [see note 22 above].

[33] *Paris et l'agglomération parisienne* [see note 10 above], Vol. 1, pp. 68 ff.

[34] *Rencontres de la géographic et de la sociologie* [see note 11 above].

[35] Chombart de Lauwe and others: *Paris et l'agglomération parisienne*, [see note 10 above], Vol. 1, p. 243.

[36] *Rencontres de la géographie et de la sociologie* [see note 11 above], pp. 53–86.

[37] Ibid. See also *L'Homme sur la terre* [see note 16 above], pp. 96–101.

[38] The headquarters of the main group, the 'Centre d'Ethnologie Sociale', is at Montrouge. There one finds interdisciplinary research on the general theme, 'evolution of social life', subsidized by the Centre National de Recherche Scientifique. An interesting offshoot, the 'Centre d'Etudes des Groupes Sociaux', works on practical problems relating to urban planning, for example, work on the decentralization policy now being implemented in Paris.

[39] 4 vols.; Paris, 1962–5. See also their *Logement et vie familiale: Étude sociologique des quartiers nouveaux* (Centre d'Étudesdes Groupes Sociaux, Paris, 1965), and *L'Attraction de Paris sur sa banlieue* (Paris, 1965).

[40] Jean Labasse's work is probably most illustrative of this new trend among French geographers; see his *L'Organisation de l'espace: Éléments de géographie volontaire* (Paris, 1966). See also Jean Gottmann: *Essais sur l'aménagement de l'espace habité* (Paris, 1966).

[41] These are some of the general results of the work, *L' Integration du citadin a sa ville et a son quartier* [see note 39 above].

[42] Donald J. Bogue: *The Structure of the Metropolitan Community* (Ann Arbor, 1949); William M. Dobriner: *Class in Suburbia* (Englewood Cliffs, N. J., 1963); Herbert J. Gans: *The Levittowners* (New York, 1967); Gerardus Antonius Wissink: *American Cities in Perspective, with Special Reference to the Development of Their Fringe Areas* (Assen, Neth., 1962).

[43] Robert Sommer: 'Man's Proximate Environment', *Journ. of Social Issues*, 22, No. 4 (1966), 59–70; reference on p. 62.

[44] Fredrik Barth: 'Ecologic Relationships of Ethnic Groups in Swat, North Pakistan', *Amer. Anthropologist*, 58 (1956), 1079–89.

[45] Hall, *The Hidden Dimension* [see note 2 above].

[46] See, for example, Walter T. Martin: *The Rural-Urban Fringe* (Eugene, Ore., 1953); Amos H. Hawley: *The Changing Shape of Metropolitan America* (Glencoe, Ill., 1956); R. E. Pahl: *Urbs in Rure: The Metropolitan Fringe in Hertfordshire*, London School of Economics and Political Science Geographical Papers No. 2, 1965.

[47] Chombart de Lauwe: *L'Attraction de Paris sur sa banlieue* [see note 39 above].

9. SENTIMENT AND SYMBOLISM AS ECOLOGICAL VARIABLES

W. Firey

Systematization of ecological theory has thus far proceeded on two main premisses regarding the character of space and the nature of locational activities. The first premiss postulates that the sole relation of space to locational activities is an impeditive and cost-imposing one. The second premiss assumes that locational activities are primarily economizing, 'fiscal' agents.[1] On the basis of these two premisses the only possible relationship that locational activities may bear to space is an economic one. In such a relationship each activity will seek so to locate as to minimize the obstruction put upon its functions by spatial distance. Since the supply of the desired locations is limited it follows that not all activites can be favoured with choice sites. Consequently a competitive process ensues in which the scarce desirable locations are pre-empted by those locational activities which can so exploit advantageous location as to produce the greatest surplus of income over expenditure. Less desirable locations devolve to correspondingly less economizing land uses. The result is a pattern of land use that is presumed to be most efficient for both the individual locational activity and for the community.[2]

Given the contractualistic milieu within which the modern city has arisen and acquires its functions, such an 'economic ecology' has had a certain explanatory adequacy in describing urban spatial structure and dynamics. However, as any theory matures and approaches a logical closure of its generalizations it inevitably encounters facts which remain unassimilable to the theoretical scheme. In this paper it will be our purpose to describe certain ecological processes which apparently cannot be embraced in a strictly economic analysis. Our hypothesis is that the data to be presented, while in no way startling or unfamiliar to the research ecologist, do suggest an alteration of the basic premisses of ecology. This alteration would consist, first, of ascribing to space not only an impeditive quality but also an additional property, viz. that of being at times a symbol for certain cultural values that have become associated with a certain spatial area. Second, it would involve a recognition that locational activities are not only economizing agents but may also bear sentiments which can significantly influence the locational process.[3]

A test case for this twofold hypothesis is afforded by certain features of land use in central Boston. In common with many of the older American cities Boston has inherited from the past certain spatial patterns and landmarks which have had a remarkable persistence and even recuperative power despite challenges from other more economic land uses. The persistence of these spatial patterns can only be understood in terms of the group values that they have come to symbolize. We shall describe three types of such patterns: first, an in-town upper-class residential neighbourhood known as Beacon Hill; second, certain 'sacred sites', notably the Boston Common and the colonial burying-grounds; and third, a lower-class Italian neighbourhood known as the North End. In each of these land uses we shall find certain locational processes which seem to defy a strictly economic analysis.

From *American Sociological Review*, 10 (1945), 140–48. Reprinted by permission of the author and the American Sociological Association.

The first of the areas, Beacon Hill, is located some five minutes' walking distance from the retail centre of Boston. This neighbourhood has for fully a century and a half maintained its character as a preferred upper-class residential district, despite its contiguity to a low-rent tenement area, the West End. During its long history Beacon Hill has become the symbol for a number of sentimental associations which constitute a genuine attractive force to certain old families of Boston. Some idea of the nature of these sentiments may be had from statements in the innumerable pamphlets and articles written by residents of the Hill. References to 'this sacred eminence',[4] 'stately old-time appearance',[5] and 'age-old quaintness and charm',[6] give an insight into the attitudes attaching to the area. One resident reveals rather clearly the spatial referability of these sentiments when she writes of the Hill:

It has a tradition all its own, that begins in the hospitality of a book-lover, and has never lost that flavour. Yes, our streets are inconvenient, steep, and slippery. The corners are abrupt, the contours perverse. . . . It may well be that the gibes of our envious neighbours have a foundation and that these dear crooked lanes of ours were indeed traced in ancestral mud by absent-minded kine.[7]

Behind such expressions of sentiment are a number of historical associations connected with the area. Literary traditions are among the strongest of these; indeed, the whole literary legend of Boston has its focus at Beacon Hill. Many of America's most distinguished literati have occupied homes on the Hill. Present-day occupants of these houses derive a genuine satisfaction from the individual histories of their dwellings.[8] One lady whose home had had a distinguished pedigree remarked: 'I like living here for I like to think that a great deal of historic interest has happened here in this room.' Not a few families are able to trace a continuity of residence on the Hill for several generations, some as far back as 1800 when the Hill was first developed as an upper-class neighbourhood. It is a point of pride to a Beacon Hill resident if he can say that he was born on the Hill or was at least raised there; a second-best boast is to point out that his forebears once lived on the Hill.

TABLE 1

Number of Upper-class Families in Boston,
by Districts of Concentration, and in Main Suburban Towns,
for Certain Years

	1894	1905	1914	1929	1943
Within Boston					
Beacon Hill	280	242	279	362	335
Back Bay	867	1,166	1,102	880	556
Jamaica Plain	56	66	64	36	30
Other districts	316	161	114	86	41
Suburban Towns					
Brookline	137	300	348	355	372
Newton	38	89	90	164	247
Cambridge	77	142	147	223	257
Milton	37	71	106	131	202
Dedham	8	29	48	69	99
Other towns	106	176	310	403	816
Total in Boston	1,519	1,635	1,559	1,364	962
Total in Suburbs	403	807	1,049	1,345	1,993
Totals	1,922	2,442	2,608	2,709	2,955

Tabulated from: *Social Register, Boston*

Thus a wide range of sentiments—aesthetic, historical, and familial—have acquired a spatial articulation in Beacon Hill. The bearing of these sentiments upon locational processes is a tangible one and assumes three forms: retentive, attractive, and resistive. Let us consider each of these in order. To measure the retentive influence that spatially referred sentiments may exert upon locational activities we have tabulated by place of residence all the families listed in the Boston *Social Register* for the years 1894, 1905, 1914, 1929, and 1943. This should afford a reasonably accurate picture of the distribution of upper-class families by neighbourhoods within Boston and in suburban towns. In Table 1 we have presented the tabulations for the three in-town concentrations of upper-class families (Beacon Hill, Back Bay, and Jamaica Plain) and for the five main suburban concentrations (Brookline, Newton, Cambridge, Milton, and Dedham). Figure 1 portrays these trends in graphic form. The most apparent feature of these data is of course, the consistent increase of upper-class families in the suburban towns and the marked decrease (since 1905) in two of the in-town upper-class areas, Back Bay and Jamaica Plain. Although both of these neighbourhoods remain fashionable residential districts their prestige is waning rapidly. Back Bay in particular, though still surpassing in numbers any other single neighbourhood, has undergone a steady

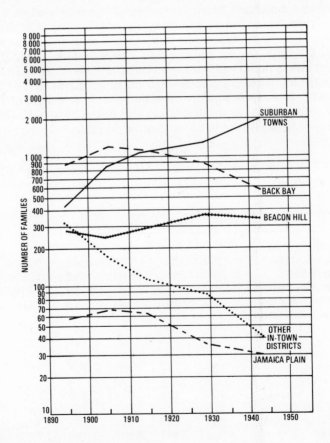

Fig. 1. Number of upper-class families in Boston, by districts of concentration, and in suburbs, for certain years.

invasion of apartment buildings, rooming houses, and business establishments which are destroying its prestige value. The trend of Beacon Hill has been different. Today it has a larger number of upper-class families than it had in 1894. Where it ranked second among fashionable neighbourhoods in 1894 it ranks third today, being but slightly outranked in numbers by the suburban city of Brookline and by the Back Bay. Beacon Hill is the only in-town district that has consistently retained its preferred character and has held to itself a considerable proportion of Boston's old families.

There is, however, another aspect to the spatial dynamics of Beacon Hill, one that pertains to the 'attractive' locational role of spatially referred sentiments. From 1894 to 1905 the district underwent a slight drop, subsequently experiencing a steady rise for 24 years, and most recently undergoing another slight decline. These variations are significant, and they bring out rather clearly the dynamic ecological role of spatial symbolism. The initial drop is attributable to the development of the then new Back Bay. Hundreds of acres there had been reclaimed from marshland and had been built up with palatial dwellings. Fashion now pointed to this as the select area of the city and in response to its dictates a number of families abandoned Beacon Hill to take up more pretentious Back Bay quarters. Property values on the Hill began to depreciate, old dwellings became rooming houses, and businesses began to invade some of the streets. But many of the old families remained on the Hill and a few of them made efforts to halt the gradual deterioration of the district. Under the aegis of a realtor, an architect, and a few close friends there was launched a programme of purchasing old houses, modernizing the interiors and leaving the colonial exteriors intact, and then selling the dwellings to individual families for occupancy. Frequently adjoining neighbours would collaborate in planning their improvements so as to achieve an architectural consonance. The results of this programme may be seen in the drift of upper-class families back to the Hill. From 1905 to 1929 the number of *Social Register* families in the district increased by 120. Assessed valuations showed a corresponding increase: from 1919 to 1924 there was a rise of 24 per cent; from 1924 to 1929 the rise was 25 per cent.[9] The nature of the Hill's appeal, and the kind of persons attracted, may be gathered from the following popular write-up:

To salvage the quaint charm of Colonial Architecture on Beacon Hill, Boston, is the object of a well-defined movement among writers and professional folk that promises the most delightful opportunities for the home seeker of moderate means and conservative tastes. Because men of discernment were able to visualize the possibilities presented by these architectural landmarks, and have undertaken the gracious task of restoring them to their former glory, this historic quarter of old Boston, once the centre of literary culture, is coming into its own.[10]

The independent variable in this 'attractive' locational process seems to have been the symbolic quality of the Hill, by which it constituted a referent for certain strong sentiments of upper-class Bostonians.

While this revival was progressing there remained a constant menace to the character of Beacon Hill, in the form of business encroachments and apartment-hotel developments. Recurrent threats from this source finally prompted residents of the Hill to organize themselves into the Beacon Hill Association. Formed in 1922, the declared object of this organization was 'to keep undesirable business and living conditions from affecting the hill district'.[11] At the time the city was engaged in preparing a comprehensive zoning programme and the occasion was propitious to secure for Beacon Hill suitable protective measures. A systematic set of recommendations was drawn up by the Association regarding a uniform 65-foot height limit for the entire Hill, the exclusion of business from all but two streets, and the restriction of apartment-house bulk.[12] It succeeded in gaining only a partial recognition of this programme in the 1924 zoning ordinance. But the Association continued its fight against inimical land uses year after year. In 1927 it successfully fought a petition brought before the Board of Zoning Adjustment to alter the height limits in one area so as to permit the construction of a four-million-dollar apartment-hotel 155 feet high. Residents of the Hill went to the hearing *en masse*. In spite of the prospect of an additional twenty million dollars' worth of exclusive apartment hotels that were promised if the zoning restrictions were withheld the petition was rejected, having been opposed by 214 of the 220 persons present at the hearing.[13] In 1930 the Association gained an actual reduction in height limits on most of Beacon street and certain adjoining streets, though its leader was denounced by opponents as 'a rank sentimentalist who desired to keep Boston a village'.[14] One year later the Association defeated a petition to rezone Beacon street for business purposes.[15] In other campaigns the Association successfully pressed for the rezoning of a business street back to purely residential purposes, for the lowering of height limits on the remainder of Beacon street, and for several lesser matters of local interest. Since 1929, owing partly to excess assessed valuations of Boston real estate and partly to the effects of the depression upon families living on securities, Beacon Hill has lost some of its older families, though its decline is nowhere near so precipitous as that of the Back Bay.

Thus for a span of one and a half centuries there have existed on Beacon Hill certain locational processes that largely escape economic analysis. It is the symbolic quality of the Hill, not its impeditive or cost-imposing character, that most tangibly correlates with the retentive, attractive, and resistive trends that we have observed. And it is the dynamic force of spatially referred sentiments, rather than considerations of rent, which explains why certain families have chosen to live on Beacon Hill in preference to other in-town districts having equally accessible location and even superior housing conditions. There is thus a non-economic aspect to land use on Beacon Hill, one which is in some respects actually diseconomic in its consequences. Certainly the large apartment-hotels and specialty shops that have sought in vain to locate on the Hill would have represented a fuller capitalization on potential property values than do residences. In all likelihood the attending increase in real-estate prices would not only have benefited individual property holders but would have so enhanced the value of adjoining properties as to compensate for whatever depreciation other portions of the Hill might have experienced.

If we turn to another type of land use pattern in Boston, that comprised by the Boston Common and the old burying-grounds, we encounter another instance of spatial symbolism which has exerted a marked influence upon the ecological organization of the rest of the city. The Boston Common is a survival from colonial days when every New England town allotted a portion of its land to common use as a cow pasture and militia field. Over the course of three centuries Boston has grown entirely around the Common so that today we find a 48-acre tract of land wedged directly into the heart of the business district. On three of its five sides are women's apparel shops, department stores, theatres, and other high-rent locational activities. On the fourth side is Beacon street, extending alongside Beacon Hill. Only the activities of Hill residents have prevented business from invading this side. The fifth side is occupied by the Public Garden. A land-value map portrays a strip of highest value pressing upon two sides of the Common, on Tremont and Boylston streets, taking the form of a long, narrow band.

Before considering the ecological consequences of this configuration let us see what attitudes have come to be associated with the Common. There is an extensive local literature about the Common and in it we find interesting sentiments expressed. One citizen speaks of: '. . . the great principle exemplified in the preservation of the Common. Thank Heaven, the tide of money making must break and go around that.'[16] Elsewhere we read: 'Here, in short, are all our accumulated memories, intimate, public, private.'[17] 'Boston Common was, is, and ever will be a source of tradition and inspiration from which the New Englanders may renew their faith, recover their moral force, and strengthen their ability to grow and achieve.[18] The Common has thus become a 'sacred' object, articulating and symbolizing genuine historical sentiments of a certain portion of the community. Like all such objects its sacredness derives, not from any intrinsic spatial attributes, but rather from its representation in people's minds as a symbol for collective sentiments.[19]

Such has been the force of these sentiments that the Common has become buttressed up by a number of legal guarantees. The city charter forbids Boston in perpetuity to dispose of the Common or any portion of it. The city is further prohibited by state legislation from building upon the Common, except within rigid limits, or from laying out roads or tracks across it.[20] By accepting the bequest of one George F. Parkman, in 1908, amounting to over five million dollars, the city is further bound to maintain the Common, and certain other parks, 'for the benefit and enjoyment of its citizens'.[21]

What all this has meant for the spatial development of Boston's retail centre is clear from the present character of that district. Few cities of comparable size have so small a retail district in point of area. Unlike the spacious department stores of most cities, those in Boston are frequently compressed within narrow confines and have had to extend in devious patterns through rear and adjoining buildings. Traffic in downtown Boston has literally reached the saturation point, owing partly to the narrow one-way streets but mainly to the lack of adequate arterials leading into and out of the Hub. The American Road Builders Association has estimated that there is a loss of $81,000 per day in Boston as a result of traffic delay. Trucking in Boston is extremely expensive. These losses ramify out to merchants, manufacturers, commuters, and many other interests.[22] Many proposals have been made to extend a through arterial across the Common, thus relieving the extreme congestion of Tremont and Beacon streets, the two arterials, bordering the park.[23] Earlier suggestions prior to the construction of the subway, called for street car tracks across the Common. But 'the controlling sentiment of the citizens of Boston, and of large numbers throughout the State, is distinctly opposed to allowing any such use of the Common'.[24] Boston has long suffered from land shortage and unusually high real-estate values as a result both of the narrow confines of the peninsula comprising the city centre and as a result of the exclusion from income-yielding uses of so large a tract as the Common.[25] A further difficulty has arisen from the rapid south-westerly extension of the business district in the past two decades. With the Common lying directly in the path of this extension the business district has had to stretch around it in an elongated fashion, with obvious inconvenience to shoppers and consequent loss to businesses.

The Common is not the only obstacle to the city's business expansion. No less than three colonial burying-grounds, two of them adjoined by ancient church buildings, occupy downtown Boston. The contrast that is presented by nine-storey office buildings reared up beside quiet cemeteries affords visible evidence of the conflict between 'sacred' and 'profane' that operates in Boston's ecological pattern.

The dis-economic consequences of commercially valuable land being thus devoted to non-utilitarian purposes goes even further than the removal from business uses of a given amount of space. For it is a standard principle of real estate that business property derives added value if adjoining properties are occupied by other businesses.[26] Just as a single vacancy will depreciate the value of a whole block of business frontage, so a break in the continuity of stores by a cemetery damages the commercial value of surrounding properties. But, even more than the Common, the colonial burying-grounds of Boston have become invested with a moral significance which renders them almost inviolable. Not only is there the usual sanctity which attaches to all cemeteries, but in those of Boston there is an added sacredness growing out of the age of the grounds and the fact that the forebears of many of New England's most distinguished families as well as a number of colonial and Revolutionary leaders lie buried in these cemeteries. There is thus a manifold symbolism to these old burying-grounds, pertaining to family lineage, early nationhood, civic origins, and the like, all of which have strong sentimental associations. What has been said of the old burying-grounds applies with equal force to a number of other venerable landmarks in central Boston. Such buildings as the Old South Meeting-House, the Park Street Church, King's Chapel, and the Old State House—all foci of historical associations—occupy commercially valuable land and interrupt the continuity of business frontage on their streets. Nearly all of these landmarks have been challenged at various times by real-estate and commercial interests which sought to have them replaced by more profitable uses. In every case community sentiments have resisted such threats.

In all these examples we find a symbol-sentiment relationship which has exerted a significant influence upon land use. Nor should it be thought that such phenomena are mere ecological 'sports'. Many other older American cities present similar locational characteristics. Delancey street in Philadelphia represents a striking parallel to Beacon Hill, and certain in-town districts of Chicago, New York, and Detroit, recently revived as fashionable apartment areas, bear resemblances to the Beacon Hill revival. The role of traditionalism in rigidifying the ecological patterns of New Orleans has been demonstrated in a recent study.[27] Further studies of this sort should clarify even further the true scope of sentiment and symbolism in urban spatial structure and dynamics.

As a third line of evidence for our hypothesis we have chosen a rather different type of area from those so far considered. It is a well known fact that immigrant ghettos, along with other slum districts, have become areas of declining population in most American cities. A point not so well established is that this decline tends to be selective in its incidence upon residents and that this selectivity may manifest varying degrees of identification with immigrant values. For residence within a ghetto is more than a matter of spatial placement; it generally signifies acceptance of immigrant institutions. Some light on this process is afforded by data from the North End of Boston. This neighbourhood, almost wholly Italian in population, has long been known as 'Boston's classic land of poverty'.[28] Eighteen per cent of the dwellings are eighty or more years old, and 60 per cent are forty or more years old.[29] Indicative of the dilapidated character of many buildings is the recent sale of a twenty-room apartment building for only $500. It is not surprising then to learn that the area has declined in population from 21,111 in 1930 to 17,598 in 1940.[30] To look for spatially referable sentiments here would seem futile. And yet, examination of certain emigration differentials in the North End reveals a congruence between Italian social structure and locational processes. To get at these differentials recourse was had to the estimation of emigration, by age groups and by nativity, through the use of life tables. The procedure consists of comparing the actual 1940 population with the residue of the 1930 population which probably survived to 1940 according to survival rates for Massachusetts. Whatever deficit the actual 1940 population may show from the estimated 1940 population is a measure of 'effective emigration'. It is not a measure of the actual volume of emigration, since no calculation is made of immigration *into* the district between 1930 and 1940.[31] Effective emigration simply indicates the extent of population decline which is attributable to emigration rather than to death. Computations thus made for emigration differentials by nativity show the following (Table 2):

TABLE 2
*Effective Emigration from the North End,
Boston, 1930–40, by Nativity*

Nativity	1930 Population	Per cent of 1930 Pop in each Nativity Group	Effective Emigration 1930–40	Per cent of Emigration accounted for by each Nativity Group
American-born (second generation)	12,553	59·46	3,399	76·42
Italian-born (first generation)	8,557	40·54	1,049	23·58
Totals	21,110	100·00	4,448	100·00

Calculated from: census tract data and survival rates.

Thus the second generation, comprising but 59·46 per cent of the 1930 population, contributed 76·42 per cent of the effective emigration from the North End, whereas the first generation accounted for much less than its 'due' share of the emigration. Another calculation shows that where the effective emigration of second-generation Italians represents 27·08 per cent of their number in 1930, that of the first generation represents only 12·26 per cent of their number in 1930.

Equally clear differentials appear in effective emigration by age groups. If we compare the difference between the percentage which each age group as of 1930 contributes to the effective emigration, and the percentage which each age group comprised of the 1930 population, we find that the age groups 15–24 account for much more than their share of effective emigration; the age groups 35–64 account for much less than their share.[32] In Table 3 the figures preceded by a plus sign indicate 'excess' emigration, those preceded by a minus sign indicate 'deficit' emigration.

In brief, the North End is losing its young people to a much greater extent than its older people.

These differentials are in no way startling; what is interesting, however, is their congruence with basic Italian values, which find their fullest institutionalized expression in the North End. Emigration from the district may be viewed as both a cause and a symbol of alienation from these values. At the core of the Italian value system are those sentiments which pertain to the family and the *paesani.* Both of these put a high premium upon maintenance of residence in the North End.

TABLE 3

Difference between Percentage Contributed by Each Age Group
to Effective Emigration and Percentage it Comprised of 1930 Population

Age Groups as of 1930	Differences between Percentages	
	Male	Female
under 5	−1·70	−0·33
5−9	+0·38	+0·04
10−14	+0·21	+2·66
15−19	+4·18	+3·01
20−24	+2·04	+2·35
25−34	−0·97	−0·07
35−44	−2·31	−1·09
45−54	−1·43	−1·17
55−64	−2·29	−1·19
65−74	−1·13	−0·59
75 and over	uncalculable	

Calculated from: Census tract data and survival rates.

Paesani, or people from the same village of origin, show considerable tendency to live near one another, sometimes occupying much of a single street or court.[33] Such proximity, or at least common residence in the North End, greatly facilitates participation in the *paesani* functions which are so important to the first-generation Italian. Moreover, it is in the North End that the *festas*, anniversaries, and other old-world occasions are held, and such is their frequency that residence in the district is almost indispensable to regular participation. The social relationships comprised by these groupings, as well as the benefit orders, secret societies, and religious organizations, are thus strongly localistic in character. One second-generation Italian, when asked if his immigrant parents ever contemplated leaving their North End tenement replied: 'No, because all their friends are there, their relatives. They know everyone around there.' It is for this reason that the first-generation Italian is so much less inclined to leave the North End than the American-born Italian.

Equally significant is the localistic character of the Italian family. So great is its solidarity that it is not uncommon to find a tenement entirely occupied by a single extended family: grandparents, matured children with their mates, and grand-children. There are instances where such a family has overflowed one tenement and has expanded into an adjoining one, breaking out the partitions for doorways. These are ecological expressions, in part, of the expected concern which an Italian mother has for the welfare of her newly married daughter. The ideal pattern is for the daughter to continue living in her mother's house, with she and her husband being assigned certain rooms which they are supposed to furnish themselves. Over the course of time the young couple is expected to accumulate savings and buy their own home, preferably not far away. Preferential renting, by which an Italian who owns a tenement will let apartments to his relatives at a lower rental, is another manifestation of the localizing effects of Italian kinship values.

Departure from the North End generally signifies some degree of repudiation of the community's values. One Italian writes of an emigrant from the North End: 'I still remember with regret the vain smile of superiority that appeared on his face when I told him that I lived at the North End of Boston. *"Io non vado fra quella plebaglia."* (I do not go among those plebeians.)[34] As a rule the older Italian is unwilling to make this break, if indeed he could. It is the younger adults, American-born and educated, who are capable of making the transition to another value system with radically different values and goals.

Residence in the North End seems therefore to be a spatial corollary to integration with Italian values. Likewise emigration from the district signifies assimilation into American values, and is so construed by the people themselves. Thus, while the area is not the conscious object of sentimental attachment, as are Beacon Hill and the Common, it has none the less become a symbol for Italian ethnic solidarity. By virtue of this symbolic quality the area has a certain retentive power over those residents who most fully share the values which prevail there.

It is reasonable to suggest, then, that the slum is much more than 'an area of minimum choice'.[35] Beneath the surface phenomenon of declining population there may be differential rates of decline which require positive formulation in a systematic ecological theory. Such processes are apparently refractory to analysis in terms of competition for least impeditive location. A different order of concepts, corresponding to the valuative, meaningful aspect of spatial adaptation, must supplement the prevailing economic concepts of ecology.

NOTES AND REFERENCES

[1] See Everett C. Hughes, 'The Ecological Aspect of Institutions', *American Sociological Review.* 1:180–9, April 1936.

[2] This assumption of a correspondence between the maximum utility of a private association and that of the community may be questioned within the very framework of marginal utility analysis. See particularly A. C. Pigou, *The Economics of Welfare*, 2nd edn., London: 1924, Part II, ch. 8. For a clear presentation of the typical position see Robert Murray Haig, 'Towards an Understanding of the Metropolis–the Assignment of Activities to Areas in Urban Regions', *Quarterly Journal of Economics* 40:402–34, May 1926.

[3] Georg Simmel, 'Der Raum und die räumlichen Ordnungen der Gesellschaft', *Soziologie.* Munich, 1923, pp. 518–22; cf. Hughes, op. cit.

[4] John R. Shultz, *Beacon Hill and the Carol Singers.* Boston, 1923, p. 11.

[5] *Bulletin of the Society for the Preservation of New England Antiquities.* 4:3, August 1913.

[6] Josephine Samson, *Celebrities of Louisburg Square.* Greenfield, Mass., 1924.

[7] Abbie Farwell Brown, *The Lights of Beacon Hill.* Boston, 1922, p. 4.

[8] Cf. W. Lloyd Warner and Paul S. Lunt, *The Social Life of a Modern Community.* New Haven, Conn., 1941, p. 107, on this pattern.

[9] *The Boston Transcript.* 12 April 1930.

[10] Harriet Sisson Gillespie, 'Reclaiming Colonial Landmarks', *The House Beautiful,* 58:239–41, September 1925.

[11] *The Boston Transcript.* 6 December 1922.

[12] *The Boston Transcript.* 18 March 1933.

[13] *The Boston Transcript.* 29 January 1927.

[14] *The Boston Transcript.* 12 April 1930.

[15] *The Boston Transcript.* 10 January, 29 January 1931.

[16] Speech of William Everett, quoted in *The Boston Transcript.* 7 March 1903.

[17] T. R. Sullivan, *Boston New and Old.* Boston, 1912, pp. 45–6.

[18] Joshua H. Jones, Jr., 'Happenings on Boston Common', *Our Boston.* 2:9–15, January 1927.

[19] Cf. Emile Durkheim, *The Elementary Forms of the Religious Life.* London, 1915, p. 345.

[20] St. 1859, c. 210, paragraph 3; Pub sts. c 54, paragraph 13.

[21] M. A. De Wolfe Howe, *Boston Common.* Cambridge, Mass., 1910, p. 79.

[22] Elisabeth M. Herlihy, ed., *Fifty Years of Boston.* Boston, 1932, pp. 53–4.

[23] See, for example, letter to editor, *The Boston Herald.* 16 November 1930.

[24] *First Annual Report of the Boston Transit Commission.* Boston, 1895, p. 9.

[25] John C. Kiley, 'Changes in Realty Values in the Nineteenth and Twentieth Centuries', *Bulletin of the Business Historical Society*, 15 (June 1941), p. 36; Frank Chouteau Brown, 'Boston: More Growing Pains', *Our Boston*, 3 (February 1927), 8.

[26] Richard M. Hurd, *Principles of City Land Values*. New York, 1903, pp. 93–4.

[27] H. W. Gilmore, 'The Old New Orleans and the New: A Case for Ecology', *American Sociological Review*. 9:385–94, August 1944.

[28] Robert A. Woods, ed., *Americans in Process*. Boston, 1903, p. 5.

[29] Finance Commission of the City of Boston, *A Study of Certain of the Effects of Decentralization on Boston and Some Neighbouring Cities and Towns*. Boston: 1941, p. 11.

[30] Aggregate population of census tracts F1, F2, F4, F5: *Census Tract Data, 1930 Census*, unpublished material from 15th Census of the United States, 1930, compiled by Boston Health Department, table 1; *Population and Housing–Statistics for Census Tracts, Boston*. 16th Census of the United States, 1940, table 2.

[31] By use of *Police Lists* for two different years a count was made of immigration into a sample precinct of the North End. The figure (61) reveals so small a volume of immigration that any use of it to compute actual emigration by age groups would have introduced statistical unreliability into the estimates. Survival rates for Massachusetts were computed from state life tables in: National Resources Committee, *Population Statistics, 2. State Data*. Washington, 1937, Part C, p. 38. The technique is outlined in C. Warren Thornthwaite, *Internal Migration in the United States*. Philadelphia, 1934, pp. 19–21.

[32] Obviously most of the emigrants in the 15–24 age group in 1930 migrated while in the age group 20–29; likewise the emigrants in the 35–64 age group migrated while in the 40–69 age group.

[33] William Foote Whyte, *Street Corner Society*. Chicago, 1943, p. xix.

[34] Enrico C. Sartorio, *Social and Religious Life of Italians in America*. Boston, 1918, pp. 43–4.

[35] R. D. McKenzie, 'The Scope of Human Ecology', in Ernest W. Burgess, ed., *The Urban Community*. Chicago, 1926, p. 180.

10. SOCIAL SPACE IN THE BELFAST URBAN AREA

F. W. Boal

The classic work of Emrys Jones[1] has provided a more comprehensive urban geography of Belfast than is perhaps available for any other city of comparable size. This is an excellent foundation on which further study is being based. Much of his work used data obtained from the 1951 census of population, and most of the analysis was restricted to the County Borough of Belfast. However, since 1951 the population of the County Borough has declined by over 44,000, while the built-up area outside the city had, at the 1966 census, a population of 161,000, or about 29 per cent of the total population of the whole urban area. On these grounds alone a further analysis seems justified. In addition, there is now a greater range of data available for the whole of the urban area, derived from the 1966 Census of Population, from the Belfast Area Travel Survey, and from various planning surveys. Finally, the availability of computers makes it possible to use new techniques for analysis of the data.

Urban social geography in general has been heavily orientated towards the description of the areal distribution of a range of socio-economic characteristics. This is in line with the social area analyses of sociologists such as Shevky and Bell.[2] However, the spatial aspects of interaction between areas has received little attention except in transportation studies and investigations of shopping patterns. Because of the system nature of urban complexes it would appear that social area analysis can be improved by a study of interaction both within and between such areas. The present study then, will consist of two principal parts: first an analysis of the whole urban area leading to its subdivision into a series of broad socio-economic regions, and second, an analysis of some aspects of interaction within the broader context established in the first part of the study.

Urban Area Analysis

Urban areas have been characterized in terms of a number of gradients. E. W. Burgess suggests a positive gradient outwards from the city centre in terms of class—working class in the inner areas grading through to the highest-income groups on the periphery.[3] Colin Clark, and subsequent workers, have demonstrated the existence of a general negative gradient of population density with distance from the city centre.[4] Both sets of gradients indicate a concentric arrangement of various socio-economic characteristics focused on the central business district. These concentric models will be taken as a point of departure in this study.

The gross population density for 119 Census data zones within the Belfast area, ranging from 0·6 km (0·35 miles) to 10·5 km (6·54 miles) from the city centre (City Hall) is shown in Figure 1. The data have been plotted on double log axes and a least-squares regression line fitted which is based on the equation, log population density = 1·88 −0·88 log distance (where density is persons per gross residential acre and distance is in tenths of a mile). The negative form of the density gradient is obvious. At the same time it is clear that individual data zones differ considerably

From *Irish Geographical Studies* ed. N. Stephens and R. Glasscock (Queen's University, Belfast), 1970, pp. 373−93. Reprinted by permission of the author and editors

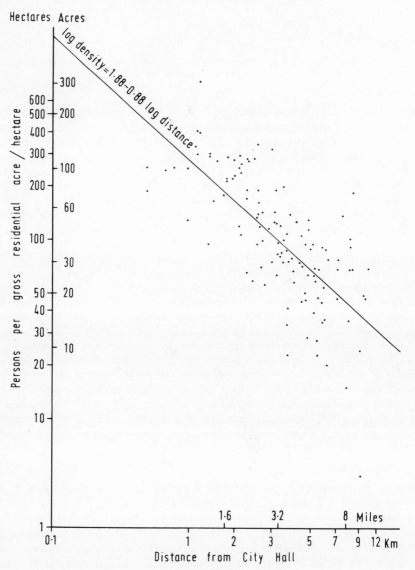

Fig. 1. The relationship between the population density of 119 census zones and their distance from the City Hall (1966).

from the general trend. These deviations from the regular 'model' density surface can be computed and mapped in terms of residuals from the regression (Fig. 2). The spatial distribution of the residuals displays a well-defined pattern and can be described in terms of thirteen sectors forming an alternating series in which density is either over- or under-predicted. Where density is over-predicted, actual densities are less than expected from the model, and conversely where under-predicted actual densities are higher than expected. The two sets of sectors are indicated in Table 1.

This suggests an over-all sector distribution of density rather than a concentric one. However, while sectors can be distinguished, within any one sector the

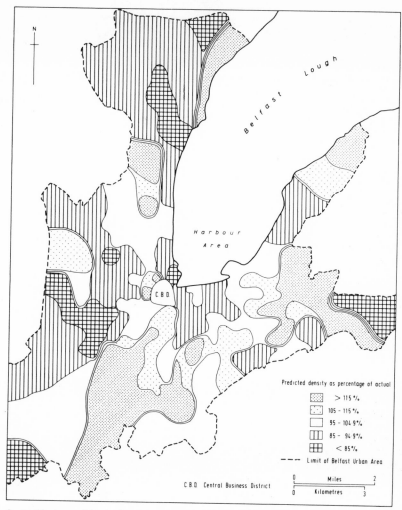

Fig. 2. Belfast: residuals from regression of density against distance from the city centre. The regression equation used to obtain residuals was log gross residential density (persons per acre) = $1\cdot88 - 0\cdot88$ log distance (miles). For locations named in text see Figure 5.

TABLE 1
Positive and negative residual sectors

Over-predicted (positive residual areas)	Under-predicted (negative residual areas)
Outer North Lough Shore	Inner North Lough Shore—Rathcoole
Antrim Road	Crumlin Road—Ligoniel
Ballygomartin Road (weak)	Springfield Road—Falls Road
Malone Road	Ormeau Road (weak)
Ravenhill—Saintfield Roads	Castlereagh Road
Upper Newtownards—Belmont Roads	Inner South Lough Shore
Outer South Lough Shore	

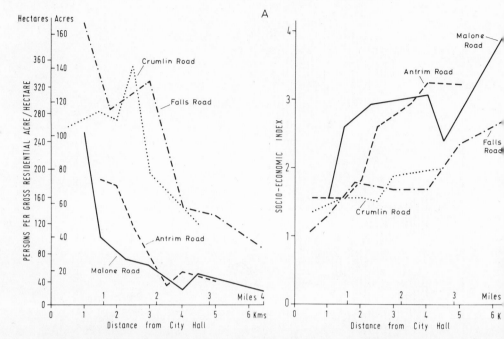

Fig. 3. Population density (A) and socio-economic status (B) measured along selected sectors in Belfast.

negatively sloped density gradient can still be distinguished, and is illustrated in Figure 3A where density is shown along two high-density and two low-density sectors. The same gradient feature, though now positive, can be demonstrated for socio-economic status (Fig. 3B). The differences between sectors and the over-all density gradient are both apparent.

Density (x) in Belfast is negatively correlated with distance (y) from the city centre (r log x. log y = -0.72) but as noted above, with distinctive differences in density levels between sectors. In European and North American cities there is also a high correlation between density and other socio-economic characteristics. Belfast is no exception, where, for instance, a general index of socio-economic status (a) based on occupation has a high negative correlation with density ($r_{a.\ x}$ = -0.70), while there is a similar negative correlation between density and car-ownership (b) ($r_{b.\ x}$ = -0.67). If we take four general indicators of socio-economic status (density, occupational index,[5] car-ownership, and male unemployment) and correlate them against a general array of variables for the 119 Belfast data zones, the correlation matrix shown in Table 2 is obtained.

The four general indicators are all highly intercorrelated. At the same time they are highly correlated with a number of other variables. It would seem possible, therefore, to substitute one of the indicators as a general socio-economic index. However, instead of using just one variable it was considered desirable to employ a technique that would involve the use of the full array of the 26 available variables. This number was finally reduced to 25 by the omission of the distance variable in case this had too strong a patterning effect on its own. The technique used was principal components analysis whereby linear combinations of variables are

TABLE 2

Correlations between selected variables for the Belfast urban area.
In addition the correlations between 25 variables and the first two
components are also given (data are untransformed).

	Density	Occupational Index[5]	Car-Ownership	Male Unemployment	Correlation between variables and component Component 1	Component 2
Per cent population ≤ 14 years						0·88
Per cent population ≥ 65 years						−0·92
Persons per household						0·73
Persons per room			−0·51	0·50	0·61	0·63
Distance from City Hall	−0·59	0·62	0·59		NA	NA
Gross residential density		−0·70	−0·67	0·72	0·78	
Gross dwelling density	0·92	−0·78	−0·72	0·57	0·81	
Occupational index	−0·70		0·86	−0·62	−0·88	
Cars per household	−0·67	0·86		−0·57	−0·89	
Per cent of population 15−19 years in full-time education	−0·64	0·70	0·75		−0·79	
Per cent of population with driving licences	−0·75	0·88	0·89	−0·65	−0·91	
Per cent of heads of household Socio-economic group A$_i$	−0·75	0·70	0·77		−0·72	
Per cent of heads of household Socio-economic group A$_{ii}$	−0·50	0·66	0·53		−0·63	
Per cent of heads of household Socio-economic group B						0·62
Per cent of heads of household Socio-economic group C	0·62	−0·74	−0·74	0·54	0·83	
Per cent population over 15 years years occupied						0·71
Per cent occupied males out of work	0·72	−0·62	−0·57		0·68	
Per cent workers employed in CBD						
Per cent journey to work by bus			−0·55		0·52	
Per cent journey to work by car	−0·75	0·88	0·91	−0·63	−0·92	
Per cent journey to work on foot	0·70	−0·72	−0·66	0·67	0·76	
Age of housing		−0·62			0·55	−0·73
Migrants as per cent of total population	−0·53	0·58	0·51		−0·61	
Internal area migrants						
In migrants from rest of Northern Ireland		0·58	0·50		−0·58	
Per cent of population Roman Catholic				0·57		

Only correlation coefficients ≥ 0·5 shown. All coefficients significant at 0·01 level.
NA−not available.

obtained which are uncorrelated, and whereby the first linear combination (component) is a normalized combination with maximum variance; the second component is uncorrelated with the first and has as large a variance as possible and so on. The initial data were standardized.

The first five principal components obtained absorbed 79 per cent of the total variance of the 25 variables as follows:

	Component					
	1	2	3	4	5	1–5
Percentage of Variance	41·4	18.0	8.8	6·4	4·5	79·1

The component scores were computed. The data zones were then ranked according to the value of their scores on each component, and then grouped by deciles. A map of the zonal groups derived from the first principal component is shown in Figure 4. The component is most highly correlated positively with the following initial variables (see Table 2): persons per room, gross residential density, gross dwelling density, percentage of heads of household in socio-economic group C (semi-skilled and unskilled manual workers), percentage of normally occupied males out of work, and percentage of people who journey to work on foot. The component is negatively associated with occupational index, car-ownership, percentage of population with driving licences, percentage of population between 15 and 19 years in full-time education, percentage of heads of household in socio-economic group A_i (managerial and professional), and percentage who make the journey to work by car. These variables are generally indicative of socio-economic status, and on this basis the first principal component has been named the socio-economic component.

The pattern displayed shows a close association with the pattern of residuals from the density analysis (Fig. 2) and the sectoral form is striking. Those zones that score highly on this component are areas of low socio-economic status, whereas at the other end of the scale are the high-status areas. Particularly striking are the low-status sectors along the inner parts of the north and south lough shores and the massive low-status sector extending west and south-west from the city centre, along the Crumlin-Ligoniel and Falls-Springfield axes, with the Shankill Road in the middle. The most clearly defined high-status sectors are on the lines of the Antrim, Malone, Ravenhill-Saintfield, and Upper Newtownards-Belmont Roads, together with the two outer lough shore areas.

One vital aspect of the low-status sector extending west and south-west from the city centre is not included in the pattern derived from the first component—this is the high degree of religious segregation that exists.[6] Unfortunately, religious data were not obtained in the 1966 population census, necessitating the use of estimates derived from a series of surveys. This provides a sample cover for about 50 per cent of the urban area, but when considered with the pattern discussed by Jones[7] a fairly complete picture can be obtained. The main elements of the highly segregated religious area in the centre and western low-status sector of the city are shown in Figure 5, where a highly segregated area is defined as having more than 90 per cent Protestants or more than 90 per cent Roman Catholics. The main Roman Catholic concentration extends from the city centre south-westwards along the spine of the Falls Road for a distance of about 6 km (3·7 miles). There are separate and much smaller concentrations north of the middle Crumlin Road (Ardoyne), immediately west of the city centre, south-east of the centre (Cromac), and east of the centre (part of Ballymacarrett). Between Ardoyne and the Falls Road sector, there is the

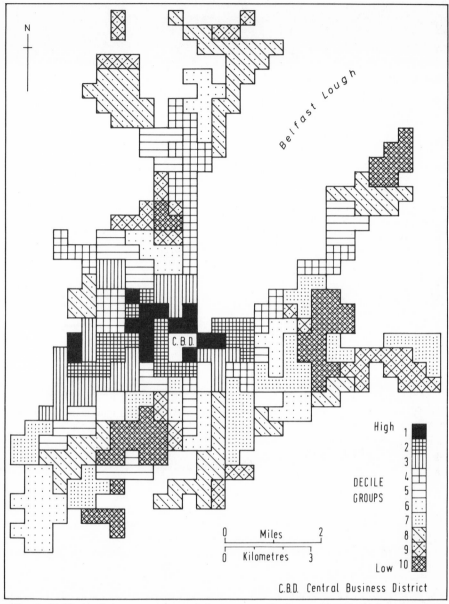

Fig. 4. Belfast urban area: census data zones ranked according to their component scores on the socio-economic component. The boundaries of the census zones have been adjusted to a grid format.

very well-developed and almost entirely Protestant Shankill Road area, while lying south-east of the Falls sector is the equally predominantly Protestant Sandy Row area.

The result is that within the western low-status area there is a Roman Catholic-Protestant alternation of sub-sectors. The actual divides between these

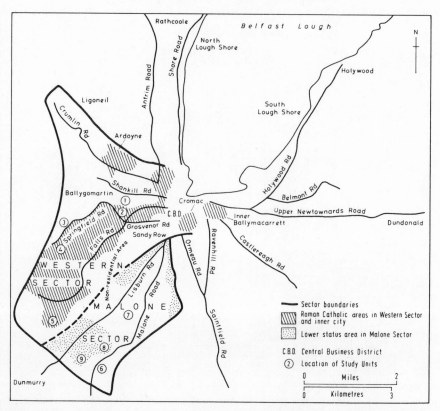

Fig. 5. Roman Catholic areas in central and west Belfast, and general key to locations mentioned in the text. Study units: (1) Shankill; (2) Clonard; (3) New Barnsley; (4) Turf Lodge; (5) Ladybrook; (6) Upper Malone; (7) Inner Malone; (8) Taughmonagh; (9) Erinvale.

Note: Dock areas excluded.

sub-sectors are, almost without exception, very sharp. In some cases the division is composed of non-residential areas, such as factory sites and railway tracks, while in others, the residential areas come into direct contact with each other, and the transition from Protestant to Catholic occurs within the width of a street of houses. An example of this is shown in Figure 6, on the divide between the Falls and Shankill sub-sectors.[8]

Thus far the basic socio-economic picture of the Belfast urban area we have obtained is one of a city-centre-focused gradient, positively sloped in terms of social status, and negatively sloped in terms of density. Superimposed on this general surface are the alternating high- and low-status sectors, while the western low-status sector displays a further set of internal sub-sectors distinguished on the basis of religion.

When the data zones are ranked on their scores for component 2 the pattern produced is much less sectoral in character. In fact, the highest-scoring zones are the peripheral ones and the low-scoring the central zones, with inner high-status areas scoring lowest of all. The initial variables most heavily weighted in this component are those associated with demographic characteristics. Zones with high

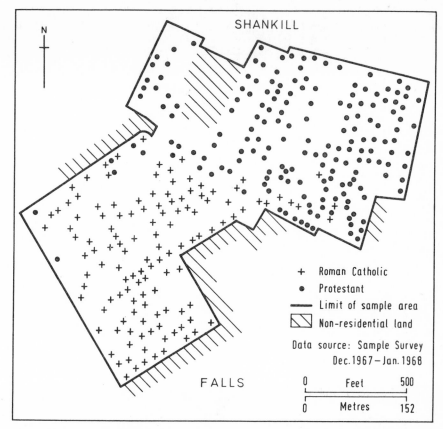

Fig. 6. Religious distribution in a small area of west Belfast at the contact of the Shankill and Falls sub-sectors. The map is based upon a 10 per cent sample of persons over the age of twenty-one.

scores have large proportions of the population under 14, a low proportion over 65, and large households. A large proportion of the population has also been involved recently in a house move, and the houses occupied are relatively new. The component picks out the growing periphery of the urban area. This growth is of very mixed socio-economic character, in that there is Local Authority and Northern Ireland Housing Trust rental housing, low- to medium-cost private estates, and a limited development of high-cost housing. Government-developed housing (Local Authority and Housing Trust) is quite widespread on the periphery and has been constructed at the outer ends of a wide range of socio-economic sectors. However, there is a predominance of rental housing on the outer fringes of low-status sectors. Where Government housing lies on the lines of higher-status sectors, the population generally has a higher socio-economic status than for similar housing on the lines of the low-status sectors. Thus, while the demographic characteristics of the urban area have a general concentric pattern, a strong sectoral influence can still be seen.

The presence of both sectoral and concentric residential patterns corresponds with the findings reported by Berry for American cities.[9] He notes that there are three dimensions of socio-economic variation: the sectoral variation of neighbour-

TABLE 3

Study unit characteristics

Sector	Study Unit Name	Type of Housing	Persons per net residential hectare (acre)	Households per net residential hectare (acre)	Religion (per cent RC)	Size of Household	Occupational Index[5]	Persons Sampled
	Shankill 1	Victorian terrace	438 (177)	138 (54)	1	3·3	1·68	158
	Clonard	Victorian terrace	353 (143)	90 (36)	98	3·9	2·27	113
Western	New Barnsley	Corporation estate*	195 (79)	34 (14)	12	5·7	2·47	101
	Turf Lodge	Corporation estate*	259 (105)	37 (15)	99	7·0	2·13	116
	Ladybrook	Semi-detached private	96 (39)	23 (9)	90	4·2	3·26	61
	Inner Malone	Large detached	34 (14)	8 (3)	14	4·1	4·11	65
	Upper Malone	Large detached bungalows	30 (12)	8 (3)	8	3·7	4·20	66
Malone	Erinvale	Mainly semi-detached private	125 (51)	33 (13)	10	3·8	3·32	77
	Taughmonagh	Corporation pre-fab' estate	107 (44)	19 (8)	13	5·7	2·58	92

*Maisonette areas excluded

hoods by socio-economic rank, the concentric variation of neighbourhoods according to family structure, and the localized segregation of particular ethnic groups. However, if we consider the religious groups as 'ethnic' the segregation pattern in the Belfast context is predominantly sectoral, as noted above. Thus, while Jones found a 'sector residential pattern' in the west,[10] the present analysis suggests the coexistence of 'sectors' and 'rings' over much of the urban area.

Before proceeding to the activity analysis it should be stressed that there is some loss of 'information' in the analysis of the Belfast data zones. This applies particularly to parts of the periphery, where the data zones are quite large and include a wide range of housing types. The general picture is not distorted greatly but locally considerable statistical homogenization has been imposed.

Activity Analysis

Up to this point, the analysis has dealt with the whole urban area, and has concentrated on standard socio-economic data. An attempt will now be made to examine a series of sample areas in much greater detail, and in particular to carry out an analysis of some activity patterns to see how activity linkages are distributed and how activity is related to the basic socio-economic structure of the urban area outlined above.

Nine study units were selected and a random sample of persons over the age of 21 was interviewed in each area. The study units were selected from the western low-status sector and the Malone high-status sector. Pairs of units were also selected to allow comparison, while holding religion, socio-economic status, and age of housing constant. The study units and certain of their characteristics are listed in Table 3 while their locations are shown in Figure 5. The sharp differences of religion within the western sector and between the two semi-detached private-housing areas, one in the western sector, the other on the outer edge of Malone, are evident.

Clearly, Shankill, Clonard, New Barnsley, and Turf Lodge are low-status areas, while Inner and Upper Malone are high-status areas. On the other hand Ladybrook, Erinvale, and Taughmonagh, do not conform to the particular low- or high-status characteristics of their respective sectors. In fact, these three areas lie on the flanks of the two sectors, Ladybrook being lower-middle income and predominantly Roman Catholic, Erinvale being lower-middle income and Protestant. Taughmonagh is a highly non-conforming insertion of Corporation housing on the central axis of the Malone sector. The non-conforming nature of these three study units is also evident in the activity analysis.

The activity analysis applied depends on the examination of a set of linkages within the Belfast urban area. The present residence of the interviewee forms one point and the links between that point and three other sets of points are established. The three other sets of points are the previous address of interviewee (if there is one), the origin points of social visits to interviewee or points interviewee visited during a one-week period, and the pre-marriage addresses of interviewee and spouse (if applicable). The first step in the analysis required the establishment of the extent to which points associated with the three social attributes (previous address, visits, and pre-marriage address) corresponded with each other for any one study unit. The extent to which the three-point distributions were congruent for each of the study units is shown in Figure 7, cells for which three or two attributes were congruent being indicated, together with the cells for which only one attribute was present.

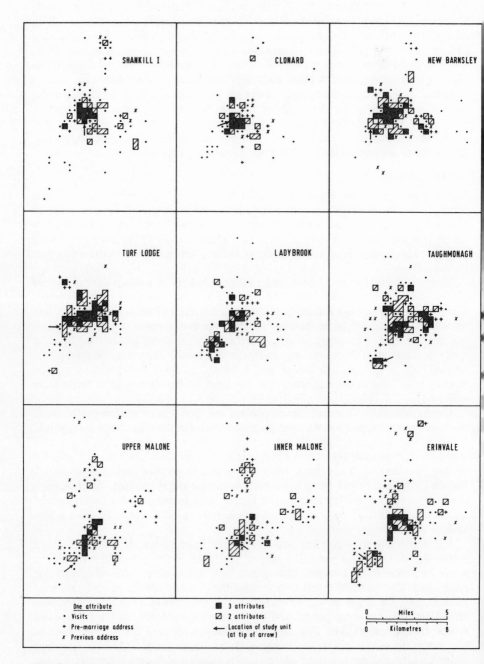

Fig. 7. Congruence of social activity attributes for sample residents in each of nine study units. The congruence is measured within a 0·5 km² grid superimposed on the Belfast urban area.

Note: the degree of concentration of attributes in the three- and two-attribute cells is not shown.

TABLE 4

Percentage allocation of previous addresses, pre-marriage addresses, and visit connections for the Malone sector sample units

Sample Units	Malone sector (percentage of urban area connections)		Low-Status sub-sector + Sandy Row (percentage of urban area connections)	Outside urban area (percentage of all connections)	
	Total	High-Status sub-sector		Northern Ireland	Abroad
Previous address					
Upper Malone	65	48	20	11	20
Inner Malone	60	52	10	11	11
Erinvale	25	4	35	20	12
Taughmonagh	15	4	24	7	4
Pre-marriage address					
Upper Malone	33	27	3	24	42
Inner Malone	25	25	0	28	30
Erinvale	24	7	30	33	9
Taughmonagh	9	2	32	11	6
Visit connections					
Upper Malone	71	66	9	17	4
Inner Malone	63	58	6	22	5
Erinvale	44	4	52	26	0
Taughmonagh	27	1	36	6	3

If we confine our attention to those cells where two or three attributes are congruent a number of features emerge. First, all the study units display 'core areas' where all three attributes are congruent. The simplest and most sharply developed are those for the inner low-status areas of Shankill and Clonard. Secondly, we can note the more elongated·well-developed cores for the outer housing estates of New Barnsley and Turf Lodge and the somewhat more fragmented core pattern for the private estate of Ladybrook. In the Malone sector two distinct patterns emerge, rather weakly developed elongated cores for the high-status Upper and Inner Malone units, and more strongly developed but discontinuous cores for the Erinvale private estate and the Taughmonagh Corporation Housing area. Viewed differently we can say that all the low- and middle-status areas display well-developed cores while the high-status units are weaker in this respect.

Well-developed cores indicate a closely knit spatial system wherein, for each study unit, there is a series of congruent linkages—the area or areas concerned are connected to the study unit in terms of visiting, an immediately previous address, and the pre-marriage location of at least one partner. In the instances in which all these linkages occur within the same area, this is taken to indicate the existence of a tightly knit 'spatial community', which Fried claims is an indication of a standard working-class community pattern, 'an overlapping series of close knit networks'.[11] The core areas occur either where there are old-established fairly static groups (Shankill and Clonard) or where there has been movement from a small part of the

TABLE 5

Percentage allocation of previous addresses, pre-marriage addresses,
and visit connections for the western sector sample units

| | Sample Units | Total | Western Sector (percentage of urban area connections) | | Outside Urban Area (percentage of all connections) | |
			Within Protestant sub-sectors	Within Catholic sub-sectors	Northern Ireland	Abroad
Previous address	Shankill	87	82	5	4	4
	Clonard	81	5	76	4	5
	New Barnsley	75	67	8	2	9
	Turf Lodge	85	5	80	0	2
	Ladybrook	87	11	76	9	14
Pre-marriage address	Shankill	91	89	2	5	1
	Clonard	85	7	78	7	8
	New Barnsley	79	71	8	7	4
	Turf Lodge	83	7	76	2	3
	Ladybrook	86	13	73	19	6
Visit connections	Shankill	83	79	4	3	1
	Clonard	93	5	88	3	2
	New Barnsley	84	76	6	5	1
	Turf Lodge	85	5	80	1	0
	Ladybrook	79	8	71	10	2

inner city to new housing areas on the urban periphery (New Barnsley, Turf Lodge, Taughmonagh, which are Local Authority housing areas, and Ladybrook and Erinvale, which are higher-status private-housing areas deriving a significant proportion of their population from a restricted section of the inner city).

The two high-status Malone areas do not show the close-knit networks to the same degree, though even here reasonably well-defined cores are evident. However, in these two cases, not only are the various social attributes less congruent within the Belfast urban area but they also show much stronger linkages outside the urban area' altogether. This is shown in Table 4 where the percentage concentration of the various attributes is given for the Malone sector and also outside the urban area.

The five study units within the western sector show high levels of concentration for all three social attributes (Table 5). A very high proportion of total interaction is restricted to the western low-status sector. A further degree of concentration can also be distinguished, in that the two predominantly Protestant study units (Shankill and New Barnsley) have very high levels of linkage within the Protestant sub-sectors, while the three Roman Catholic units have strong links within the Catholic sub-sectors. The different 'orientation' of the Protestant and Roman Catholic sub-sectors can also be indicated in terms of newspaper readership and support for certain football teams. In this case Catholic loyalties lie with Glasgow Celtic and the *Irish News*, while Protestant loyalties lie with Linfield football club and there is an 'inverted' loyalty to the *Irish News*. Probably television and the *Belfast Telegraph* evening paper are the two news and cultural media that both sectors have in common but there is little else (Table 6).

The three outer units within the western sector (New Barnsley, Turf Lodge, and Ladybrook) show clearly the centre-periphery nature of much interaction, for previous addresses are located in the inner parts of the subsectors as are pre-marriage addresses. The tendency towards out-migration along sectors has been noted previously by Jones,[12] and is a generally observed feature of residential moves within the Belfast urban area. If a move to a new house is contemplated, people express a strong preference for a location in the outer reaches of the sector within which they already reside. This is clearly related to familiarity and ease of movement from the new housing area back to the 'home' district.

The study units in the Malone sector display a less concentrated set of linkages in terms of the sector itself. Even so the two high-status units (Upper and Inner

TABLE 6

Newspaper readership, football team support, and presence of television sets, Western sector study units

	Percentage Roman Catholic	Percentage reading *Irish News*	Percentage supporting Glasgow Celtic	Percentage supporting Linfield	Percentage reading *Belfast Telegraph*	Percentage with TV sets
Clonard	98	83	73	0	58	77
Turf Lodge	99	74	63	0	70	97
Ladybrook	90	39	11	0	62	100
Shankill	1	3	0	74	68	86
New Barnsley	12	3	1	63	72	97

Malone) do show considerable degrees of sector concentration in terms of previous addresses and visit connections, even though there are significant linkages outside the urban area altogether. For these two areas the pre-marriage address is more dispersed, both within and outside the urban area, though the urban area distribution is almost entirely restricted to high-status sectors.

The two lower-status units in the Malone sector are the most weakly linked in terms of the sector within which they are present. This is because both units are non-conforming as far as the socio-economic characteristics of most of the sector are concerned. On social-status grounds they have low probabilities of connection with the high-status predominant portion of the sector. However, both study units show strong links with an inner low-status area (Sandy Row), which until now we have considered part of the western sector. In terms of potential interaction this interpretation needs to be relaxed because the innermost parts of all sectors west of the river are close to each other and it is questionable to which sector they should be allocated. From the restricted evidence available it would appear that Sandy Row is more strongly linked to the lower-status outer parts of the Malone sector than to the outer parts of the western sector, particularly since the outer parts of the western Protestant sub-sector are 'cut-off' from Sandy Row by the overwhelmingly Catholic sub-sector of Falls.

The non-conforming nature of Erinvale and Taughmonagh is further emphasized when the distances of the linked points from the study units are considered. For instance, the mean distance of visit links for Taughmonagh is not significantly different from that for Upper Malone, while it is significantly greater than that for Inner Malone (p=0·05) despite the considerable socio-economic differences between the units.

The pattern of connectivity which has been analysed would seem to be influenced by a number of factors. First, linkages will occur predominantly with areas which are similar in socio-economic and religious characteristics. Secondly, the linkages are further constrained by distance, and by the general accessibility pattern of the various potential linkage areas to any particular study unit. Where there is a high dependence on walking and use of buses, distances are small unless movement is channelled in and out along a radial road where there is a good bus service. With the present radial arrangement of bus routes between city centre and

TABLE 7

Mobility potential of households in the sample units

	Cars per household	Percentage of households with no car	Percentage of households with telephone
Shankill	0·14	85	2
Clonard	0·29	71	7
New Barnsley	0·19	82	5
Turf Lodge	0·24	77	2
Ladybrook	0·77	23	16
Upper Malone	1·55	2	96
Inner Malone	1·68	6	99
Erinvale	0·77	30	35
Taughmonagh	0·35	67	0

periphery, lateral (inter-sector) movement is difficult, particularly where the spine roads of the sectors are far apart. As noted earlier, however, since the spine roads are much closer together in the inner parts of the city, inter-sector movement is easier here. The availability of a car and to some extent of a telephone also tends to free movement from the radial network. But all the low-status study units have two-thirds to three-quarters of households without cars, and in the western sector there is no significant difference between the inner and outer low-status areas (Table 7). Thus, in this case peripheral location is not compensated for by higher personal mobility using a car and consequently, movement by bus on the spine roads is a major constraint on linkage patterns.

At the other end of the spectrum lie the two high-status Malone units where practically every household has at least one car, and about half the households have two or more cars available. About three-quarters of the households in the middle-status units (Erinvale and Ladybrook) have cars. The existence of a telephone is even more marked in the inequality of its distribution, ranging from just about saturation in the Malone units to almost insignificance in the low-status areas. The telephone distribution pattern suggests a whole sub-system of interaction as far as the high-status areas are concerned.

The lack of cars and to some extent of telephones in the low-status units, together with the enforced radial nature of bus travel, suggests why so much social interaction is sectoral in nature, and the constraints of religion and social status further affect the pattern. In this context it is still striking to observe the degree to which the interaction for the Malone high-status units is also restricted to a considerable extent to the Malone sector, despite much greater potential physical mobility. There are elements of Fried's 'close knit networks'[13] present here too.

Conclusion

This analysis has disclosed the existence of clearly developed sectors in the Belfast urban area. The 'static' socio-economic sector pattern disclosed in the earlier part of the study is further emphasized by the sectoral congruence of selected activity systems. The sector pattern, when viewed both from a social-pattern and activity-analyses viewpoint, indicates very high levels of segregation, that is segregation by socio-economic group and by religious affiliation.

It remains to comment briefly on the significance of these sector-segregated patterns from a planning standpoint. Currently segregation based on religion is viewed with disfavour by external observers, while in the past, in many cities, segregation by class has been looked upon with equal disfavour, although these attitudes are not generally held in the segregated areas concerned. In fact, one could argue that highly segregated sectors are the most efficient form for the existing system of interaction. Where areas that are non-conforming in terms of the general character of the particular sector occur, this only seems to generate more extended ·linkages to other areas that do conform. On the other hand, it could be argued that the existing segregated activity patterns are a consequence of the homogeneous sectors or sub-sectors. In the Belfast area, in so far as people have any residential choice, they exercise it by moving from less segregated to more segregated housing groups or else they move within an existing highly segregated sector. In the case of one Corporation housing estate which initially was integrated in terms of religion, subsequent moves have produced an almost entirely Roman Catholic estate. The Ladybrook and Erinvale private estates are both highly segregated, with only 10 per cent of the particular minority religious group present in each case. Catholics have opted for Ladybrook, Protestants for Erinvale. This highlights a further factor in segregation, namely the availability of schools. As might be expected the voluntary (Roman Catholic) schools, and the Roman Catholic churches, are restricted to a large extent to the Catholic sectors. A Catholic family buying a house, or obtaining a rented-housing allocation outside the Catholic sectors is faced subsequently with long and difficult school journeys, a particularly important factor in the case of primary schools.

Planning proposals for the Belfast urban area have been produced recently,[14] and these suggest that 'the strengthening of the identity and sense of community of townships and city sectors is important socially'. To achieve this a structuring of the urban area into a series of 'Districts' is proposed. While the 'Districts' may have meaning where they focus on pre-existing outlying settlements such as Dunmurry, Dundonald, and Holywood (Fig. 5), the 'Districts' proposed for much of the rest of the area run quite counter to existing community identities. The findings of the current study indicate that well-defined areas with marked identity already exist whereas the proposed new 'Districts' break right across these. This is particularly true for the proposed West Belfast District which would not allow the strengthening of existing communities. The only intention can be to restructure completely the western sector by attempting to link into one 'District' at least four sharply defined sub-sectors. This aim should have been stated unequivocally and the advantages and disadvantages of such a policy carefully assessed.

In the Belfast urban area physical segregation and social segregation are highly correlated. Whether physical desegregation, in terms of religion and social class, would lead to social desegregation (that is, social interaction) is open to question. The possible consequences of physical desegregation need to be examined in depth. In fact, actual experiment may be the most effective, though not necessarily the least painful way of providing the necessary data. Analyses such as the present study, or experiments as suggested above, cannot provide substitutes for judgement as to the desirability of desegregation, but they can provide a firmer basis on which the judgement can be made.

ACKNOWLEDGEMENT

The survey work on which part of the study is based was made possible by generous grants from the Frederick Soddy Trust, the James Munce Partnership, and The Queen's University of Belfast. I would also like to thank Miss J. Orr, Mr. W. McGaughey, and Mr. G. Bullock of the Department of Geography in the university for their assistance, and Building Design Partnership for providing data for the Belfast urban area.

NOTE

This chapter was completed in September 1968. The communal disturbances during 1969 and 1970, many of which occurred in the vicinity of the edges of the religious subsectors in the western part of the city, are, in consequence, not discussed here.

REFERENCES

[1] E. Jones, *A Social Geography of Belfast* (London, 1960).
[2] E. Shevky and W. Bell, *Social Area Analysis* (Stanford Calif., 1955).
[3] E. W. Burgess, 'The Growth of the City', in R. E. Park and E. W. Mackenzie, eds., *The City* (Chicago, 1927).
[4] C. Clark, 'Urban Population Densities', *J. Roy. Stat. Soc.* 114 (1951), 490–6.

[5] The Occupational Index is derived from the formula:

$(0.05 \times P_1) + (0.04 \times P_2) + (0.03 \times P_3) + (0.02 \times P_4) + (0.01 \times P_5)$ where $P_1, P_2, \ldots P_n$ are percentages of heads of households in the given area whose socio-economic groups are $1, 2 \ldots$ n respectively. See R. Travers Morgan and Partners, *Travel in Belfast* (Belfast, 1968), p. 188.

[6] See E. E. Evans, 'Belfast: The Site and the City', *Ulster J. Arch.* 3rd Ser. 7 (1944), 25–9, and E. Jones, op. cit., pp. 172–206.

[7] E. Jones, op. cit., p. 196.

[8] F. W. Boal, 'Territoriality on the Shankill-Falls Divide, Belfast', *Irish Geography*, 6, No. 1 (1969), 30–50.

[9] B. J. L. Berry, 'Internal Structure of the City', *Law and Contemporary Problems* (Winter 1965), p. 115.

[10] E. Jones, op. cit., p. 273.

[11] M. Fried, 'Functions of the Working Class Community in Modern Urban Society—Implications for Forced Relocations', *J. Amer. Inst. Planners*, 33, No. 2 (March 1967), 92.

[12] E. Jones, op. cit., pp. 145–6.

[13] M. Fried, op. cit., p. 92.

[14] Building Design Partnership, *Belfast Urban Area—Interim Planning Policy* (Belfast, 1967), pp. 72–106.

11. SOCIETY, MAN, AND ENVIRONMENT

J. Mogey

Ever since I went as an undergraduate apprentice with Estyn Evans into the hills
and byeways of Ulster, digging in the horned cairns of prehistoric settlers, or
looking at the ruins of recently deserted huts and cottages, the problems of the
interaction between the physical environment and human society have been with
me. I have them still as intellectually unfinished business and in this paper I will try
to untangle one of the sociological strands of these puzzles. The argument that the
environment controls or directly affects man is, at its simplest, geographical
determinism and like all simple causal explanations for human behaviour fails to
stand up to testing. Yet the belief that some influences on human affairs come
directly from the physical environment is so persistent that the intellectual
exploration of these problems remains attractive. Although our society has now
acquired tremendous capacities to alter the landscape, some explanation of the
impact of the physical environment as a complex variable on social life is
important.

Adaptation to Environment

Geographers talk of 'man', sociologists of 'human behaviour' and 'society'. Many
other disciplines use the term 'human being', in the sense of a creature functioning
as a single biological entity in an environment. Some even talk of the 'real' world as
distinct from the world of thought and ideas. In this sense the 'real' world in its
effect on mankind means, so far as I can judge, the direct, unmediated influence of
climate, soil, latitude, germs, etc., on the biological functioning of the individual.
So we have studies of the effects of altitude on the oxygen levels of the atmosphere
and the consequence of these levels either for the performance of athletes or on the
lung capacity of Andean peasants.[1] The correlations so established are statistically
meaningful and the results reported are interesting. None the less something
important is missing in these equations. They overlook the fact that human
behaviour is social and therefore has to be learned. We never react merely as
biological pawns buffeted by external forces. All human life is social life. We cannot
really talk meaningfully of man and society. Man is society. He is created by his
society and in one sense creates the society anew every generation. Continuity and
order in societies come about through the overlap of the generations or, in other
words, through socialization. By means of language the repetition of accumulated
and transmitted knowledge is easier than an entirely new creation of the human
social fabric.

Every society has as one aspect of its social matrix its means of adaptation to its
environment: these means represent one part of its solution to the problems of
survival. They consist of techniques and desired objectives and both are learned.
Even the capacity to learn has to be learned. Harlow has shown that Rhesus
monkeys given adequate food, shelter, and comforting from a mechanical mother

From *Man and His Habitat* ed. R. H. Buchanan, E. Jones and D. McCourt (London: Routledge
and Kegan Paul Ltd; New York: Barnes and Noble Books, 1971), pp. 79–92. Reprinted by
permission of the publishers.

develop biologically but do not develop the capacity to interact sexually or socially with other Rhesus monkeys.[2] Studies of autistic children reveal that biological, sociological, and psychological capacities develop in different ways: it is now suspected that most accounts of feral children are really folk tales to explain the appearance of autism in the midst of otherwise normally socialized children.[3] If we wished to study the interaction of biology and environment in a culture-free group, these unfortunates might be the only possible subjects.

The existence of societies as the primary matrix for human living complicates enormously the problems of understanding the adaptive processes. By these I mean the attitudes, values, and techniques held by members of a society towards the external world. Societies are variable and rarely stable. They affect each other in complex ways and adapt to the physical or biological world with many distinctively different solutions to common problems.

It is this variability from place to place, coupled with the liability of societies to change, that makes arguments from the environment to man, or human behaviour, so treacherous. It is easy to demonstrate that most specific social changes at the present time are not accompanied by, and therefore not to be explained by, changes in any environmental conditions. Natural disasters, earthquakes, tornadoes, floods, if rare, do not necessarily lead to changes in social life; if they are frequent and expected, the society has adapted to their recurrence and continues without any basic change. Consider two simple biological facts to which all societies have to adapt: (a) that only women bear children, and (b) that only sexual intercourse with a male makes conception possible. The variety of socially approved arrangements for impregnating the females of the world gives us some first idea of the complexities of the social problems of adaptation.[4] In addition, every society knows of several unapproved conditions for achieving pregnancy.

These considerations lead to the basic theme of this paper—that the problems of adaptation are social problems. In consequence, it follows that explanations about variations in adaptive processes and about adaptive innovations—which is an isomorphic statement—are to be looked for in variations of other elements of sociological systems, and not in changes of either ecological or biological systems.[5]

Studies of the acceptance of new seeds, fertilizers, tools, and methods of husbandry by rural sociologists illustrate the social nature of innovations. These studies prove over and over again that the acceptance of efficient and profitable new ideas in agriculture is a slow and complex social process.[6] To the rural sociologist, an innovation has been accepted only when a majority of a community practise it without outside encouragement.

The almost universal social rule against incest points to the next step in this argument. Since parent-child and sibling incest are universally taboo, the basic social structural unit of society cannot be the family, any more than it can be the isolated individual.[7] The existence of this taboo means that for continuity beyond one generation a minimum of two families, which exchange children as mates, must exist.[8] Such a unit, existing in a territory and meeting all its problems of survival and continuity, is a community. These statements hold good even though the incest taboo is often broken; its existence as a universal rule of society means that the community must also exist as a universal social group. The work of Murdock has established this empirically.[9]

The community has as important a role in socialization as in survival, for no family ever completely socializes a child. Simple communities are marked by closed boundaries although the closure is never so complete that all external influences are excluded. Such communities are endogamous and may appear like extended kinship groups. The existence of work teams, religious practices, and educational processes within all communities marks them as functioning units of all societies. To the geographer the community appears as a settlement pattern, and the geographical classification of types of villages and open-country, single-family houses is a body of fact much neglected by sociologists.

The Role of Community in Adaptation

We reach at this point the first proposition in the sociological analysis of adaptation: the community is the structural unit of society through which the adaptive processes work. If this is accepted then we have to abandon the simple deterministic type of statement such as that water is essential to settlement. Rather the reverse is more plausible: a water supply becomes significant only because of settlement. In the Irish countryside I was amazed at the number of farmhouses that had no domestic water supply. One abandoned farmhouse we used as headquarters for a field project on Inishmore, Co. Fermanagh, was more than half a mile from the nearest source of drinking-water. This spring was not beside any other house. Considering that any shallow well in Ireland will fill with drinkable water, this fact might be explained by a preference for spring water with a consequent neglect to dig a well for every farmhouse. The point being made here is that adaptive patterns as the dependent variable are explained by the community as the independent variable. The community factor isolated in this example is the meaning or value assigned to spring water.

The variety of meanings that can be assigned to any single adaptive process is great; however, it is presumably not infinitely great. One illustration of such variety comes from studies in New Mexico. Living in the same physical and climatic area, a geographical tableland occupying a corner of the high plateau, are two irrigation agriculture communities, one of Pueblo Indians and one of Mormons, two ranching communities, one Spanish-American and one Navajo Indian, and a specialist dry-zone bean-farming group of Texan Presbyterians. That is to say, there are five distinctive communities in a single geographical area. The desires of the members of these communities, their ways of co-operating to reach their desired objectives, the obligations they feel towards their spouses, children, and kinsmen, their religious beliefs, and their technology all differ.[10] A second illustration from the Old World is afforded by Israel. Over the past forty years there has been a substitution of Israeli Jews for Arab Palestinians; here we have two different communities living side by side in the same environment.

These community differences are so striking that we could say, justifiably, that members of each community looked at, and therefore lived in, different physical environments. All the physical and ecological variables, the climate, and the territory are similar for all five communities in New Mexico and the two in Israel. From the viewpoint of the inhabitants, each community behaves differently in the face of the environment. Perhaps we could say that the society creates the environment as a system of meanings in the same way as it may be said to create the individual. At this point, however, we seem to have substituted a sociological determinism for the earlier geographical determinism. The parallel is more apparent than actual. The earlier argument was that variables in the physical environment affected human behaviour directly. The present argument is that the definition of desires and the availability of techniques determine what effect the physical environment can have on community. Both of these arguments are over simple. We must look more closely both at the structural elements and social processes of the community, and also at the environment as a matrix of possibilities, given certain levels of technology.

Major Environmental Areas

Taking the environment first, some areas of the world are evidently more suited to human life than others. Geographers have for a long time recognized natural ecological regions of the world such as 'areas of increase', where a small effort will bring a lot of return in subsistence, or 'areas of difficulty', where great effort is needed to reach a bare subsistence level. A recent attempt at a more precise classification recognizes four environmental types:

Type 1 Areas of no agricultural potential including tundra, desert, tropical savanna, swamps, and mountain ranges.
Type 2 Areas of limited agricultural potential such as the tropical forest of South America.
Type 3 Areas of improvable agricultural potential including temperature forest lands of Europe and the U.S.A. as well as irrigation areas like parts of California, Iran, Iraq, or Utah.
Type 4 Areas of unlimited agricultural potential where climate, soil, terrain, and fertility are for all practical purposes inexhaustible. These areas include the seats of all Old World and New World civilizations.

The recognition of agriculture as a cultural technique in the development of communities and societies is implicit in this classification.[11] It is the response of the environment to the adoption of a new way of living by the community that is important.

This is but one aspect of adaptation. The appearance of agriculture is not more crucial than the emergence of groups of full-time craft specialists, the urban revolution, or the rise of complex local societies, in the emergence of civilizations. Consequently to associate in a direct fashion the agricultural responsiveness of the environment and the rise of a complex civilization is to overlook a major sociological fact: that adaptation is not a simple stimulus-response process but exists as a complex of causes and a complex of consequences.

Earlier we mentioned the small intermarrying community as one polar type of human settlement: one form of this is often called a 'closed corporate peasant community'.[12] These communities have very clear boundaries but are never closed in any absolute sense. Even the pre-Neolithic fishers of Ireland imported some goods: in the next archaeological period Irish Neolithic tombs already show objects of jade from Brittany, amber from the Baltic, and glass from Portugal or the Mediterranean. In spite of this, we may assume that ideas and techniques were accepted slowly. Modern examples of closed corporate peasant communities abound as villages of subsistence farmers in all continents. One important sociological characteristic of these communities is the lack of a leadership structure. Although reports of village headmen are common, most groups resemble the Skara Brae prehistoric community where every hut was the same size and had the same equipment, showing a minimal degree of status differentiation. Each had only one fireplace: this was interpreted to mean a single family or at any rate one wife per hut.[13] Rights in lands were often redistributed at intervals, in the manner of the infield-outfield economy of the proto-historic Scots and Irish clachan settlements, so that families had equal shares. A study of a modern Tennessee corporate community showed that this redistribution was managed by an outside auctioneer who apparently reached decisions through a formal public bidding, but in reality all decisions were in accordance with prior discussions with the community.[14] There is a parallel here to the classification of farms in Northern Ireland as either Protestant or Catholic when they are put up for auction. Such corporate groups are often communities of equals, where every adult member takes responsibility for the affairs of the community. The Amish of the United States are a typical example of such a group.[15] In such communities the goal of equality of life chances has been reached: fraternity, too, is an ideal characteristic, thanks to intermarriage. The preferred marriage partners in Tennessee in 1965 were double first cousins. If within the community all are of equal status, this can only be maintained from generation to generation by some mechanism such as the redistribution of basic resources, and by strict attention to boundary maintenance to keep traditional ways strong and the strangers who carry new ideas such as achievement, or individual betterment, out. Dozens of examples from India to Ireland are available to illustrate this ideal system of adaptation. The community adapts by applying its traditional skills to its own environment and by distributing the resources produced by these skills to maintain its own status system.

If the community is the group that controls the adaptive processes in any society, then it follows that different community types will follow differing adaptive processes. This means that there may be no one explanatory theory in a strict sense that can cover all the varieties of adaptation. In this paper the adaptive processes are considered one part of solutions to complex problems of community survival. Survival, however, is a wider concept than simply the adaptation of a community to its environment. It encompasses internal processes of change as well as the relationship of one community to other external social systems which are part of its environments.

Types of Communities

No adequate typology of communities exists for our purpose. Most classify communities by the state of technology into: (a) simple hunters, fishers or gatherers, (b) horticultural, using the hoe, (c) agricultural, using the plough, (d) mercantile, and (e) industrial. Many variants on this scheme exist.[16] The levels of technology represent the major innovations of human societies as they seek to provide resources such as food, shelter, and safety for their members. The innovations of domesticated animals, crop husbandry, urban settlement, and industrial organization are the adaptations that are to be explained by any theory of adaptation. But if our arguments are correct, for the study of adaptation the classification criteria must include not only techniques but also community values. Therefore an alternative classification of communities based on their value systems must now be constructed. Two complex variables may be used: first, the pattern of status in the community which may be either 'egalitarian' or 'hierarchal'; secondly the way by which status is acquired which may be either by birth or caste ('ascriptive') or by merit or performance ('achievement'). The first unit of a classificatory scheme drawn up on this basis has been introduced as the closed corporate community. The value system of such a community is 'ascriptive egalitarianism'. Using the structural variables of ascription and achievement together with egalitarianism or its opposite—status differentiation or a hierarchy of social ranks—we can arrive at the following typology:

TABLE 1

Value System	Ideal Community Type	Example
Ascriptive equalitarian	closed corporate	Tennessee
Ascriptive hierarchy	feudal	Japan
Achievement equalitarian	utopian	Israeli kibbutz
Achievement hierarchy	modern industrial	U.S.A.

Explanations for the appearance of major new innovations in any community have been advanced by many theorists. The diffusion theory placed all major social, technological, religious, and political innovations in one regional area and explained their appearance elsewhere by export procedures. This was hardly satisfactory.[17] An alternative explanation is the environmental challenge and response theory: there appear to be better grounds for this theory, since it allows for multiple centres of innovation.[18] Moreover, the desire to reach new goals, or to use new techniques to reach existing goals, is not adequately accounted for by environmental challenges. Another widely accepted theory of innovations is that they are the contribution of Great Men, uniquely gifted individuals. Adaptive innovations represent major changes in both goals (values) and techniques. While Great Men have made their contribution at intervals, the fact of change is constant, though its rate may vary.[19] Lacking any good, well-tested hypotheses, the assumption that innovations are always present and that many small innovations may on occasion be combined into a major adaptive change seems justified as a quantitative approach to the problem.[20]

Recent work in comparative culture gives, through the analysis of newly collected data, some common value configurations or patterns. Most of these reports use the nation or some combination of nations as a spatial aspect of the analysis. One study of 2,500 cultural measures of sixteen California Indian tribal groups finds two distinct patterns: (a) a 'wealth-oriented, competitive, individualistic, sedentary' one, characteristic of ten of the tribes and (b) a 'more co-operative, outgoing, nomadic' one, characteristic of six of the tribes.[21]

Studies based upon data from the responses of samples of population in modern nation states are more difficult to interpet, partly because of sampling problems, partly because of methodological differences, and partly because of the variety of instruments used. Some use multivariate analysis, some simpler correlation techniques, and, while some report empirical factors arising out of clusters of responses in the data, others assume *a priori* clusters of values and therefore can only report simple frequencies. However, all find common or invariant values to report. Amongst the values two seem to have common aspects that are revelant to the theme of adaptation. These are variously phrased as A(I) vigorous order versus unadapted rigidity; A(II) act and enjoy life through group participation; B(I) cultural pressure and complexity versus direct expression of energy; B(II) constantly master changing situations.[22]

These research efforts, yielding empirical values as illustrated above and testing *a priori* normative values as in the New Mexico research, are building a body of knowledge that can in the future enrich the potentiality of the theory of adaptation. The classification of communities mentioned earlier used two complex variables as if they were dichotomous; in reality, each is, in all probability, multidimensional. The basic attitude of each of these community types towards the twin elements that affect the adaptive process, values and techniques, can also be treated as if they were dichotomous: they may resist innovations (—) or they may accept them (+). Using this approach, we get the table below:

TABLE 2

| Community Type | Changes in | |
	Values	Techniques
Ascriptive equalitarian	—	—
Ascriptive hierarchy	—	+
Achievement equalitarian	+	—
Achievement hierarchy	+	+

The Ascriptive Equalitarian community is small in size, traditional in culture, closed as to marriage, and almost always archaic in its technology. Ascriptive hierarchies, the community base of feudal empires, while traditional in their value system are still innovative in their approach to technology. This is a structural consequence of the existence of a hierarchy that includes an *élite*. Even under ascriptive rules, any *élite* position is not secure: these types of upper status positions require the use of power to maintain their claim to the majority of the surplus produced by the community. Even though the holders of these positions use religious leaders to support their privileged position, the continuity of *élites* over several generations is always problematical.[23] The exercise of power requires constant watchfulness coupled with eagerness to adopt new techniques such as cross-bow, armour, gunpowder, or fortifications to maintain a superior position.

Communities based both on equalitarian access to the resources they produce and on achievement are so rare in the natural history of communities we may simply note that they run the continuous risk of becoming ascriptive equalitarian communities after the founding generation has died. This process may explain in part the failure of many utopian communities, though not all utopian communities aim at equality.

Achievement hierarchies represent a major social innovation—the bureaucratic organization. Bureaucracies are hierarchies of specialist roles directed specifically at problem solving as their normal task. A bureaucracy, therefore, by its structure and recruitment, is an instrument of innovation. It functions to solve problems of adaptation.

In this sense, the bureaucracy is almost as old as human civilization. The organization of specialists into a single social structure goes back to the first urban centres: early priest-kings operated through this form of social organization. Although the recruitment pattern may not have been based on tests for merit, early documents show the controls that were placed on officials to be efficient, timely, and industrious.

There is no explicit or implicit order to the statement of these types of communities: no evolutionary sequence or stages of development are intended. If there is any quantitative change through time, it refers only to the rate of increase in the search for, and acceptance of, adaptive innovations. Neither is the typology complete, for bureaucratically organized achievement hierarchies have their own internal rigidities which can lead to ritual performance rather than creative problem solving.

Some of the theoretical ideas in this paper may be tested later with data taken from the Ethnographic Atlas. The lack of data from two points in time that relate to a variety of community types makes possible only a rough test. As data banks about the contemporary world are established, more extensive tests can be carried out.[24] One small-scale field test is reported for the Philippines. In it the degree of receptivity to community development innovations was sought to be explained. Out of twenty-three variables that had some relationship to receptivity of innovations, three are more important than others: (a) highest grade (of education) completed; (b) preference for democratic-type leadership in job tasks; (c) rating of house and grounds for good order. Both (a) education and (b) leadership seem from the text to refer directly to achievement values and hierarchical position based on capacity or performance rather than inheritance. The third probably refers to family co-operation between husband and wife. Other variables such as 'size of farm' and 'size of largest field' are statistically less strong and are weaker than 'clique popularity' and 'having held a local office'. Within the small-scale local peasant community this report shows that achievement and acceptance by peers are both strongly related to the acceptance of innovations.[25]

To take the analysis further the interrelations between other orders of values than those appropriate to status would have to be examined. The goals of the community or the society in the areas of political, religious, economic, and familial values would have to be added to the simplified matrix presented in this paper. That task is much beyond its scope. In it we have argued that the existence of leaders as a consequence of a status hierarchy is not, by itself, enough to account for either the emergence or acceptance of adaptive innovations. Consequently the Great Man theory of social change does not explain the acceptance of adaptive innovations. The environment as a static and relatively unchanging element to which community social systems have to adapt if they are to survive cannot in itself account for the fact of change. Change is a universal social fact: adaptation to the environment is one element of social change. In explaining the process of innovation and acceptance of adaptive changes, this paper has looked at two structural elements of community social systems: (a) the patterned arrangement of the roles they provide in family, work team, religious group, and political system; and (b) the value system that underlies the community rules whereby individuals may legitimately occupy these roles.

The basic propositions advanced in this paper are:

1. The community is the unit of social structure through which environments affect human behaviour. This process is called adaption or adaptation.
2. Any adaptive innovation requires modification both of the value system and also of the techniques of the community if it is to be acceptable.
3. In equalitarian communities rates for the appearance of adaptive innovations will be low.
4. The mere presence of a status system which supports a set of leaders does not guarantee the ready acceptance of innovations.
5. Adaptive innovations are frequent and acceptable in communities with bureaucratic organizations because they have values based on achievement and a status hierarchy that demands performance.
6. Bureaucratic organizational systems have their own internal rigidities which may impede their performance in the process of adaptation. More work on the interrelations of value systems and techniques in political, religious, and family systems is clearly essential.

This paper claims only to be an exploration of one sociological strand in the study of adaptation: it is offered in the hope that others may consider it a constructive beginning, worthy of being extended and tested with appropriate data.

NOTES

[1] C. Monge, 'Biological Basis of Human Behaviour', in A. L. Kroeber (ed.), *Anthropology Today*, Chicago, 1953.

[2] H. F. Harlow, 'The Nature of Love', *American Psych.* 13 (1958), 673–85.

[3] B. Bettelheim, 'Feral Children and Autistic Children', *American J. Sociol.* 64 (1959), 445–67. W. F. Ogburn, 'The Wolf Boy of Agra', *American J. Social.*, 64 (1959), 449–54.

[4] M. Levy et al., *Aspects of the Analysis of Family Structure*, Princeton, N.J., 1965. Marriage rules in different societies approve child marriage, grandparent-grandchild marriage, monogamy, polygyny, polyandry, the existence of wives and mistresses, concubinage, cicisbeism, and so on. Levy points out that in spite of the extreme variety of these rules actual behaviour in marriage is much less variable.

[5] An early statement of this purposive and sociological approach is given by the concept of 'telesis' in L. F. Ward, *Pure Sociology*, New York, 1903, pp. 457–576.

[6] E. A. Wilkening, 'Joint Decision Making in Farm Families as a Function of Status and Role', *American Sociol. Rev.* 23 (1958), 187–92; E. M. Rogers, *Social Change in Rural Society*, New York, 1960.

[7] R. Middleton, 'Brother-sister and father-daughter incest in ancient Egypt', *American Sociol. Rev.* 27 (1962), 602–11, gives an opposite point of view.

[8] T. Parsons, 'The Incest Taboo in Relation to Social Structure and the Socialization of the Child', *British J. Sociol.* 5 (1954), 101–17.

[9] G. P. Murdock, 'Statistical Relations Among Community Characteristics' in P. F. Lazarsfeld and M. Rosenberg (eds.), *The Language of Social Research*, Glencoe, Ill., 1955, pp. 305–11.

[10] F. R. Kluckholn and F. L. Strodtbeck, *Variations in Value Orientations*, Evanston, Ill., 1961.

[11] B. J. Meggers, 'Environmental Limitations to the Development of Culture', *American Anthrop.* 56 (1954), 801–24. Quoted from J. B. Bresler (ed.), *Environments of Man*, Boston, 1968.

[12] E. Wolf, 'Closed Corporate Peasant Communities', *Southwestern J. Anthrop.* 13 (1957), 1–13.

[13] V. G. Childe, *Scotland Before the Scots*, London, 1946.

[14] E. M. Mathews, *Neighbor and Kin*, Nashville, Tenn., 1965, pp. 14–20.

[15] S. A. Freed, 'Suggested Type Societies in Acculturation Studies', *American Anthrop.* 59 (1957), 58–68.

[16] G. Lenski, *Power and Privilege, a Theory of Social Stratification*, New York, 1966.

[17] W. J. Perry, *The Children of the Sun*, New York, 1923.

[18] A. J. Toynbee, *A Study of History*, London, 12 vols., 1934–59.

[19] S. Hook, *The Hero in History: a Study in Limitation and Possibility*, Boston, 1955.

[20] W. Moore, *Social Change*, New York, 1965.

[21] K. F. Schuessler and H. E. Driver, 'Factor Analysis of Sixteen Primitive Societies', *American Sociol. Rev.* 21 (1956), 393–9. Quoted from R. M. Marsh, *Comparative Sociology*, New York: Harcourt, Brace & World, 1967, pp. 220–2.

[22] R. M. Marsh, op. cit., pp. 221–7

[23] S. Keller, *Beyond the Ruling Class*, New York, 1963.

[24] R. B. Textor, *A Cross Cultural Summary*, New Haven, Conn., 1967, p. 208 with 2,000 pp. tables; A. D. Coult and R. Habenstein, *Cross Tabulations of the World Ethnographic Sample*, Columbia, Mo., 1965.

[25] F. C. Madigan, 'Predicting Receptivity to Community Development Innovations', *Current Anthropology*, 3, No. 2 (1962), 207–8.

PART THREE:

PROCESSES

12. THE BALANCED COMMUNITY

Homogeneity or Heterogeneity in Residential Areas?

H. J. Gans

In 'Planning and Social Life', which appeared in the May 1961 issue of this journal, I discussed the influence of propinquity and homogeneity on social relations. I tried to show that architectural and site plans can encourage or discourage social contact between neighbours, but that homogeneity of background or of interests or values was necessary for this contact to develop into anything more than a polite exchange of greetings. Without such homogeneity, more intensive social relations are not likely to develop, and excessive heterogeneity can lead to coolness between neighbours, regardless of their propinquity. Homogeneity is even more fundamental in friendship formation, and its presence allows people to find friends near by, whereas its absence requires them to look further afield for friends.

These observations can be combined with a variety of value judgements, each resulting in alternative planning recommendations. I argued that positive, although not necessarily close, relations among neighbours and maximal opportunity for the free choice of friends both near and far from home were desirable values, and concluded that a moderate degree of homogeneity among neighbours would therefore be required.

The advocacy of moderate homogeneity was based on a single set of values, those concerning the quality of social life. Communities have many other functions besides sociability, however, and planning must therefore concern itself with other values as well. With such values in mind, many influential planners have advocated the balanced residential area, containing a typical cross-section of dwelling-unit types and population characteristics, notably age groups and socio-economic levels.[1]

Population heterogeneity has generally been advocated for at least four reasons:[2]

1. It adds variety as well as demographic 'balance' to an area and thus enriches the inhabitants' lives. Conversely, homogeneity is said to stultify, as well as to deprive people of important social resources, such as the wisdom of the older generation in the suburbs.

2. It promotes tolerance of social and cultural differences, thus reducing political conflict and encouraging democratic practices. Homogeneity increases the isolation between area residents and the rest of society.

3. It provides a broadening educational influence on children, by teaching them about the existence of diverse types of people and by creating the opportunity for them to learn to get along with these people. Homogeneity is thought to limit children's knowledge of diverse classes, ages, and races, and to make them less capable of association with others in later years.

From *Journal of the American Institute of Planners* 27 . 3 (1961), 176–84. Reprinted by permission of the author and the editor of the journal.

4. It encourages exposure to alternative ways of life, for example, by providing intellectually inclined neighbours for the child from a bookless household, or by offering the mobile working-class family an opportunity to learn middle-class ways. Homogeneity freezes people in present ways of life.

These are actually ends to be achieved through population heterogeneity, and should be discussed as such. Two questions must then be answered:

1. Are the ends themselves desirable?
2. Is the balanced community a proper means for achieving them; that is, is it a logically and empirically verifiable means, free of undesirable by-products or consequences?

No one can quarrel with the ends. A society of diverse people taking pride in their diversity, enriching their own and their children's lives by it, and co-operating to achieve democracy and to alleviate useless social conflict is a delightful and desirable vision. I believe that the achievement of this vision is a legitimate planning goal, and the means to achieve it should be explored.

Whether or not the goal can be achieved simply by requiring diverse people to live together is debatable, however. Even if the planning or legislating of population heterogeneity could be implemented—which is doubtful at present—it is questionable whether a heterogeneous and balanced community would result in the envisaged way of life. Many other societal conditions would have to be altered before such a way of life were possible, notably the present degree of economic and social inequality that now exists in the typical metropolitan area's population.

The data needed to determine the ends-means relationships I have suggested are not yet available, so that only tentative conclusions can be reached. The discussion will be limited to heterogeneity of age, class, and race—these being the most important criteria affecting and differentiating community life.[3]

Heterogeneity and Social Relations

The belief in the efficacy of heterogeneity is based on the assumption that if diverse people live together, they will inevitably become good neighbours or even friends and, as a result, learn to respect their differences. The comments about the importance of homogeneity in social relations in my previous article suggest that this assumption is not valid. A mixing of all age and class groups is likely to produce at best a polite but cool social climate, lacking the consensus and intensity of relations that are necessary for mutual enrichment. Instances of conflict are as probable as those of co-operation. For example, some old people who live in a community of young couples may vicariously enjoy their neighbours' children—and vice versa—but others will resent the youngsters' noise and the destruction they wreak on flowerbeds. Likewise, some older residents may be founts of wisdom for their younger neighbours, but others are insistent advocates of anachronistic ideas. In a rapidly changing society, the knowledge that the older generation has gathered by virtue of its experience is outdated more quickly than in the past, when social change was less rapid.

Class differences also result in a mixture of good and bad consequences. I noted in the earlier article that most neighbour disputes arise about the children and that they stem from differences in child-rearing norms among the classes and among parents of different educational backgrounds. People who want to bring their children up one way do not long remain tolerant of the parents of a playmate who is being reared by diametrically opposed methods. People with higher incomes and more education may feel that they or their children are being harmed by living among less advantaged neighbours. The latter are likely to feel equally negative about the 'airs' being put on by the former, although some may want to keep up, especially in matters concerning the children. This can wreck family budgets and, occasionally, family stability as well. Social and cultural mobility is difficult enough when it is desired, but it may become a burden to families who are forced into it involuntarily.

The negative consequences of heterogeneity are not inevitable, but they occur with regularity, even among the most well-intentioned people. As a result, a markedly heterogeneous community that spells enrichment to the planner— especially to the one who sees it only through maps, census reports, and windshield surveys—may mean endless bickering and unsettled feuds to the people who actually live in it.

Indeed, the virtues ascribed to heterogeneity are more often associated with the degree and type of population homogeneity found in the typical new suburb. Much has been written about the alleged dangers of homogeneity, but, frequently, these allegations are based on the false assumption that, because the suburbs as a whole are statistically more homogeneous than cities as a whole, suburbanites are all *alike*. Even if they were alike in age and income—which is not true—they would still be different in occupation, educational level, ethnic and religious background, and regional origin, as well as temperament.

In actual fact, many suburban subdivisions are more heterogeneous than the urban neighbourhoods from which some of their residents came. For example, in Levittown, New Jersey, many people felt that they were encountering a greater mixture of backgrounds than where they had lived before.[4] The fact that most people were similar enough in age and, to a lesser extent, income, enabled them to become friendly with people of different occupations, religions, ethnic backgrounds, or regional origins for the first time in their lives. Many felt that they had been enriched by experiencing this diversity. This would not have been possible if marked differences in age and income had also been present. It would seem, therefore, that in the large 'brand name' suburbs, at least, the relatively greater homogeneity of age and income provides the cultural and social prerequisites which allow people to enjoy their neighbours' heterogeneity with respect to other, less basic characteristics.

Heterogeneity and Democracy

Heterogeneity is also thought to engender the tolerance necessary for the achievement of local democracy and for the reduction of social and political conflict. When differences between people are small, residents of an area can develop tolerance towards each other; they can even agree to ignore some important differences that stand in the way of consensus. More extreme population heterogeneity is not likely to have the same result.

Sizeable differences, especially with regard to fundamental social and economic interests, are not erased or set aside by the mere fact of living together. For example, many suburban communities today are split over the question of school expenditures. Upper-middle- and middle-class residents, for whom high-quality schooling is important regardless of price, cannot often find a common meeting ground with lower-middle-class residents, who may have different definitions of quality and who place less urgent priority on getting their children into a 'good' college, or with working-class residents for whom tax economy is often—and of sheer necessity—the most important consideration.[5] Under such conditions, heterogeneity is not likely to encourage greater tolerance, and the struggle between competing points of view may be so intense that the relatively fragile norms of democratic procedure sometimes fall by the wayside. Homogeneity facilitates the workings of the democratic process, but this is no solution for a pluralist society such as ours. Nevertheless, heterogeneity itself does not facilitate the achievement of the democratic norms of community decision-making.

Heterogeneity and the Children

The value of population heterogeneity for children is based on the assumption that they discover other age-groups and classes through visual contact, and that they learn how to live with them through the resulting social contact. In actual fact, however, children develop their conceptions of society and the ability to get along with diverse types from the actions and attitudes of the persons with whom they come into close and continual social contact—especially parents, playmates, and teachers. Mere visual contact does not, however, result in close contact. Although a city child may see all segments of society, he is not likely to come into close contact with them. Even if he does, there is no guarantee that he will learn to be tolerant of differences, especially if he has learned to evaluate these differences negatively at home or elsewhere. Parental attitudes or direct prohibitions can thus discourage a child from playing with other children whom he sees everyday. Conversely, a suburban child, is still likely to learn about them—and to evaluate them—from comments made by his parents. If these parents are well educated, the child may even learn to become tolerant of people he has never seen. (In reality, city children get out of their own neighbourhoods much less often than is sometimes imagined, and they may not see people of other ages, classes, and races unless they happen to live in particularly heterogeneous or changing residential areas.)

This issue may be illustrated by the relationship between the races. White city children probably see more non-whites, at least from a distance, than do suburban children, although even in suburbs like Levittown and Park Forest, enough families hire domestic help to insure some visual contact with non-whites. If community heterogeneity had the positive effects attributed to it, we should expect that city children, who do see more non-whites, would exhibit greater racial tolerance than suburban ones. This has not happened, however,

In fact, the opposite is probably true. Children exhibit little or no racial intolerance until they are old enough to understand the attitudes and behaviour patterns of their parents and other adults. These reactions reflect the current economic and social inequality of the white and non-white populations. If children could be isolated from such reactions, they might grow up with more tolerance than they now do. This is, of course, not possible. Consequently, until the inequality between the races is removed, there is little hope for a pervasive change in inter-racial understanding, either in the city or in the suburb.

The older city child differs from his suburban peer in that he is more likely to have close contact with children of diverse background, for example, of class and race, because urban schools usually draw from a wider variety of residential areas than suburban ones. Although researchers are still undecided whether close contact will increase tolerance and understanding—or under what conditions it is likely to have more positive than negative effects—such contacts should be encouraged wherever possible.[6] This would suggest the desirability of heterogeneous schools, in the suburbs as well as in the city.

Heterogeneity and Exposure to Alternatives

Heterogeneity is also valued for the opportunity it provides for exposure to alternative and, by implication, better ways of life. Elizabeth Wood's recent argument for the balanced neighbourhood stresses this value. She is concerned primarily with public housing and argues that middle-class ones with organizational leadership and with models to inspire them to accept middle-class standards. If public housing projects and the neighbourhoods in which they are located are homogeneously working class or lower class, the population is deprived of the two functions supposedly performed by the middle class.[7]

Middle-class people have traditionally supplied leadership in settlement houses and similar institutions located in working-class neighbourhoods; however, these institutions have not attracted large working-class clientele except from among the socially mobile and from children.[8] The latter tend to use the facilities, while ignoring the middle-class values being propagated by the staff. Middle-class people are also likely to be more active in voluntary associations, such as clubs, civic groups, and tenant organizations, than working-class people, but their activity is usually limited to organizations with middle-class goals, and these are shunned by working-class people. Such organizations do, however, provide leadership to the latter, by offering guidance to the socially mobile, and by pursuing activities which may benefit every class in the area. Occasionally, a middle-class person may also function as a leader of a predominantly working-class organization, although this is rare.

Instances of middle-class leadership abounded in the annals of public housing during the 1930s and the 1940s. Today, however, public housing attracts or accepts mainly the deprived lower-class population, which stays away from middle-class institutions and does not often join voluntary associations of any kind. The deprived population needs and wants help, but so far, it has not often accepted leadership from the types of middle-class institutions and persons who offer it.

No one knows what motivates working-class people to adopt middle-class standards, or whether the presence of middle-class neighbours is likely to do so.[9] The new suburban communities could be studied advantageously from this viewpoint. My own impression is that heterogeneity enables those already motivated towards social mobility to learn from their middle-class neighbours and that, in some instances, the exposure to such neighbours can inspire previously unmotivated individuals to change their ways. As previously noted, close contact can have negative as well as positive consequences, for working-class people are as likely to resent the 'uppity' behaviour of middle-class residents as they are to adopt it. Success in teaching alternative ways of life seems to be dependent on three conditions. *First*, the people involved must have the necessary economic wherewithal and the social skills required for the new way. *Second*, sociologists of social stratification have found that ideas and values are diffused from one class to the one immediately 'above' or 'below' it, rather than between classes that diverge sharply in income, education, and other background characteristics. Consequently, positive effects are more likely to be achieved under conditions of moderate population heterogeneity. Extreme heterogeneity is likely to inhibit communication and to encourage mutual resentment, whereas moderate heterogeneity provides enough compatibility of interests and skills to enable communication—and therefore learning—to take place. *Third*, the 'teachers' must be sympathetic to the needs and backgrounds of their students, and must have sufficient empathy to understand their point of view.

Wood suggests that heterogeneity be implemented through community facilities and neighbourhood institutions, and that these be used to encourage the exposure to alternative ways, since the mixture of classes can be accomplished more easily than in residential arrangements. (A similar use of community facilities has recently been proposed by some planners and community organization officials concerned with the social aspects of urban renewal, in order to aid slum dwellers to adapt to life in non-slum urban surroundings.)

I have already noted, however, that such agencies have had little success so far in converting working-class clients to middle-class points of view. Although the lack of success can be explained on the basis of cultural differences between the classes, the existing research has not yet led to policy suggestions as to how these differences may be bridged. My impression is that much of the emphasis—and hope—placed on community facilities and professionally trained staff is naïve. These two elements are important, but success is likely only if the persons chosen to work in such facilities have empathy for their clients' culture and needs. This quality may be more important than professional training, but it is not easily learned, for it entails much more than sympathy and good intentions. Unfortunately, empathic personalities are rare. Consequently, the encouragement of heterogeneiety in community facilities is desirable, but it cannot by itself motivate people to expose themselves to new alternatives.

Implications for Planning

I have tried to show that the advantages of heterogeneiety and the disadvantages of homogeneity have both been exaggerated and that neither is unqualifiedly good or bad. Extreme forms of either are undesirable. Complete, or near-complete homogeneity, as in a company town where everyone has the same kind of job, is clearly objectionable. Total heterogeneity is likely to be so uncomfortable that only those who want no social contact with neighbours would wish to live under such conditions. Even then, it would be tolerable only in apartment buildings in which visual contact between residents is minimal. Both extremes are rarely found in actual communities. In considering planning implications, we need concern ourselves primarily with more moderate forms.

Specific implications for planning policy are best discussed in two steps, at the level of block life, and at the level of area-wide community life. At the block level, the arguments of this and the earlier article suggest that the degree of heterogeneity advocated in the balanced community concept—which comes close to total heterogeneity—is unlikely to produce social relationships of sufficient intensity to achieve either a positive social life or the cultural, political, and educational values sought through the balanced community. The ideal solution is sufficient homogeneity with respect to those characteristics that will assure:

1. Enough consensus between neighbours to prevent conflict;
2. Positive although not necessarily intensive relationships between neighbours with respect to common needs and obligations;
3. The possibility for some mutual visiting and friendship formation for those who want it in the immediate vicinity.

This should provide sufficient heterogeneity to create some diversity as well. At the present time, no one knows how this solution could be defined operationally, that is, what mixture of specific characteristics would be likely to provide the kind of homogeneity suggested above. Consequently, existing subdivisions with differing degrees of homogeneity and heterogeneity should be studied, and adventurous builders should be encouraged to experiment with mixing people and house types. Planners and students of urban life could observe the results systematically and provide the evidence needed for more specific guides for planning. These guides would not spell out detailed dwelling-unit or population mixtures but would indicate only the types of population compositions which should be avoided because they bring about the undesirable effects of too much homogeneity or heterogeneity.

At the community level, and especially at the level of the politically defined community, population heterogeneity is desirable.[10] It is not a proper means to the ends for which it has been advocated, although a moderate degree of heterogeneity may aid in the achievement of the educational and exposure values. Rather, its desirability must be argued in relation to two other values. *First*, ours is a pluralistic society, and local communities should reflect this pluralism. *Second*, and more important as long as local taxation is the main support for community services, homogeneity at the community level encourages undesirable inequalities. The high-income suburb can build modern schools with all the latest features; the low-income suburb is forced to treat even minimal educational progress as a luxury. Such inequity is eliminated more efficiently by federal and state subsidy than by community heterogeneity, but the latter is essential as long as such subsidies are so small.

The ideal amount and type of heterogeneity can only be guessed at, since so little is known about the impact of population characteristics within various sectors of community life. Two general statements can be made, however.

First, enough homogeneity must be present to allow institutions to function and interest groups to reach workable compromises. In areas with a wide range of population types, the balanced community—that is, a local cross-section of the entire area—would probably experience intense political and cultural conflict. Since local institutions, including government, have little power to affect—and to ameliorate—the basic causes of such conflict, they would be unable to handle it constructively. Conflict itself is not unhealthy, but irreconcilable conflict is socially destructive, and nothing would be gained by instituting population heterogeneity within political units which cannot deal with the negative consequences of conflict.

Second, enough heterogeneity must be provided in the community so that important facilities and services can be financed and enabled to find sufficient clients to allow them to function. Economic or social ghettos, either of the very rich or the very poor, are thus not desirable. (Cultural ghettos, such as those of ethnic groups, are not a problem, as long as they are voluntary ones and are able to provide non-ethnic facilities for those who want to get out of the group.)

The generality of these proposals illustrates clearly how little is known about the consequences of homogeneity and heterogeneity. More specific planning guides require a thoroughgoing research programme that would explore the consequences of different types and degrees of population mixture for a variety of planning values. No one can now predict the conclusions of such research. For example, I have suggested that schools with heterogeneous student bodies are desirable. Systematic studies may show, however, that children learn better among homogeneous peers. The tracking system that exists in many high schools, and even in elementary schools, suggest this possibility. Moreover, such studies might also show that the heterogeneous elements of the student body come into visual contact, but do not achieve any real social contact. If the learning benefits resulting from homogeneity are greater than the social benefits of a mixed student body, a more homogeneous school system might be desirable. Such a system would, however, conflict with yet another value, that of the school as a symbol and an institution of democratic pluralism. Needless to say, comparison of different types of values is not an easy task. Nevertheless, the importance of the balanced-community concept in contemporary planning thought, and the constant rejection of the concept in the housing market, suggest that policy-oriented research along this line is badly needed.

An Appraisal of Present Conditions

It should be clear from the preceding comments that I place little value on heterogeneity as an end in itself. Consequently, I see no overwhelming objections against the patterns of population distribution that exist in today's suburban subdivisions and new communities. I noted earlier the beneficial effects of the kind of population mixture found in Levittown. In addition, the fact that most developments are built in or near older towns, and therefore fall into existing political subdivisions, usually creates additional heterogeneity at the community level.

Thus it would seem that the present system, in which the housing industry supplies subdivisions which are homogeneous in price and where the buyer decides what he can afford or wants to pay, makes for a degree of heterogeneity that is satisfactory both from the point of view of the residents and from that of society as a whole. Three qualifying comments must be added, however. *First*, acceptance of house-price homogeneity should not be interpreted as a justification for accompanying by-products, and especially for racial or religious discrimination. Specifically, if an individual chooses to move into an area where the residents differ from him in age, income; race, religion, or ethnic background, he has not only the right to do so, but he also has the right to governmental support to uphold his action. If this wreaks havoc with the block's social life or the community's consensus, it is an unfortunate but irrelevant consequence. Freedom of choice, civil rights, and the protection of minority interests are values of higher priority than peaceful social life or consensus. *Second*, the homogeneity of population that results from the homogeneity of house price is on the whole voluntary, differing radically from the enforced homogeneity of slums and public-housing projects, which force deprived people into clearly labelled economic ghettos. *Third*, the fact that the present suburban housing-market arrangements may be satisfactory with respect to population mixture does not excuse their inability to house low- and even medium-income families.

Towards A Reformulation of the Issue

At the present time, population heterogeneity as advocated by planners is not workable. Neither home purchasers nor tenants seem to want it, and the housing market is not organized to provide it. (Planners themselves rarely practise what they preach, and usually reside in areas inhabited by people of like values and class background.) Consequently, it is unlikely that heterogeneity can be implemented through planning or other legislative and political means. Lack of feasibility is not a legitimate objection, *per se*. However, I have tried to show that heterogeneity does not really achieve the ends sought by its advocates.

Moreover, even if it could be implemented, it would not solve the problems that currently beset our communities. *Indeed, the opposite is closer to the truth; population heterogeneity cannot be achieved until the basic metropolitan-area social problem is solved.* This I believe to be the economic and social inequalities that still exist in our society, as expressed in the deprivations and substandard living conditions of the lowest socio-economic strata of the metropolitan-area population. These conditions in turn produce some of the residential patterns that restrict population heterogeneity. For example, the present homogeneity of the age and class in cities and suburbs results in part from the desire of middle-class and working-class families to avoid contact with the deprived population and with the way it is forced to live. Thus the city—and especially its inner areas—becomes the abode of the very rich, the very poor, and those who cannot get away.

The planner's advocacy of heterogeneity is in part a means for dealing with this problem; he hopes that the mixing of classes will iron out these inequalities. The intent is noble, but the means are inappropriate. What is needed instead is the raising of substandard incomes, the provision of greater occupational and educational opportunities to the deprived population, and the development of institutions that will create opportunities tailored to their needs and cultural wants. These programmes should receive first priority in future metropolitan-area policy-making.

The elimination of deprivation cannot be implemented solely or even primarily by city planning as now practised. Nor are physical planning methods of much relevance. Some policies may fit into the newly emerging field of local social planning, but many can be achieved only through economic and legislative decisions at the national level. Some of the programmes in which city planners are involved do, however, bear a direct relation to the basic goal; and changes in city-planning policies would, therefore, be helpful in achieving it. For example, urban-renewal programmes that give highest priority to the improvement of housing conditions of the poorest city dwellers would be more desirable than, and considerably different from, those presently supported by the city planning profession.[11] Similarly, school planning which seeks better methods and facilities for educating lower-class children—the average as well as the gifted—is more important than concern with space standards that are currently applicable only to high-income, low-density communities.[12] Also, a more serious attempt to solve the recreation problems of inner-city children should complement, if not replace, the current preoccupations with marinas and with regional parks for well-to-do suburban residents.

I am suggesting that the city-planning profession should pay less attention to improving the physical environment of those who are already comparatively well served by private and public means, and pay more attention to the environmental conditions of the deprived population. Such a change in planning emphasis will not by itself solve the problem (even an intensive national programme geared to reduce all inequality cannot erase immediately the inequities of a century), but it will be making a contribution towards the eventual solution.

The reduction of inequalities may also have some positive consequences for population heterogeneity. At first, greater social and economic equality would result in greater homogeneity of income, education, and the like. This homogeneity would, however, extend to a larger number of people the opportunity to make choices, and this in turn is likely to result in more heterogeneity of attitude and behaviour. Thus, if more people have the discretionary income and the skills to make choices, they will begin to express and to implement preferences. This can create a demand for greater diversity in housing, recreation, taste, and in many other aspects of life.

It must be stressed, however, that the resulting heterogeneity would be qualitatively different from the type that exists today. The disappearance of ways of life based on deprivation would do away with such phenomena as the street life of the overcrowded slum which now provides a measure of variety to the social and physical landscape of a middle-class society. Thus, there would undoubtedly be less clearly visible *cultural diversity*, especially since ethnic differences and exotic immigrant neighbourhoods are also disappearing. Conversely, the ability of people to make choices should result in greater expression of *individual preferences*.[13] Even now, home-owners in the Park Forests and the Levittowns make more individual changes in their houses than do the owners of urban row-houses.

There is no reason to expect that homogeneity of class and age will ever be totally eliminated in residential areas. But it is possible that a somewhat closer approximation to the kind of residential heterogeneity advocated by planners may be realized when the extreme cultural differences have disappeared and when a greater number of people have more freedom of choice with respect to residence.

Appendix

Heterogeneity for Aesthetic Values

My argument has dealt primarily with population heterogeneity, but planners have also advocated heterogeneity of house types, primarily for aesthetic reasons. In the past, it was thought that aesthetic values could be achieved only through custom-built housing, and the discussions of the topic stressed the evils of mass production. Today the issue is: how much heterogeneity should be provided in mass-produced housing to create aesthetic values. No one, including the builder himself, is opposed to beauty; but considerable disagreement exists over priorities and about the definition of aesthetic standards.

The issue of priorities is basically economic, and the debate rages about the price consequences of house-type heterogeneity. I feel that the aesthetic benefits of house-type diversity are not sufficient to justify depriving anyone of a new house because he cannot afford to pay for variations in floor plans or elevations. No one wants what Vernon De Mars has called cookie-cutter developments, although the home buyer with limited means may have no other alternative, and he may subsequently build his own individuality into the house when he can afford to do so. Builders of mass-produced housing should of course be encouraged to vary designs and site plans as much as possible, as long as the added cost does not price anyone out of the market who would otherwise be able to buy. Planners and architects should be able to use their professional skills to help builders to achieve variety; but, too often, their recommendations add too much to costs and prices.

In recent years, planners have advocated a mixture of dwelling-unit types, mainly to cut down suburban sprawl, but also to provide aesthetic variety. Unfortunately, architects have not yet designed saleable row-houses or duplexes, and the universal dislike of these house types among most home buyers has not created the incentives necessary for experimentation by builders or their designers. Some sophisticated consumer research to discover what people dislike about the higher-density dwelling-unit types is necessary before acceptable new versions can be developed.

The second issue results from the lack of agreement on aesthetic standards. Although everyone seeks beauty, concepts of beauty and of what is beautiful or ugly differ between professionals and laymen, as well as between people of different socio-economic backgrounds and educational levels. Unfortunately, the American dedication to cultural pluralism specifically excludes aesthetic pluralism. As a result, demands for more beauty in housing usually favour the aesthetic standards of a single group, the well-educated, upper-middle-class professional.[14] Indeed, much of the critique of suburban housing and of suburbia generally is a thinly veiled attack by this group on the aesthetic principles and on the over-all taste level of the middle- and working-class population.

There is at present no democratic method for reconciling the aesthetic disagreement. Since differences of taste have not been proved to be socially or emotionally harmful, or inimical to the public interest, there is no justification for an undemocratic implementation of a single aesthetic standard. In a democracy, each person is, and should be, free to pursue his concept of beauty. Aesthetic pluralism may hurt the aesthetic sensibilities of the better-educated people, but until every one has the opportunity to acquire their level of education, such hurts must be borne as a price—and a small one—of living in a democracy. No one should be discouraged from advocating and propagating his own aesthetic standards, but public policy must take the existence of taste differences into account. Needless to say, this does not justify promoting ugliness or taking architectural shortcuts under the guise of aesthetic pluralism. Architectural and site designs should, however, respect the aesthetic standards of those people for whom they are primarily intended. This requires some knowledge—little of it now available—about diverse aesthetic standards, and cannot be based on uninformed guesses about such standards by either architect or builder. Public buildings exist for the benefit of all cultural groups, and should therefore appeal to what is common in all aesthetic standards; or better still, promote architectural innovation. Cognizance of the diversity of aesthetic standards will of course add additional heterogeneity to the landscape.[15]

NOTES AND REFERENCES

This is the second of two articles exploring the relationships between homogeneity, heterogeneity, and propinquity in social relations. The first, entitled 'Planning and Social Life: Friendship and Neighbor Relations in Suburban Communities', appeared in the May 1961 issue of this journal.

[1] See, e.g., Catherine Bauer, 'Social Questions in Housing and Community Planning', *Journal of Social Issues*, 7 (1951), 23; Lewis Mumford, 'The Neighborhood and the Neighborhood-Unit', *Town Planning Review*, 24 (1954), 267–8; Howard Hallman, 'Citizens and Professionals Reconsider the Neighborhood', *Journal of the American Institute of Planners*, 25 (1959), 123–4; Elizabeth Wood. *A New Look at the Balanced Neighborhood* (New York: Citizen's Housing and Planning Council, December 1960). Reginald Isaacs's critique of the neighbourhood plan is based on a similar point of view. See, e.g., 'The Neighborhood Theory', *Journal of the American Institute of Planners*, 14 (1948), 15–23.

[2] A fifth reason, the contribution of heterogeneity to aesthetic values is discussed at the end of the article. I shall not deal at all with economic reasons, for example, with the desirability of age heterogeneity in order to prevent tax burdens resulting from the flood of school-age children in suburban communities.

[3] Comments made in the May 1961 article about race as a symbol of class differences (especially on page 137 and in note 12) apply here also.

[4] Communities like Park Forest and Levittown may be more heterogeneous in class than smaller and higher-priced subdivisions. The low house-price attracts two types of owners: mobile young couples who will eventually buy more expensive houses as the husband advances in his career; and somewhat older families in which the husband has reached the peak of his earning power and who are buying their first, and probably last, house. These communities are also more likely than smaller subdivisions to attract newcomers to the metropolitan area, which creates a greater diversity of regional origins.

[5]In some suburbs, this conflict is complicated by religious differences. Moreover, Catholic families, who may have to support two school systems, often have lower family incomes than do the members of other religious groups.

[6]For an interesting study of the attitudes which young children bring to an inter-racial nursery school, and of the role of close contact in affecting the inter-racial relationship, see Mary E. Goodman, *Race Awareness in Young Children* (Cambridge: Addison-Wesley Press, 1952). The general problem is discussed in George E. Simpson and J. Milton Yinger, 'The Sociology of Race and Ethnic Relations'; in Robert K. Merton, Leonard Broom, and Leonard S. Cottrell, Jr. (eds.), *Sociology Today* (New York: Basic Books, 1959), pp. 397—8.

[7]Wood. op. cit., pp. 18—21.

[8]For an analysis of the working-class client's view of the settlement house, see Albert K. Cohen, *Delinquent Boys: The Culture of the Gang* (Glencoe, Illinois: The Free Press, 1955), pp. 116—17.

[9]There is some evidence that students react positively to the exposure to alternatives. Alan B. Wilson found that some working-class high-school students adopt middle-class standards if they attend a predominantly middle-class school, and that some middle-class students adopt working-class standards if they attend a predominantly working-class school. See his 'Class Segregation and Aspirations of Youth', *American Sociological Review*, 24 (1959), 836—45. Students are socially more impressionable than adults, however, and the school is a more persuasive social environment than a residential area or a voluntarily attended neighbourhood institution.

[10]The planner has traditionally concerned himself more with the neighbourhood than with either the block or the political community. The neighbourhood is not a meaningful social unit, however, since the significant face-to-face relationships occur on the block. Moreover, it is not a political unit and thus cannot make decisions about its population composition. The neighbourhood is therefore not a relevant unit for considering this issue.

[11]For details, see Herbert J. Gans, 'The Human Implications of Current Redevelopment and Relocation Planning', *Journal of the American Institute of Planners*, 25 (1959), 23—5. In contrast, it may be noted that the recent AIP policy statement on urban renewal refers only to the removal of blight and has nothing to say about the improvement of housing conditions of those who live in blighted areas. 'Urban Renewal', *Journal of the American Institute of Planners*, 25 (1959), 221.

[12]See John W. Dyckman, 'Comment on Glazer's School Proposals', *Journal of the American Institute of Planners* 25 (1959), especially p. 199.

[13]The two types of heterogeneity and their implications for American society are explored more fully in Herbert J. Gans, 'Diversity is Not Dead', *New Republic*, 144 (3 April 1961), 11—15.

[14]It is therefore no coincidence that the illustrations of aesthetically desirable blocks in most planning reports are usually from high-income residential neighbourhoods. See, for example, Henry Fagin and Robert C. Weinberg, eds., *Planning and Community Appearance* (New York: Regional Plan Association, Inc., May 1958).

[15]For a discussion of aesthetic differences and taste levels, see Russell Lynes, 'Highbrow, Lowbrow', in *The Tastemakers* (New York: Harper and Brothers, 1954), Chapter 13. For an excellent discussion of aesthetic pluralism in a democracy, see Lyman Bryson, *The Next American* (New York: Harper and Brothers, 1952), Chapter 10. Some of the policy implications of my point of view are discussed in Herbert J. Gans, 'Pluralist Esthetics and Subcultural Programming', *Studies in Public Communications*, No. 3 (Summer 1960).

13. BEHAVIOURAL ASPECTS OF THE DECISION TO MIGRATE

J. Wolpert

During the decade 1950–60, there were sufficient changes from previous patterns of migration streams in the United States to warrant some re-examination and re-evaluation of model-building attempts in migration analysis. It must be admitted that the gravity model and its elaborations appear to lose explanatory power with each successive census. When flows are disaggregated, the need becomes greater selectively to determine unique weights for areas and unique distance functions for subgroups of in- and out-migrants. The Stouffer model of 'competing migrants'[1] provided a rather poor prediction of migration streams for the 1955–60 period. Perhaps the most successful of spatial interaction models, which does take into consideration the spatial arrangement of places of origin and destination, is sufficiently rooted in the 1935–40 depression-period movements so as to present serious deficiencies when applied to recent streams. Plots of migration distances defy the persistence of the most tenacious of curve fitters.

The defenders of the wage theory of economic determinism find some validity for their constructs, so long as net, and not gross, migration figures are used and regional disaggregation does not proceed below the state level, thereby neglecting much of the intrastate heterogeneity.[2]

The extremely scanty empirical evidence of the 'friends and relatives effect' in directing migration has given birth to a generation of models which, although offering the solace of a behavioural approach, provide little explanation of the actual process involved.[3] Perhaps the most serious gap occurs in the transition from micro- to macro-model and in the selection of appropriate surrogates for testing. Here, the inadequacy of published data in the United States appears to have its most telling effect. Though almost every conceivable method of combining existing data into useful indicators has been tried, explanation through surrogates hardly provides an analysis which is independent of the bias which is introduced.

A good deal of useful information has come from the analysis of migration differentials by categories of occupation, income, race, and, especially, age.[4] However, predictive models have not been designed to include these findings and to consider the interdependence of these characteristics in migration behaviour. Demonstrating the potential usefulness of the migration differential approach is one of the objectives of this paper.

A composite of interesting ideas about migration behaviour has been incorporated within Price's ambitious proposed simulation model.[5] On the basis of selected characteristics of individuals and of places of origin and destination, migration probabilities are generated reflecting empirically observed regularities. As far as it is known, the model has not become operational—the task for simulating

From *Papers of the Regional Science Association*, 15 (1965). Reprinted by permission of the Regional Science Association.

United States migration would overtax the most modern computer. The only successful attempt in this direction has been Morrill's study of the emerging town development in south central Sweden.[6]

The use of Monte Carlo simulation models in migration analysis does offer a viable and promising approach, especially considering the rather persistent tendencies for critical elements or parameters to remain stable over time. Thus, although the streams show considerable variation over time, and the characteristics of the population and of places continuously change, stability persists in migration behaviour.

To illustrate this observation it may be noted that Bogue, Shryock, and Hoermann,[7] in their analysis of the 1935–40 migration streams, summarize with the following statements that could as well be applied to the 1955–60 streams:

1. Basic shifts in the regional and territorial balance of the economy guided the direction and flow of migration streams.
2. The two factors that seem to contribute most to the mobility of the population are above-average educational training and employment in white-collar occupations.
3. Any theory of economic determinism in migration is inclined to be incomplete.

It appears, therefore, that understanding and prediction of migration streams require determining of the constants in migration behaviour with distinguishing these from the variables with respect to population composition and place characteristics which evolve differentially over time.

As indicated, attempts at model building in migration research have largely focused on variables and surrogates such as distance and ecological characteristics of places exerting 'push and pull' forces[8] to the exclusion of behavioural parameters of the migrants. The model suggested here is of doubtful usefulness as an exact predictive tool. It borrows much of its concepts and terminology from the behavioural theorists, because of the intuitive relevance of their findings to the analysis of mobility. Verification will be only partial because of the general absence in this country of migrational histories. Instead, greater reliance will be placed upon evidence from a variety of sources and special studies. The framework of the analysis must be classified as descriptive or behavioural and partially dynamic.

Clearly, the focus must remain with the process of internal migration, i.e. a change of residence which extends beyond a territorial boundary. Some attempt will be made, however, to relate this process of 'long distance' movement to the more general topic of mobility which encompasses not only shifts within areal divisions but also movement between jobs and social categories. This larger zone of investigation is referred to as the 'mover-stayer' problem.[9]

The central concepts of migration behaviour with which we shall be concerned are: (1) the notion of place utility, (2) the field theory approach to search behaviour, and (3) the life-cycle approach to threshold formation. Before translating these concepts into an operational format within a proposed model, some attempt will be made to trace their relevance to migrational decisions.

Place Utility

Population migration is an expression of interaction over space but differs in certain essential characteristics from other channels of interaction, mainly in terms of the commodity which is being transported. Other flows, such as those of mail, goods, telephone calls, and capital also reflect connectivity between places, but, in migration, the agent which is being transported is itself active and generates its own flow. The origin and destination points take on significance only in the framework in which they are perceived by the active agents.

A degree of disengagement and upheaval is associated with population movements; thus, households are not as readily mobile as other phenomena subject to flow behaviour. Yet, it would be unrealistic to assume that sedentariness reflects an equilibrium position for a population. Migrational flows are always present, but normally the reaction is lagged and the decision to migrate is non-programmed. Thus, migration is viewed as a form of individual or group adaptation to perceived changes in environment, a recognition of marginality with respect to a stationary position, and a flow reflecting an appraisal by a potential migrant of his present site as opposed to a number of other potential sites. Other forms of adaptation are perhaps more common than change of residence and job. The individual may adjust to the changing conditions at his site and postpone, perhaps permanently, the decision to migrate. Migration is not, therefore, merely a direct response or reaction to the objective economic circumstances which might be incorporated, for example, within a normative transportation model.

In designing the framework for a model of the migration decision, it would be useful at the outset to enumerate certain basic descriptive principles which have been observed to have some general applicability and regularity in decision behaviour. To a significant degree these principles have their origin in the studies of organizational theorists.

We begin with the concept of 'intendedly rational' man[10] who, although limited to finite ability to perceive, calculate, and predict and to an otherwise imperfect knowledge of environment, still differentiates between alternative courses of action according to their relative utility or expected utility. Man responds to the perception of unequal utility, i.e. if utility is measured broadly enough to encompass the friction of adaptation and change.

The individual has a threshold of net utility or an aspiration level that adjusts itself on the basis of experience.[11] This subjectively determined threshold is a weighted composite of a set of yardsticks for achievement in the specific realms in which he participates. His contributions, or inputs, into the economic and social systems in terms of effort, time, and concern are rewarded by actual and expected attainments. The threshold functions as an evaluative mechanism for distinguishing, in a binary sense, between success or failure, or between positive or negative net utilities. The process is self-adjusting because aspirations tend to adjust to the attainable. Satisfaction leads to slack which may induce a lower level of attainment.[12] Dissatisfaction acts as a stimulus to search behaviour.

Without too great a degree of artificiality, these concepts of 'bounded rationality'[13] may be transferred to the mover-stayer decision environment and a spatial context. It is necessary, only to introduce a place subscript for the measures of utility. *Place utility*, then, refers to the net composite of utilities which are derived from the individual's integration at some position in space. The threshold reference point is also a relevant criterion for evaluating the individual's place utility. According to the model, the threshold will be some function of his experience or attainments at a particular place and the attainments of his peers. Thus, place utility may be expressed as a positive or negative quantity, expressing respectively the individual's satisfaction or dissatisfaction with respect to that place. He derives a measure of utility from the past or expected future rewards at his stationary position.

Quite different is the utility associated with the other points which are considered as potential destinations. The utility with respect to these alternative sites consists largely of anticipated utility and optimism which lacks the reinforcement of past rewards. This is precisely why the stream of information is so important in long-distance migration—information about prospects must somehow compensate for the absence of personal experience.

All moves are purposeful, for an evaluation process has preceded them, but some are more beneficial, in an *ex post* sense, because of the objective quality of search behaviour, the completeness of the information stream, and the mating of anticipated with realized utility. If migrations may be classified as either successes or failures in a relative sense, then clearly the efficiency of the search process and the ability to forecast accurately the consequences of the move are essential elements.

Assuming intendedly rational behaviour, then the generation of population migration may be considered to be the result of a decision process which aims at altering the future in some way and which recognizes differences in utility associated with different places. The individual will tend to locate himself at a place whose characteristics possess or promise a relatively higher level of utility than in other places which are conspicuous to him. Thus, the flow of population reflects a subjective place-utility evaluation by individuals. Streams of migration may not be expected to be optimal because of incomplete knowledge and relocation lag but nor may we expect that individuals purposefully move in response to the prospect of lower expected utility.

The process of migration is conceived in the model as: (1) proceeding from sets of stimuli perceived with varying degrees of imperfection, and (2) involving responses in a stayer-mover framework.

The stayers are considered lagged movers postponing the decision to migrate for periods of time extending up to an entire lifetime. Thus, the mover-stayer dichotomy may be reduced to the single dimension of time—when to move.

Distinction must clearly be made between the objective stimuli which are relevant for the mover-stayer decision and the stimuli which are perceived by individuals and to which there is some reaction. The stimuli which are instrumental in generating response originate in the individual's action space which is that part of the limited environment with which the individual has contact.[14] Thus, the perceived state of the environment is the action space within which individuals select to remain or, on the other hand, from which to withdraw in exchange for a modified environment.

Field Theory Approach to Search Behaviour

Though the individual theoretically has access to a very broad environmental range of local, regional, national, and international information coverage, typically only some rather limited portion of the environment is relevant and applicable for his decision behaviour. This immediate subjective environment or action space is the set of place utilities which the individual perceives and to which he responds. This notion of the action space is similar to Lewin's concept of life space—the universe of space and time in which the person conceives that he can or might move about.[15] Some correspondence may exist with the actual external environment, but there may also be a radical degree of deviation. The life space is a surface over which the organism can locomote and is dependent upon the needs, drives, or goals of the organiser and upon its perceptual apparatus.[16] Our concern is with man in terms of his efficiency or effectiveness as an information-collecting and assimilating organism and thus with his ability to produce an efficient and unbiased estimation or evaluation of the objective environment. It is suggested that the subjective action-space is perceived by the individual through a sampling process whose parameters are determined by the individual's needs, drives, and abilities. There may not be a conscious and formal sampling design in operation, but, nevertheless, a sampling process is inherently involved in man's acquisition of knowledge about his environment.

Both sampling and nonsampling errors may be expected in the individual's perceived action-space—a spatial bias induced by man's greater degree of expected contact and interaction in his more immediate environment, as well as sampling errors introduced because of man's finite ability to perceive and his limited exposure and observation. The simple organism which Simon describes has vision which permits it to see, at any moment, a circular portion of the surface about the point in which it is standing and to distinguish merely between the presence or absence of food within the circle.[17]

The degree to which the individual's action-space accurately represents the physically objective world in its totality is a variable function of characteristics of both man and the variability of the environment. Of primary emphasis here are the consequences of man's fixity to a specific location—the spatial particularism of the action-space to which he responds.

What is conspicuous to the individual at any given time includes primarily information about elements in his close proximity. Representing the information bits as points, the resulting sampling design most closely resembles a cluster in the immediate vicinity of the stationary position. The individual may be considered at the stationary position within the cluster of alternative places, each of which may be represented by a point on a plane. The consequences of this clustered distribution of alternatives within the immediate vicinity of the individual is a spatially biased information set, or a mover-stayer decision based upon knowledge of only a small portion of the plane.

Cluster sampling may be expected to exhibit significantly greater sampling bias for a given number of observations than random sampling; its most important advantage is in the reduction of the effort or cost in the collection of information. In the absence of a homogeneous surface, however, the difference in cost may be more than outweighed by the loss in representativeness of a given cluster.

The local environment of the individual may not, of course, be confined purely to his immediate surroundings. The action-space may vary in terms of number and intensity of contacts from the limited environmental realm of the infant to the extensive action-space within which diplomats, for example, operate. The degree of contact may perhaps be measured by the rate of receipt of perception of information bits.[18] Mass communications and travel, communication with friends and relatives, for example, integrate the individual into a more comprehensive spatial setting but one which is, nevertheless, still biased spatially. Mass communications media typically have coverage which is limited to the service area of the media's transmission centre. Here a hierarchy of nodal centres exists in terms of the extent of service area and range of coverage. Thus the amount of transmission and expected perception of information by individuals is some function of the relative position of places within the network of communcation channels. The resident in the area of a primary node has an additional advantage resulting from his greater exposure to information covering a relatively more extensive area of choice. His range of contact and interaction is broader, and the likelihood of an unbiased and representative action-space is greater.

The Life Cycle Approach to Threshold Formation

Another significant determinant of the nature and extent of the individual's action-space (i.e. the number and arrangement of points in the cluster) consists of a set of factors which may be grouped under the heading of the 'life cycle'. Illustrative of this approach is Hägerstrand's analysis of population as a flow through a system of stations.[19] Lifelines represent individuals moving between stations. The cycle of life almost inevitably gives rise to distinct movement behaviour from birth, education, and search for a niche involving prime or replacement movements. Richard Meier also has examined this notion of the expanding action-space of the individual from birth through maturity.[20] The action space expands as a function of information input—and growth depends on organization of the environment so that exploration becomes more efficient. Associated with the evolution of the individual's action-space through time is a complex of other institutional and social forces which introduce early differentiation. Differences in sex, race, formal education, family income, and status are likely to find their expression early in shaping the area of movement and choice. Although the action-space is unique for each individual, still there is likely to be a good deal of convergence into a limited number of broad classes. The congruity and interdependence of the effects of race, family income, education, and occupation are likely to result in subgroups of individuals with rather homogeneous action-space.

In Lewin's concept, behaviour is a function of the life-space, which in turn is a function of the person and the environment.[21] The behaviour-influencing aspects of the external (physical and social) environment are represented through the life-space. Similarly, but in a more limited fashion, the action-space may be considered to include the range of choice or the individual's area of movement which is defined by both his personal attributes and his environment. Most prominent among the determinants of the alternatives in this action-space which are conspicuous to the individual is his position on one of divergent life cycles and location in terms of the communication networks linking his position to other places. His accumulated needs, drives, and abilities define his aspirations—the communication channels carry information about the alternative ways of satisfying these aspirations. To illustrate this structure in terms of the simple organism, we may turn to Simon's model of adaptive behaviour.[22] The organism he describes has only the simple needs of food getting and resting, the third kind of activity of which it is capable is exploration for food by locomotion within the life space where heaps of food are located at scattered points. In the schema, exploration and adaptive response to clues are necessary for survival; random behaviour leads to extinction. The chances of survival, i.e. the ability to satisfy needs, are dependent upon two parameters describing the organism (its storage capacity and its range of vision) and two parameters describing the environment (its richness in food and in paths). Of course, with respect to the human organism, aspirations require the fulfilment of many needs, and thresholds are higher. Exploratory search is aided by clues provided by the external environment through communication channels which extend the range of vision.

Other Behavioural Parameters

The discussion was intended to develop the concept of action-space as a spatial parameter in the mover-stayer decision. Thus the action-space of the individual includes not only his present position but a finite number of alternative sites which are made conspicuous to him through a combination of his search effort and the transmission of communicators. The action-space refers, in our mover-stayer framework, to a set of places for which expected utilities have been defined by the individual. A utility is attached to his own place and a relatively higher or lower utility has been assigned to the alternative sites. The variables here are the absolute number of alternative sites and their spatial pattern of arrangement with respect to his site. The sites may consist of alternative dwellings within a single block, alternate suburbs in a metropolitan area, or alternative metropolitan areas. The alternatives may not all present themselves simultaneously but many appear sequentially over time.

There are other components of behavioural theories which are relevant in the analysis of migration, especially with respect to the problem of uncertainty avoidance. We have already mentioned the sequential attention to goals and the sequential consideration of alternatives. The order in which the environment is searched determines to a substantial extent the decisions that will be made. In addition, observations appear to confirm that alternatives which *minimize uncertainty* are preferred and that the decision maker *negotiates for an environment of relative certainty*. Evidence shows also that there is a tendency to *postpone decisions* and to rely upon the *feedback of information*, i.e. policies are reactive rather than anticipatory. Uncertainty is also reduced by imitating the successful procedures followed by others.[23]

The composite of these attempts to reduce uncertainty may be reflected in a lagged response. A lapse of time intervenes in a cause-and-effect relationship—an instantaneous human response may not be expected. As with other stimulus-response models, events are paired sequentially through a process of observation and inference into actions and reactions, e.g. unemployment and outmigration. As developed in economics, a lag implies a delayed, but rational, human response to an external event. Similarly, with respect to migration, responses may be measured in terms of elasticity which is in turn conditional upon factors such as complementarity and substitutability. A time dimension may be added to measures of elasticity, and the result is a specific or a distributed lag—a response surface reflecting the need for reinforcement of the perception of the permanance of change.

Framework of a Proposed Operating Model

The model which is proposed attempts to translate into an operational framework the central concepts with which we have been concerned: the notion of place utility, the field theory approach to search behaviour, and the life cycle approach to threshold formation.

The model is designed to relate aggregate behaviour in terms of migration differentials into measures of place utility relevant for individuals. The objective is a prediction of the composition of in- and out-migrants and their choice of destination, i.e. by incorporating the stable elements which are involved in the changes in composition of population of places.

Inputs into the system are the following set of matrices:

1. Matrix A, defining the migration differentials associated with the division of the population by life cycles and by age, represented respectively by the rows and columns.

2. Matrix B, representing the distribution of a place's population within the life cycle and age categories.

3. Matrices C, D, E, and F, representing respectively the gross in-, out-, and net-migration and 'migration efficiency'[24] for each of the cell categories corresponding to Matrix B.

The rates for the A matrix are determined on an aggregate basis for the United States population by means of the 'one in a thousand' 1960 census sample. These rates are then applied to the B matrix entries for specific places to predict the expected out-migration rates of profile groups at these places. The differences between the expected rates and those observed in the C, D, E, and F matrix tabulations are then used to provide a measure of the relative utility of specific places for the given profile groups which may be specified as a place utility matrix. The net migrations, whether positive or negative for the given cell, represent the consensus of cell members of the utility which the place offers relative to other places which they perceive. The migration efficiency measures not only the relative transitoriness of specific subgroups of the population but also the role of the specific place as a transitional stepping-stone or station for certain groups.

There is an additional matrix, Matrix G, representing the parameters of search behaviour which are characteristic of the subgroup populations. These are specified in terms of the number of alternatives which are perceived and the degree of clustering of these alternatives in space. The destination of the out-migrants predicted by means of the G-matrix entries are tested against the observed migration flows in order to derive measures of distance and directional bias.

The concepts of place utility, life cycle, and search behaviour are integrated, therefore, within the classification of the population into subgroups. Preliminary testing has revealed a significant degree of homogeneity of migrational behaviour by subgroup populations in terms of differential rate of migration, distance, and direction of movement. The classification procedure, involving the use of multivariate analysis, is designed to provide a set of profile or core groups whose attributes may be represented by prototype individuals. The differential migration rates of Matrix A are assumed, therefore, to be parameters in the migration system, at least for the purposes of short-term forecasting. Individuals move along each row as they grow older and, to some extent, move in either direction along age columns as socio-economic status changes over time, but the migration rates for the cells remain relatively constant.

Similarly, the utility to the population subgroups of the specific places of origin and destination shift over the long term but remain relatively constant in the short run. For long-term forecasting, exogeneous measures of economic trends in specific places would be necessary inputs.

NOTES AND REFERENCES

[1] Samuel A. Stouffer, 'Intervening Opportunities and Competing Migrants', *Journal of Regional Science*, 2 (1960), 1–26.

[2] Cicely Blanco, 'Prospective Unemployment and Interstate Population Movements', *Review of Economics and Statistics*, 46 (1964), 221–2; Donald J. Bogue, Henry S. Shryock, Siegfried Hoermann, 'Streams of Migration Between Subregions', Scripps Foundation Studies in Population Distribution, 5 (1957), Oxford, Ohio; Robert L. Bunting, 'A Test of the Theory of Geographic Mobility', *Industrial and Labor Relations Review*, 15 (1961), 76–82; Robert L. Raimon, 'Interstate Migration and Wage Theory', *Review of Economics and Statistics*, 44 (1962), 428–38; Larry A. Sjaastad, 'The Relationship Between Migration and Income in the United States', *Papers and Proceedings, Regional Science Association*, 6 (1960), 37–64.

[3] Clark Kerr, 'Migration to the Seattle Labor Market Area, 1940–42', *University of Washington Publications in the Social Science*, 11 (1942), 129–88; Philip Nelson, 'Migration, Real Income and Information', *Journal of Regional Science*, 1 (1959), 43–74.

[4]Donald J. Bogue, Henry S. Shryock, and Siegfried Hoermann, op. cit.; Hope T. Eldridge and Dorothy Swaine Thomas, *Population Redistribution and Economic Growth, United States, 1870–1950*. Philadelphia: American Philosophical Society, 1964; Dorothy S. Thomas, 'Age and Economic Differentials in Internal Migration in the United States: Structure and Distance', *Proceedings, International Population Conference*, Vienna, 1959, pp. 714–21; George L. Wilber, 'Migration Expectancy in the United States', *Journal of the American Statistical Association*, 58 (1963), 44–53.

[5]D. O. Price, 'A Mathematical Model of Migration Suitable for Simulation on an Electronic Computer', *Proceedings, International Population Conference*, Vienna, 1959, pp. 665–73.

[6]Richard L. Morrill, 'The Development of Models of Migration', *Entretiens de Monaco en Sciences Humaine*, 1962.

[7]Donald J. Bogue, Henry S. Shryock, and Siegfried Hoermann, op. cit.

[8]Ibid.; Roger L. Burford, 'An Index of Distance as Related to Internal Migration', *Southern Economic Journal*, 29 (1962), 77–81.

[9]Leo Goodman, 'Statistical Methods for the Mover-Stayer Model', *Journal of the American Statistical Association*, 56 (1961), 841–68.

[10]Herbert A. Simon, 'Economics and Psychology', in Sigmund Koch, ed., *Psychology: A Study of a Science*, 6, New York: McGraw-Hill, 1963.

[11]R. M. Cyert and J. G. Marsh, *A Behavioral Theory of the Firm*. Englewood Cliffs, N.J.: Prentice-Hall, 1963; Kurt Lewin, *Field Theory in Social Science*. New York: Harper and Row, 1951; Joseph W. McGuire, *Theories of Business Behavior*. Englewood Cliffs, N.J.: Prentice-Hall, 1964; S. Siegal, 'Level of Aspiration and Decision Making', *Psychological Review*, 64 (1957), 253–63; Herbert Simon, op. cit., 1963; William H. Starbuck, 'Level of Aspiration Theory and Economic Behavior', *Behavioral Science*, 8 (1963), 128–36.

[12]R. M. Cyert and J. G. Marsh, op. cit.

[13]Herbert Simon, op. cit., 1963.

[14]Kurt Lewin, op. cit.

[15]Ibid.

[16]Herbert A. Simon, 'Rational Choice and the Structure of the Environment', *Psychological Review*, 63 (1956), 129–38.

[17]Ibid.

[18]Richard L. Meier, *A Communications Theory of Urban Growth*. Cambridge, Mass.: Massachusetts Institute of Technology Press, 1962.

[19]Torsten Hägerstrand, 'Geographical Measurements of Migration', *Entretiens de Monaco en Sciences Humaines*, 1962.

[20]Richard L. Meier, 'Measuring Social and Cultural Change in Urban Regions', *Journal of the American Institute of Planners*, 25 (1959), 180–90; Richard L. Meier, op. cit., 1962.

[21]Kurt Lewin, op. cit.

[22]Herbert Simon, op. cit., 1956.

[23]R. M. Cyert and J. G. Marsh, op. cit.

[24]Migrational efficiency refers to the ratio of net migration to total gross migration. See H. S. Shryock, 'The Efficiency of Internal Migration in the United States', *Proceedings, International Population Conference*, Vienna, 1959, pp. 685–94.

14.   ON THE DEFINITION OF MIGRATION

T. Hägerstrand

As a rule, migration of the population is regarded in two ways. In one case, it is considered as a whole, as one of the book-keeping entries in the total population balance of different areas. In the other case, there is greater detailed interest in mobility as an aspect of individual human behaviour. The commentary which follows below is concerned with the latter side of the question, in some respects from a microscalar viewpoint, which is not usual. The reason for the choice of the scale is my belief that a great deal can be learnt in regard to the macro aspects if familiarity has first been attained with some elementary microscopic features.

It is customary to introduce the basic concepts of the formal population theory with the aid of Becker's scheme. In this, the individual is represented as a straight *line of life*, which begins on a *day of birth* and ends at a *point of death*. In the scheme, time is the universally prevailing physical dimension, even to the extent that both the x and y co-ordinates represent time—naturally in itself on good foundations. If the question is now raised of how the individual occupies himself, while the line of life inexorably goes straight forward in time towards the point of death, the answer is—if we keep to the corresponding level of abstraction—that he indefatigably moves in the other physical dimension, in space. He moves there to be able to tend to this economy, and to satisfy his need of co-operation with other individuals.

It is not difficult to provide a graphic illustration of the individual's path in space-time, though it should be noted that we satisfy ourselves with a space which has just length and breadth, so that we can allow the abandoned third dimension to represent time (Fig. 1). Nothing is said here about the absolute values of either the space or the time scale. We can have in mind an hour in a living-room, a day in a town, or a whole life in a country. In fact, we are concerned with an entire hierarchy of movements, in which each lower level can be regarded as oscillations around a vertical line at a higher level.

Movements in space are regulated by an infrastructure of what we can term *stations*. The most important of these, reckoned in length of stay, are homes and workplaces. The primary sources of Swedish population statistics provide inexhaustible material from which one can, for the purpose of demonstration, pick random samples of the life-path of separate individuals, or the system of life-paths spent in common with others.

Figure 2 gives the skeleton of the history of a rural family. Admittedly, only one case is demonstrated, but it is typical of its environment and its period of time. The time scale runs from 1840 to 1940. The dwelling is the localizing unit. For as long as the individual stays in a certain house, his life-path is indicated as vertical, with an unbroken line for a man, and a dotted line for a woman. Children are put immediately to the right of their parents. A circle denotes the point of birth, and a cross the point of death. Horizontal arrows indicate migratory movements made either into or out of the houses. Return to a place which has been lived in before is

From *Scandinavian Population Studies*, 1 (1969), 63–72. Reprinted by permission of the author and The Population Research Institute of Helsinki.

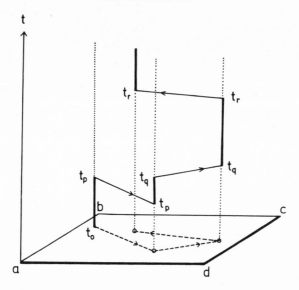

Fig. 1. Part of the time-space path of an individual. Dotted vertical lines represent stations. Movements take place between stations at times t_p, t_q, and t_r. Dashed lines project movements on the landscape.

indicated. However, space has not permitted scalar representation of the distance of geographical movement.

At the age of four, our man accompanies his family on his first migration. At the age of 17, he leaves home to work as a farm-worker on a number of farms not very far away. We omit the further fate of his family.

From the age of one, our woman accompanies her family on a number of short moves backwards and forwards between a couple of nearby smallholdings. At the age of 16, she leaves her home to work in domestic service on some neighbouring farms. The two people meet while they are working on the same farm, and marry after two years, at the respective ages of 26 and 24. Soon after this they move to the first home of their own, and a son is born there. Shortly, the young family moves back again, and stays there for a long period. Six further children are born.

The man dies without any more migrations, at the age of 66. Two years later, his widow and an unmarried daughter move away to join the youngest son. The older brothers and sisters have left their home for the first time at ages varying between 17 and 22. It is characteristic that they have returned home once or more during their search for their own, entirely independent positions.

This example, and many like it, demonstrate clearly that the life cycle almost inevitably gives rise to a rather distinct migratory behaviour. When an individual has left home, there follows a period of oscillation between different stations—often with intermediate returns home. This is a period of training for an occupation and searching—perhaps it could be termed a career period. This can proceed for some time after the formation of a family. We know from the general age distribution of migrants that rather many small children are in course of movement with their parents. None the less, mobility diminishes sharply at the age of 25 to 30 years. A shorter period of movement is again discernible once occupational activity has eased.

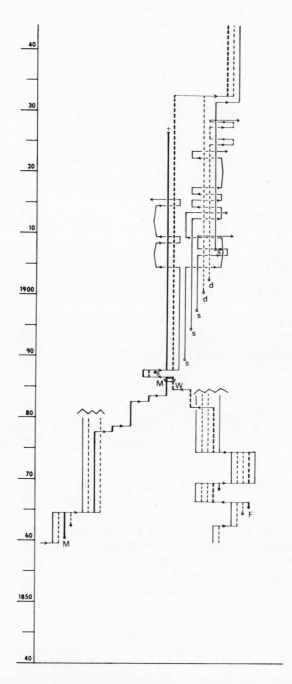

Fig. 2. Time-space paths of a family between 1860 and 1945. Solid vertical lines represent males, dashed vertical lines females. Horizontal arrows mark the time of movements between dwellings (distance not taken into account). M = husband, W = wife, s = son, d = daughter, o = birth, + = death.

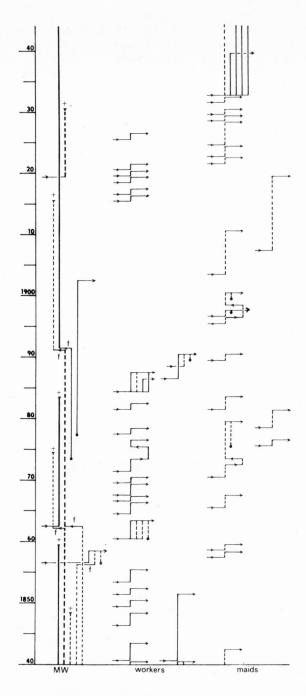

Fig. 3. Time-space paths in individuals living on an owner-operated farm with servants. Family members to the left, servants to the right. Here stations represent functional positions rather than dwellings.

The pattern of the life-path naturally varies with the economic structure of the community and its work organization. In rural districts, for example, land-ownership and the circumstances of tenancy appear to influence the movement pattern of individuals. This can be demonstrated by a couple of diagrams in which the life-paths are throughout viewed from the aspect of the fixed stations.

Figure 3 represents a farm which is owned by the farmer. The life-paths have been arranged in functional groups, with the family to the left, and male and female servants to the right. The life-path of the owning family is very stable during the course of time. At the first inheritance (1862), the farm was transferred to the youngest daughter, and her husband, who moved in. At the next inheritance (1891), the oldest son took over. He married a woman who moved in after the death of the mother. Gradually, the other children have moved away and not returned.

Never the less, the turnover of male and female servants has been great, if account is taken of the individuals concerned. But seen from the functional viewpoint—or station aspect—the picture is a different one. We find that the work has been organized in a very stable way. To a major extent, there has been work for one male and one female servant. During some periods, servant families filled both functions. This picture of a succession of young individuals, who stream through a station with no more than brief stays, closely agrees with what was observed earlier in regard to the individual's life cycle in a farming environment.

The movement pattern is completely different on a tenant farm (Fig. 4). During the century, thirteen different families have been occupants, with stays over periods varying between one and 19 years. In one case only is there a transfer from father to son. Here, male and female servants make but occasional appearance. To a great extent, the croft has functioned as a station for young families (note the abundance of births), who were still in movement. Families have moved in and out as groups, and individual migrations have been few in number.

It is not particularly difficult to imagine how the life-paths of individuals, when they find their way between the stations of space while time goes by, form an intricate, but far from unordered fabric. Of course, it is impossible to describe this fabric satisfactorily with the aid of such detailed examples as those presented above. More global methods are called for, which could indicate in figures the most important types of event in the system. However, it should have become sufficiently apparent that the methods practised to date for statistical description of migration are rather far removed from the physical realism required for a developed life-path model. What we achieve is a measurement of the number of discrete events per unit of space and time. Against this, we cannot as yet describe in figures a phenomenon with such features of continuity as a life-path in space and time, and even less a number of paths. Let us look at what is done in practice.

Assume that we are going to describe a part of a life-path such as that indicated in Figure 5. The full number of movements between stations is seven. Statistically, we can do no more than catch the movements which pass over an administrative border during a certain period of time. They can be taken as changed places of residence at the beginning of the period compared with those at its end, or as the number of border crossings during the period. A comparison is made between a period of five years and one of ten, and of a minor and a major administrative area.

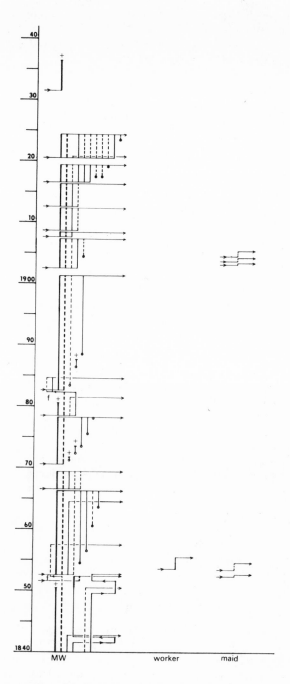

Fig. 4. Time-space paths of individuals on a tenant farm. Family members to the left, servants to the right.

The contribution of the individual to the gross movement number then becomes:

	Changed residence	Migratory movements registered
Case (1)	Small area 1 out-migration 5 years	3 (2 out + 1 in)
Case (2)	Small area 0 » 10 years	4 (2 out + 2 in)
Case (3)	Large area 1 » 5 years	1 (1 out)
Case (4)	Large area 0 » 10 years	2 (1 out + 1 in)

Thus the statistical picture is extremely variable in regard to one and the same migratory behaviour, dependent upon how we impose our check borders in space and time. Generally, it applies that—by reason of the great distance friction that migrants usually display—the smaller the regional unit is, the greater is the probability that a movement will be registered. Moreover, it applies that the longer the time chosen, the greater is the probability that, in respect of the same individual, he will appear more than once in registered migration events. As a consequence of these circumstances, it is very difficult to make comparative measurements of relative mobility on the basis of the statistical data available.

Today, a further complication of the difficulties associated with measurement is that the concept of migration itself can be said to be linked with the experiences and ideas of the agrarian community. Migration was rather inevitably the same as to change home and workplace at the same time. As a consequence, there was hardly any difficulty, from the aspect of definition, of what was of importance to register. That at such an early stage a beginning was made in noting migrations, in any event in Sweden and Finland, depended otherwise naturally not upon any scientific interest in human behaviour, but upon the desire of the clergy to exercise social and religious control, and later upon fiscal and military demands. The result is that now we have a generally accepted definition of migration, which beyond minor variations implies a change of residence between administrative units.

Data compiled according to this definition now provide an insight worse than before of how the individual steers his life-path in the system of dwellings and workplaces. We have hardly adapted the statistical description to phenomena created by the greater freedom of movement and the more complicated community structure.

If we—using the terminology of the life-path model—descend to the station level, we find today at least three separate population distributions, viz. the population of permanent housing (night population), the workplace population (day population), and the population in leisuretime accommodation. All of these have their interest, both from a purely behavioural aspect, and with respect to practical economy and community planning.

The migratory movements which give rise to these different population distributions can be complicated with regard to place relations. If we keep to the relation between home and workplace, we find that a person can change his home between two communes without thereby changing his place of work. He can change his workplace from one commune to another without changing his home. He can at one time change both home and workplace, whereby two, three, or four separate communes are affected, all dependent upon the home-workplace constellations before and after the migration. In this spectrum of possibilities, it may be so that

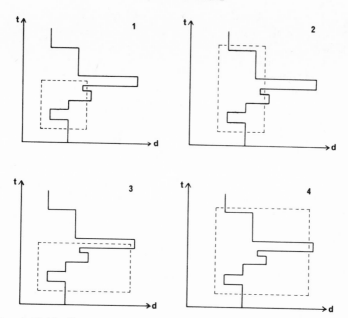

Fig. 5. An individual's movements between dwellings over time. Number of registered movements is a function of the time-space size of registration unit. Case 1: small area, short time; 2: small area, long time; 3: large area, short time; 4: large area, long time.

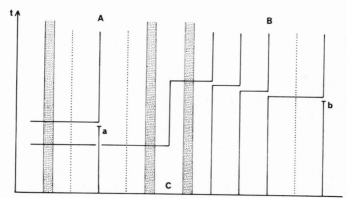

Fig. 6. Two hypothetical situations when a job-vacancy starts movements. A: stations for unskilled workers. B; stations for professionals. C: advanced educational system.
a: a vacancy is filled immediately by a young individual leaving his home. b: a vacancy is filled by successive promotion which finally draws a young individual who has passed some required educational threshold into the labour-force.

the economic consequences of the mobility to the community are primarily linked with the place of residence. If this is the case, a strong motivation is given to the importance attached by the current definition of migration to the change of home. Nevertheless, it is hardly possible to disregard the fact that, when it is a matter of finding data for a causal analysis of migrations, the mobility between workplaces, or quite simply that between work functions, is of more deeply seated interest than that concerned with the mobility between homes. Let us return to the life-path model in a time-space to indicate what this means (Fig. 6).

The life-paths originally enter the stations of working life from the parents' home. The stations placed to the left (A) are assumed to be of a type which does not call for special occupational training or experience. On the other hand, the stations to the right (B) cannot be reached by other than those who have passed a training threshold, and moreover have in general acquired practical working experience.

If a vacancy (a) arises in area A, it can in principle be filled promptly by a young, untrained person. Accordingly, *one* vacancy need not give rise to more than *one* movement.

If a vacancy (b) arises in one of the more qualified functions in B, this should, on the other hand, lead to a series of successive movements. For example, we could think that an elderly company director is replaced by a younger one from another company. In its turn, this leads to the promotion of a sales manager, who is in his turn replaced by the promotion of an assistant manager. Only the last-mentioned vacancy leads to a new professional man making his first entry into professional life. But he does not come direct from home: he has come via a training institution. In the example chosen, *one* vacancy brings about *four* movements, excluding the youngest individual's much earlier movement from home to the training establishment. Naturally, movements can take place in a company without movements between communes, but it is just as probable that the chain stretches out between a series of different places.

I am convinced that the majority of movements are replacement movements. They arise to fill vacancies, which in final cases are due to deaths or superannuation. Dependent upon the demands in regard to training and age imposed upon those who will fill the vacancy, there come into being long or short *movement chains*. These of course affect the volume of not only the functional mobility, but also the geographical. The dominance of replacement movements surely also explains why the large number of gross migrations registered is in fact accompanied by relatively small net profits and losses. Even when the primary vacancy relates to a new workplace, it means often enough a chain of replacement movements for it to be filled. Naturally, queues can arise in the system, which means that youngsters must remain for an abnormally long time in the home, or must content themselves with jobs which lie beneath the training threshold they have passed. Emigration out of the country provides another solution. However, if the reserve of young people is inadequate, stations begin to be abandoned in the less attractive part of the system. If this is not sufficient either, then filling up through immigration from abroad begins. If things are viewed in this way, it is not a matter for surprise that the immigrants get the jobs with less pay. The citizens proper have greater opportunities to lie further advanced in the movement chains.

The system aspect of movement is an area of research which has been rather neglected. It is naturally easier to ask people why they move, and then regard the whole as a function of the desires and evaluations of individual persons. I believe, however, that it would also be rewarding to look at the community as an enormous channel system, in which we more or less consciously regulate the streams by means of organizational arrangements which open and close channels. A large training institution in an economic wasteland is, for example, of necessity an effective machine for the creation of out-migration, if it is not at the right moment matched by a regional expansion of commercial and industrial life with vacancies which correspond to the examination given.

From a statistical aspect, we know just nothing of such things. And I believe that we shall find it difficult to achieve anything worthwhile with them if our compilation of data does not match the way in which society has become more complex since the days when movement was first registered as changes of dwellings between administrative units.

15. SYSTEMS APPROACH TO A THEORY OF RURAL-URBAN MIGRATION

A. L. Mabogunje

In the growing literature on the study of migration, two theoretical issues have attracted the greatest attention, namely, why people migrate and how far they move. A simple model for explaining the reasons why people move has been formulated in terms of the 'pull-push' hypothesis.[1] This has been elaborated variously to take account of internal migration movements of the rural-rural, rural-urban, or urban-urban types and international migrations. The issue of how far people move has, in turn, given rise to the formulation of a surprisingly large number of models of varying degrees of statistical or mathematical sophistication. In most of these models the distance covered is treated as either the sole independent variable or as one of many independent variables explaining the number of migrants moving to particular destinations. Morrill[2] has provided a valuable summary of these models and suggests that they can be classified broadly into deterministic and probabilistic models.

Most of these theoretical formulations have been applied to conditions in the developed countries of the world and especially to urban-to-urban migrations. Their relevance for handling migratory movements from rural to urban areas and particularly in the circumstances of underdeveloped countries has hardly been considered. Yet, it is these areas of the world where rural-urban migrations are presently taking place that afford the best opportunity for testing theoretical notions about this class of movements.

It is suggested that Africa in particular is a unique area from which to draw important empirical evidence about this type of movements. Similarly valuable data, however, can also be derived from examining the history of some of the advanced countries of the world. It is, of course, true that in Africa attention to date has been focused to a disproportionate extent on seasonal and other non-permanent transfers of population from rural to urban areas, that is, on what has been referred to as a 'constant circulatory movement' between the two areas.[3] But, it will be shown that this type of movement represents a very special case of rural-urban migration. To make the point clear, it is necessary to offer a definition of the latter. Essentially, rural-urban migration represents a basic transformation of the nodal structure of a society in which people move from generally smaller, mainly agricultural communities to larger, mainly non-agricultural communities. Apart from this spatial (or horizontal) dimension of the movement, there is also a socio-economic (or vertical) dimension involving a permanent transformation of skills, attitudes, motivations, and behaviour patterns such that a migrant is enabled to break completely with his rural background and become entirely committed to urban existence. A permanence of transfer is thus the essence of the movement.

Rural-urban migration also represents an essentially spatial concomitant of the economic development of a region. Indeed, it has been suggested that one of the basic goals of economic development is to reverse the situation wherein 85 per cent

From *Geographical Analysis*, 2 (1970), 1–18. Copyright © 1970 by the Ohio State University Press. Reprinted by permission.

of the population is in agriculture and lives in rural areas while only about 15 per cent is in non-agricultural activities and lives in the cities.[4] Rural-urban migration represents the spatial flow component of such a reversal. It is a complex phenomenon which involves not only the migrants but also a number of institutional agencies, and it gives rise to significant and highly varied adjustments everywhere in a region.

It can be argued with a great deal of justification that few of the theoretical models provided so far have considered migration, especially rural-urban migration, as a spatial process whose dynamics and spatial impact must form part of any comprehensive understanding of the phenomenon. It is the main contention of this paper that such an understanding can best be achieved within the framework of General Systems Theory.[5] This approach demands that a particular complex of variables be recognized as a system possessing certain properties which are common to many other systems. It has the fundamental advantage of providing a conceptual framework within which a whole range of questions relevant to an understanding of the structure and operation of other systems can be asked of the particular phenomenon under study. In this way, new insights are provided into old problems and new relationships whose existence may not have been appreciated previously are uncovered. In this paper no attempt is made to define major components and relationships in a formal, mathematical manner. The emphasis here is on a verbal analysis of the ways in which the system operates. This, it is hoped, will enable us to identify areas where present knowledge is fragmentary and where future research may be concentrated with some profit.

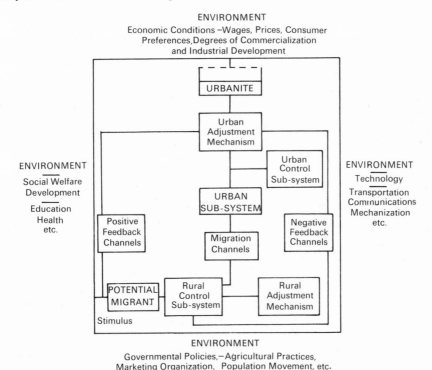

Fig. 1. A system schema for a theory of rural-urban migration.

Defining the System of Rural-Urban Migration

A system may be defined as a complex of interacting elements, together with their attributes and relationships.[6] One of the major tasks in conceptualizing a phenomenon as a system, therefore, is to identify the basic interacting elements, their attributes, and their relationships. Once this is done, it soon becomes obvious that the system operates not in a void but in a special environment. For any given system, this environment comprises 'the set of all objects a change in whose attributes affects the system, and also those objects whose attributes are changed by the behaviour of the system'. Thus, a system with its environment constitutes the universe of phenomena which is of interest in a given context.

Figure 1 indicates the basic elements in the rural-urban migration system as well as the environment within which the system operates. It shows that a systems approach to rural-urban migration is concerned not only with why people migrate but with all the implications and ramifications of the process. Basically, the approach is designed to answer questions such as: why and how does an essentially rural individual become a permanent city dweller? What changes does he undergo in the process? What effects have these changes both on the rural area from which he comes and on the city to which he moves? Are there situations or institutions which encourage or discourage the rate of movement between the rural area and the city? What is the general pattern of these movements, and how is this determined? These, and other such questions, define the problems for which we require a theory of rural-urban migration.

It can be shown theoretically that areas with isolated and self-sufficient villages such as were found in many parts of Africa until recently, are not likely to experience rural-urban migration, since, in any case there would be hardly any cities in such areas. The fact that today such movements characterize many parts of the continent and are lately assuming spectacular proportions means that rural areas are in general no longer isolated or self-sufficient. It is therefore relevant to ask: what forces have contributed and continue to contribute to the decline in these conditions of isolation and self-sufficiency in the rural areas? They are, in the main, forces set in motion by increasing economic development. In most African countries, this was brought about initially by the colonial administrations and further reinforced in recent years by the activities of the new African governments. Decreasing isolation means not only improvement in transportation and communication links but also greater integration of the rural economy into a national economy. Such integration makes the rural economy more responsive to changes in wages and prices, consumer preferences, and the over-all demand pattern within the country. It also subjects it to a wide range of governmental legislation or official policies over which, in many cases, the rural community has little or no control. Decreasing isolation also means greater social and cultural integration of rural and urban areas such that levels of expectations in both areas begin to converge towards a recognizable national norm of what is the 'good life'. The breakdown of isolation brings the rural areas within the orbit of one or more urban centres and sharpens the awareness and desire of villagers for the ever-increasing range of goods and services which the urban centres have to offer. To acquire these, the villagers have to produce more agricultural goods and enter into an exchange relation with the city. Alternatively, they may move into the city to sell their labour direct in exchange for wages with which to buy goods and services.

This then is the environment within which the system of migration from rural to urban areas operates. This is the environment which stimulates the villager to desire change in the basic locale and rationale of his economic activities and which, in consequence, determines the volume, characteristics, and importance of rural-urban migration. Moreover, it is an environment which is constantly changing, and these changes affect the operation of the system. Hence, for any theory of rural-urban migration to be of value it must take into account this dynamic aspect of the problem.

The basic elements in the system of migration are shown in Figure 1. It identifies first the potential migrant who is being encouraged to migrate by stimuli from the environment. Few studies have concerned themselves with the universe of potential migrants. More often, the tendency has been to study only those who successfully made the move. Even for these, attention is given mainly to classificatory characteristics such as age, sex, religion, education, and ethnic or racial origin rather than to an analysis or understanding of the background to their move.[8] There is, of course, no doubt that what this variety of information is meant to indicate is the pattern of distribution of the 'propensity to migrate' within the rural population. But this is neither explicitly stated nor formulated. Moreover, an equally valuable concept which this variety of information might have been used to explore is that of 'migration elasticity'.[9] This relates not so much to the propensity to migrate but to how long impulses or stimuli from the environment must be transmitted to a potential migrant before he makes the desired move.

Within the systems framework, attention is focused not only on the migrant but also on the various institutions (sub-systems) and the social, economic, and other relationships (adjustment mechanisms) which are an integral part of the process of the migrant's transformation. The two most important sub-systems are the rural and the urban control sub-systems. A control sub-system is one which oversees the operation of the general system and determines when and how to increase or decrease the amount of flow in the system. A simple example is provided by the thermostat which controls the amount of heat that flows within a given area. If we accept the existence of control sub-systems in this type of migration movement, the problem then is to identify which institutions operate in this manner both in the rural and the urban areas.

In the rural areas, a true control sub-system would, of course, be the family, both nuclear and extended. In the first place, it is the family that holds back potential migrants until they are old enough to undertake the move. Even when they are of an age to move, the family still acts as a control sub-system in many ways. In some places, it enables members of both sexes to move out; in others, members of one sex tend to get away more easily than those of the other. Where the potential migrant is married, the issue of whether he can move alone or with his wife and children may depend on the customary role of the sexes in agricultural activities, the age at which marriage is encouraged, and the circumstances and age at which a young man may expect to be economically independent of his parents. More important as a control mechanism is the relation of family members to the family land, especially as this relation is expressed through the lineage system and the inheritance law. An inheritance law that encourages most of the land to go into the hands of the first child (the primogeniture rule) will tend to stimulate more migration of the other children[10] compared to one based on the equality of access (partible inheritance rule) by all the children. In either case, the size of the farmland, the nature of the major agricultural products, and the prevailing prices for these would also be of decisive significance.

Apart from the family, the village community itself may act as a control sub-system. Its controlling role is not often direct but is obvious in either a positive or a negative way in the various activities which it sponsors or encourages. Thus, a village community which attempts to improve its economic conditions, for instance, through co-operative farming or marketing, may discourage, at least in the short run, permanent migration. On the other hand, a village community which puts emphasis on social betterment, for example, through education, may inadvertently stimulate migration to the city through training the younger generation to be more enlightened and more highly motivated. A pertinent aspect of the study of rural-urban migration is thus to assess how different rural communities react to migration away from the village. Such assessment should involve more than the opinion survey of the older generations. It should include an investigation of village activities and administration, and of the degree of cohesiveness in the community.

The urban control sub-system operates at the opposite end of the migrant's trajectory to encourage or discourage his being absorbed into the urban environment. Absorption at this level is of two kinds: residential and occupational. Basically, the control sub-system here can be identified with the city administration and other employment agencies operating under national laws and statutes. The city administration can ensure availability of relatively cheap and adequate housing in quantities which could make the transition of the rural migrant either difficult or easy. Apart from housing, the activities of the city administration in providing reception centres as well as various amenities and services may be a vital factor in gradually inducing a migrant to commit himself to the urban way of life.

A major factor in this commitment is, of course, the securing of an employment. In the city, there are numerous employment agencies offering, at any one time, very limited opportunities for the migrant. A pressing problem in the control sub-system is how to bring together and make known these disparate, but sometimes impressive, lists of vacancies. In some urban communities, this function of collation is left entirely to the press and their advertising columns. In others, a labour exchange is provided. The effectiveness with which these organizations function can be crucial for the inflow of migrants. However, once the migrant has secured an employment, a number of other factors determine his final commitment. Among these are: the type of job he secures, whether seasonal or permanent, the opportunity the job offers for improvement in his skill and for advancement in his status, the provisions available for security against the normal hazards of industrial life, and his eventual retirement due to old age.

At both the village and the city level, the decision of the migrant to move from or to move into the community sets in motion a series of adjustments. With regard to the village community, the mechanism for these adjustments should operate in such a way as to lead to an increase in the *per capita* income of the community. At least theoretically, the loss of one of the productive units in the village should lead to an increase of the productive capacity available to the remaining units; otherwise such losses from the rural area would eventually lead to a significant drop in agricultural production, to food shortage, and to famine. That these do not occur in many places means that some adjustments do take place to maintain aggregate productivity from these areas. The Ardeners[11] in their study of the Hsu of the Cameroons, for instance, point out that, in spite of the fact that as much as 40 per cent of the adult male population in the village was absent, food production did not show any significant drop. Studies of other communities in Africa have indicated similar observations.[12] However, what is involved in the adjustment to rural-urban migration is more than the minor arrangements by which the farmlands belonging to seasonal or short-term migrants are tended in their absence by their wives, their friends, or other members of their families. What is involved here are the ways and methods by which rural communities permit migrants to renounce partially or wholly their rights to productive resources in the rural areas.

One of the major research frontiers in rural-urban migration studies is the understanding of how this renunciation is accomplished. In Africa, for instance, such renunciation must be seen against the background of a complex land tenure situation and the fact that sale of land is regarded as basically a foreign concept. There is some evidence that one of the implications of rural-urban migration is to encourage a growing individualization of land-holding (with or without enclosuring) and a disposition to treat land as a marketable commodity. In the Eastern Region of Nigeria, for instance, rural-urban migration has been leading to a new pattern of land distribution and ownership. This is especially so in those areas not too far from the major urban centres.[13] It would appear, however, that initially it is the usufruct (or right to beneficial usage) on the land and not ownership that is regarded as negotiable. As a result, leasehold or annual rental of agricultural land has become widespread in many parts of West Africa and serves as a means of reallocating land which would otherwise remain unutilized because its owners have migrated to the cities. In some other cases, it is the right to exploit tree crops such as the oil-palm, cocoa, or rubber that is exchanged for monetary considerations either by outright payment or by share-cropping arrangement. In all cases, the effect of the renunciation of the migrant's claims on land or other resources is to enable some members of the village community to increase their net income by the expenditure of their often under-utilized labour. The more complete the renunciation by the migrant, the greater the acceptance of the idea of outright sale or alienation of land. Renunciation, by providing increased capacity in land or other resources, also encourages attempts at production on individual farms, and a reduction in the subsistence sector of the village economy.

Sometimes, however, this process of adjustment is induced by government and has the effect of widely stimulating migration from the rural areas. This was in fact, what happened in Britain in the eighteenth and nineteenth centuries with the various Enclosure Acts. In Africa, especially in East and Central Africa, the same process can be witnessed today. Thus, in Rhodesia, the Native Land Husbandry Act of 1951 individualized agricultural holdings and occasioned the loss by many farmers of their right to cultivate former family land. This disenfranchisement, as was only to be expected, gave rise to a flood of migrants most of whom had no alternative but to become permanently committed to wage employment and psychologically attuned to surviving in an urban environment.

In the urban areas, the mechanism of adjustment is basically one of incorporating the migrant into a new frame of reference more relevant to his needs in the city. In this respect, a city can be described as an assemblage of interacting interest groups. Part of the process of becoming a member of such a community would thus be to identify closely with one or more of these groups. The mechanism of incorporation in the urban areas, in contrast to the adjustment process in the rural areas, has been the subject of a number of studies. In particular, attention has been called to the role of ethnic unions and various voluntary organizations such as the Church, trade unions, occupational associations, and recreation societies in helping the rural migrant to adjust to his new environment.[14]

Finally, of the various elements of the system, there is the city *qua* city, seen as part of an urban sub-system. What aspects of urban life and activities are relevant for the understanding of rural-urban migration? To answer this question, it is important to visualize the city as comprising a hierarchy of specializations. In other words, a city is a place where everyone is trying to sell specialized skill. The more specialized the skill, the greater the demand for it, and hence the higher the price it commands on the market. Within this conceptual framework, the illiterate, unsophisticated rural migrant is seen as belonging to the lowest level of the hierarchy. A corollary is that the higher a person moves up within the hierarchy, the greater his commient to the urban way of life and the less the probability of his reversion to rural existence. This is one reason why the type of job which a rural migrant secures in the city can be so crucial to how soon he becomes committed to urban life. This is also one reason why those countries, such as Rhodesia, which are anxious to ensure that the African does not become an urban resident, pursue a discriminatory policy with regard to his acquisition of skill in urban employment. Yet, as Masser pointed out, even in Rhodesia the propensity to return to the village after migrating to the city decreases with the minimal rise in the skill of the migrant.[15]

Another interesting aspect of this concept of the city is that upward mobility within the hierarchy of specializations is often accompanied by changes in residential location within the city. This is no doubt a function of rising income, but it is also closely related to the length of stay in the city and the increasing commitment of a migrant to spend the remaining part of his working life there. There have been many studies of the residential pattern and varying length of stay of migrants in urban areas. Unfortunately, a good number of these studies have been concerned more with indicating the ethnic basis of this pattern than with investigating the dynamic factor of skill differentiation and status advancement which is operating to blur out the importance of ethnicity. As a result, this rather crucial dimension of rural-urban migration has tended to be neglected. Its investigation should yield some rather interesting results.

One final aspect of the examination of cities as a hierarchy of specializations relates to the significance of size. What effect has the size of a city on the type of migrants attracted to it? Clearly, small urban centres have fewer tiers of specializations and more restricted employment opportunities than the larger ones. Yet, competition for positions in them may be less intense. Are certain types of migrants attracted to such centres first and then able to 'leap-frog' gradually to bigger and bigger centres? What type of migrants would make direct for the larger cities? Does rural-urban migration into the larger cities take place in the manner of 'a series of concentric migratory contractions' suggested by Ashton[16] for Britain in the eighteenth century? According to Ashton, the larger industrial centres attracted a number of workers and their families who were living in the larger market towns on their perimeters. These towns in turn made good their losses from the surrounding villages, the villages from the hamlets, and the hamlets from the farms. In this way, there was no sharp discontinuity in the pattern of life with which the migrant was familiar. Are there conditions, for instance, the nature of the transportation network and development, which would make such a pattern of migration appropriate for Britain of the eighteenth century but not for Africa in the twentieth century? Or, does this pattern reflect stable human reaction to a permanent spatial dislocation of existing networks of social contacts?

The Energy Concepts in Systems Analysis

A system comprises not only matter (the migrant, the institutions, and the various organizations mentioned) but also energy. In the physical sense, energy is simply the capacity of a given body to do work. It can be expressed in a number of ways, but two forms of it are relevant here. There is 'potential energy' which is the body's power of doing work by virtue of stresses resulting from its relation either with its environment or with other bodies. The second form is 'kinetic energy' which is the capacity of a body to do work by virtue of its own motion or activity.

In a theory of rural-urban migration, potential energy can be likened to the stimuli acting on the rural individual to move. What is the nature of these stimuli? As pointed out earlier, a number of studies have tried to identify why people migrate and have come up with a variety of answers generally subsumed under the push-and-pull hypothesis. This suggests that people migrate from rural areas to the cities because of one of two general causes: overpopulation and environmental deterioration in the rural areas (the push factor) or the allurement or attraction of the city (the pull factor or the so-called 'bright-light theory'). The push factor, it is claimed, explains migrations directed to earning extra income to pay the annual tax or to take a new bride or to buy a few manufactured articles or to escape oppressive local *mores*. The pull factor, on the other hand, explains migrations undertaken as a modern form of initiation ceremony to adult status or as the basis for later receiving preferential admiration of the village girls or as the product simply of an intense curiosity about the city.

These explanations, to the extent that they have any theoretical validity at all, are relevant only at the aggregate level. These are notwithstanding the results from completed questionnaire surveys requiring individuals to indicate the reason or reasons for their migration into the city. But, as Richards[17] and Gulliver[18] stress, the battery of questions usually asked of migrants hardly ever reveals anything about why they moved. In Africa, the great number of temporary migrants to the cities on whom most studies have been concentrated, are involved in making no major decisions other than on the length of time they can or have to be away from home. The reasons for their migration are very often manifold and usually not easy to articulate in a few, simple sentences. What the questionnaire does, in fact, is to suggest to the migrant a set of equally plausible reasons, besides the obvious one of coming to earn extra income.

Within the systems framework, the explanation of why people migrate must be in terms of differential individual responses to the stimuli both from the environment and from within the system. It differs from the pull-and-push hypothesis in putting the emphasis at the individual level, not on why people migrate from particular areas but why any person from any village would want to migrate to the city. The stimulus to migrate is related to the extent of the integration of rural activities into the national economy, to the degree of awareness of opportunities outside of the rural areas, and to the nature of the social and economic expectations held by the rural population not only for themselves but also for their children. Indeed, the notion of 'expectations' or 'aspirations' is central to an understanding of the ways in which the stimulus from the environment is transmitted to individuals, and for that reason it is a crucial variable in the theory of rural-urban migration. What determines the variation in the level of individual expectations in rural areas and conditions individual responses to the stimulus to migrate? Clearly, for a given cohort in any rural area, one can, at least theoretically, conceive of individuals who respond promptly to the stimulus and others who take a much longer time to respond. One may in fact ask whether there is a threshold below which the stimulus cannot be expected to act and an upper limit beyond which its impact is no longer felt? How are these limits defined—by age, wealth, natural alertness, or family position? In short, two problems in the theory of rural-urban migration which still require resolution concern the nature and significance of rural expectations and their relation to the differential effectiveness of the stimulus to migrate.

Once an individual has been successfully dislodged from the rural area, we can assume that he is translating his 'potential energy' into its 'kinetic form'. The major issues concern not only the act of moving but also the cost, the distance, and the direction of movement. These three variables clearly determine the crisscross channels of migration as well as their destinations. Again, as already indicated, this aspect of migration studies has received considerable theoretical attention. Starting with Ravenstein's laws of migration[19] which try to establish the relation between distance and the propensity to move, there have been various attempts to seek understanding through using the gravity model,[20] and the intervening opportunities model.[21] There have also been other studies which have tried to understand the pattern of migration channels through probabilistic models.[22]

As soon as a migrant has moved from the rural to the urban area, his role in the system is greatly amplified. Basic to an understanding of this amplified role is the concept of 'information', a central notion in the theory of communications. Information can be defined simply as bits of messages in a system which lead to a particular set of actions. Thus, one can easily assume that the first migrant from a village to a city would soon start to transmit back to the village information about his reception and progress in the city. Ignoring for the moment the question of 'information content', it can be shown that the level of information can be measured in terms of decisions.[23] A particular set of decisions can be compared with the random choice from a universe of equally probable decisions. Its deviation from the latter becomes a measure of the level of information. It also represents a statement of the level of order or organization existing within the system. Information is thus a crucial feature of the operation of a system since it determines at any point of time the state of organization of the system.

Of equal importance is the notion of 'feedback' which has been the focus of the field of Cybernetics. This can be explained quite simply in terms of stimulus-response behaviour. A stimulus affects a receptor which communicates this message to some controlling apparatus and from this to an effector which gives the response. In feedback, the effector's activity is monitored back to the receptor with the result that the system's behaviour is in some way modified by the information. The feedback process can have one of two effects. It can further amplify the deviation (in this case by stimulating further migration), or it may counteract the deviation by encouraging a return to the initial situation. Deviation-amplifying feedbacks are regarded as positive; deviation-counteracting feedbacks as negative.

The notion of a 'most probable or random state' is one that needs further clarification. Imagine a situation in which migrants from a village are lost to their communities as soon as they move out and send back no information on their reactions to the cities to which they moved. Later migrants then, not knowing where the first set of migrants went to might choose any city in the system, almost in a random manner. Over time, the distribution of migrants from individual villages may come to approximate a situation in which the number of migrants from any village to a city is proportional to the size of that city. This is the most probable state in which no order or organization is evident in the system. Conceptually, it can be seen as a state of maximum disorder, or a state of maximum 'entropy'.

Yet, the general experience is that migrants are never lost in this sense to their village or origin but continue to send back information. If the information from a particular city dwells at length on the negative side of urban life, on the difficulties of getting jobs, of finding a place to live, and on the general hostility of people, the effect of this negative feedback will slow down further migration from the village to this city. By contrast, favourable or positive feedback will encourage migration and will produce situations of almost organized migratory flows from particular villages to particular cities. In other words, the existence of information in the system encourages greater deviation from the 'most probable or random state'. It implies a decrease in the level of entropy (or disorder) or an increase in negative entropy (negentropy). The result is greater differentiation in the pattern of migration which reflects some form of organization. Thus, experience of rural-urban migration in many parts of the world emphasizes this organized nature of the moves. In many North African cities, for instance, it is not uncommon for an entire district or craft occupation in a city to be dominated by permanent migrants from one or two villages.[24] Furthermore, this element of 'organization' resulting from the operation of feedback in the system underlies the varying rate of population growth among cities.

A major area of research into rural-urban migration thus concerns the flow of information between the urban and the rural areas. Considerable work on this question has been undertaken in Europe and the United States and some of the results are of great interest. Hägerstrand, for instance, insists that we must distinguish between 'active' and 'passive' migrants.[25] The former are those who seek out suitable destinations which, in their eyes, guarantee future prosperity; the latter are those who follow impulses (feedbacks) emanating from persons of their acquaintance, primarily those who had made 'fortunate' moves. One implication of this distinction is that in a theory of rural-urban migration, the crucial moves which we need to understand and explain are those of the active migrants. In the aggregate, these moves are likely to be complex and not easily explained in terms of a few choice variables.

A number of other studies have concentrated on the measurement of the information field of a potential migrant as a means of understanding the general pattern of his behaviour in space.[26] Individual information fields may be aggregated to produce community mean information fields, and these have been used in studies which attempt to predict the volume and pattern of migratory movements.[27]

Relation Between a System and its Environment

Systems can be classified into three categories depending on the relationship they maintain with their environment; first, the isolated systems which exchange neither 'matter' nor 'energy' with their environment; second, the closed systems which exchange 'energy' but not 'matter'; third, the open systems which exchange both 'energy' and 'matter'. The distinction between the categories, however, is largely one of scale and depends on which elements are regarded as belonging to the system and which to the environment. Thus, if the scale was to be reduced significantly, an open system could become an isolated system.

Given the system in Figure 1, it can be seen that rural-urban migration is an open system involving not only an exchange of energy but also of matter (in this case, persons) with the environment. The persons concerned would be defined as all those, who having migrated into cities, have become involved in making local decisions or formulating national policies and legislation on economic and other matters which do affect the volume, character, and pattern of migration. The energy. exchange has to do with the increasing economic activities resulting from rural-urban migration and affecting the over-all economic and social conditions of the country.

One major implication of viewing rural-urban migration as an open system is the fact that it enables us to explore the principle of equifinality in so far as it applies to this phenomenon. This principle emphasizes that the state of a system at any given time is not determined so much by initial conditions as by the nature of the process, or the system parameters. In consequence, the same results may spring from different origins or, conversely, different results may be produced by the same 'causes'. In either case, it is the nature of the process which is determinate, since open systems are basically independent of their initial conditions. This principle is of considerable importance in studying rural-urban migration in different parts of the world since there has been a tendency to regard this movement in countries such as in Africa and Asia as a special kind different from elsewhere in the world. There is, of course, no doubt that initial conditions in Africa today are vastly different from what they were in countries such as Britain and the United States at the times of the massive migrations there of people from the rural areas into the cities. But, according to the principle of equifinality, as long as we keep in mind the particular system's parameters, an understanding of the migration process as it affected and continues to affect those developed countries may throw considerable light on what is currently happening in many parts of the underdeveloped world.

Growth Process in the System

From what has been said so far, it must be assumed that one of the concomitants of the continued interaction between the system and its environment will be the phenomenon of growth in the system. This will be indicated by, among other things, a rise in the volume of migration from the rural to the urban areas. Within a system framework, this phenomenon involves more than a simple growth or increase in the number of people moving from one area to another. It is much more complex, involving not only the individual components of the system but also the interaction between them and the system as a whole.

Boulding[28] has identified three types of growth processes that may occur in a system. The first is 'simple growth' and involves the addition of one more unit of a given variable such as a migrant, a farm, a vehicle, or a retail establishment. The second type is 'population growth', a process which involves both positive and negative additions. In general, this type of growth depends on the surplus of births (positive additions) over deaths (negative additions) and applies to variables which have an age distribution and regular rates of births and deaths. The third type is 'structural growth', the growth process of an aggregate with a complex structure of interrelated parts. This process often involves a change in the relation of the components since the growth of each component influences and is influenced by the growth of all other components in the system. Structural growth shades imperceptibly into structural change since, in most cases, it is not only the over-all size of the structure that grows but also its complexity.

In viewing rural-urban migration as a system, growth, in the form of structural growth, is an important dimension for more detailed investigation and study. What effects have an increase in the volume of migration on the character of the cities? What effects have the growth in the size and complexity of the cities on the types of migrants, on villages and their spatial distribution, on farms and their areal extent, on the crops grown and their qualitative importance, on the types of equipment used and on the average income of families in the rural areas? What effects have changes or growth in these variables on the volume and characteristics of migrants and on further growth and complexity in the urban areas?

It may be argued, of course, that to conceive of a theory of rural-urban migration in this broad, systematic framework is to suggest a catchall embracing a wide range of changes taking place in a country at any given time. In a sense, this is deliberate since part of the object of this paper is to call attention to the paramount importance of 'flow phenomena' in the spatial processes modifying the character of any country. Thus, just as the flow of water acts as a major sculpturing agent in the physical geography of any area of the world, the flow of persons (migration), of goods and services (trade and transportation), and of ideas (communication) is a crucial agency in shaping the human geography of a country.

More than this, there is the fact that growth in such 'flow phenomena' creates form. Growth in the flow of rural-urban migrants affects the pattern of population distribution, the areal size and internal configuration of cities, the types of buildings in rural areas, the size and arrangements of farms, and the number, size, and network density of rural roads. These, in a sense, are simply the results of the way the system tries to adjust to growth processes. However, as Boulding has pointed out, there is a limit to the extent to which the system can go on making these adjustments. 'Growth', states Boulding, 'creates form; but form limits growth. This mutuality of relationship between growth and form is perhaps the essential key to the understanding of structural growth.'[29]

This paper has tried to show how a theory of rural-urban migration can gain in incisiveness and breadth by being construed within a General Systems Theory framework. The conceptualization of the problem in this way emphasizes the structural congruencies or isomorphy with other problems. Further, one of the major attractions of this approach is that it enables a consideration of rural-urban migration no longer as a linear, uni-directional, push-and-pull, cause-effect movement but as a circular, interdependent, progressively complex, and self-modifying system in which the effect of changes in one part can be traced through the whole of the system. Such a circularity gives special prominence to the dynamic nature of rural-urban migration and allows the process to remain as one of considerable interest over an indefinite period of time. In other words, it emphasizes rural-urban migration as a continuous process, occurring in most countries all the time though at different levels of complexity. In this respect, the systems approach also serves as a normative model against which one can seek to explain obvious deviations. If the movement of people from the rural to the urban areas is not generating the set of interconnected effects which the theory leads us to expect, we may ask why. We may then investigate the various elements in the system to ascertain which of them is not functioning in the proper way. Alternatively, we may examine critically the politico-economic environment (such as, for example, the situation in those areas of the world where discriminatory policies exist based on race or caste) in order to appreciate those features that do impair the efficient operation of the system. In either case, the basic systems approach would provide the most important insight to the many dimensions of the problem. More than that, it would emphasize the crucial role of rural-urban migration as one of the most important spatial processes shaping the pattern of human occupation of the earth's surface.

NOTES AND REFERENCES

[1] R. Herberle, 'The Causes of Rural-Urban Migration: a Survey of German Theories', *American Journal of Sociology*, 43 (1938), 923–50; J. C. Mitchell, 'Migrant Labour in Africa South of the Sahara: the Causes of Labour Migration', *Bulletin of the Inter-African Labour Institute*, 6 (1959), 8–16.

[2] R. L. Morrill, 'Migration and the Spread and Growth of Urban Settlement', *Lund Studies in Geography* Ser. B, 26 (1965).

[3] J. C. Mitchell, 'Wage Labour and African Population Movements in Central Africa', in *Essays on African Population*, ed. K. M. Barbour and R. M. Prothero. New York, 1962, p. 232.

[4] W. A. Lewis, *Theory of Economic Growth*. London, 1955, p. 333.

[5] L. von Bertalanffy, 'An Outline of General System Theory', *British Journal of the Philosophy of Science*, 1 (1950), 134–65; id., 'General System Theory', *General Systems Yearbook*, 1 (1956), 1–10; id., 'General System Theory–a Critical Review', *General Systems Yearbook*, 7 (1962), 1–20.

[6] A. D. Hall and R. E. Fagen, 'Definition of System', *General Systems Yearbook*, 1 (1956), 18.

[7] Ibid., p. 20.

[8] A. Diop, 'Enquête sur la migration toucouleur à Dakar.', *Bulletin de l'Institut Français d'Afrique Noire*, Ser. B, 22 (1960), 393–418.

[9] J. Wolpert, 'Migration as an Adjustment to Environmental Stress', *Journal of Social Issues*, 22 (1966), 92–102.

[10] C. M. Arensberg, *The Irish Countryman, an Anthropological Study*. New York, 1937.

[11] E. Ardener, Shirley Ardener, and W. A. Warmington. *Plantation and Village in the Cameroons*. London, 1960, pp. 211–29.

[12] R. M. Prothero, 'Migratory Labour from North-Western Nigeria', *Africa*, 27 (1957), 250.

[13] N. I. Ndukwe, 'Migration, Agriculture and Trade in Abriba Town'. Unpublished MS., Department of Geography, University of Ibadan, 1964; A. I. Onwueke, 'Awka Upland Region, the Land of Migrant Farmers'. Unplushed MS., Department of Geography, University of Ibadan, 1966.

[14] M. Banton, *West African City*. London, 1957; id., 'Social Alignment and Identity in a West African City', in *Urbanization and Migration in West Africa*, ed. Hilda Kuper. Los Angeles, 1956, pp. 131–47; K. Little, *West African Urbanization*. London, 1965.

[15] F. I. Masser, 'Changing Pattern of African Employment in Southern Rhodesia', in *Geographers and the Tropics: Liverpool Essays*, ed. R. W. Steel and R. M. Prothero. London, 1964, p. 229.

[16] T. S. Ashton, *An Economic History of England: The Eighteenth Century*. London, 1966 ed., pp. 15–17.

[17] A. I. Richards, ed., *Economic Development and Tribal Change*. Cambridge, 1954, p. 66.

[18] P. Gulliver, 'Nyakyusa Labour Migration', *Rhodes-Livingstone Journal*, 21 (1957), 59.

[19] E. G. Ravenstein, 'The Laws of Migration', *Journal of the Royal Statistical Society*, 48 (1885). 167–235; 52 (1889), 242–305.

[20] S. C. Dodd, 'The Interactance Hypothesis: A Gravity Model Fitting Physical Masses and Human Groups', *American Sociological Review*, 15 (1950), 245–56; J. W. Stewart, 'Demographic Gravitation: Evidence and Applications', *Sociometry*, 11 (1948), 31–57.

[21] S. A. Stouffer, 'Intervening Opportunities: A Theory Relating Mobility and Distance', *American Sociological Review*, 5 (1940), 845–67; id., 'Intervening Opportunities and Competing Migrants', *Journal of Regional Science*, 2 (1960), 1–26.

[22] G. Kulldorf, 'Migration Probabilities', *Lund Studies in Geography*, Ser. B, 14 (1955).

[23] L. von Bertalanffy, op. cit.

[24] J. I. Clarke, 'Emigration from Southern Tunisia', *Geography*, 42 (1957), 99–101; G. Marty, 'A Tunis: éléments allogènes et activités professionnelles', *Revue de l'Institut des Belles Lettres Arabes*, Tunis (1948), pp. 159–88.

[25] T. Hägerstrand, 'Migration and Area: Survey of a sample of Swedish Migration Fields and Hypothetical Considerations on their Genesis', in *Migration in Sweden, a Symposium*, ed. D. Hannerberg et al., Lund Studies in Geography, Ser. B, 13 (1957), p. 132.

[26] D. F. Marble, and J. D. Nystuen, 'An Approach to the Direct Measurement of Community Mean Information Fields', *Papers and Proceedings, Regional Science Association*, 11 (1962), 99–109; R. L. Morrill, and F. R. Pitts, 'Marriage, Migration and the Mean Information Field: a Study in Uniqueness and Generality', *Annals of the Association of American Geographers*, 57 (1967), 401–22.

[27] R. L. Morrill, op. cit.

[28] K. Boulding, 'Toward a General Theory of Growth', *General Systems Yearbook*, 1 (1956), 66–75.

[29] K. Boulding, op. cit., p. 72.

16.   AN ASPECT OF URBANIZATION
IN SOUTH-EAST ASIA:
THE PROCESS OF CITYWARD MIGRATION

T. G. McGee

In developing areas the sequence of events leading to urbanization is perhaps different from that noted in nineteenth-century Europe and North America.[1]

Introduction

In the period since 1945 the urban areas of South-East Asia[2] have grown rapidly. As Table 1 reveals, the increase of towns of over 100,000 population has been well in excess of the increase of the total population with the one exception of the Philippines. Such a rapid growth has not always been characteristic of these urban areas. It has been estimated that . . .

Between 1800 and 1850 the large city population of Asia increased by about 25 per cent in contrast with an increase of 184 per cent in Europe and America combined. Between 1850 and 1900, Asian large city population increased by about 60 per cent as contrasted with an increase of over 210 per cent in Europe and America. In the first half of this century, however, the large city population of Asia has grown by almost 450 per cent as compared with only 160 per cent in Europe and America.[3]

This urban growth has not been distributed evenly among the various size categories of the urban areas. In general, it is the larger cities which have accounted for a sizeable portion of the numerical increase in town populations—a trend given early emphasis by the nature of the colonial economy—continuing today as the most characteristic feature of South-East Asian urbanization. The tendency for the urban hierarchy of many South-East Asian countries is to be dominated by '. . . one great metropolis, "the primate city", a great city which dominates the urban situation'.[4] Table 1 suggests that while the percentage increase of the larger towns is not always as fast as the rest of the town population, they are still accounting for a considerable portion of the increased urban population. In fact, the slower rate of growth of some of the larger cities such as Bangkok and Manila is almost certainly due to the out-movement of population from the crowded city core. Thus, Manila City grew by 109·3 per cent between 1947 and 1960: in the same period Quezon City on its boundaries grew by a marked increase of 268·5 per cent. The slowing down of the growth rate of the large cities in some cases simply indicates the growth of suburbanization.

There is scant evidence on what have been the main components in this considerable increase of population in urban areas. Natural increase has been of some importance although comprehensive data on rural-urban differentials in fertility and mortality are extremely difficult to find. For instance, evidence on fertility differentials is contradictory, and it is difficult to establish a clear pattern. Some evidence suggests that fertility may be lower in urban than in rural areas, but at the same time there are some indications that family size tends to rise with

From *The Urbanization Process in the Third World* (London: G. Bell & Sons Ltd., 1971), pp. 97–120. Reprinted by permission of the publishers.

income[5] in many of the South-East Asian countries. If this is so, it might count as a factor in increasing urban fertility as urban incomes are almost invariably higher than rural ones in South-East Asia. However, the greatest factor in increasing the populations of the South-East Asian cities has probably been the reduction in the mortality rate, particularly the infant mortality rate.[6]

TABLE 1

South-East Asia
Growth of Urban Population in Selected Countries

Country	Period	Per cent Increase of Towns 100,000 +	Per cent Increase of Largest Town	Per cent Increase of Total Population
Burma (1)	1941–58	40·5 (2·2)[a]	35·3 (1·4)	20·3 (1·1)
Federation of				
Malaya (2)	1947–57	51·8 (5·1)	79·7 (7·9)	27·9 (2·7)
Indonesia (3)	1930–60	170·6 (5·6)[b]	357·7 (11·9)	60·6 (2·0)
Phillippines (4)	1948–60	44·3 (3·4)[c]	16·5 (1·3)	43·4 (3·6)
Thailand (5)	1947–60	118·0 (8·4)	115·0 (8·2)	59·2 (4·5)

Notes:
[a]Figures in brackets are the yearly rates of increase.
[b]This figure is calculated for the *Kotapradja* of Indonesia which include some towns of below 100,000 population.
[c]The low rate of increase in the Philippines is probably not correct, and when it is possible to analyse the 1960 Census in detail it seems likely that the rate of increase will be much higher.
Sources:
(1) United Nations Department of Economic and Social Affairs, *Demographic Yearbook*, 1960, New York, p. 306.
(2) H. Fell, *1957 Population Census of Malaya*, Report Number 14, Kuala Lumpur, p. 8.
(3) William A. Withington, 'The Kotapradja or "King Cities" of Indonesia', *Pacific Viewpoint*, 4, No. 1 (March 1963), 76.
(4) The United Nations Department of Economic and Social Affairs, *Demographic Yearbook*, 1960, New York, pp. 323–4.
(5) Thailand. Central Statistical Office, National Economic Development Board, *Thailand Population Census 1960. Whole Kingdom*, Bakok, 1962, pp. 4–7.

Another factor contributing to the increase in city populations has been the expansion of the size of urban areas. In the period between 1947 and 1957 Kuala Lumpur expanded from 18 square miles to 30 square miles in size and in the process incorporated villages which had formerly been adjacent to the city.[7] Heeren has described a somewhat similar process in the case of Djakarta.[8] Another aspect of this growth of city populations has been the creation of new 'satellite towns' which are, in many cases, simply new residential suburbs of the city. Typical of such areas are Petaling Jaya, close to Kuala Lumpur; Kebajoran Baru, adjacent to Djakarta and Quezon City, which is now the capital of the Philippines. In addition to these middle-class areas, there is a proliferation of squatter areas surrounding the city which has sometimes induced city authorities to expand city boundaries in order to provide better living conditions.

While there is no doubt that natural increase and urban extension have accounted for some of this increase, it is impossible to disagree with U.N.E.S.C.O. when it comments that 'rural-urban migration has undoubtedly accounted for the overwhelming share of urban growth in the region'.[9] Yet, surprisingly, it is the one component of population growth in urban areas which is most inadequately treated. Historically, of course, rural-urban migration has always contributed the major part of the urban growth of South-East Asia. In the period after 1800 when the majority of cities in South-East Asia were being established by colonial powers, such as Bangkok, the majority of cities of South-East Asia were being peopled by rural migrants. But, in many cases, they were not internal migrants but rather immigrants from other countries—Europeans, Chinese, Indians, and Arabs. The most numerous group were the Chinese, and they tended to assume a dominant numerical and commercial position in the cities. Surprisingly most of them came from rural backgrounds[10] and yet they adapted to the urban areas with great ability. Thus the colonial city was an alien creation to the local groups whose migration to the city was not extensive during the colonial period.

However, the post-World War II period has seen the rise of the political independence of these powers and with it the assumption of control by the indigenous groups. The cities are no longer alien and thus there has been created a psychological and political situation which is encouraging to the rural migrant. In addition, the independent powers have endeavoured to create new industries in the city which have provided greater job opportunities for the rural migrants. Virtually every country in South-East Asia is now experiencing a rapid rural-urban movement. A 1954 Djakarta survey showed 73 per cent of the Indonesian houseaheads interviewed were born outside the city;[11] in 1960, 26·6 per cent were born outside Bangkok;[12] 47·7 per cent outside Phnom Penh;[13] 34 per cent outside Singapore;[14] and an estimated 50 per cent outside Kuala Lumpur.[15] These figures clearly indicate the importance of in-migration to the cities of South-East Asia. The rest of this paper is concerned with the patterns of rural-urban migration, and in particular, with investigating the question of whether the rural-urban movements in South-East Asia have any similarities with those that occurred in Western Europe during the industrial revolution. The next section investigates the character of rural-urban migration in Western Europe and puts forward some generalized conclusions with which to compare the process in South-East Asia.

Formulating a European Model

The problems of constructing a model of the mechanisms and dynamics of rural-urban migration in Western Europe during the period of the industrial revolution are numerous. First, there is the problem of finding and assembling population data which cover the whole of western Europe. Despite the lack of census material there are several studies on three Western European countries which are of great value; studies by Redford,[16] Smelser,[17] Ravenstein,[18] and Saville,[19] of population movements during the English industrial revolution; the results of research by Thomas,[20] Hägerstrand,[21] and Pred[22] in Sweden, and the work of Pickney,[23] Wrigley,[24] and Dickinson[25] in France, Germany, and Belgium. A study of these sources provides a considerable body of evidence on the nature of rural-urban migration from which a broad model of rural-urban migration can be constructed.

Secondly, it is difficult to construct a model of rural-urban migration which incorporates the uneven temporal and regional impact of the industrial revolution. The economic, social, and technical changes wrought by the industrial revolution began first in Great Britain during the eighteenth century, came later to Northern France and Belgium, and did not really occur in Germany until after 1871. Its impact was felt even later in the northern countries such as Sweden, and not until the twentieth century in Eastern Europe and Russia. This 'uneven time impact' unquestionably influenced the type and manner of rural-urban migration which occurred in various countries.

There is also the third problem of the time span of the industrial revolution. There is, for instance, clear evidence that the type and character of rural-urban migration changed considerably as the industrial revolution progressed. Thus, in some countries, seasonal migration to the cities changed to permanent migration; single migration to family migration; and male migration to female migration. Finally, there is the debatable question of the relationship between industrialism and the growth of towns. While there may be no reason to argue with Davis and Golden's claim that the 'achievement of high levels of urbanization anywhere in the world had to wait for (*the relatively short periods of*)* the industrial revolution'[26] if it is applied on a world-wide level, it should be remembered that in Western Europe there already existed large cities such as Paris and London which grew rapidly at the same time as the newer industrial towns such as Manchester.

Broadly speaking, then, migration to the cities of Western Europe varied with each regional and temporal stage of the industrial revolution. The first stage of migration which had been occurring for many centuries was the movement of seasonal labour into the larger cities. Thus Redford reports that much of 'the general dock-labour around Paris . . . was done by seasonal migrants from Brittany and Normandy'.[27] There were also seasonal movements of masons from the central massif areas to Paris. Such patterns of seasonal labour were common in other cities. In England in the second half of the eighteenth century when country factories were being established they tended to employ a highly mobile transitory labour force who habitually sought seasonal occupations. Redford comments that the early mill-owners had great difficulty in getting such people to settle down, and in fact recruiters were sent into the country to obtain labour.[28]

In these early phases such labour tended to be single and dominantly male. Thus the beginnings of rural to urban movement in the early phases of the industrial revolution were essentially based on impermanent populations who took some time to stabilize in the urban areas.

The second type of movement—the shift to permanent residence in the city—occurred during what may be called the 'main' period of the industrial revolution; the period of industrial concentration based on steam power, coal, and iron production which occurred during the nineteenth century. This period can be said to have induced rural-urban migration from two sources. First there was a movement of industrial workers from declining industrial areas to newer ones. Secondly, agricultural workers were also moving to the cities in search of jobs. In most of Britain 'The motive force controlling the migration was the positive attraction of the industry rather than the negative repulsion of agriculture'[29] despite the fact that the years between 1815 and 1850 were depression years in agriculture. Most of the migration to English cities during this period was family migration. In the case of the industrial migrant 'the father of a family would in most cases pursue a declining trade as long as he could, hoping for a turn in the tide; in the last resort he moved with his family to the nearest town. The unspecialized labour of the children was there readily absorbed.'[30]

Because of the family nature of this migration it was probably much less selective in terms of sex and age groups than was the later migration. Migration was in most cases short-distance migration characterized by a step pattern. '. . . The

*The words in italics are mine.

great majority of migrants went only a short distance, and migration into any centre of attraction having a wide sphere of influence was not a simple transference of people from the circumference of a circle to its centre, but an exceedingly complex wave-like motion.'[31] In general the largest cities attracted the largest proportion of the urban population growth at this time. Thus the London County area grew by one and a half million population between 1800 and 1850 while Manchester, the centre of the industrialism of the north, only increased its population by 279,000.[32] In addition the volume and length of population movement to the cities was a positive function of city size.[33] Finally, there is the important role that specific cultural groups such as the Irish played in the patterns of rural-urban migration. Thus the seasonal visits of the Irish harvesters to England was the beginning which eventually led to permanent settlement in England. This pattern, coupled with the severe economic conditions in Ireland, led to a mass movement of Irish labourers to England, the majority of whom settled in the large towns.[34]

Finally, there is the third period of the industrial revolution when population movements to the cities were increasingly characterized by a dominance of females. In England and Wales, Saville points out that, 'In the second half of the nineteenth century . . . women were more migratory than men. Generally by the end of the century, the urban areas showed a higher proportion of females to males, at all ages, than the rural areas.'[35] This was largely because in the rural areas employment opportunities for females were declining faster than those for males and thus women were being pushed out of the countryside at a faster rate. Thomas supports this pattern with evidence for Sweden for a somewhat later period.

This then is a brief résumé of the main characteristics of rural-urban migration during the period of the industrial revolution in Western Europe. Six main features of rural-urban migration emerge.

(a) The largest cities tended to attract the greatest number of migrants though not necessarily growing as fast as the newer industrial cities.

(b) Rural-urban migration was generally short-distance migration with the one proviso that the larger the city, the greater the distance from which it would attract migrants.

(c) In terms of migration differentials three main features can be observed;

   (i) During the earlier part of the revolution the migration pattern tended to be made up of single seasonal workers. This changed to a pattern of family migration during the 'main' phase of the industrial revolution, although during the later parts of the industrial revolution, single migration was more characteristic.

   (ii) Migrants tended to be concentrated into what have been called the 'migration prone' age groups between 15 and 35 years although this pattern was not so clear during the family phase of rural-urban movement.

   (iii) The sex differentials of the migrants varied considerably from country to country and phase to phase of the industrial revolution. During the earliest phases it was largely male dominated, but later it was evenly balanced between males and females and finally passing into a phase where migration was dominated by females.

(d) There was a tendency for certain cultural groups such as the Irish to figure prominently in the rural-urban movements.

(e) Finally if the simple, 'push-pull' framework of motivation for migration is accepted, it seems clear that the 'pull' factors of increasing opportunities for employment in the new industrial cities and large towns acted as a far more important motivating force than any 'push' factors such as the decline of agricultural employment opportunities.

In the next section of the paper a comparison is made between the process and dynamics of rural-urban migration in Europe described above and cityward movement in South-East Asia today.

South-East Asian Comparisons

As has already been mentioned, data on the various aspects of rural-urban movement in South-East Asia are scarce, but enough information can be culled from recent census material and some specific surveys of rural-urban migration to enable some comparisons with the European model. It would be reasonable to assume that the different cultural milieu, the different historical era, and the technical improvements of the present day would have meant that the pattern of rural-urban migration in South-East Asia would vary strikingly from that of the industrial revolution in Europe, but as the following analysis suggests there are striking similarities.

(1) Rural-urban Migration and the Larger Cities

Most evidence suggests that the larger cities of South-East Asia today are attracting a greater proportion of the rural migrants than the smaller cities. It is true that evidence on the growth rates of the larger cities suggests that they are not growing as fast as the smaller cities in many cases. But this growth pattern must be seen in the context of increasing suburbanization and the establishment of satellite towns on the fringes of many of these larger cities. For instance, while the population of Manila City grew by only 166,000 between 1948 and 1960, the population of Metropolitan Manila increased by almost 1 million people.[36] Care should be taken in viewing such a process as similar to the pattern of conurbation which occurred in urbanized areas such as Manchester and London during the industrial revolution, for the process of urban expansion is advancing into agricultural land and incorporating agricultural villages, not the merging of urban areas. Thus although the growth rates of some of the larger cities may be slowing down, in the total metropolitan areas there can be little doubt that the rate of increase exceeds other urban areas.

(2) Migration and Distance

One of the most generally accepted features of migration during the industrial revolution was that it tended to be short-distance migration with the one provision that the larger the city, the greater the area from which it drew its migrants. In general present-day patterns in South-East Asia seem remarkably similar. For instance, in 1960 approximately 50 per cent of the population which had been born outside Phranakhorn Changwad (which incoroporates the population of Bangkok and Thonburi Municipalities) came from within a 50-mile radius of the city.[37] In Singapore an analysis of the exchange of identity cards showed that the majority of migrants had come from the adjacent state of Johore.[38] In a survey of Malay migration to Kuala Lumpur carried out by the author in 1962–3, 20 per cent of the migrants had come from the state in which Kuala Lumpur is located and the majority of these migrants came from kampongs within 30 miles of the city.[39] The 1953 survey of migrants to Djakarta reported that 21 per cent of the Javanese migrants to the city came from the *Kabupaten* of Bogor, a regency which is only about half an hour from the city by bus or train.[40] The highest percentage of migrants who had been born in a surrounding district were the 40 per cent of Cambodian national migrants in Phnom Penh city who came from the Kandal province.[41]

Historically, of course, the short-distance migration law did not apply to the South-East Asian cities at least from the colonial era onwards. During the initial phases of the establishment of colonial cities in South-East Asia, the cities were peopled by migrants who frequently travelled great distances; the Chinese were by far the most ubiquitous and sometimes travelled the greatest distances; but there were Indians, Arabs, and Europeans as well. In addition, at least in some areas such as Java, there was a movement of local people to the cities, but in general the cities remained alien creations attracting alien migrants. With the passing of immigration restrictions, the cities of South-East Asia can no longer grow from such long-range migration and the patterns of migration are swinging to the characteristic short-distance migration of the West European industrial revolution. Even today the cities still attract migrants from considerable distances such as the *samlor* drivers who move from north-east Thailand to Bangkok and the Minangkabaus movement from Sumatra to Djakarta. Such movement, it is suggested, may be as much due to earlier established patterns of cityward movement and of the cultural distinctiveness of such groups as to the superior attraction of the city.

(3) Step Migration

A third feature of the migration patterns during the industrial revolution was a tendency for people to move to the larger cities in a series of moves from rural to small town and then to larger urban area in a pattern which has been labelled 'step migration'. Once again historically South-East Asia has not followed this pattern entirely. Many of the Chinese who came from long distances originally made the transition from rural to urban environment in one step. Today it is difficult to establish whether 'step migration' is more prevalent. In the Malay migrant survey carried out in Kuala Lumpur over 90 per cent of migrants had moved more than twice before settling in the city. This probably, however, reflects the role that Kuala Lumpur plays as the political capital of the Federation. The post-Independence period has seen the gradual disappearance of the 'expatriate' administrators and the adoption of a government policy which is replacing them largely by Malays. Thus there has been a shift of many public servants, who have seen many moves to Kuala Lumpur.[42] However, the 1964 Djakarta survey reports 'that by far the great part (80·4 per cent) of the migrants moved directly to the capital'.[43] In view of the high percentage of direct migrants reported in the Djakarta survey in contradistinction to the Kuala Lumpur experience, the evidence might suggest that improved transport facilities, particularly road transport, have greatly eased the problems of the migrant trip, and that improved education has increased the knowledge of the urban environment, making it easier for the migrant to settle in the larger city. But it would seem that until further evidence is available, a conclusion on the patterns of South-East Asian step migration will have to be left in abeyance.

(4) Migration Demographic Differentials

One of the clearest indications of rural-urban migration has been the rural-urban differences in sex ratios. It has been noted that rural-urban migration during the industrial revolution went through a series of phases from dominantly male migration, to an evenly balanced migration and finally to a largely female migration. As Table 2 shows the majority of South-East Asian large cities have sex

TABLE 2

Sex Ratios of Largest City and
Capital or Group of Cities of 100,000+

Country	Year of Census	Males per 100 Females
BURMA (1)	1953	104
Cities of 100,000 +		111
INDONESIA (2)	1961	97
Djakarta		105
SINGAPORE (1)	1947	122
Singapore City		122
THAILAND (3)	1960	104
Cities of 100,000 +		104
FEDERATION OF MALAYA (4)	1957	106
Kuala Lumpur		113
SARAWAK (1)	1947	101
Kuching		106
NORTH BORNEO (1)	1951	107
Sandakan		119
BRUNEI (1)	1951	122
Belait (12,551)		155
PHILIPPINES (5)	1960	101
Manila City		93
CAMBODIA (6)	1959	100
Phnom Penh		105

Sources:

(1) The data for sex ratios of Burma, Singapore, Sarawak, North Borneo, and Brunei were taken from Philip M. Hauser (ed.), *Urbanization in Asia and the Far East*, U.N.E.S.C.O., Paris, 1957, pp. 124–5.
(2) Department of Foreign Affairs, Republic of Indonesia, *Indonesia, 1962*, p. 38.
(3) Central Statistical Office, Economic Development Board Thailand, *Thailand Population Census, 1960*, Bangkok, pp. 4–7.
(4) H. Fell, *1957 Population Census of the Federation of Malaya*, Report Number 14, Kuala Lumpur, 1960, pp. 53–5.
(5) Bureau of the Census and Statistics, *Census of the Philippines, 1960*, 'Manila', Vol. 1, Manila, 1960, pp. 30–2.
(6) The total population figures for Cambodia were taken from Tan-kim Huon, *Géographie du Cambodge*, Phnom Penh, 1961, p. 72. The figures for Phnom Penh came from an unpublished cyclostyled document incorporating the 1959 Cambodian Census results for Phnom Penh.

ratios which are much more heavily weighted in favour of males than the national figures. Only part of this male dominance in the cities can be explained by the fact that, with the exception of Cambodia and Indonesia, the national sex ratios have a higher ratio of males to females than is characteristic in most Western countries. More significant, perhaps, is the influence of immigrant communities, particularly the Chinese, for these communities generally have highly unbalanced sex ratios heavily weighted in favour of males in addition to having a high percentage of their population concentrated in the main urban areas (see Table 3). Even allowing for these above factors the male (with the exception of the Philippines) dominant sex ratios of the urban areas points to a dominantly male migration from rural to urban areas. This is further emphasized by the tendency of the populations to become more masculine as the localities become more urban which—the U.N.E.S.C.O. Report confirms—'. . . reflects primarily the sex composition of migrants from rural areas and villages to towns and cities'.[44]

A further indication of not only the male-dominant character of this migration, but also its age selectivity can be obtained from the age-specific sex ratios shown in Table 4 and the age-divergency graphs (Figure 1). In 1957 the U.N.E.S.C.O. Report commented: 'The excess of males over females in urban areas is greatest, in most cases, at ages 15–59, and more particularly at ages 15–39',[45] and in general this is supported by both Table 4 and the divergency graphs. What is interesting is the exception of the Philippines which has a clear majority of females in the city and a striking dominance of females in the age group 15–24. Other countries also show indications of a breakdown of the male-dominant sex ratios in this younger age group. Whether or not this increase in the number of females in urban areas represents the beginning of a trend towards the female-dominant pattern of migration already accomplished in the Philippines is an interesting question. Certain evidence from Cambodia suggests that some of this female movement may be marriage movement. For instance, there were over twice as many married women in the age group between 15 and 24 years as men. Thus a pattern is established of a young single man moving first to the city and after he has earned enough money and established himself he sends back to his village for a wife to be found for him. His new wife then joins him in the city. Evidence for this pattern has been provided by the Kuala Lumpur survey.

However, there is no doubt that the male-dominated rural-urban migration patterns which had characterized the Philippines in 1948 have changed dramatically to a dominantly female movement to the city (Figure 1c). The reasons for this movement of females have been suggested by Hunt.[46] First, the rapid increase of manufacturing, much of it located in Manila City, has created favourable employment opportunities for the females who are frequently found more efficient for the routine work involved in industrial assembly. Secondly, we must consider the large numbers of females who pass on to college education in the Philippines and the fact that these institutions are highly concentrated in Manila City. Finally, the female movement represents far-seated social changes in the nature of Filipino society in which the equality of the sexes is becoming an increasingly important feature. Thus the dominantly male character of rural-urban migration in South-East Asia is similar to the earlier phases of the industrial revolution and there are even indications that if the Filipino pattern becomes characteristic of South-East Asia the swing to female-dominant migration which occurred in Western Europe may occur also.

(5) Migration—Family or Single Migration?

It was earlier pointed out that migration during the industrial revolution varied greatly as to whether it was single or family migration. In the earlier stages of the industrial revolution it was more frequently family migration, though in the later period it became increasingly single migration. There is little evidence on this aspect of rural-urban migration from South-East Asia. The Kuala Lumpur and Djakarta surveys indicate that about 50 per cent of the migrants were married and travelled with their families, and it has been suggested that such family migration 'may constitute the "normal" migrational type'.[47] Single men form an important component of the remainder, although there are a significant number of married migrant males who leave their family behind on their first visit to the city. The role of marriage of the single men in the town with women in their home villages which

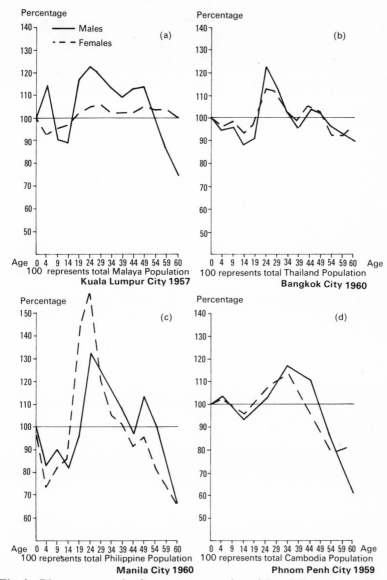

Fig. 1. Divergency-graph of age structure, selected South-East Asian cities.

has already been mentioned may be of considerable significance in bringing females into the urban milieu.[48]

(6) Rural-urban Migration and Cultural Distinctiveness.

One of the features of the movement to cities during the industrial revolution was that not all of the movement fitted into the neat set of laws elaborated by Ravenstein.[49] In particular there was the movement of distinct cultural groups such as the Irish, which was partly motivated by the grinding poverty in their homeland, partly motivated by earlier patterns of seasonal agricultural migration to England and the possibility of cheap boat transport. Such movement, of course, did not conform in all its characteristics to many of the so-called migration laws. There

TABLE 4

Ratio of Males to Females for Total Population
and Main City by Specific Age Groups

PHILIPPINES (1969) (1)	Total Population	Manila City
15—24	102·4	73·6
25—34	95·4	92·7
35—44	97·4	96·4
Total Population	101·4	93·2
CAMBODIA (1959) (2)	Total Population	Phnom Penh
15—24	96·3	98·2
25—34	94·3	104·3
35—44	97·5	120·7
Total Population	99·7	105·0
THAILAND (1960) (3)	Total Population	Phranakhorn (Bangkok)
15—24	101·4	108·6
25—34	99·5	106·1
35—44	101·3	108·0
Total Population	100·3	103·7
FEDERATION OF MALAYA (1957) (4)	Total Population	Kuala Lumpur
15—24	99·3	117·6
25—34	99·0	116·0
35—44	110·5	123·0
Total Population	106·0	113·0

Sources:
(1) The Manila Figures were calculated from Bureau of Census and Statistics, *Census of the Philippines, 1960*, 'Manila', Vol. 1, Manila, 1960, pp. 30—3.
   The total population figures were calculated from United Nations Department of Economic and Social Affairs, *Demographic Yearbook, 1960*, New York, 1960, pp. 216—17.
(2) The total population figures were calculated from Tan-kim Huon, *Géographie du Cambodge*, Phnom Penh, 1961, p. 72. The figures for Phnom Penh were calculated from an unpublished cyclostyled document incorporating the 1959 Cambodian Census results for Phnom Penh.
(3) The figures for Thailand were taken from the Central Statistical Office, Economic Development Board, Thailand, *Thailand Population Census, 1960*, Bangkok, 1960. The figures for Phranakhorn Changwad which is made up largely of Bangkok Municipality from *Thailand Population Census, 1960, Changwad Series, Changwad Phranakhorn.*
(4) The figures for the Federation of Malaya and Kuala Lumpur were taken from H. Fell, *1957 Population Census of the Federation of Malaya*, Report Number 14 and *1957 Population Census, State of Selangor*, Report Number 2, Kuala Lumpur, 1960.

have been many examples of culturally distinctive migrant groups in the cities of South-East Asia. Such groups frequently tend to travel the longest distances and have the most highly specialized jobs. Some examples are the movement of migrants from north-east Thailand to Bangkok and their tendency to group in *samlor* driving;[50] the large community of Boyans, from the small island of Bawean off the coast of Java, heavily concentrated in the driving and occupations which are concerned with horse racing;[51] and the movement of Minangkabaus from Sumatra to Djakarta where they tend to have a large proportion of the better government and clerical jobs.[52] It is not possible to explain the migration of such groups,

TABLE 3

Numbers of Chinese in Selected South-east Asian Countries and some Features of their Urban Patterns

Country	Date of Population Estimate	Size of Chinese Population	Chinese as a Percentage of Total Population	Percentage of each Country's Chinese Population Living in Major Urban Area	Chinese as a Percentage of Total Population Living in Major Urban Area	Sex Ratios of Chinese in Urban Area
Indonesia	1950s	2,500,000	2·5	12·0	10·2	—
Thailand	1960	384,000	1·5	51·3	9·2	155·9
Philippines	1948	250,000	1·0	36·0	3·4	136·3
Burma	1950s	300,000	1·5	—	—	—
Federation of Malaya	1957	2,333,756	37·0	8·3	63·4	103·0
Cambodia	1959	275,000	5·6	22·8	17·6	116·2

Notes: Accurate contemporary figures of the Chinese in South-East Asian countries are difficult to locate. Few national censuses identify the Chinese population by any other form than place of birth which means the Chinese populations are frequently underestimated in such documents.
Sources: National censuses cited in the other tables were used in the preparation of this Table.

frequently over long distances, purely in economic terms. Frequently they have a type of culture which can be said to be 'migrant prone'. Thus the Minangkabau group are characterized by a matriarchial social structure in which land passes through the female line. Such a situation does not offer the male many economic opportunities, and he frequently moves to the city. Such out-migration causes no major dislocation in the social and economic structure of the community from which he departs; in fact such out-movement was recognized in the past as a formal institution of the society, which allowed men to travel away from the village— *merantau.*[53] There are many other examples in South-East Asia of 'migrant prone' groups, and it would seem that any set of general characteristics of rural-urban migration would have to incorporate them in some way or other.

(7) Migration Motivations

Perhaps the best-established generalization on the nature of South-East Asian rural-urban migrations, next to the statement that such migration is largely male-dominated, has been the claim that such migration is generally motivated primarily by 'push' rather than 'pull' factors. This statement is reiterated again and again in many of the works on Asian migration. For instance, the U.N.E.S.C.O. publication reports—'It gives a clue to one of the most important features of Asian rural-urban migration, namely the *push* of people from the countryside to the cities rather than the pull of industrial and employment opportunities in urban areas.'[54] This is, of course, in direct contrast to the experience of the industrial revolution in Western Europe where there was close connection between the economic demands for labour exerted by the rapidly growing urban industry and the growth of cities. It has also led to the statement that many of the countries of South-East Asia are 'over-urbanized' because they have too high a level of urbanization in relation to the level of economic development.[55] Such a situation creates many of the problems of unemployment, social and economic discontent which characterize many of the South-East Asian cities. Rural migrants come to the cities because of the pressure of population and lack of jobs in the rural areas only to find that a similar situation is in existence in the city. Thus rural poverty is replaced by urban poverty. The process has been chronicled not only academically but also in many of the writings of South-East Asian novelists; in harrowing terms by Mochtar Lubis in Indonesia,[56] Kerima Polotan in the Philippines,[57] and in a more light-hearted manner in Anthony Burgess's trilogy of Malaya.[58]

Yet, despite all the problems that result from rural-to-urban migration, the process still goes on and at an apparently faster rate, and the cities grow bigger and bigger. The fact that the migration still continues does lead to a situation where the simple 'push-pull' hypothesis of rural-urban migration does not seem to be an entirely adequate framework within which to assess the whole process of migration.[59] As the Report of the Population Conference held in Teheran comments, the rapid increase in urban population should not be regarded merely as a demographic phenomenon 'but rather as part of the whole fabric of strains and tensions which is inherent in a rapid process of social change, unaccompanied by a corresponding pace of economic growth'.[60]

It is thus a condition of society which is responsible for increased mobility— increased education facilities and improved communications make the rural dweller far more aware of the urban environment. The growth of nationalism acutely fostered by the new governments make the rural dweller more aware of the role he has to play in the new state. Political instability associated with the process of imposing national unity frequently forces the rural dweller into the city. The associated problem of getting economic development off the ground at times of such political instability means that development is not rapid enough to suggest to the rural dweller that his opportunities will be better in the rural areas than in the city. Thus push-and-pull symptoms are simply evidences of a wider condition of society, but it does indicate that the model of Western European rural-urban migration needs to be modified substantially in the Asian situation.

Implications for Policy Planning for the Future of South-East Asian Cities

The broad conclusions of this preliminary comparison of the patterns of rural-urban migration in Western Europe and South-East Asia are obvious. In many of the specific details of rural-urban migration patterns the South-East Asian migrations bear remarkable similarities. Migration has been shown to be largely short-distance migration in both areas; the larger cities are attracting more migrants; there are evidences of step migration; the question of whether migration is single or family migration still seems to be rather confused as is the evidence for Europe. There is a tendency for migrants to be generally in migratory age groups; for similar patterns of specific groups being more 'prone' to migration; and there is even a trend (clearly evident in the Philippines) which seems to indicate an increasing tendency of migration to the cities to become female dominant.

It is only in the general context of the motivations for migration that South-East Asia seems to be different, but even here there is at least the factor of a general condition of society which is conducive to rural-urban migration. This is not to say that South-East Asian governments view the process of rural-urban migration with favour. Many take the view that such a process is unhealthy, not only because of the social and economic erosion it causes in rural communities, but also because of the problem of urban overcrowding, poverty, and unemployment which occurs in the cities. This is sometimes associated with an almost idealistic belief that the rural life is somehow morally better and the increasing urbanization will lead to a steady corruption of society. There are modern-day Cobbetts as well. Such an attitude, although it can perhaps be best understood in the light of contemporary nationalisms and their attempt to build a truly indigenous culture in reaction against the alien impositions of colonialism, is scarcely realistic, in view of the inevitability of urbanization in the region. While it may be accepted that piecemeal policies of rural and urban development may stem the process in part, the most obvious need is for the collection of information in great detail, on the process of rural-urban migration. Only from such information can over-all planning schemes be formulated which take advantage of the modern technological advances of this era, as well as increased government control. With such information and carefully designed plans which aim at increased industrialization in the cities as well as rural development, it may be possible to alleviate many of the pressing problems of rural-urban migration which characterize South-East Asia today.

NOTES AND REFERENCES

[1] Economic Commission for Asia and the Far East, 'Draft Report of the Asian Population Conference', Twentieth Session, 2–17 March 1964, Teheren, Iran (unpublished), p. 105.

[2] South-East Asia is defined for the purpose of this paper as including Brunei, Burma, Cambodia, Indonesia, Laos, Malaysia, North Vietnam, the Philippines, South Vietnam, and Thailand.

[3] Philip M. Hauser (ed.), *Urbanization in Asia and the Far East*, U.N.E.S.C.O. Research Centre on the Social Implications of Industrialization in Southern Asia, Calcutta, 1957, p. 59.

4 Ibid., p. 87. Other articles dealing with this aspect of South-East Asia urbanization are D. W. Fryer, 'The Million City in South east Asia', *Geographical Review*, October 1953, pp. 474–94; and Norton S. Ginsburg, 'The Great City in Southeast Asia', *American Journal of Sociology*, 60, 5, pp. 455–62.

5 See, for instance, Department of Statistics, Federation of Malaya, *Household Budget Survey of the Federation of Malaya, 1957–58*, Kuala Lumpur, 1958.

6 This is well illustrated by the Malaysian community in Singapore whose crude death rate fell from 17·8 per 1,000 in 1947 to 10 per 1,000 in 1957. See T. G. McGee, 'The Population of Malaysia: A Preliminary Analysis' in Wang Gungwu (ed.), *Malaysia: A Handbook*, London, 1964.

7 See pp. 121–47, [in the original publication].

8 H. J. Heeren, 'The Urbanization of Djakarta', *Ekonomi dan Keuangan*, 11 November 1955, p. 699.

9 Philip M. Hauser (ed.), op. cit., p. 154.

10 See Victor Purcell, *The Chinese in Southeast Asia*, London, 1961; G. William Skinner, *Chinese Society in Thailand: An Analytical History*, New York, 1957; and William H. Newell, *Treacherous River: A Study of Rural Chinese in North Malaya*, Kuala Lumpur, 1962.

11 H. J. Heeren, op. cit., p. 702.

12 Central Statistical Office, Economic Development Board, Thailand, *Thailand Population Census, 1960, Changwad Series, Changwad Phranakhorn*, Bangkok, 1961, pp. 8–11.

13 Unpublished cylostyled document incorporating the 1959 Cambodian Census results for Phnom Penh.

14 Department of Statistics, Singapore, *1957 Census of Population, Singapore*, Preliminary Release, No. 7, Singapore, 1959, pp. 2–3.

15 See p. 126 [in the original publication].

16 Arthur Redford, *Labour Migration in England, 1800–1850*, London, 1926.

17 Neil J. Smelser, *Social Change in the Industrial Revolution: An Application of Theory to the Lancashire Cotton Industry, 1770–1840*, London, 1959.

18 E. G. Ravenstein, 'The Laws of Migration', *Journal of the Royal Statistical Society*, 48 (June 1885), 167–235; 52 (June 1889), 241–305.

19 John Saville, *Rural Depopulation in England and Wales, 1851–1951*, London, 1957.

20 Dorothy Swaine Thomas, *Social and Economic Aspects of Swedish Population Movements, 1750–1933*, New York, 1941.

21 Torsten Hägerstrand, 'Migration and Area Survey of a Sample of Swedish Migration Fields and Hypothetical Considerations on Their Genesis', in David Hannerberg, Torsten Hägerstrand, Bruno Odeving, *Migration in Sweden: A Symposium*, Lund Studies in Geography, Series B, Human Geography, 13, Lund, 1957.

22 Allan Pred, *The External Relations of Cities during the 'Industrial Revolution'*, The University of Chicago, Department of Geography, Research Paper, Number 76, Chicago, 1962.

23 David H. Pickney, 'Migrations to Paris during the Second Empire', *The Journal of Modern History*, 25 (1 March 1953), 1–12.

24 E. A. Wrigley, *Industrial Growth and Population*, Cambridge, 1961.

25 Robert E. Dickinson, *The West European City*, London, 1951.

26 Kingsley Davis and Hilda Hertz Golden, 'Urbanization and the Development of Pre-Industrial Areas', *Economic Development and Cultural Change*, 3 (1954–5), 8.

27 Arthur Redford, 1926, op. cit., p. 4.

28 Ibid., pp. 20–1.

29 Ibid., p. 21.

30 Ibid., p. 160.

31 Ibid., p. 160

32 G. D. H. Cole and Raymond Postgate, *The Common People, 1746–1946*, London, 1963, p. 137.

33 Robert E. Dickinson, *The West European City*, London, 1951, pp. 447–8.

34 Arthur Redford, op. cit., Chapters VIII and IX.

35 John Saville, op. cit., p. 31.

36 Carlos P. Ramos, 'Manila's Metropolitan Problem', *Philippine Journal of Public Administration*, 5 No. 2 (April 1961), 92.

37 Central Statistical Office, Economic Development Board, Thailand, *Thailand Population Census, 1960, Changwad Series, Changwad Phranakhorn*, Bangkok, 1961, pp. 8–11.

38 See T. G. McGee, 'Malays in the City: A New Social Structure for Malaya?', unpublished paper read to the Malaysia Society, Wellington, New Zealand, 1 July 1964, p. 2.

[39] Ibid., p. 6.

[40] H. J. Heeren, op. cit., p. 703.

[41] Unpublished cyclostyled document incorporating the 1959 Cambodian Census results for Phnom Penh.

[42] T. G. McGee, 1964, op. cit., p. 8.

[43] H. J. Heeren, op. cit., p. 704.

[44] Philip M. Hauser (ed.), op. cit., p. 108.

[45] Ibid., p. 109.

[46] Chester L. Hunt, 'Changing Sex Ratio in Philippine Cities'. Paper presented to the I.G.U. Regional Conference on South-East Asia held at Kuala Lumpur, April 1962.

[47] H. J. Heeren, op. cit., p. 705.

[48] T. G. McGee, 1964, op. cit., p. 7.

[49] E. G. Ravenstein, op. cit.

[50] Robert B. Textor, 'From Peasant to Pedicab Driver', *Yale University Cultural Report Series*, 9, New Haven, 1961.

[51] Jacob Vredenbregt, 'Bawean Migrations: Some Preliminary Notes', *Bijdragen, Tot de Taal-, Land-, en Volkenkunde*, 120, 1964, pp. 109–37.

[52] Ruth T. McVey (ed.), *Indonesia*, New Haven, 1963.

[53] T. G. McGee, 1964, op. cit., pp. 6–7.

[54] Philip M. Hauser, op. cit., p. 133.

[55] See B. F. Hoselitz, 'Generative and Parasitic Cities', *Economic Development and Cultural Change*, 3, No. 3, 1955.

[56] Mochtar Lubis, *Twilight in Djakarta* (tr. Claire Holt), London, 1963.

[57] Kerima Polotan, *The Hand of the Enemy*, Manila, 1962.

[58] Anthony Burgess, *Beds in the East*, London, 1959.

[59] See William Petersen, 'A General Typology of Migration', *American Sociological Review*, 23, No. 3, (June 1958), 256–66.

[60] Economic Commission for Asia and the Far East, *Draft Report of the Asian Population Conference*, p. 91.

17.   FILTERING AND NEIGHBOURHOOD CHANGE

W. F. Smith

'Filtering' is an indirect process for meeting the housing demand of a lower-income group. When new quality housing is produced for higher-income households, houses given up by these households become available to the lower-income group. Though it is a 'well-recognized phenomenon',[1] filtering provides an issue of public policy which has long commanded the attention of housing economists—whether or not it is fundamentally desirable that low-income housing needs be met in this way. The answer to this question can affect the character and pattern of cities, and hence the forecasts of demand for every existing residential neighbourhood. In this chapter we show that the filtering concept and the questions it provokes have played important roles in the development of urban analytical technique, shifting this from a cartographic approach to more rigorous matrix analysis.

The filtering issue today can be traced to an empirical study made during the 1930s by Homer Hoyt.[2] That study offered a concept which would explain and predict the location within a city of certain types of residential uses—the so-called 'sector theory'. The theory, in turn, implied a succession of occupancy in dwellings originally built for higher-income families. Thus filtering was the dynamic element in the sector theory.

Hoyt's entire study has been subjected to much criticism by other urban economists. In such an important field criticism was nearly inevitable because of the manner in which the sector theory was originally put forward. Hoyt's study called attention to a number of variables affecting the character and evolution of residential neighbourhoods, variables such as the distribution of income in the community as a whole, the community's rate of growth and changes in its composition, the quality level of new construction, and, of course, the spatial distribution of socio-economic groups and of construction activity. Having identified these variables, however, Hoyt failed to present an operational framework in which they might be integrated. He provided only a generalized historical description with vague suggestions about the interrelation among the variables.

Another failing of the original Hoyt study was that it raised policy questions without analysing their broad implications. The study can be criticized on this score because the work was done for a public agency and was thus to influence public policy. This gave critics of the sector theory even more reason to quarrel with Hoyt and to view his theory as a *justification* of the historical pattern of urban development, a pattern which to many persons seemed undesirable. Rightly or wrongly, Hoyt was soon accused of espousing as 'ideal', a form of urban development which he had actually merely described.

Both of these defects in Hoyt's sector theory—the non-operational nature of his concepts and his avoidance of implied policy questions—could be remedied by creating a model of competitive equilibrium. With a theoretical structure for

From *Research Report No. 24* (1964), 1–16. Reprinted by permission of the Center for Real Estate and Urban Economics, Institute of Urban and Regional Development, University of California, Berkeley.

translating any given set of demand and supply conditions into an equilibrium pattern of residential neighbourhoods, the implications of policy or other exogenous changes can be worked out.

The present study is an effort to provide and to illustrate just such an analytical framework as a more flexible tool for both forecasting and policy formulation than the sector theory. First, however, we should explore the sector theory and some of its criticisms and developments in some amount of detail.

The Sector Theory

Hoyt's essential notion was that as a city grows the fashionable residential district moves outward from the centre, always in the same direction. Obsolete houses left behind by the well-to-do become occupied by the poor, particularly the recent immigrants, so that the wedge-shaped path taken by the high-income group contains both extremes in the income spectrum. This sector is the most vital, the most active, and the most troublesome. Middle-income families group themselves about the well-to-do, hoping that some of the status of the fashionable areas will rub off on them.

The study in which the sector theory was first presented provided a number of specific rules which seemed to determine the direction which fashionable residential development would take. It moves towards high ground, for example, along the best transportation routes, and avoids 'dead ends' which would impede further outward movement. Pre-existing commercial nuclei may exert a pull on high-income residential development, and real-estate promoters may succeed in bending the normal direction of this growth.

These points constitute the sector theory 'proper'. In Hoyt's original study, however, there are at least two other major components. He discusses and illustrates the impact of the community's rate of growth upon the pattern of neighbourhood change: '... the rapidity of population growth is one of the most important determinants of the differences in the speed with which high-grade neighbourhoods move to new locations.'[3]

The other major component of Hoyt's neighbourhood study is a series of qualifications by which he seeks to offset the inflexibility and the simplification of his model. For example, he explains that: 'The rate of neighbourhood change may vary even between cities growing in population at the same rate. The component elements of the added population are of extreme importance.'[4] Thus, if there were a great wave of poor immigrants, the cast-off mansions of the rich would not suffice to house them; the predetermined pattern of movement within the city would have to be altered in some unspecified way. In this portion of his study Hoyt seems to anticipate, if not to satisfy, some of his later critics.

Firey's Cultural Ecology

Hoyt's simplified and 'deterministic' description of residential patterns was attacked by Walter Firey in his book *Land Use in Central Boston*.[5] Firey, a sociologist, found the sector theory inadequate as an explanation for the irregular pattern of residential settlement in the Boston area. He wrote: 'The spatial distribution of upper class families is apparently more variable than the Burgess-Hoyt theories appreciate. Whatever forces are responsible for it must be sought in less simple and tangible factors than those of inevitable radial extension or inevitable ringlike expansion.'[6]

Chief among the 'less simple and tangible factors' were 'spatially referred values', according to Firey, meaning that cultural attachments could confound the neat determinism of the sector theory. Fashionable districts might spring up wherever an atmosphere of gentility was once centred, and then such districts might persist in or recover such character again and again, long after the sector theory would have moved them into new suburban tracts. Cultural cohesion among low-income minority (especially immigrant) groups might account for their clustering in the slums, rather than a need for hand-me-down housing. The filtering mechanism seemed to Firey too much apart from human volition and non-economic motivations.

Perhaps the most imaginative part of Firey's work is his suggestion of a grand balancing of several objectives from among several cultural groups, within the limited confines of the metropolis. We read:

... there is always a problem of allocating space. In such allocation there must always be a *proportionalization of ends* [emphasis Firey's]. This arises out of the fact that every community has a multiplicity of component ends, and not merely one or a few ends. Hence it becomes necessary to achieve a certain 'balance of sacrifices' in order that every component end of the community will in some degree be attained.[7]

The further exposition of this idea is rather badly bungled by Firey, but it is not too difficult to read into it an appeal for the development of some mathematical programming technique by which the resources of the community, both real and cultural, may be divided among groups of the population in some optimal way.

Filtering as a Source of Low-income Housing

The concept of filtering certainly ante-dates Hoyt's study of residential neighbourhoods. For example, a British government report in 1929 contained this statement: When post-war building began, it was hoped that there might be a gradual movement of the working-class population of the slums into better houses. This might occur in two ways, either the slum dweller might go direct into a new house or a process of 'filtering up' might occur under which the slum dweller would move from the slum into a better pre-war house, the tenant of which would, in his turn, move into a new house. Both of these processes have, of course, occurred, but on a disappointingly small scale.[8]

By making the filtering process an essential element in his model of residential dynamics, Hoyt implicitly raised an important policy issue. If public policy seeks to raise housing standards among low-income groups, must it—or should it—work through the filtering process? From the standpoint of housing welfare, is the filtering process desirable? Is it even inevitable?

It seems clear that Hoyt originally had no intention of grappling with this issue. In reply to criticism on the filtering issue as it affects low-income housing he said: '... the purpose of the study was economic and "social" factors, or ability to pay and need, will make a hash of both economics and social welfare.'[9]

Yet the policy issue was there, the more emphatically because Rodwin could charge that Hoyt's sector theory was developed as a policy tool, to be applied by and through the Federal Housing Administration. The charge is contained in these words:

Perhaps Hoyt may not have intended it as such, but there is a strong emphasis in the study in favor of preserving the better nieghborhoods rather than improving the poorer ones. That suspicion is further supported by the fact that the study was made for the Federal Housing Administration whose interest and experience to date have been primarily to protect its insured loans and which has shown little interest in other points of view.[10]

As a reflection of Hoyt's qualifications or his method of attack this remark by Rodwin seems to misfire. An objective, empirical review of urban development cannot be said to be 'in favour of' one course of public action as opposed to some other. Hoyt did not even attempt to justify his sector theory as a normative description of ideal competitive allocation.

There is validity to the point raised by Rodwin, however, in the sense that if the normal market process—i.e. filtering down of older houses—appears to provide only inadequate dwellings for the lower-income population, perhaps somewhat stronger and more direct measures are required. The argument, as developed with particular force by Ratcliff in his *Urban Land Economics*,[11] seems to have evolved in the following way:

1. It is perceived that housing markets usually build new dwellings chiefly for the well-to-do; older dwellings filter down to lower-income families—i.e. Hoyt's empirical generalization is accepted.
2. A social judgement is made that housing of low-income families is deficient. It is proposed to subsidize the construction of new dwellings for them.
3. Some groups—presumably real-estate interests—object, point out that in the course of time houses now being built will be available to the poor through the filtering process. Hence no interference with the market is required.
4. Welfare-minded economists retort that too great a period of time is involved, since the social pyramid is so narrow at the top and so wide at the bottom. In the great length of time needed to transmit a small volume of new housing to families now ill housed, the filtered units will—in fact must—deteriorate. When they arrive at the lowest income level they will represent no improvement. Hence direct new construction is required to meet the low-income needs.

The discussion had about reached this point in 1949, when Ratcliff's book appeared. It was less specifically developed by Ratcliff and Ernest Fisher as early as 1936 when the two reviewed housing programmes in Europe.[12] As part of that review the two economists attempted to test the validity of the theory that housing standards may be improved through filtering. They did this by observing the experience of certain European countries, and their conclusion was: '. . . that no evidence has been adduced . . . that dependence can be placed on this procedure for a substantial improvement in the housing conditions of the lower-income group. Cures of a more positive nature are demanded.'[13]

Their 'test' of the theory, however, is unconvincing. In England they observed that between 1920 and 1930 there had been a high rate of building, chiefly for upper-income demand. Concurrently, '. . . from 25,000 to 35,000 unfit houses were demolished . . .' and '. . . a total of 5,943,462 dwellings were repaired.'[14] Further, 'The 1931 census indicates a definite improvement in the extent of overcrowding in the preceding decade. The average number of persons per occupied house dropped from 4·85 in 1921 to 4·38 in 1931.' On the other hand, the doubling rate was unchanged at 1·21 families per occupied house; the average size of families, clearly, had decreased.

In Holland it was noted that construction volume had been stimulated by government aid. A government official was quoted: 'Owing to the numerous unoccupied dwellings and the general fall in rents many flats of inferior standard have fallen empty and will be difficult to let.' However, the reviewers conjectured that migration back to rural areas could account for some of the vacancy of low-rent dwellings.

The principal 'test' of the filtering theory in the Fisher-Ratcliff study turns out to be a theoretical one. With the aid of an abbreviate frequency distribution of dwellings in England and Wales by rent, the authors point out that to supply 10 per cent of the lowest group with better dwellings through the filtering process the housing stock at the highest level would have to grow by 45 per cent, because the number of units in the former group is four and a half times that of the latter. The authors considered such a volume of building to be unlikely: '. . . if the producers of housing are well informed of the demand situation there will be no overproduction in any grade of housing, and no surplus will be created.'[15] This argument is repeated with only minor embellishments in Ratcliff's 1949 book.[16]

This theoretical argument, that any 'surplus' of housing would curtail new construction, could leave the sector theory without its mainspring and would seem to contradict Ratcliff's candid admission that filtering is a 'well recognized phenomenon'. All new construction for a population already housed is necessarily redundant in a physical sense, but not in an economic sense. But the 'no surplus' idea has a more fundamental flaw. A *subsidized* filtering process can indeed provide the requisite surpluses which will permit upgrading of low-income housing. Ratcliff (in particular) has made it appear that to achieve improvement in housing standards the choice is between an unsubsidized market-filtering process and a subsidized public housing programme. He has said 'Filtering cannot be forced.'[17] This seems to overlook the fact that public policy can, and often does, stimulate the filtering process. There is the FHA, the Home Loan Bank Board, The Federal Savings and Loan Insurance Corporation, and the legion of freeway builders to lure the relatively well-to-do suburban areas of new housing, leaving their older homes to families of relatively lower income. More direct inducements to accelerate filtering are also possible. Perhaps Ratcliff meant to say that filtering cannot be forced *without some public subsidy or other effort,* though it is difficult to imagine how a market process can be 'forced' to accelerate *except* by a public programme.

Because of this theoretical lapse Ratcliff (and Fisher) cannot be said to have provided the sector theory with a normative test. They were obviously arguing *ex parte* for public housing, obscuring rather than creating a set of equilibrium relationships.

Rodwin and the Issue of a Competitive Market

Of course, it is not obvious from Hoyt's work that the filtering process or the working out of the sector theory reflects an efficient, competitive allocation of urban resources by the private market. Perhaps the historical regularities which permitted Hoyt to develop his generalized descriptions of urban development stem from more or less universal imperfections in the housing market. If this be the case the sector theory is robbed of its usefulness as a benchmark of ideal behaviour or as an instrument of policy.

Rodwin makes almost this charge in his extensive evaluation of the sector theory which appeared in 1950. He says:

Throughout the analysis, Hoyt has been dealing with the operation of a relatively laissez-faire competitive economy. Real estate, however, is a notorious and oft cited example of just such market imperfections. Housing, in particular, reflects an additional complication because its long production period and durability contribute to serious and prolonged marketing errors and maladjustments.[18]

But is the urban housing market so imperfectly competitive? Rodwin mentions the following conditions for 'ideal' market performance:

'perfect knowledge and mobility'—but the entire brokerage profession (which

some would claim to be overpopulated) and a major portion of newspaper lineage are devoted to the dissemination of knowledge; as for mobility, Hoyt's empirical observations are very largely a documentation of population movement.

'*maximization of profit, many buyers and sellers, free entry and departure of productive factors*'—but there can be little dispute that these conditions exist in one of the most atomistic of all commodity markets.

'*homogenous products*'—but product homogeneity is a requirement of two-dimensional *analysis*, not of optimal resource allocation. It is the function, after all, of an economic system to allocate resources among an essentially infinite range of heterogeneous products. The defect of analytical equipment ought not to be attributed to a type of product which is inherently heterogeneous, but Rodwin does so.

There are two other critical estimates of the market process in Rodwin's essay. As noted above, he calls attention to the durability of housing as an impediment to efficient market adjustments. Here he rather spectacularly misses the point of the filtering discussion and the sector theory; the movement of population through the housing stock is the competitive market's way of making use of a durable but deteriorating inventory. This is surely the import of Hoyt's bold generalizations. Rodwin presumably would not see in the used-car market, or in the markets for used machine tools, passenger airplanes, or household appliances a culpable market organization; why then for used houses? It is the nature of the product to go through a succession of less affluent or less particular users; there is nothing necessarily 'imperfect' about the process of handing things down.

Lastly, Rodwin calls attention to the fact that land uses which are determined solely by private market considerations can give rise to notorious external dis-economies or 'social costs'. Factories produce smoke, and automobiles produce congestion. There are sins of neglect, too:

To compete in the urban land and housing market, uses must be income producing and rather high at that. Uses like playgrounds, parks and good minimum standard housing for low-income groups cannot or at any rate have not been adequately served under such a mechanism.

The need for public remedies for such conditions clearly is a value judgement on Rodwin's part, with which one may agree or disagree. Valid or not, however, the point hardly reflects on the sector theory or the filtering concept as a description of the urban market. One cannot blame a market for acting like a market.

Rodwin's low estimate of the housing market's performance—in which many other economists, planners, and urbanists, generally concur—is not based upon a convincing demonstration that this particular market is ineffectively organized. Nor does Rodwin's disillusion with the market-place make the sector theory seem less capable of predicting how the clockwork of the market-place will tick. Rodwin's complaint is fundamentally with social attitudes, not with the sector theory. His intuition that the filtering process somehow harms low-income people cannot be supported with the analytical tools at his command. It remains an intuition.

Grigsby's Empirical Method

With the publication in 1963 of William Grigsby's *Housing Markets and Public Policy*, the sector theory's cartographic representation of housing market inter-actions gave way to a matrix approach. Though he concedes that his new formulation is 'tentative and exploratory',[19] Grigsby examines and describes promising new tools for urban analysis. He deals explicitly with the concept of filtering, pointing out that '. . . filtering is, in a sense, the subject of the entire book since, broadly speaking, it is the principal dynamic feature of the housing market.'[20] The analytical portions of the book, then, can be construed as a new treatment of the filtering question.

How to define filtering, particularly for purposes of empirical measurement, has been a persistent problem, and Grigsby provides a good review of alternative definitions. The 'traditional' definition is Ratcliff's:

This process [filtering] . . . is described most simply as the changing of occupancy as the housing that is occupied by one income group becomes available to the next lower income group as a result of decline in market price, i.e., in sales price or rent value.[21]

This definition has been found to be unsatisfactory in practice.[22]

The specific objection to Ratcliff's definition is that it speaks of changes both in *occupancy* (i.e. income level of occupants) and in *value*, as though the two were necessarily related. But in practice one may fall while the other changes in different degree, or different direction, or remains the same.

A reformulation was provided by Fisher and Winnick.[23] 'Filtering is defined as a change over time in the position of a given dwelling unit or group of dwelling units within the distribution of housing rents and prices in the community as a whole.' Thus, they chose to measure filtering in terms of changes in relative value rather than in terms of incomes of occupants.

Grigsby who generally seems to prefer the Fisher-Winnick reformulation suggests still another concept—that of filtering as an improvement in real housing standards among low-income families. That is, filtering would be said to occur only if low-income housing standards have been raised. He says:

Such a definition would hold that filtering (changes in house prices and rents) must be measured while holding income, quality, and space per person constant, or in more relaxed form, that filtering occurs only when value declines more rapidly than quality so that families can obtain either higher quality and more space at the same price, or the same quality and space at a lower price than formerly.[24]

This welfare concept of filtering does not play a role in Grigsby's stimulating discussion of market mechanisms. It is not consistent with his expressed belief that filtering is 'the principal dynamic feature of the housing market',[25] for the market may not in fact produce welfare effects.

The welfare issue seems to reduce to this: *optimum use* of given resources should not be confused with *improvement* in the supply or quality of those resources. In the traditional economic jargon, Rodwin, Ratcliff, and others have failed to distinguish the problem of allocation from that of growth. Optimization in the use of a durable good requires shifting it about among different classes of users as its relative usefulness declines or rises. The shifting-about, in itself, affects welfare only as it is an efficient or an inefficient reallocation. Other market circumstances being unchanged, filtering in response to deterioration of the housing stock could well leave aggregate and individual housing welfare unchanged.

If filtering is to be understood as a basic pattern of market behaviour then it must be defined as a response to any change in conditions of supply or demand—in the number or types of households or in their incomes, in the physical quality of the stock or any portion of it, or in construction of particular kinds of new units. The response must be measured in terms of occupancy of particular houses or neighbourhoods by some different class of households.

This is still not a completely precise formulation; such is not required, for the data available to the student of a particular market will usually force him to adopt some workable definition. The important point is that the welfare question is best left either to deliberately contrived (and controlled) empirical tests (unlikely without massive financial support), or to careful deductive reasoning based on an operational model and realistic market data. The former is not yet available. The following chapter of the present study presents a hypothetical example of the latter.

If filtering is thought of simply as a change in the allocation of housing units among households of different types, the method of analysis most appropriate to this concept would clearly involve a *matrix* of relationships among submarkets. This is precisely the formulation which Grigsby develops in his analytical chapters. Defining a set of submarkets in the Philadelphia metropolitan area, he illustrates flows among these submarkets on the basis of unpublished National Housing Inventory data and certain assumptions about the 'second choices' which different households would make if their actual location were not available to them. The object is to provide a 'matrix expressing relative degrees of substitutability among submarkets . . .'[26]

Such a matrix is potentially capable of predicting market responses—i.e. shifts among submarkets, or filtering—which would result from certain essentially exogenous changes in market conditions, such as alterations in the characteristics of dwelling units. The matrix form permits an analyst to give appropriate attention to the *indirect* links between submarkets which might not be directly substitutable; thus:

Bargain house prices in Area A might be completely ingored by potential home buyers in Area C if the latter area were too far distant. These prices might, however, attract a segment of the market from Area B to Area A. This shift might in turn create values in B which would serve to capture a segment of the potential in C.[27]

In this way the entire housing market is seen to be interconnected.

Later portions of the Grigsby book examine issues of new residential construction volume, maintenance of residential structures, and residential renewal. The intention is to make use of the matrix concepts developed in earlier chapters, but the effort is not successful. Grigsby discusses the manner in which the existing stock of houses acts to discourage new construction, the extent to which expenditures on maintenance of the quality of the existing stock (as an alternative to new construction) are justified, and the renewal strategy which will get the best response from the private market.

The problem is that Grigsby's matrix model is not operational (nor does he claim that it is). It cannot simulate market responses to, say, redevelopment of a central slum area, or to development of a suburban middle-income tract. Hence his conclusions with respect to new construction, maintenance, and renewal do not flow out of the model.

The sector theory has been transformed into a matrix. Conceptually the matrix should be able to provide answers to welfare-type questions such as those having to do with the housing standards of low-income families as affected by subsidized or unsubsidized filtering, by renewal or public housing. It may also prove to be a much more precise tool for forecasts of construction activity and neighbourhood change. In the following chapters efforts to develop it along such lines will be illustrated.

The sector theory was an empirical generalization which described the experience of many cities approximately but of no cities exactly. It generalized from events that were conditioned on certain social structures, technologies, and public policies; wherever or whenever these things differ from those which Hoyt observed his implied forecasts of neighbourhood changes are invalidated. The very agency which commissioned Hoyt's study has been as instrumental as any other single force in changing those conditions.

The sector theory was never intended, explicitly, to answer the welfare questions which so concerned its critics. But those questions must be answered as public resources in increasing volume are being directed towards improvement in housing standards. A more flexible means of describing competitive market interactions, particularly in response to alternative hypothetical public programmes, was clearly needed.

The basic source of confusion over filtering stems from this close association of welfare issues with patterns of movement in an unregulated private market. This confusion would be heightened by a *definition* of filtering—i.e. of the basic dynamic force—in terms of achievement of a welfare aim.

In a mixed economy, the most effective model for all purposes is one which generates private market responses to all manner of exogenous forces, such as mortgage insurance, rising real incomes, shifts in tastes, public housing, population growth, increased property taxes, or earthquakes. As we are interested in changes in the use made of specific neighbourhoods, the model must be considerably disaggregated. Then the impact of any proposed welfare programme can be traced through each neighbourhood in the community, and its real effect on housing welfare assessed.

NOTES AND REFERENCES

[1] The phrase is Ratcliff's. Richard U. Ratcliff, *Urban Land Economics* (New York: McGraw-Hill, 1949), p. 321.

[2] Homer Hoyt, *The Structure and Growth of Residential Neighborhoods in American Cities* (Washington, D.C.: Government Printing Office, 1939).

[3] Hoyt, op. cit., p. 84.

[4] Ibid., p. 88.

[5] Walter Firey, *Land Use in Central Boston* (Cambridge, Mass.: Harvard University Press, 1947).

[6] Ibid., p. 55.

[7] Ibid., p. 326.

[8] 'A Policy for the Slums', report of a special committee of the National Housing and Town Planning Council (London: P. S. King and Son, Ltd., 1929), p. 16. (Quoted in *European Housing Policy and Practice*, by Ernest M. Fisher and Richard U. Ratcliff, Federal Housing Administration, 1936, p. 61.)

[9] Homer Hoyt, 'Residential Sectors Revisited', *The Appraisal Journal* (October 1950).

[10] Lloyd Rodwin, 'The Theory of Residential Growth and Structure', *The Appraisal Journal* (July 1950).

[11] Ratcliff, op. cit. (see especially Chapter 11).

[12] Ernest M. Fisher and Richard U. Ratcliff, op. cit. (especially Part IX).

[13] Ibid., p. 66.

[14] Ibid., p. 60.

[15] Ibid., p. 64.

[16] Ratcliff, *Urban Land Economics*, p. 321.

[17] Ibid., p. 322. In his book Ratcliff himself contradicts the earlier 'no surplus' idea. On page 332 he says: 'It has been demonstrated here that filtering cannot take place except in the presence of a surplus.'

[18] Rodwin, op. cit.

[19] William Grigsby, *Housing Markets and Public Policy* (Philadelphia: University of Pennsylvania Press, 1963), p. 28.

[20] Ibid., p. 99.

[21] Ratcliff, *Urban Land Economics*, pp. 321–2.

[22] For example, Grebler in his empirical study of New York's lower east side writes: 'Commonly accepted notions of the operation of the filtering process are found to be ambiguous and inadequate when subjected to an empirical test, and a reformulation of the theory of filtering, which lends itself to verification, is suggested.' Leo Grebler, *Housing Market Behavior in a Declining Area* (New York: Columbia University Press, 1952), p. 17.

[23] Ernest M. Fisher and Louis Winnick, 'A Reformulation of the "Filtering" Concept', in *Social Policy and Social Research in Housing*, Robert K. Merton, ed. (New York: Association Press, 1951). Though Grebler's book (op. cit.) was published in 1952 it was available to Fisher and Winnick earlier and is referred to by them.

[24] Grigsby, op. cit., pp. 95 ff.

[25] Ibid., p. 99.

[26] Grigsby, op. cit., p. 50.

[27] Grigsby, op. cit., pp. 34–5.

18. SOCIAL INTERACTION AND URBAN OPPORTUNITY: THE APPALACHIAN IN-MIGRANT IN THE CINCINNATI CENTRAL CITY[1]

G. A. Hyland

The metropolitan areas of the United States are undergoing a dialectic process in which both centralization and dispersion increase in magnitude with the growth of the metropolis (2, p. 143). The urban industrially based national economy has centralized in metropolitan nodes. The nodes themselves are undergoing an outward population diffusion, with a concommitant dispersion of urban physical plant, a dispersal reflecting the volume of in-migrants, the natural increase of the urban population, and a rapidly developing taste for greater space in urban living made possible by rising incomes and progress in the technology of transport mechanics. The majority of the national population is becoming an integral part of a vast 'spatially extensive' community operating in an intricate urban system, which has a mesh of metropolitan nodes of diffusion.[2]

The paradox in this process is that urban vacuums are being created at the cores of metropolitan nodes. These voids are being filled by people of a lower socio-economic class migrating into the city. It has been postulated that these people have transplanted a pre-industrial rural-village structure into the centre of a metropolitan area, a structure in which social interaction is very much affected by geographic distance (6). This represents an anomaly: a people living in a place-based community.

The Cincinnati central city has two major in-migrant groups: the rural southern black and the Appalachian white. The central city, in Cincinnati as elsewhere, has traditionally been the port-of-entry for acculturating in-migrants and has witnessed the through-movement of numerous upward socially mobile ethnic groups, on their way out to the suburbs (7). This paper will examine the social interaction network of the Appalachian in-migrant and its ramifications for urban acculturation and access to the social and economic opportunities in the metropolitan area. Before embarking on the empirical analysis let us define a conceptual base.

The Urban Language and the Stratification of the Population

The individual enters the urban environment to gain access to the income and facilities associated with urban-industrial society. People clustering in urban agglomerations are simply reducing their physical distance from the centres of employment. The share of income that the individual receives is a function of his ability to operate and compete in an urban environment. This ability could well be measured in terms of the individual's adeptness at the *urban language*, a knowledge of the facility with the urban communication process. The level of proficiency in the urban language decides the degree of urbanity: 'Urbanity is more profitably conceived as a property of the amount and variety of one's participation in the cultural life of a world of creative specialists, of the amount and variety of information received' (3, p. 88).

From *Antipode*, 2 . 2 (1970). Reprinted by permission of the editor of the journal.

For the lifetime residents of an urban area, the process of the learning of the urban language has its beginnings in early childhood. For the rural in-migrant, the process may only effectively begin upon entering the urban area. The mechanism for learning the urban language may be both an informal and a formal socialization process. The informal process involves family training, contacts with the extended family, and contacts made with friends and voluntary organizations; the formal process involves educational institutions, employment training programmes, and mass media. Together these processes create an *urban awareness* for the individual, which makes his presence in the urban environment both comfortable and profitable. Basically, the learning of the urban language can be looked upon as a process of acculturation to that particular environment. The degree of acculturation dictates the socio-economic stratification of the urban population. It follows, therefore, that facility in the urban language is a key to income and status, and the power associated with the two.

Mobility

Before considering the social interaction aspect of the urban language-learning process, it is necessary to introduce the concept of *mobility*. This is a fundamental concept because the urban physical plant, designed as it is to encourage interaction, nevertheless covers a large area. For any individual, the utility of urban facilities is a function not only of their type and purpose, but also their accessibility, both physical and conceptual.

Transactions operate through movement over a network of distances. The distances between urban functions have increased since the pedestrian era, through the carriage era, to that of public transportation and the private automobile. If the population's mobility matches the increase in distances between urban functions, then in actuality there has been no change in scale; the *ratio of extensions* has remained the same (8, p. 189).

Mobility problems arise when some of the population does not have access to the form of transportation moulding the dimensions of the urban environment. These particular individuals are becoming a smaller proportion of the total population, so their mode of transport, predominantly pedestrian, dictates virtually none of the urban form. Add to this the fact that the distances over which urban transactions take place have increased enormously under the effect of mechanical transportation and the plight of the mobility-deprived population becomes greater. They are less able to use urban functions important to their social and economic well-being. Mass use of the private automobile in fact may well have increased the number of low-mobility urban residents by undermining the economic viability of public transportation systems (9, p. 175). These non-participants in the modal means of transport have a distorted *ratio of extensions.* They become a seriously handicapped group of people as regards mobility.

One such group may well be the low socio-economic urban in-migrant of the inner core residential zone. As the means of transportation have improved, the mobility of some groups has decreased. This observation led McLuhan to comment that 'the annihilation of space permits easy annihilation of travellers as well' (10, p. 95).

Social Interaction: The Media of Exchanges

The growth and development of urbanization have been closely related to improvements in the means of communication which are basic to any of the

multitudinous functions that occur in the urban area. These basic concepts have
been incorporated into a general theory by Meier (11). The urban area is viewed as
a *transaction-maximizing system* in which the agglomerations have a multiplier
effect on interactions of the population (12, p. 1295). The urban population
provides a concentration of both senders and receivers at any given point of time,
while the physical plant provides the channels for communication.

Social interaction is the media through which urban transactions take place. The
social interaction network develops during socialization and mirrors the rising
proficiency in urban language for an individual. The variety and breadth of the
contacts will determine how the individual's proficiency matures. It may well be
that there is a 'take-off' point in the urban language-learning process, the
attainment of which can be frustrated through the spatial restrictions concomitant with mobility handicaps and residential segregation. The low-income
central-city resident may well become a non-participant in meaningful social
interaction. What presently are the educational facilities of the central city like?
What are the job opportunities that exist around the core of the city, what kind of
information filters through the social interaction network of a spatially restricted
group? Are there place-based communities in the central city? Webber believes that
there are: 'Here in the Harlems and South Sides of the nation are some of the last
viable remnants of preindustrial societies, where village styles are most nearly
intact. Here in the slum blocks of the central city may be the only pure place-based
social neighborhoods we have left' (5, p. 1102).

The Central City Appalachian In-migrant in Cincinnati

Basically, the central city Appalachian in-migrant is concerned with three distinct
environments, the Appalachian homeland, the urban central city, and the
metropolitan area. We can conceptualize these environments as three sets within
which are distinct elements, socio-economic population characteristics, physical
plant, opportunities, and social interaction (Fig. 1).

Appalachia, broadly defined, includes the entire state of West Virginia, and
portions of twelve Southern and eastern-seaboard states (Fig. 2).[3] From these
economically depressed areas the Appalachian has sought opportunity in such
Midwestern industrial cities as Chicago, Detroit, Indianapolis, Dayton, and
Cincinnati. This paper will confine itself to those migrants presently living in the
Cincinnati central city.[4] Of the migrants under study, almost two-thirds came from
eastern Kentucky.[5] For the majority of this Cincinnati sample, therefore, the 'set
A' environment (the east Kentucky mountain counties) is the initial socialization
area. The region in question is undoubtedly one of the most depressed in the

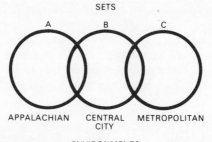

SETS

APPALACHIAN   CENTRAL   METROPOLITAN
                CITY

ENVIRONMENTS

Fig. 1.

nation, with all but five counties having a median annual family income of less than $3,000. The disintegration of economic viability may be traced to the absolute decline of the soft-coal-mining industry and internal change in the mining industry (from a labour-intensive to a mechanical capital-intensive structure). Almost every in-migrant studied, including those not from eastern Kentucky, was from a mining community.

The perspective of the Appalachian, however, has widened to embrace an understanding of economic opportunities existing in the neighbouring 'flatland' urban centres. This awareness has probably been brought about (or certainly reinforced) by knowledge that it was national economic forces, outside the sphere of Appalachia, that led to the decline of coal-mining. Other equally important changes in reducing Appalachian isolation have been the growth of local and national government, especially with armed service, during, and since, World War II, transportation network improvement, and the infiltration of media (*Time-Life* photographs not withstanding). But once the process was ongoing, nothing was more important than feedback, principally through kinship networks, from migrants who had already arrived in the cities to the north.[6] Cincinnati is the most proximate large metropolitan area to the mountain counties of eastern Kentucky, which had a combined net population loss of over 150,000 persons in the decade between 1950 and 1960. It is the most southern and Midwestern cities, with part of its metropolitan area in Kentucky, and its proximity allows weekend home visits or a relatively easy complete return home if the migration fails.

If all the places in which the in-migrant has lived for more than one year are placed in order from the place of birth, the result is a *migration sequence* (Table 1). With the exception of four in-migrants, the sample population began their lives in mining towns of less than 10,000 people. The important point in this characteristic is that for these in-migrants the initial environment was not rural, but small town. The information for the sequence was gathered to discover if the in-migrants were gradually exposed to a more urban environment as they moved from town to town. A group of this sample did go through a series of small towns before arriving at a large urban area. Nevertheless, further exploration demonstrated that these were, in the main, other mining towns. The inference from this would seem to be that the migrant was trying to replicate his occupational role in a similar cultural milieu. In several cases the migrant has spent a number of years in Cincinnati, or a comparably sized urban area, only to return to a mining town to begin the sequence again. Conceptually the migrant on his first arrival in the 'city' could be thought of as occupying the intersection of sets A and B (Fig. 1). His reluctance to settle in Cincinnati could be interpreted as a desire to try every alternative avenue to adopting an environment hostile to his whole socialization process.

An interesting feature of these sample migration sequences is the number of female migrants who move from a small mining town immediately to Cincinnati. One of the respondents said in the course of an interview, 'I went back to Kentucky to get a wife.' It is possible that many of these women moved to Cincinnati to marry an already established migrant.

The Cincinnati Central City

The central city port-of-entry is the most frequently chosen area of embarkation for the low-income Appalachian in-migrant. There are minor ports-of-entry in the old industrial suburbs, but the analysis here will confine itself to those Appalachians presently dwelling in the central city. Basically, there are two forces

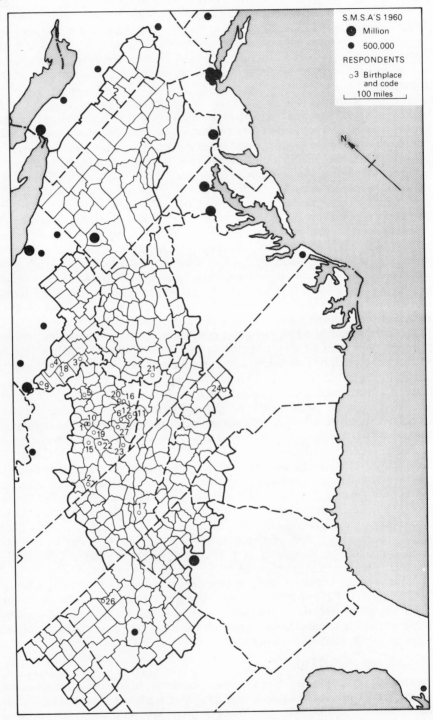

Fig. 2. Appalachia: Location of respondents' birthplaces.

TABLE 1

The Appalachian In-Migrants
The Migration Sequence

1	Estill, Ky.	F	105	B--E--D--*
2	Clinton, Ky.	F	175	A--*
3	Scioto, O.	M	90	B--A--A--A--*
4	Highland, O.	F	50	C--*
5	Rowan, Ky.	F	90	B--*--B--*
6	Perry, Ky.	F	155	A--*--H--*
7	Wayne, W. Va.	F	120	B--A--E--*
9	Clermont, O.	F	25	f--*
10	Estill, Ky.	F	105	B--*--A--*--J--E--*
11	Letcher, Ky.	F	170	A--B--f--*--J--*
12	Letcher, Ky.	M	165	A--A--*
14	Oklahoma, Olka.	F	740	H--A--E--*--E--*
15	Rockcastle, Ky.	F	125	A--H--B--*
16	Floyd, Ky.	M	155	A--H--*
17	McMinn, Tenn.	M	260	D--A--*
18	Adams, O.	F	55	A--A--*
19	Jackson, Ky.	M	120	A--*--A--*--F--D--F--*
20	Floyd, Ky.	F	150	A--*
21	McDowell, W. Va.	F	205	A--*
22	Laurel, Ky.	F	140	A--B--*
23	Bell, Ky.	F	175	B--*
24	Davie, N.C.	F	315	A--D--G--*--A--*
26	Morgan, Ala.	M	350	E--X--E--?--?--D--H--*
27	Leslie, Ky.	F	155	A--*

A City with less than 2,499	F 50,000–99,999
B 2,500–4,999	G 100,000–249,000
C 5,000–9,999	H 250,000–499,999
D 10,000–24,999	I 500,000–999,999
E 25,000–49,999	J 1,000,000 and over

Cincinnati is in the I-size class but to emphasize its position in the sequence it is represented by an asterisk.

f–this symbol represents a farm dwelling
X–this symbol represents a period in service
?–this is a place that was unidentifiable

The number at the beginning of the sequence is the distance in miles from the respondent's birthplace to Cincinnati.

at work in the residence selection process: the aggregative and the segregative. The aggregative forces are: (a) the psychological and material benefits of dwelling with people of a similar cultural experience; (b) the fact that knowledge of the urban residential areas is a function of communication, through feedback, from the migrants already living in the central city port-of-entry. The segregative forces are: (a) the income constraints of the in-migrant, which lead him to seek out real or imagined cheap housing, dwellings that are on the lower end of the housing filter process; (b) discrimination against large 'hillbilly' families in the housing market. Huelsman, an anthropologist who has extensively studied Appalachians in both Cincinnati and Dayton, vividly portrays the process:

The migrant to Dayton usually gets here in a wheezing old car full of kids with hungry bellies and maybe a guitar. In the pocket of his faded blue work shirt is a letter from a second cousin or an uncle with an address near Fifth and Brown or Tecumseh St. in East Dayton.

Given any kind of choice, the migrants would probably decide they would rather live near each other. It's easy to come across friends and kin from the same county just a block or two away. They have the same background, share common values and the oldtimers in the port of entry probably offer a lot of practical help to the just-arrived friend or kinsman from eastern Kentucky. The newcomers soon learn where the flats for rent are, that you usually pay by the week and in advance. They also learn that it's pretty hard to get a Dayton landlord to rent to a family from eastern Kentucky with a lot of kids, except of course in the port of entry (14, pp. 99–100).

When the intra-urban migration sequence (Table 2 and Fig. 3) is analysed, it becomes apparent that the aggregative and segregative forces not only lead the in-migrant to the central city port-of-entry, but, for some, are enduring parameters for their urban experience as regards place of residence.[7] Discounting present place of residence, a full 60 per cent of all past residences of the migrants have been within the immediate vicinity of the study sample area. The migrants appear to be highly residentially mobile in a very spatially restricted area. Not all are as spatially restricted as the in-migrant below (Table 3); nevertheless, these particular individuals have had a very limited urban residential experience, despite a considerable period of time in Cincinnati.

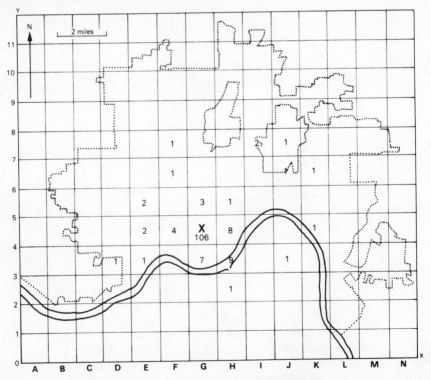

Fig. 3. Place of residence, past and present. City of Cincinnati: the grid co-ordinate system.

TABLE 2*

No.	Yrs. In Cincinnati	Residential Sequence											
1	15	3H(1)	X(5)										
2	11	X(6)											
3	0·5	X(2)											
4	22	3G(1)	3H(4)	X(4)									
5	28	X(4)	4F(2)	X(1)									
6	14	5G(1)	X(4)										
7	15	X(3)	7J(1)	X(1)	3G(1)	X(1)							
9	42	3H(1)	X(2)										
10	23	X(4)	4H(1)	3D(1)	X(1)	4H(1)	X(1)						
11	6	5G(1)	X(1)										
12	9	4F(1)	4H(1)	X(2)	4H(1)	X(2)	4H(1)						
14	17	4E(1)	4H(1)	X(1)	4E(1)	X(1)	5H(1)	X(2)					
15	18	X(3)	7F(1)	X(1)	3J(1)	X(1)	7I(2)	6K(1)	6F(1)	X(3)	5E(2)	4K(1)	X(3)
16	10	X(1)											
17**	45	X(3)											
18	43	X(1)	4H(1)	X(8)	4H(1)								
19	18	3E(1)	X(1)	4F(1)	X(1)								
20	23	X(1)	3G(1)	X(6)	2H(1)	X(2)							
21	52	X(2)											
22	13	X(10)											
23	8	X(1)											
24	15	3G(2)	5G(1)	3G(1)	3G(1)	X(5)							
26	7	6J(1)	X(1)	3G(2)	X(1)								
27	14	3H(3)	X(3)										

* This table should be read in conjunction with Figure 3. The grid co-ordinate system in the Figure is composed of the major axes of a much finer grid employed in the plotting of the points for the standard denational ellipses (Fig. 4). The figure co-ordinates have been numbered along the Y-axis and alphabetized along the X-axis. In the table above the co-ordinates are given for each respondent's place of residence. For example respondent (4) upon entering Cincinnati lived in a dwelling in square 3G, he then moved to square 3H, and while living in that square lived sequentially in four different houses; he then moved to the square in which the study area was located (actually 4G but designated for clarity as X). He has lived sequentially in four houses there.

** This respondent was not fully co-operative and the complete sequence was not completed.

TABLE 3

First Residence   914 Palace Ave.

1327 Xanadu St.

1336 Xanadu St.

1323 Xanadu St.

1330 Xanadu St.

Present Residence1414 Xanadu St.

For the in-migrant who takes up permanent residence in the metropolitan area, four stages of acculturation are postulated:

1. the port-of-entry slum; 2. the stable lower-class community; 3. the lower-middle-class community; 4. the highest 'ambition' of the Appalachian in-migrant, 'the owning of an acre or two of land in the suburbs or true farm country, where one may till one's own ground and reap its fruit and do some trucking or squirrel hunting and fishing in time away from work' (15, pp. 273–4). This would be the optimal progression for the in-migrant, the final stage replicating the initial Appalachian environment. Nevertheless, any stage could be the limits of the urban experience for the migrant. The second generation may then go on to follow a quite different progression. The in-migrant can easily fail to 'make it' at any stage and fall back to the preceding stage, as in some cases in this sample (Fig. 3). It is quite possible that some of the sample migrants prematurely moved up a stage. Conceptually, they could be said to have occupied the intersections of Sets B and C (Fig. 1). The sample group, as a whole, have spent a mean of twenty years in the port-of-entry. These Appalachians, then, are those that have never left the port-of-entry, or those who have attempted, but failed to reach the next stage, and a very small group of those who are beginning the sequence. Nevertheless, the predominant type of Appalachian in this sample is the migrant who has failed to reap the benefits of the urban environment.

Social Interaction and the Urban Language

An analysis by Fried of the relocation of Boston West End Italian Americans revealed a series of findings. Fried was in the fortunate position of being able to interview locatees before and after relocation. He was particularly interested in their degree of preparedness for their locational change. He demonstrated the fact that low socio-economic central-city residents, when relocating, suffer from the change in inverse proportion to the range of their social interaction network (16, p. 145).

The social interaction of the sample of Appalachian in-migrants mirrors their intra-urban residency pattern: with a few exceptions it is limited to their immediate neighbourhood. Employing the standard deviational ellipse technique, different types of social interaction may be graphically displayed (Fig. 4).[8]

As regards social interaction among friends, the range of the network would seem to be a function of distance from the neighbourhood. In the study, the questionnaire based social interaction on the house visit. In doing so, the schedule underestimated the in-migrant's contact field. As with other migrant groups, sidewalk culture is characteristic of Appalachian people. The custom of sitting on the stoop outside the home in the warmer weather is an important feature leading to a great deal of contact. One respondent remarked that she was glad that summer was coming in because then she would see people again. Another respondent made no mention of house visits for social interaction. However, the interview was

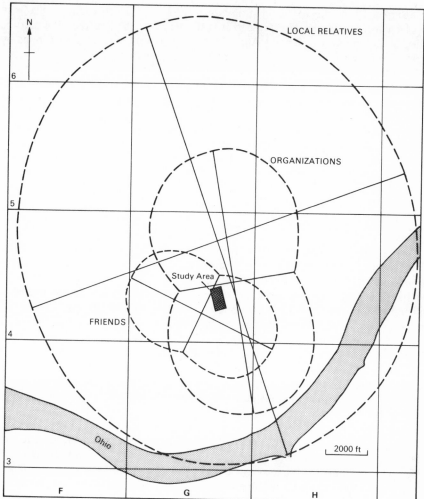

Fig. 4

conducted in the street outside his house and during its course, no fewer than six persons passed the time of day with him. It is safe to assume that all such interactions are restricted to the neighbourhood. In marked contrast to the friendship network (the smallest ellipse) is local relatives' social interaction (the widest ellipse shown in Fig. 4).

Only a third of this sample possessed an automobile, while up to a half had some access to one, usually in the extended family. This was not potentially a very mobile group. Yet making house visits to local relatives, whether near or far, seemed almost a moral duty. The distances that seemed to discourage extensive friendship networks did not deter wide-ranging forays to visit kin. The role of kinship networks is vital to an understanding of the Appalachian. It is the kinship network that precipitated migration, and often the initial employment.[9] It is the kinship network that provides a buffer to the complex urban environment. It would seem that the social machinery of the extended family does perform a valuable function in the existing communication of economic opportunity. Conversely, if friendship patterns are based on propinquity, and Appalachians tend to live with Appalachians, and if also the house visit is the realm of the kin, then the cultural milieu of the in-migrant remains Appalachian. The psychological buffer formed by the kinship network can also be a barrier to urban acculturation.

The third ellipse, intermediate in size (Fig. 4), is the interaction involving clubs, organizations, churches, and places of entertainment. Giffin's analysis of Appalachian participation in social activities saw real differences from their neighbours of different origin:

However, one difference of considerable importance was the finding that adults from the southern Appalachians participate much less often in voluntary organizations such as lodges, unions, neighbourhood clubs, and community centre activities. Such organizations can perform important functions in helping newcomers to learn the ways of urban living and avail themselves of widened opportunities as well as to discharge some community responsibilities. But until such organizations can discover how to create more interest among Southern Appalachian newcomers, this means of urbanization will continue to be under-utilized (13, p. 84).

Basically, his conclusions were borne out by the particular sample under study. Of the twenty-four respondents, only seven had any contact with organizations at all, and only two attended the meetings of the Central City Neighborhood Council, the political outlet of the area. The respondent who was strongly committed to political action lamented the lack of political integration when she complained that it was practically impossible to galvanize any support for action on very real causes for grievance. Only one third of the respondents recorded any church-going at all; these did not belong to the formal congregations of the central city, but for the most part attended store-front churches: 'The in-migrant, uneasy in the large structured services of the congregations of organized religion, seeks out the store-front church with its individualistic fundamental creeds, and small neighbor-hood congregations. It has been postulated that the store-front church is the urban adaptation of the rural village church' (17).

Entertainment was of only marginal importance to the group of Appalachians interviewed; any places of entertainment visited were, in the main, around their locale. Up to a third of the respondents left the city now and again to go fishing or walking. This adds virtually nothing to their social interaction network, but it does demonstrate their strong desire to follow some aspects of their initial life style.

With the significant exception of kinship visits and some residential sallies to the periphery of the central city, this group does approach Webber's place-based community; that is one in which the social organization is territorially coterminous with neighbourhood place: 'The concentration of activities and relationships within a single area produces a geographical and social localism, a primary and, at times, exclusive concern with people and places within the compass of the neighbourhood' (Hoggart, *The Uses of Literacy*, as cited in 18, p. 70).

Social and Economic Amenities of the Central City Core

The aggregative and segregative forces that guided the nineteenth-century immigrant to the central city core also placed him in close proximity to the largest centres of employment, the CBD, the wholesaling warehouse area, and the rapidly expanding industries clustering around the centre of communication. Another advantage was that the trauma of adjusting to the industrial revolution was an adaptation process shared by both the native-born American and the immigrant.

Now both industry and retailing have diffused throughout the urban area, while wholesaling from warehouses has virtually disappeared. The employment structure has now only a limited demand for the semi-skilled or unskilled worker. Not only does the worker of the present urban economy have to be equipped with a more advanced education, but he also has to be ready to retrain for a new employment position if the technology of his work changes. The established urban worker is subject to the dislocations of frictional-structural unemployment, while the in-migrant is subject to the burden of chronic structural unemployment (9, p. 212). As regards occupational mobility the in-migrant is both spatially and structurally disadvantaged.

Of the Appalachians in the sample, a third were retired, disabled, or welfare-dependent, and the employment places of the remainder were spread throughout the urban area, and only five had employment in and about the core of the central city.

Concomitant with the diffusion of employment has been the diffusion of the urban population and income. The public-school system of the nineteenth-century central city, prompted by nativist fears of cultural inundation, was actively involved in the Americanization and urbanization of the immigrants. Today the school system in the same area finds itself more and more disadvantaged financially. All of the children of the respondents attended schools within a radius of one mile of their homes. The Appalachian in-migrant is educated with other in-migrants.

Health care in the central city core is a problem shared by all of its residents, yet each group has its own unique attitudes towards health care:

Back home in the mountains, because of geographic and economic inaccessibility, there is an almost total absence of any notion of disease prevention or active health maintenance. If the mountaineer comes from impoverished conditions, he may accept a chronic or subclinical state of ill health as normal, and ignore physical 'dullishness' (19, p. 514).

Individualism is the most pervasive trait of the Appalachian male. The idea of leaning on the community for support is foreign to him. 'The idea that some nebulous entity called the "city" imposes law and justice and demands allegiance, or will in turn give help and support, is simply incomprehensible to the Appalachian newcomer' (15, p. 274). Institutions, such as hospitals or welfare bureaux, are formidable in the eyes of the in-migrant. Delinquency rates among the youth of Appalachian in-migrants have been attributed to a failure on the part of the parents to modify their very loose control over their children, a control suited to the village communities they have known, but not to the heterogeneous population of the anonymous urban environment (14). The problems of health and crime in the adaptation process are more of the many problems the in-migrant faces. Given these social problems and the changes in urban structure, it is not surprising that Webber views the role of the port-of-entry as not merely having changed, but having been eliminated:

It is just possible that the Appalachians, Negroes, Puerto Ricans, and Mexican-Americans now concentrated within the central ghettoes of metropolitan areas are not just the most recent wave of newcomers to these districts, as some scholars have suggested. The others were able to pass through, but today's residents could fail to make it (5, p. 1102).

Summary

The Appalachian is a white, Protestant, English-speaking, native-born American. He has become an urban in-migrant to seek out the economic opportunity that his initial environment can no longer provide. He is an individual with an extremely strong attachment to his place of birth, and comes to the city with great reluctance. He hopes that he will be able to retire 'back home' in old age, or at least replicate his former life style in the metropolitan environment.

The central city core port-of-entry is the first step in his urban acculturation sequence. The aggregative and segregative forces of residence selection strengthen the social cohesion of his fellow in-migrant group. Social interaction within this group, with the notable exception of kinship visiting patterns, is spatially limited. The in-migrants form place-based communities (a characteristic of many in-migrant groups).

However, due to the economic and social structural changes of the urban environment, the central city core perhaps no longer provides the basis of a viable urban acculturation process.

Given the limited results of the Appalachian regional development programme, it is unlikely that the flow of out-migration will be stemmed. The Appalachian will continue to form a substantial proportion of the in-migrants arriving in the industrial areas of the Midwest. The quasi-institutional status of the port-of-entry, as an agent of acculturation to the urban environment, will have to be re-evaluated. The port-of-entry must be viewed not as a blight to be removed, but as a corridor for potentially upward socially mobile groups.

NOTES

[1] Much of the research for this paper was completed while working on an M.A. thesis at the University of Cincinnati, under the direction of Dr. David L. Ames (1). A widened version of the original proposal has been incorporated into the *Migrant Peoples' Study* of the Miami Valley Project, University of Cincinnati.

[2] A spatially extensive community is composed of a population with cosmopolitan characteristics regarding their social interaction. It is one pole of a social interaction continuum conceptualized by Webber (3, 4, 5). The other pole is the place-based community in which the social interaction of the population is spatially limited, in fact confined principally to their immediate neighbourhood.

[3] The area on the map with the county outlines is the area designated by the Appalachian Commission.

[4] The sample consisted of twenty-four respondents from a two-block area to the north-east of the Cincinnati CBD. There were originally twenty-seven respondents but three were born in Cincinnati, and although they were each married to Appalachians, were not included in the sample. The interview schedule basically probed the migrant's population characteristics, migration sequence, Cincinnati residency sequence, physical mobility, neighbourhood perception, and social interaction. It was to the last category that the great weight of the schedule was given. Naturally, because of the smallness of the sample, the greatest caution should be exercised in interpreting the conclusions.

[5] These particular two blocks seem to represent the proportion of east Kentuckians that are generally found in Cincinnati among groups of Appalachian in-migrants. Roscoe Giffin, in a study of the parents of five school districts in Cincinnati, found that of the Appalachian fathers, two-thirds came from eastern Kentucky (13, pp. 79–84).

[6] When questioned on their motivations for coming to Cincinnati, there was little variation in the responses: a desire to improve their economic well-being, coupled with a knowledge of someone living in the Cincinnati area.

The responses of the twenty-four respondents were classified thus: economic well-being: 6, contact in Cincinnati area: 5, economic well-being and contact in Cincinnati area: 6, occupational health reasons: 1 work opportunity and personal reasons: 3, personal: 2, don't know: 1.

[7] During the initial research the metropolitan area was divided areally through the use of a grid to allow the plotting of past and present residences as well as social interaction. The

principal co-ordinates in Fig. 2 delimit useful areal (arbitrary) units for a simple distribution map.

[8]The standard deviational ellipse for set of points is calculated by the following method. Employing an arbitrary cartesian grid, the mean centre of the points is calculated. A new grid, composed of orthogonal axes in the same scale as the first, is centred on the mean centre. The deviation of each point, from the x-axis, is employed to calculate the *standard deviation*. The axes are then rotated, say by 10 degrees, and the procedure repeated. If all the standard deviations along the x-axes are joined, an *ellipse* will be described. Fig. 4 is an example of some of the ellipses described.

[9]Some plants literally do their hiring through a kinship network, a system eminently satisfactory to both management and employees (15, p. 276).

REFERENCES

1 Hyland, Gerard A. 'A Social Interaction Analysis of the Appalachian In-Migrant: Cincinnati S.M.S.A. Central City.' Unpublished M.A. Thesis, Department of Geography, University of Cincinnati, 1970.

2 Wolf, Laurence G. 'The Metropolitan Tidal Wave in Ohio, 1900–2000.' *Economic Geography*, 45. 2 (April 1969).

3 Webber, Melvin M. 'The Urban Place and the Nonplace Urban Realm', in M. Webber et al., *Explorations into Urban Structure* (Philadelphia: University of Pennsylvania Press, 1964), pp. 79–137.

4 Webber, M. M. and Webber, C. 'Culture, Territoriality and the Elastic Mile.' *Papers and Proceedings of the Regional Science Association*, 13 (1964), 59–70.

5 Webber, M. M. 'The Post-City Age.' *Daedalus*, Summer 1968.

6 Gans, Herbert. *The Urban Villagers*. Glencoe, Illinois: 1962.

7 Miller, Zane L. *Boss Cox's Cincinnati: Urban Politics in the Progressive Era*. New York: Oxford University Press, 1968.

8 Gutkin, E. A. *The Twilight of Cities*. New York: The Free Press of Blencoe, 1962.

9 Thompson, Wilbur. *A Preface to Urban Economics*. Washington: 1966.

10 McLuhan, M. *Understanding Media: The Extensions of Man*. New York: American Library Inc., 1964.

11 Meier, R. L. *A Communication Theory of Urban Growth*. Cambridge: Joint Center for Urban Studies of M.I.T. and Harvard University, 1962.

12 C166 Meier, R. L. 'The Metropolis as a Transaction-Maximizing System.' *Daedalus*, Fall 1968, pp. 1295–9.

13 Giffin, Roscoe. 'Appalachian Newcomers in Cincinnati', in Ford (ed.), *The Southern Appalachian Region*, pp. 79–84.

14 Huelsmann, B. 'Southern Mountaineers in City Juvenile Courts.' *Federal Probation*, December 1969.

15 Powles, William E. 'The Southern Appalachian Migrant: Country Boy Turned Blue-Collarite' in Shostak and Gomberg, *Blue-Collar World*, pp. 270–281.

16 Fried, Marc. 'Transitional Functions of Working-Class Communities: Implications for Forced Relocation' in M. Kantor (ed.), *Mobility and Mental Health* (Chicago: C. C. Thomas 1965), pp. 123–165.

17 McNeal, Alvin. 'The Distribution of Store-Front Churches in the Greater Cincinnati Area.' Unpublished M.A. thesis, Department of Geography, University of Cincinnati, 1969.

18 Fried, M. and J. Levin. 'Some Social Functions of the Urban Slum' in B. J. Frienden and R. Morris (eds.), *Urban Planning and Social Policy* (Basic Books, 1968).

19 Porter, E. Russell. 'From Mountain Folk to City Dwellers.' *Nursing Outlook*, July 1963, pp. 514–515.

19. CHANGING RESIDENCE IN THE CITY*
A REVIEW OF INTRA-URBAN MOBILITY

J. W. Simmons

Every year about 20 per cent of the population of the United States changes residence. Although many moves are made by a small number of highly mobile persons, 50 per cent of the entire population moves within a five-year period. Given the extent of this movement, the distribution and characteristics of the population remain remarkably stable: the in-migrants to an area, for the most part, resemble the out-migrants in numbers and attributes. Over a sufficient period of time, however, migration is an important instrument in altering the spatial patterns of social and demographic variables, and under certain conditions it leads to dramatic short-run changes in small areas—for example, the rapid growth of a new subdivision or the expansion of a ghetto by 'blockbusting'.

The present study is concerned with an important, but relatively neglected, aspect of migration, namely changes in residence that take place within a city,[1] Measured in one-year intervals, the intracounty mobility rate is 12 to 13 per cent, or about two-thirds of all moves (Table 1).[2] Many of these relocations take place in the same neighbourhood or on the same block, but longer moves determine most of the growth or decline of population in different parts of the city and virtually all the changes in relative income levels and ethnic or racial concentrations.

Migration has been widely studied and several excellent reviews of the subject are available,[3] but these have limited application to movement within urban areas because economic opportunity, the mainstay of migration theory at the interstate and international levels, is largely irrelevant to movement within a commuting area or to patterns of gross migration. As a result, the investigation of intra-urban mobility has been primarily the realm of the sociologist rather than of the economist, but the many facets of the topic cover the whole range of the behavioural sciences. This study attempts to synthesize the subject under three headings. First, *who moves*? What information do we have about the sociological and psychological characteristics of movers? Is it possible to predict the mobility rates for various categories of population? Second, *why do they move*? What socio-psychological and economic factors cause a given household to move? Here the emphasis is on the decision-making unit, the family. Finally, the almost completely neglected question, but the one of greatest concern to students of the urban structure, *where do they move*? Are there spatial regularities in the relocation process? How does the household go about finding a new home? What is the relation between the supply of different kinds of housing and the demand by various consumer units?

Who Moves?

The spatial distribution of demographic characteristics is a major factor in

*This study was undertaken with the support of a grant from the Canadian Council on Urban and Regional Research.

differentiating mobility rates throughout the city, and the housing and access requirements of various life-cycle groups dominate the patterns of flow. The large number of intra-urban residential movements largely reflects the high rates of mobility of a few age groups.

TABLE 1

Migration in Urbanized Areas in the United States, 1955–60
(In percentages)

Residence in 1955	Central City	Fringe	Total
Same house as in 1960	48·5	47·5	47·8
Different house in United States	47·5	50·0	48·0
Same county	33·6	28·7	31·4
Different county	13·9	21·1	16·6
Same state	5·7	10·1	7·3
Different state	8·3	11·0	9·3
Abroad	1·8	1·4	1·6
Moved, residence in 1955 not reported	2·5	1·1	1·9

Source: United States Census of Population: 1960, Subject Reports: Size of Place, *Final Report PC(3)–1B* (Bureau of the Census, Washington, D.C., 1963), Table 1.

Almost all the research on intra-urban relocation before 1950 was concerned with the measurement of mobility rates. Sociologists in the 1920s and 1930s stressed mobility as a cause of urban social problems, but the absence of census data on rates of movement forced each investigator to develop his own measures. Caplow's detailed review of the early studies of intra-urban mobility reveals the wide variations in mobility rates, derived at different times and from numerous sources of information.[4] A controversial point is whether mobility rates are increasing or decreasing over time. The measuring techniques are so imperfect and so dissimilar that it seems unlikely the question will be resolved. The general impression gained from the pre-World War II studies is that intra-urban mobility in the first quarter of the century was greater than it is today. Albig,[5] using city directories, found a steady decline in intra-urban mobility rates from more than 50 per cent a year in 1903–10 to 20 per cent in 1930–2, and Goldstein[6] also identified a decline, though not so marked. On the other hand, an unpublished study by Rossi,[7] based on the life histories of a sample population, indicates continuously increasing intra-urban mobility.

Once the United States Bureau of the Census began to gather information on mobility, researchers had the tool they needed to turn their attention to the study of process. The 1940 Census of Population asked about place of residence in 1935, though moves within areas smaller than a county were not aggregated. The 1950 census, however, provided information for the year 1949–50 on intracounty moves, tabulating it for urban places and by census tracts.[8] The 1960 census broadened the categories (Table 1) and extended the time period to five years, 1955–60.[9] For comparisons over time, the Current Population Reports[10] have produced annual estimates of national and regional mobility rates since 1948, though no data are provided for specific cities or parts of cities. These reports indicate little fluctuation in intra-urban mobility rates between 1948 and 1965.

The census materials make it possible to obtain information on gross migration rates for different subsets of the population, defined either on the basis of

TABLE 2

Percentage of Males Moving within City Annually

			Age		
	18—24	25—34	35—44	45—64	65 +
EDUCATION (in years)					
0—8	–	24·1	14·2	8·5	6·6
9—11	–	26·2	10·7	7·8	5·2
12	–	18·9	11·1	7·0	5·4
13 or more	–	19·4	10·3	7·5	5·9
OCCUPATION					
White collar	27·2	19·9	9·4	6·3	3·0
Manual	30·4	22·9	12·0	8·2	5·9
Service	25·6	25·5	16·7	9·0	5·9
Farm	15·9	11·1	9·5	6·8	2·0
EMPLOYMENT					
Self-employed	15·9	14·1	8·1	4·8	2·5
Wage and salary	28·8	22·0	11·5	8·1	4·7
Unemployed	22·3	26·4	17·2	11·7	–

Source: 'Mobility of the Population of the United States' [see text footnote 2].

destination or on socio-economic characteristics. The life cycle[11] causes many of the apparent variations in mobility rates for different areas and for different socio-economic groups, since the differentials attributable to occupation, income, and so on are minor (Table 2). The annual intracounty mobility rate for children under five is about 20 per cent, then it declines to about 12 per cent for teenagers, maximizes at more than 30 per cent for persons in their twenties, and drops again to less than 10 per cent for those over forty-five (Fig. 1).[12] A slight tendency

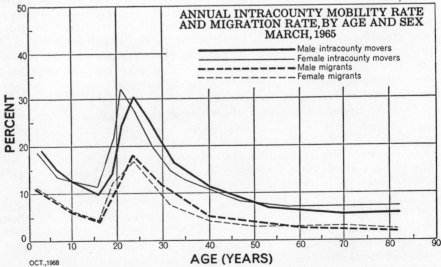

OCT.,1968

Fig. 1. Annual intra-county mobility rate. *Source:* 'Mobility of the Population of the United States March 1964 to March 1965' (see text footnote.2).

towards greater mobility for lower-income groups complements their lower migration rates. Farmers, the self-employed, and home-owners have lower mobility rates.[13] For these people investment creates a higher threshold to be overcome before moving, and ownership itself may indicate a psychological commitment to an area.

Mobility rates vary within the metropolitan area. Rates of in-movement (Figs. 2 and 3) are generally highest in the city centre and in the most recently developed suburbs. The distribution of out-migration is more significant because this measure is much less sensitive to the addition of new housing. Rates of out-migration from the city centre are about double those of the suburban area, and Moore[14] explains about 60 per cent of the variation as being a function of distance. Mobility rates are also slightly higher in low-income sectors of the city. The impression obtained from an examination of the spatial pattern of mobility is of the large number of moves in all parts of the metropolitan area.

The effect of the size of the observation unit, in this case the city, is a measurement problem common to all migration studies.[15] Large cities provide more migration opportunities than small cities, and a large observation unit allows people to move further without crossing a boundary. The growth rate is another factor that tends to increase mobility within a city. Rapid growth stimulates new housing investment, creates a ready market for older properties, and accelerates the process of suburbanization, invasion, and succession. In Canadian cities the percentage of intrametropolitan movers, 1956–61, using 1956 as the base, can be expressed as a function of city population and growth:

Per cent movers = $-28\cdot67 +10\cdot24$ log population $+0\cdot45$ growth rate.

Population explains 52 per cent, and growth 26 per cent, of the variation in the intrametropolitan migration rate. The first is a systematic measurement error owing to the definition of mobility that is used; the second accelerates movements that take place for other reasons.

Why Do They Move?

Housing needs generated by life-cycle changes cause the majority of moves and produce high rates of out-movement in all parts of the city, but the reasons for changing residence within the city vary with the characteristics of the mover. The large number of movers in the age group fifteen to twenty-five weights the over-all pattern towards their particular needs and dissatisfactions, but other sub-populations—for example, the aged or the residents of a particular part of the city—may have different reasons for moving. A great deal of social change can take place without significantly altering the mobility rate, but a variety of social factors may modify the out-movement of subpopulations from certain areas.

The decision to move can be examined from several points of view. The social psychologist sees the household as acting under various kinds of stress; the economist views the move as maximizing satisfaction of the household requirements; and the human ecologist treats it as an element in a larger pattern of movements or as part of the processes of growth and succession. From any point of view, however, the decision to move is complex. It is concerned, on the one hand, with the needs and values of the household, which change over time, and, on the other, with the characteristics of the environment, which encompasses home, neighbourhood, and alternative locations.

Types of Social Change

In order to overcome the time and money costs of moving, some attraction or

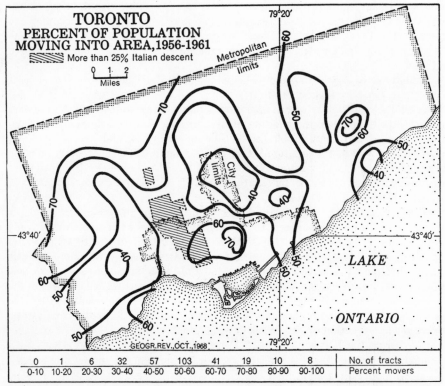

Fig. 2. Movement into the Toronto area, 1956–1961. *Source:* Migration, Fertility, and Income by Census Tracts'. *Census of Canada,* 1961 (CX–1, Ottawa, 1965).

dissatisfaction is required. The most obvious factor is social change that alters the relationship between a household and its environment. The size, age, or income of a household may change; the environment may be altered by such things as blight, invasion by other cultural groups, or increased land values. More likely, both the household and the environment change simultaneously, but at different rates. Three major clusters of social variables should be examined for their contributions to mobility: urbanization, including demographic characteristics and life style; economic status, combining measures of income, occupation, and education; and segregation, identifying ethnic or racial origin and religion.[16]

The evidence indicates that the urbanization, or life-cycle, factor is the most powerful inducement to people to change their residence. Rossi,[17] after his intensive series of interviews and follow-up studies on residential relocation, concluded: 'the major function of mobility [is] the process by which families adjust their housing to the housing needs that are generated by the shifts in family composition that accompany life cycle changes'. The sharp variations in mobility rates shown in Figure 1 reinforce Rossi's statement. The life-cycle stages (Fig. 4) account for at least five of the eight or nine moves that might be expected in a lifetime, as an individual grows up, leaves home, marries, has children, and ages. The cluster of moves in quick succession in the fifteen-to-twenty-five age bracket is evident. Although some of the life-cycle adjustments occur through intercounty migrations, many people have far more complex life cycles, with several moves at

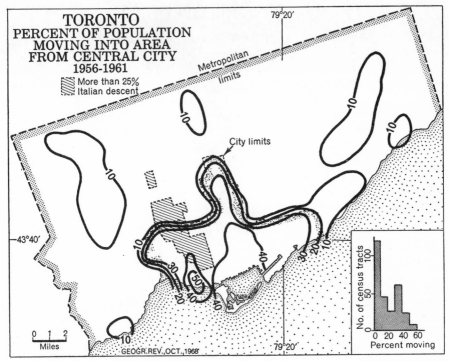

Fig. 3. Movement into the Toronto area from the central city, 1956–61. *Source:*
'Migration, Fertility, and Income by Census Tracts', *Census of Canada*, 1961
(CX–1, Ottawa, 1965).

certain stages, such as childhood, maturity, and marriage. Most movers are
dependents, accompanying the head of the household; thus the family
characteristics, rather than those of the individual, are the critical factor. Rossi[18]
classified about one-third of the moves he studied as forced, coming as an aftermath
of other major events such as eviction, marriage, death, or sudden loss of income.
The most common reason for the voluntary moves is the need for more space for a
growing family. Less frequently, there is the adjustment to a smaller unit when the
family is grown, though often this move is not made until the household is broken
up by illness or death.

Often in combination with the housing adjustment, the family may choose, or
be compelled, to change its neighbourhood. Several studies of the adjustment of
low-income families to new neighbourhoods indicate that the loss of kinship and
other contacts creates severe problems, which can lead to return movements.[19] But
the variety of life-styles already experienced by middle-class households gives them
more flexibility. For instance, a young man may flee the suburbs for a mildly
Bohemian area in the city, exchange it for a more respectable town-house district
on his marriage, and later seek a low-density suburb for his children. New
low-density housing and, particularly, the opportunity to own rather than to rent
attract the young family. On the basis of research to date, it is difficult to
determine which comes first: do people change their way of life and then seek a
more suitable environment, or do the physical surroundings modify the way of
life?[20]

MOVES DURING THE LIFE CYCLE

AGE	STAGE	MOVES
0	Birth	
	Child	1
10	Adolescent	
20	Maturity	1
	Marriage	1
30	Children	1
40		
	Children mature	
50		
60		1
	Retirement	
70		
	Death	
80		

Fig. 4. Moves during the life cycle.

In general, any alteration in the demographic characteristics of a neighbour-hood—most frequently the over-all ageing of the population—coincides with the changes taking place in the households. Even if a family were out of phase with the age structure of the neighbourhood, it seems unlikely that this form of stress would be sufficiently severe to lead to a move. One generator of mobility is the demographic change associated with the redevelopment cycle in the central city. Old houses are converted to rooming houses or are replaced by high-rise apartments, thereby increasing the neighbourhood density. These areas, however, constitute only a small part of the city and generally undergo gradual adjustment in the wake of out-movements for other reasons.

Economic and Social Status

Economic status includes income, occupation, and certain housing variables. Since urban areas are strongly differentiated with respect to class, a person who changes his social status might be expected to change the location of his residence. However, Lipset and Bendix,[21] using two class categories, found that only 30 per cent of North Americans leave the social class in which they were raised, and hence residential relocation is required only once in the lifetime of a third of the population. Even if a more complex set of social-class categories were used, so that almost everyone changed categories, only one move in a lifetime would be explained by social mobility. More effective, perhaps, are the income changes that take place without altering relative social class. Each household reaps the advantage of the annual 2–3 per cent increase in the standard of living, and while working in the same job a man's disposable income may increase as he gains seniority and shifts expenditures from children and appliances to housing and other goods. The effect is to remove the cost constraint that may have restricted the adjustment of housing needs. During the same period, of course, the original housing, even if adequate in size and location, becomes less attractive relative to the total housing stock. In this way, housing 'filters down' to lower-income groups while people 'filter up' to better housing.[22]

The majority of moves adjust housing within neighbourhoods of similar characteristics (Table 3). About 80 per cent of intracity movement takes place within census tracts of the same class or adjacent classes.[23] The economic status of a neighbourhood changes as one social class replaces another; the rich buy out the poor or the poor make life uncomfortable for the rich. The tendency for higher-income people to move outside the city limits accelerates the filtering down of housing opportunities and the net movement of lower-income groups into higher-income areas. In most instances these movements are gradual, and do not increase the rate of migration. Even urban renewal projects, which may relocate thousands from a given area during a period of two or three years, account for only a small part of the total mobility in a city.[24]

Studies of ethnic and racial groups have generated a complex, and often contradictory, body of theory about their intra-urban movements.[25] The assimilation processes that European minorities underwent in the nineteenth and the early twentieth centuries are less relevant to present-day groups, who have different problems and who live in cities with dissimilar patterns of interaction and opportunity. The Negro ghetto is larger and more permanent than the enclaves of the earlier minority groups, and many recent European immigrants have avoided the ghetto stage entirely.

TABLE 3

Moves among Social Areas
(In percentages)

| Social Class | Social Class of Destination Tract | | | | |
	I (high)	II	III	IV	V (low)
I (high)	63·8	12·0	11·3	8·2	4·8
II	8·2	51·0	20·6	13·3	6·8
III	6·1	18·8	50·4	16·7	8·1
IV	5·1	13·0	21·0	52·7	8·1
V (low)	4·1	13·2	17·3	17·4	48·1

Source: Goldstein and Mayer, *Metropolitanization and Population Change in Rhode Island* [see text footnote 23], p. 51.

The traditional ethnic community had a core area where much of the assimilation took place, and from which the successful immigrants, either as individuals or as groups, moved out socially and spatially. If the flow of in-migration slackened, the core area itself might be relocated, particularly if spatial assimilation had been a group process. The net effect was a decline in the concentration of such ethnic groups, but their movements have not had an appreciable effect on mobility rates. Members of ethnic groups move for the usual reasons—for example, the need for better housing—and the communities expand gradually.[26] The ethnic factor acts as a constraint only on the number of possible alternatives, explaining 'where' people move rather than 'why' they move.

The expansion of the Negro ghettos in Northern cities increases mobility more dramatically. Typically, the highly segregated and rapidly growing Negro areas can expand only into nearby white neighbourhoods.[27] If the whites panic, the turnover takes place rapidly, affecting as many as 75 per cent of the dwellings in two or three years. The mobility rate for Negroes increases as the normal rate of white out-migration (about 50 per cent in five years) is accelerated by racial and economic fears. The crucial aspect in the change-over is not the accelerated white out-migration but the almost total cessation of white in-migration.[28] Negro in-migrants of the same socio-economic level as the whites fill the vacuum.[29] Even in a city the size of Chicago, with a large and rapidly growing Negro population, the number of moves stimulated by racial shifts is small in proportion to total moves. An examination of the 1960 data for the south side of the city reveals that about 10 per cent of the census tracts had high mobility rates, but even these high rates were less than 50 per cent above the normal rate. Racial shifts generated from 3 to 5 per cent of all movements in that part of the city.[30]

Individual Decisions

The final set of factors that induces a change of residence reflects personal problems in adjusting to the environment, beyond the effects of physical needs and the constraints of class and culture outlined above. Evidence for these personal aspects of mobility is provided by Rossi,[31] who found it necessary to evaluate the complaints about dwellings along with life-cycle and tenure information in order to predict mobility. The complaints generated by the differences between expectation and reality as perceived by the household are not predictable from any socio-economic measures; nor are conflicts with neighbours, which may make an area untenable. Some persons are chronically restless and dissatisfied; others blunder in their evaluation of alternative neighbourhoods or are unable to adjust their life style to a particular environment. All these things affect an individual's perception of the cost, of the characteristics of the dwelling unit, and of the immediate social and economic environment. Rossi's comparison of the perception of housing by residents and by an 'objective observer' (Table 4) sheds some light on the source of complaints. Agreement is best for the most significant variable, the dwelling-unit size. Only a few complaints concerned location, in the sense of access, and these had little effect on mobility.

In order to explain expectations of movement, Lansing and Barth[32] combined two social variables (age of household head and crowding) with three attitude variables (satisfaction with housing, neighbourhood, distance from city centre) and

TABLE 4

Area Characteristics and Their Perception by Residents

Attribute	Ranking			
	Oak Lane	West Philadelphia	Kensington	Central City
LOCATION				
Observed	4	1	3	2
Perceived	3	2	1	4
PHYSICAL FACILITIES				
Observed	1	2	3	4
Perceived	2	3	1	4
DWELLING-UNIT SIZE				
Observed	1	3	2	4
Perceived	2	3	1	4

Source: Rossi, *Why Families Move* [see text footnote 4], pp. 26–30.

obtained results that confirmed Rossi's work. Rossi has also associated mobility with the perceived difference in social class between residents and their neighbours.[33]

The role of the goals and knowledge of the individual household in the decision to move is difficult to evaluate, though recent studies of environmental perception may be of some assistance.[34] A theoretical structure has been provided by Wolpert's behavioural model of migration.[35] Each social group has a constant propensity to move, which is related to its *threshold of utility*—that is, the degree of differentiation of place utility between where people are living and alternative locations necessary to make them move. Place utility is the measure of attractiveness or unattractiveness of an area relative to alternative locations, as perceived by the individual decision maker, and as evaluated according to his particular needs.[36] For instance, elderly working-class people have a very high threshold of utility: only an earthquake could make them move. Elderly middle-class people have a slightly lower threshold: they can be lured away by Florida sunshine. Young people, on the other hand, require little incentive to leave home.

Thus place utility both initiates relocation and determines the new location. But the theory of search behaviour also explains locations. The individual evaluates the alternatives with which he is familiar: nearby places, communities where friends and relatives live, areas visited in travel, places described by mass media. Generally these alternatives are clustered around one or two locations. The decision process, however, is complicated by the possibility of time lags after changes in the household-environment relationship, the tendency to minimize uncertainty, and the option of adjusting to the existing situation. In a later paper Wolpert[37] enlarges the threshold-of-utility concept into a strain-stress model in which an individual migrates as a form of adaptation to stress exerted by his environment. The two elements—the change in the individual over time and the stress exerted by the environment—are modified by the susceptibility of the individual.

To summarize, then, within a moderately growing city more than 50 per cent of the intra-urban mobility results from the changing housing needs generated by the life cycle. Abu-Lughod and Foley[38] estimate that about 30 per cent of intra-urban moves are involuntary, with 10 per cent following the creation of new households and 20 per cent resulting from demolition, destruction by fire or eviction. Perhaps another 10 per cent reflect changes outside the life cycle, such as social mobility, ethnic assimilation, and neighbourhood invasion. The most meaningful aspects of the housing adjustments are the size and facilities of the dwelling unit, followed by the social environment of the neighbourhood. The physical site and access to other parts of the city are relatively insignificant. All studies reject job location as an important reason for moving.[39] Given the high rate of mobility generated by the life cycle, changes in the numbers and characteristics of the population within an area generally reflect a change in the pattern of in-migration.

Where Do They Move?

Knowing why a family moves tells us little about its final destination. This is apparent when maps of intra-urban migration are studied.[40] Flows and counterflows crisscross the urban area, and these major regularities, such as the tendencies to move nearby and within the same sector, are determined by the procedure for seeking a new home rather than the reason for leaving the old. Once the decision to move has been made, the family takes another set of factors into consideration. The selection of a new home depends not only on demand conditions (the priorities that the family assigns to different housing characteristics) but also on supply constraints (the cost and quantity of different types of housing in different parts of the city). Then, too, the search procedure used by a family to examine and evaluate alternative locations is significant.

Both the supply and demand sides of the housing market strongly influence the choice of a place to live.[41] The supply of housing is differentiated by such variables as tenure, number of rooms, age, and location; the demand for housing is a function of such characteristics of the urban population as income, point in the life cycle, family size, and place of employment. The demand submarkets have varying degrees of independence from other submarkets; often a family will find it difficult to choose between quite different alternatives—for example, an ageing duplex in a central location or a suburban bungalow. Housing surveys and the economics of the construction industry provide the supply schedules for each submarket, and knowledge of past behaviour patterns and surveys of consumer preference permit the construction of housing-demand curves for each subpopulation.[42] Grigsby[43] has constructed matrices that show movements of households between demand submarkets and relationships between supply and demand categories. Because of the large number of variables differentiating housing submarkets and household characteristics, matrices relating supply and demand are complex. However, the number of housing alternatives is lessened by the fixed supply of housing in the short run and the correlations among housing characteristics. For instance, the majority of the smaller dwelling units are for rent, and older housing is found near the city centre.

Each family chooses from the housing available at any one time,[44] but relatively little is known about the complex selection process. Some data are available, but the survey methods—the form of questionnaire, the location of the sample, the timing—vary so much that the data are almost useless. The hierarchy of criteria is still hypothetical,[45] but cost undoubtedly plays a major role. Each household has a housing budget, which is a function of its 'normal' income, defined as a long-run expected income of the family.[46] A crucial option is whether to own or to rent, a decision related both to income and to life-cycle characteristics. The other important consideration is the amount of space required. Social factors (access to downtown, familiarity of the neighbourhood, ethnic groupings) further complicate the decision.

Spatial Aspects of the Housing Market

The division of the housing stock into locational submarkets does not, in itself, severely reduce the supply of available dwelling units. Mobility rates are high enough that some housing units are available in virtually every area. Generally, a wide range of cost alternatives also exists throughout the city, if one is willing to trade size for cost. Only in a few instances (the eighteenth-century home, the $300,000 mansion, the 50-cent flophouse) would availability and cost alone define the location. The location constraint operates in conjunction with other variables, and the requirement of living in a certain neighbourhood becomes difficult to fulfil only when housing of a certain size or standard is specified. More often location comes so far down on the hierarchy of criteria that the location of a dwelling results from decisions about other factors.

Submarkets may be defined at all levels of the decision-making process. One can consider in turn the submarket of cheap housing, cheap apartments, cheap suburban apartments, and so on, each of which has spatial implications because of the distribution of that phenomenon. But a submarket at any level need not be confined to one location, since cheap housing, for instance, can be found in several areas of a city. In general, as the submarket is defined more precisely, the housing characteristics restrict the number of possible locations until the final decision focuses on a single house.

The distribution of various kinds of housing will affect the direction of flow. Although the variety of housing found in the central city is increasing, as old houses are subdivided and new apartments are erected, the range of choice in that area is restricted in two ways. Housing in the central part of the city, particularly the single-family dwelling, is old, lacks many amenities, and is therefore rejected by some families. Also, densities are much higher in the central areas, following the variations in land costs. It should be remembered that the relative importance placed on access, space, and other criteria varies with the household and with the neighbourhood. People who live downtown have already opted for access; suburban dwellers have placed more importance on space and quiet. But the selection of an appropriate population density by a family is seldom explicit; it emerges from such decisions as whether to seek a single-family house or how big a lot to look for.

TABLE 5

Family Migration, Providence, 1950–59
(In percentages)

Destination	I (high)	II	III	IV	V (low)	Total
Within tract	18.3	20.0	22.5	28.1	29.1	24.2
Within city	35.1	38.3	46.0	48.3	45.6	43.9
Outside city	46.8	40.7	31.5	24.6	25.2	31.9

Social Class of Origin Tract

Source: Goldstein and Mayer, *Metropolitanization and Population Change in Rhode Island* [see text footnote 23], p. 51 (Table 18).

The best factor for predicting the location of a new residence is the location of the former house. All the evidence indicates that most moves are short, within familiar territory, and reflect both satisfaction with the neighbourhood and location with respect to the urban structure. For example, a number of studies show that about a quarter of all moves take place within a census tract (Table 5).[47] The short moves may produce a net spatial change in one direction (as suggested by the process of decentralization)[48] or they may just be at random. The high rate of local movement provides a large number of opportunities for in-migrants throughout the metropolitan area and indicates that a household should be able to satisfy its housing requirements relatively easily.

The large number of local moves, adjusting housing needs within the same social area, overshadow longer moves that may involve a change in the social environment of the mover. The decline of moves with distance becomes more irregular when other factors, such as the location of housing alternatives, come into play. However, it is possible to describe the probability of relocation of a migrant as a function of distance, and several formulas have been suggested, with various theoretical bases and empirical demonstrations.[49] In each case the models posit a sharp initial decline in the relocation rate, which then levels off.[50] Although few curves have been fitted to urban areas, the general relationship seems to hold, despite the distortions introduced by the patterns of social variation in the city. For the simplest expression of distance decay, the Pareto equation,

$$\text{in-migration/population} = a/ (\text{distance})^b,$$

several estimates have been made of the parameter b:[51] Åsby, Sweden (1950), $b = 1\cdot6$; Cleveland (1933–6), $b = 2\cdot5$; a group of small Midwestern cities (1930), $b = 1\cdot8$.

The tendency of movers to choose destinations nearby has two possible reasons. The household may deliberately select a nearby location in order to maintain spatial familiarity, social contacts, institutional links or to maintain its access to the city as a whole, while adjusting housing size or tenure. The decline in the number of desinations with distance, however, suggests that short moves may also reflect imperfections in the housing market, especially since location is relatively unimportant and nearby alternatives are more likely to be evaluated than distant ones. Rossi found that almost 50 per cent of all housing units were obtained through personal contact.[52]

Cultural Constraints

The tendency to relocate in the same neighbourhood may reflect the requirements, voluntary or involuntary, of being near people of similar origin or interest or of access to certain institutions. The effect of the cultural constraints is to emphasize movements within sectors as demonstrated by Caplow[53] and by Green.[54] Households are able to adjust their housing and access costs without crossing the sectoral boundaries, defined by nonresidential land use or by the location of other income and cultural groups. The tendency for high-income movers to relocate in the same sector forms a central part of Hoyt's theory of the residential structure.[55] Hoyt suggests a number of reasons for this, among them the attraction of site characteristics, such as shorelines, and of fast transportation, both of which are essentially sectoral phenomena. However, the most prized residential sites in the city often are not intrinsically different from less desirable sites, but they represent the cumulative effect of high-income areas attracting prestige commercial establishments and community leaders, which in turn attract high-income residents. Minority groups are also sensitive to linkages. Entire Jewish communities have been transplanted from the old urban core to the suburbs as they climb the economic ladder; Negroes find tremendous internal and external forces opposing their movement out of the ghetto.

Families in higher social classes tend to move further (Table 5). More of them move outside the census tract, outside the central city, and outside the metropolitan area. Their evaluation procedures are apt to be more thorough and to embrace a more complex set of constraints. For these families, the cost of moving, estimated to be at least 10 per cent of house value,[56] requires a substantial change in dwelling or environment to make it worthwhile. At the lowest end of the income scale, however, the slightest financial crisis may prevent the payment of rent and require relocation, and any change in the family structure creates pressures for adjustment.

We have assumed here that people tend to remain in the same income or ethnic environment when they move. Moves by the upwardly mobile or by ethnic families who are rapidly assimilating are less easy to predict, but these form only a small part of total moves. The time lag may be of considerable importance: movers select a neighbourhood according to their perception of its characteristics in the near future, characteristics which may resemble the neighbourhood they are leaving as it was five, ten, or twenty years ago. The degree of contiguity of income and culture areas will also have an effect. A city may have only one high-income area or it may have half a dozen, providing alternative locations.

Access to the Rest of the City

As we have seen, the consensus of studies of consumer preference is that the location of the house is generally less important than the characteristics of the dwelling unit. For most people the three aspects of location that have the most importance are the social environment (nearness of friends and institutional amenities); the physical environment (quiet, maintenance, and design); and access to the city as a whole or to places of work. After trying unsuccessfully to explain differences in stated access preference by measures of income, life cycle, and family activity, Lansing and Barth[57] concluded that access was relatively unimportant to most people and that location decisions reflect other kinds of preference, such as privacy, cost, and type of dwelling. Yet access becomes an important factor in the decision if only because of the constraints it imposes on the supply side. The supply and demand for access have generated consistently declining housing costs along the continuum of submarkets moving outward from the city centre to the suburbs, as Alonso and Wingo have shown theoretically, and Brigham, Muth, and Seyfried have demonstrated empirically.[58] This pattern reflects the differential access to the rest of the city. Housing costs also vary sectorally with changing access to higher social-class amenities and sometimes with certain site characteristics such as water frontage or elevation. Although Yeates[59] has demonstrated a steady decline in the effect of access over time as the reduction of transport costs lessens the importance of centrality and man-made amenities outweigh natural advantages, strong radial variations in housing costs remain.

Considerable evidence indicates that the majority prefer to live further from, rather than closer to, the CBD; they find the quiet, the spaciousness, and the general suburban image more attractive than downtown.[60] Most of the demand for residences in the city centre is generated by a relatively few families. For instance, the white middle-to-high income group is older and has a family structure and employment characteristics that differ from those of their counterparts in the suburbs. The most significant difference is the almost total absence of school-age children.[61] Although access is important to this group, they are concerned with the availability of social amenities rather than with employment.[62]

The high cost of housing near the city centre is not a response to overwhelming demand but a result of competition from other land uses and of a slowly increasing demand for residences, while the supply of housing is fixed or decreasing. Almost all the net addition to the city's housing occurs in the outer, suburban, parts of the metropolitan area. The dwelling units added by increasing the housing density in the central area are counterbalanced by the removal of other residential units to accommodate other land uses. The result of this imbalance is a continuous increase in housing costs in the city centre, which is amplified by the perception of future urban development as seen by investors. The constant-cost isopleth moves steadily outward, requiring outward movement for families with fixed income and housing needs. Different types of housing vary in response to access costs, depending on supply and demand. Single-family homes, requiring a minimum lot size, cannot support population densities above a certain level.

The movement away from the city centre because of personal preference and cost is encouraged by the proportion of housing opportunities found on the outskirts. A city growing at the rate of 10 per cent a year, with an overall annual mobility rate of 20 per cent, will generate one-third of all housing opportunities on the periphery. It can be shown, using simple assumptions and calculus, that a large majority of the population will have a higher proportion of their housing opportunities further from the city centre than their present residence. The result is a persistent net movement outward as the city grows (Table 6). For instance, about 10 per cent of the 1956 population of the central city (Toronto) moved beyond the city limit, but many other moves within the city and the fringe had the same decentralizing effect. A similar outward bias shows up in Caplow's table[63] and on Green's maps,[64] and is an important assumption in Burgess's discussion of city structure.[65]

Certain groups are much more likely to move outward—households with young children, renters wanting to own, and people with preferences for low-density areas. Alonso and Kain have tried to explain these location decisions from economic theory, given different preferences for space.[66] Caplow notes that there is also a countercurrent, with young people forming new households at the city centre and older households ready to trade space for access.[67] There is no evidence of a greater propensity towards decentralization on the part of higher-income groups,[68] but this may have been true in the past. Rodwin[69] points out that the constraints of income, transportation, and cultural values used to prevent low-income people from moving to the suburbs.

TABLE 6

Gross Movement Patterns in the Toronto Metropolitan Area

Origin	Destination		
	Fringe	Central City	Total
Fringe	343,500	17,900	361,400
Central City	63,000	197,800	260,800
TOTAL	406,500	215,700	622,200
Population (1961)	1,152,100	672,400	1,824,500
Population (1956)	834,400	667,700	1,502,100

Access plays an important role in the development of new suburban areas. Virtually every model of urban growth introduces the effect of access, generally to the CBD, but frequently to the areas of employment, and to shopping centres, schools, and highways as well. Several studies have developed empirical relationships. Hansen[70] used density and access to the city centre, to other residential areas, and to jobs to predict 87 per cent of the variation in a measure of development (new dwellings divided by possible sites). All his variables correlated strongly with the dependent variable and with one another. In a series of multiple regressions Chapin and Weiss[71] evaluate the effect of a number of growth factors, and find that 60 per cent of the urban development in a given area could be explained by eight factors: poor land, access to employment, assessed value, distance to major street, residential amenities, distance to school, sewers, and zoning, in that order. A study by Kaiser,[72] which develops the Chapin-Weiss model further, indicates that the contributions to development are, in order of importance, socio-economic rank, contiguous residential subdivision, public utilities, zoning protection, and access to employment. The change in order, together with the propinquity effect noted earlier, suggests that urban growth may be related primarily to access to older residential areas which serve as sources of migrants and that access to the city centre is meaningful only to the extent that it acts as a surrogate.

The Journey to Work

The relationship between job and residence is a particular form of access, which is defined for each employment location. All families are concerned to some extent with their location relative to the CBD, but only a few hundred may care about their relationship with a specific industrial area. Although few people move in order to be closer to their jobs, the place of employment may act as a constraint when it comes to selecting a dwelling. Several studies show a weak but consistent decline in the employment field with distance.[73] Lansing[74] notes that only 36 per cent of movers explicitly defined a maximum time for the journey to work in searching for a new home, though 92 per cent of those who did, kept within the limit.

PLACE OF WORK AND MIGRATION

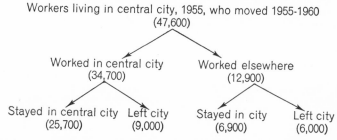

Fig. 5. Place of work and migration. *Source:* Goldstein and Mayer: 'Residential Mobility, Migration and Commuting in Rhode Island' (see text footnote 4) p. 58.

A number of factors offset the apparent attraction of reduced travel time. Many drivers enjoy the journey to work;[75] many more do not mind it. When Goldstein and Mayer analysed the interactions between commuting and migration in Providence, Rhode Island (Fig. 5), they found that more than 25 per cent of those who worked in the central city moved out of the city. They outnumbered (9,000 to 6,000) those who worked elsewhere and moved, presumably to reduce the journey to work. However, the probability of outward movement is much higher for persons working outside the central city. When these and similar data are examined for all towns in Rhode Island, the pattern of employment location is found to be closer to the pattern of mover origins than of destinations. Apparently the majority prefer to live further from, rather than closer to, downtown. However, many members of the labour force do not make the location decision, but follow the head of the household; others, such as retail clerks or handymen, can find local employment wherever they live. For the population as a whole, the journey to work tends to increase with each move, reflecting the residential decentralization process.[76] The only workers who consistently relocate closer to their jobs are those employed in the suburbs. Thus continuing decentralization of employment may lead to the increased importance of job location in predicting residence location. Job changes and residence changes have approximately the same frequency of occurrence.[77]

Information on the effects of the journey-to-work constraint on different income groups is inconsistent. Lansing finds few differences; Lapin indicates a longer work trip for middle-income clerical, sales, and blue-collar workers; and Lowry and Duncan show higher-income persons to be further away from job locations.[78]

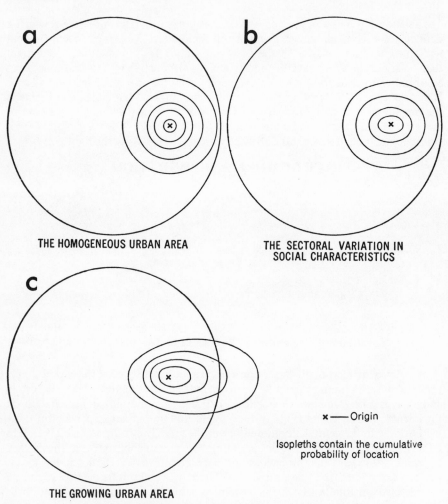

Fig. 6. Hypothetical intra-urban migration fields.

To summarize, then, the destination of an intracity move is determined by the interaction of a series of constraints. Some are imposed by the needs and preferences of the household, and others by the distribution of different kinds of housing. Despite the complexity of the decision process, it is possible to make some generalizations about the shapes of the migration field around a point of origin in a hypothetical city (Fig. 6). The most powerful regularity is the tendency to relocate near the origin, producing a migration field that declines equally in all directions. Superimposed on this is the effect of sectoral variations in income and ethnic characteristics coupled with the barrier of downtown, which together distort the migration field along a sectoral axis. Finally, the growth of the city, increase of housing costs in the inner city, and expansion of housing alternatives on the outskirts skew the migration field away from the city centre towards the suburbs.

Future Research: Problems and Implications

The spatial differentiation of residential attributes is largely the result of the cumulation of intra-urban moves. Unfortunately, the type of data available has caused urban research to focus on the static distributions instead of on the processes that generate urban patterns. Yet so many significant urban phenomena—for example, social segregation, the housing market, and urban growth—operate through the mechanism of intra-urban mobility that it merits systematic study.

Perhaps the most remarkable aspect of intra-urban mobility is the stability of the social characteristics of neighbourhoods in spite of the high mobility rates throughout the city. The tendency of movers to relocate nearby maintains the spatial equilibrium, but the occasional dramatic social change within a neighbourhood is a reminder of the complexity of the adjustments between form and process that lead to social differentiation. The equilibrium between in-migration and out-migration encompasses a great variety of factors—physical characteristics of the city, economic conditions, and, particularly, the values and perceptions of the population—which may contradict or reinforce one another.

Regular, consistent measures of area-to-area flows are critically needed for a better understanding of intra-urban location. Current census data that give mobility rates for in-movers identify only a limited number of origins; these are useful, but not sufficient. The development of models that will explain and predict patterns of flow, and hence spatial change, within the city will require a full matrix, identifying flows from every subdivision of the city to every other subdivision. The problems of filing and storing such information become enormous, since n areas generate n^2 possible flows, and one metropolitan area might comprise twenty to thirty communities (10^3 flow dyads) or several hundred census tracts (10^5 flow dyads). Recent technological advances make possible the use of such data.[79] The problem of gathering an adequate sample from interviews or city directories overwhelms the private researcher, particularly when it is desirable to obtain socio-economic information at the same time.[80] The most promising avenue is the compilation of change-of-address data gathered for other purposes but capable of modification to provide the necessary variables. Public-utilities data, transportation studies, and various kinds of government files have also been used.

The other necessary set of variables is housing measures, based on many small areas and classified by the critical aspects of location, cost, tenure, number of rooms, and quality. These measures of opportunity, when combined with existing data on the social characteristics of the population, can be used to predict the volume of in-movers and out-movers.

Although the accumulation of pertinent data should lead to better models of intra-urban migration in the short run, the prospects over a longer period are more uncertain. The housing needs of the population under thirty-five dominate the mobility pattern, but a large hazy area of perception, preference, and institutional effects is also concerned. The attitudes towards a given neighbourhood can shift more rapidly than the physical characteristics of the area, and the actions of planning boards, real-estate associations, and mortgage brokers are capricious.

It is increasingly apparent that virtually all the elements that enter into location decisions reflect individual perception and evaluation of needs and opportunities, which are shaped in turn by the values and habits of various subcultures. Households with similar social characteristics but different life styles prefer widely different housing and neighbourhood conditions. Even such a basic element as size of house is perceived differently; some households prefer large units and others, even the more affluent, prefer a smaller number of rooms.[81] Location preferences are more obviously tied to the background or to the role aspirations of the household. The problem of planners, who try to design urban environments on the basis of such a tenuous structure of likes and dislikes, is brought out forcefully in *Environment for Man*,[82] a collection of papers that demonstrates clearly the uncertainties and conflicting interpretations of human needs as seen by professional planners. In the absence of rigid functional requirements for urban residential areas, the alternatives seem to be either the aesthetics of the professional planner or the preference of the man in the street as interpreted in the market-place. The returns to planners in understanding and modifying preferences are enormous. A shift in middle-class norms regarding the value of access to downtown could be more significant than all the urban renewal to date; changing attitudes towards land tenure could modify the suburban landscape; and a desire for a greater variety of social contacts could alter the social-spatial distribution of the entire city.

NOTES AND REFERENCES

[1] Henry S. Shryock, Jr.: *Population Mobility within the United States* (University of Chicago. Community and Family Study Center, 1964), p. 10. Shryock, following the practice of the Bureau of the Census, restricts the use of the term 'migration' to movements across county lines. The present study, then, is primarily of mobility rather than of migration, though larger cities may include more than one county—if not within the city itself, at least as part of the Standard Metropolitan Statistical Area. Many census aggregations refer to intracounty movements, but data provided for individual census tracts data measure intrametropolitan moves.

[2] 'Mobility of the Population of the United States, March 1964 to March 1965', *Current Population Repts.*, Ser. P–20, *Population Characteristics*, No. 150, U. S. Bureau of the Census, Washington, D.C., 1966.

[3] The models available are reviewed by Walter Isard: *Methods of Regional Analysis* (New York and London, 1960, Chap. 3, Migration Estimates); Gunnar Olsson: *Distance and Human Interaction: A Review and Bibliography*, Regional Sci. Research Inst. Bibliogr. Ser. No. 2, Philadelphia, 1965; and E. G. Moore: 'Models of Migrations and the Intra-Urban Case', *Australian and New Zealand Journ. of Sociology*, 2 (1966), 16–37. Shryock (op. cit. [see note 1], p. 435) discusses sources of data. Juhan Wolpert ('Behavioral Aspects of the Decision to Migrate', *Papers Regional Science Assn.* 15 (1965), 159–69) and Torsten Hägerstrand ('Migration and Area', in *Migration in Sweden*, Lund Studies in Geogr., Ser. B, Human Geography, No. 13, 1957, pp. 27–158) present important contributions to the theory.

[4] Theodore Caplow: 'Incidence and Direction of Residential Mobility in a Minneapolis Sample', *Social Forces*, 27 (1948–9), 413–17. Other good bibliographies are found in Sidney Goldstein: *Patterns of Mobility, 1910–1950* (Philadelphia, 1958), 244–9, and in Peter H. Rossi: *Why Families Move* (Glencoe, Ill., 1956), pp. 185–95. See also Janet Abu-Lughod and Mary Mix Foley: 'Consumer Strategies', in *Housing Choices and Housing Constraints* (by Nelson N. Foote, Janet Abu-Lughod, Mary Mix Foley, and Louis Winnick; New York, 1960), pp. 71–271. Studies deriving mobility rates include Andrew W. Lind: *A Study of the Mobility of Population in Seattle*, Univ. of Washington Publs. in the Social Sciences, No. 3, 1925, pp. 1–64; T. Earl Sullenger: 'A Study in Intra-Urban Mobility', *Sociology and Social Research*, 17 (1932–3), 16–24; idem: 'The Social Significance of Mobility: An Omaha Study', *Amer. Journ.*

of Sociology, 55 (1949–50), 559–64; William Albig: 'The Mobility of Urban Population', *Social Forces*, 11 (1932–3), 351–67; idem: 'A Method of Recording Trends in Urban Residential Mobility', *Sociology and Social Research*, 21 (1936–7), 120–7; idem: 'A Comparison of Methods for Recording Trends in Urban Residential Mobility', ibid. 21 (1936–7), 226–33; Sidney Goldstein and Kurt B. Mayer: *Residential Mobility, Migration and Commuting in Rhode Island*, Rhode Island Development Council, Planning Division Publ. No. 7, Providence, 1963. An incredible amount of data (eight 321 x 321 flow matrices) was assembled in the 1930s, but remains largely unanalysed (see Howard Whipple Green: *Movements of Families within the Cleveland Metropolitan District*, Real Property Inventory of Metropolitan Cleveland, Repts. Nos. 3, 5, 7, 9, 11, 13, 15, and 17; Cleveland [issued annually, 1934–421]). The data, however, stimulated the seminal paper by Samuel A. Stouffer: 'Intervening Opportunities: A Theory Relating Mobility and Distance', *Amer. Sociol. Rev.*, 5 (1940), 845–67.

[5] Albig, 'A Method of Recording Trends in Urban Residential Mobility' [see note 4 above]. The decline is great enough to overcome errors in his sources.

[6] Op. cit. [see note 4], pp. 211 ff.

[7] Quoted in Abu-Lughod and Foley, op. cit. [see note 4], p. 161.

[8] *United States Census of Population*: 1950, Vol. 2, *Characteristics of the Population*. Based on a 20 per cent sample of persons.

[9] *United States Census of Population*: 1960, Vol. 1, *Characteristics of the Population*. My headings in Table 1 differ slightly from those listed in the Census—that is, 'Central City of SMSA', 'Other Part of SMSA', 'Outside SMSA'. In addition, the Census of Housing, 1960, identifies the date of movement into the present residence: 1958 to mid-1960; 1954 to 1957; 1940 to 1953; 1939 or earlier.

[10] 'Mobility of the Population of the United States' [see note 2], issued annually since 1948, uses a national sample of 30,000 families.

[11] John B. Lansing and Leslie Kish ('Family Life Cycle as an Independent Variable', *Amer. Sociol. Rev.* 22 (1957), 512–19) point out that the stage of family formation is more accurate than age alone in predicting expenditure, housing characteristics, and, undoubtedly, mobility. Most data, however, are tied to age, and the two variables are used interchangeably in this discussion.

[12] The concentration of movement in a short period in the life-span accounts for the phenomenon of repeated migration, in which a single person or household moves several times during the period of study. See Sidney Goldstein: The Extent of Repeated Migration, *Journ. Amer. Statist. Assn.*, Vol. 59, 1964, pp. 1121–1132, and also his 'Repeated Migration as a Factor in High Mobility Rates', *Amer. Sociol. Rev.*, Vol. 19, 1954, pp. 536–541.

[13] Rossi, op. cit. [see note 4], p. 69.

[14] Moore (op. cit. [see note 3], p. 26), using data from Brisbane, Australia. Lind (op. cit. [see note 4], Fig. 1) shows the pattern of out-migration in Seattle, where the highest rates in the central area are two or three times as great as in the suburbs. Albig ('The Mobility of Urban Population' [see note 4]) finds the same pattern, but with the central area about 50 per cent higher. See also Elsa Schneider Longmoor and Erle Fiske Young: 'Ecological Interrelationships of Juvenile Delinquency, Dependency, and Population Mobility: A Cartographic Analysis of Data from Long Beach, California', *Amer. Journ. of Sociology*, 41 (1935–6), 598–610; and Green (op. cit. [see note 4]), in each of his Cleveland reports.

[15] The effect of size has been studied theoretically by Gunnar Kulldorff (*Migration Probabilities*, Lund Studies in Geogr., Ser. B., Human Geography, No. 14, 1955), and empirically by Bertil Wendel ('Regional Aspects of Internal Migration and Mobility in Sweden, 1946–1950', in *Migration in Sweden* [see note 3], pp. 7–26).

[16] Theodore R. Anderson and J. A. Egeland: 'Spatial Aspects of Social Area Analysis', *Amer. Sociol. Rev.* 26 (1961), 392–8, Brian J. L. Berry: 'Cities as Systems within Systems of Cities', *Paper Regional Science Assn.* 13 (1964), 147–63; Robert A. Murdie: *Ecological Structure and Chance in Metropolitan Toronto*, Univ. of Chicago, Dept. of Geogr. Research Papers (forthcoming).

[17] Rossi, op. cit. [see note 4], p. 9. Rossi was able to predict a large proportion of mobility on the basis of a mobility index, based on age, household size, and tenure preference (p. 76). Similar results were obtained by R. Wilkinson and D. M. Merry: 'A Statistical Analysis of Attitudes to Moving', *Urban Studies*, 2 (1965), 1–14. See also Abu-Lughod and Foley, op. cit. [see note 4], p. 155.

[18] Op. cit. [see note 4], p. 135.

[19] See, for example, Michael D. Young and Peter Willmott: *Family and Kinship in East*

London (Chicago and London, 1957); Marc Fried: 'Grieving for a Lost Home', in *The Urban Condition* (edited by Leonard J. Duhl; New York, 1963), pp. 151–71.

[20] A continuing investigation into the effect of physical environment and way of life is being undertaken by William Michelson: 'An Empirical Analysis of Urban Environmental Preferences', *Journ. Amer. Inst. of Planners*, 32 (1966), 355–60. See also the review of the adjustment process by Robert Gutman: 'Population Mobility in the American Middle Class',in *The Urban Condition* [see note 19], pp. 172–83, and by Herbert J. Gans: 'The Effects of the Move from City to Suburbs', ibid., pp. 184–98; idem: *The Levittowners* (New York, 1967).

[21] Seymour M. Lipset and Reinhard Bendix: *Social Mobility in Industrial Society* (Berkeley and Los Angeles, 1959), Table 2–1. Goldstein (*Patterns of Mobility* [see note 4], p. 185), using six categories, found that less than 50 per cent of those he studied shifted during a ten-year period.

[22] For a detailed discussion of the filtering process, see William G. Grigsby: *Housing Markets and Public Policy* (Philadelphia, 1963), Chap. 3.

[23] Sidney Goldstein and Kurt B. Mayer: *Metropolitanization and Population Change in Rhode Island*, Rhode Island Development Council, Planning Division Publ. No. 3, Providence, 1961, p. 51, Table 18). Green (op cit. [see note 4], Rept. No. 11, p. 63) obtained similar results in Cleveland.

[24] For instance, of a total of more than 1,200,000 moves in Chicago (1955–60) only about 80,000 persons were relocated because of public demolition activities, including urban renewal, public housing, and expressways ('Housing and Urban Renewal Progress Report' [Chicago Community Renewal Program, 31 December 1964], Fig. 7; and United States Censuses of Population and Housing, 1960. *Final Rept. PHC (1)–26*, 'Census Tracts, Chicago, Illinois').

[25] Patterns of residential segregation are discussed in Davis McEntire: *Residence and Race* (Berkeley and Los Angeles, 1960), pp. 9–101, and in Stanley Lieberson: *Ethnic Patterns in American Cities* (New York, 1963). For particular cities, see Paul Frederick Cressey: 'Population Succession in Chicago: 1898–1930', *Amer. Journ. of Sociology*, 44 (1938–9), 59–69; Richard G. Ford: 'Population Succession in Chicago', ibid. 56 (1950–1), 156–60; Christen T. Jonassen: 'Cultural Variables in the Ecology of an Ethnic Group', *Amer. Sociol. Rev.* 14 (1949), 32–41; John Kosa: 'Hungarian Immigrants in North America: Their Residential Mobility and Ecology', *Canadian Journ. of Econ. and Polit. Sci.* 22 (1956), 358–70.

[26] When the mobility rates for Metropolitan Toronto were plotted the large Italian area (more than 100,000 persons) of recent origin and its surroundings showed slightly greater mobility on one map (Fig. 2).

[27] For a discussion of the process in Northern cities, see Otis Dudley Duncan and Beverly Duncan: *The Negro Population of Chicago* (Chicago, 1957); Chester Rapkin and William G. Grigsby: *The Demand for Housing in Racially Mixed Areas* (Berkeley and Los Angeles, 1960); Richard L. Morrill ('The Negro Ghetto: Problems and Alternatives', *Geogr. Rev.* 55 (1965), 339–61) and Kari E. Taeuber and Alma F. Taeuber: *Negroes in Cities* (Chicago, 1965). These writers have shown that the ghetto in Southern cities expands differently because access to the urban fringe allows Negroes to move directly into new housing.

[28] This has been documented by Rapkin and Grigsby, op. cit. [see note 27], pp. 52–72.

[29] Taeuber and Taeuber, op. cit [see note 27], pp. 156 and 180.

[30] 'Census Tracts, Chicago, Illinois' [see note 24], Table 1.

[31] Op. cit. [see note 4], p. 92–4.

[32] John B. Lansing and Nancy Barth: *Residential Location and Urban Mobility: A Multivariate Analysis* (Inst. for Social Research, Ann Arbor, Mich., 1964), p. 18.

[33] Rossi, op. cit. [see note 4], p. 34.

[34] Studies of individual perception of the environment are presented in two collections of papers: R. W. Kates and J. F. Wohlwill, eds.: 'Man's Response to the Physical Environment', *Journ. of Social Issues*, 22, No. 4 (1966); and David Lowenthal, ed.: *Environmental Perception and Behavior*, Univ. of Chicago, Dept. of Geogr., Research Paper No. 109, 1967. Significant studies of urban phenomena include Kevin Lynch: *The Image of the City* (Cambridge, Mass., 1960); Robert L. Wilson: 'The Livability of the City'. in *Urban Growth Dynamics* (edited by F. Stuart Chapin, Jr., and Shirley F. Weiss, New York, 1962), pp. 359–99; and George L. Peterson: 'A Model of Preference: Quantitative Analysis of the Perception of the Visual Appearance of Residential Neighborhoods', *Journ. of Regional Science*, 7 (1967), 19–31. So far urban studies relate to the selection of neighbourhood rather than to motivations for moving.

[35] Wolpert, op. cit. [see note 3].

[36] Further evidence is provided by Peter Gould: (*On Mental Maps*, Michigan Inter-University Community of Mathematical Geographers Discussion Paper No. 9, 1966), who obtained consistent structures of location preferences for individuals.

[37] Julian Wolpert: 'Migration as an Adjustment to Environment Stress', in *Man's Response to the Physical Environment* [see note 34], pp. 92–102.

[38] Abu-Lughod and Foley, op. cit. [see note 4], p. 135. Peter H. Rossi ('Why Families Move', in *The Language of Social Research* [edited by Paul F. Lazarsfeld and Morris Rosenberg; Glencoe. Ill., 1955], pp. 457–68; reference on p. 459) suggests slightly smaller values.

[39] Rossi, *Why Families Move* [see note 4], p. 85; Howard S. Lapin: *Structuring the Journey to Work* (Philadelphia, 1964), p. 163.

[40] Maps of mobility-desire lines are found in Lind (op. cit. [see note 4], p. 28), in Albig ('The Mobility of Urban Population', [see note 4], pp. 352–3) and in Green (op. cit. [see note 4], Rept. No. 9, p. 52, and Rept. No. 11, pp. 54–5). Caplow (op. cit. [see note 4], p. 416) tabulated his data by rings from the city centre, in order to examine the degree of decentralization. No one has yet produced an urban counterpart to the remarkable work by C. Warren Thornthwaite: *Internal Migration in the United States* (Philadelphia, 1934), in which flow lines summarize the whole pattern of interstate migration, or the study by Daniel O. Price: 'Distance and Direction as Vectors of Internal Migration, 1935–40', *Social Forces*, 27 (1948–9), 48–53.

[41] One of the most stimulating discussions of the housing market is found in Grigsby (op. cit. [see note 22], Chap. 11). Other studies that approach the city's housing market from the point of view of supply and demand are Chester Rapkin and William G. Grigsby: *The Demand for Housing in Eastwick* (Redevelopment Authority of the City of Philadelphia, 1960), and their *Residential Renewal in the Urban Core* (Philadelphia, 1960); and Beverly Duncan and Philip M. Hauser: *Housing a Metropolis–Chicago* (Glencoe, Ill., 1961).

[42] The San Francisco Community Renewal Program has undertaken a project that will measure and predict the present and future supplies of housing stock and housing demand as a policy aid in renewal planning (Ira M. Robinson, Harry B. Wolfe, and Robert L. Barringer: 'A Simulation Model for Renewal Programming', *Journ. Amer. Inst. of Planners*, 31 (1965), 126–33. Michelson analyses the demand by one set of consumers, those likely to prefer downtown high-rise apartments (William Michelson: 'Potential Candidates for the Designer's Paradise: A Social Analysis from a Nationwide Survey', *Social Forces*, 46 (1967–8), 190–6.

[43] Op. cit. [see note 22], pp. 64–9, 51, and 54, respectively.

[44] Grigsby differentiates between the total stock of housing and the amount on the market at one time. Certain submarkets, such as owner-occupied single-family dwellings, have a lower turnover than others, and the supply of this type of housing for rent or sale is disproportionately low at any one time (ibid., p. 83).

[45] The best information to date in this area is the national sample of interviews carried out by the Survey Research Center, Institute for Social Research, University of Michigan, Ann Arbor: John B. Lansing and Eva Mueller: *Residential Location and Urban Mobility* (1964); Lansing and Barth, op. cit. [see note 32]; John B. Lansing: *Residential Location and Urban Mobility: The Second Wave of Interviews* (1966). An interesting gaming approach developed by Wilson (op. cit. [see note 34]) asks people to spend a given amount of money on various housing features.

[46] Margaret G. Reid (*Housing and Income* [Chicago, 1962]) finds that housing expenditures are tied more closely to average incomes than to actual incomes because of the short-term fluctuation in the latter. Housing expenditures form a higher proportion of income as income increases, and as tenure shifts from renting to owning (p. 378). See also Louis Winnick: 'Economic Constraints', in *Housing Choices and Housing Constraints* [see note 4], pp. 3–67.

[47] For the years 1933 to 1937, Green (op. cit. [see note 4]) obtained values of 31, 28, 30, 26, and 24 per cent of moves within the same tract in Cleveland. Caplow (op. cit. [see note 4 above], p. 417) gives 25 per cent for Minneapolis, 1940–8; Albig (*The Mobility of Urban Population*, [see note 4], Table 6) indicates in Danville, Rock Island, and Moline, Illinois, 1929–30, that 25 to 30 per cent of the moves were less than 1,200 feet.

[48] Richard Dewey: 'Peripheral Expansion in Milwaukee County', *Amer. Journ. of Sociology*, 54 (1948–9), 118–25; reference on p. 120. Dewey states that most out-movement occurs by a succession of short moves, but provides no substantiating data.

[49] See Kulldorff, op. cit. [see note 15], and Hägerstrand, op. cit. [see note 3], pp. 112–26. See also Richard L. Morrill: 'The Distribution of Migration Distances', *Papers Regional Science Assn.* 11 (1963), 75–84.

[50] See the discussion of the migration field in Olsson, op. cit. [see note 3], pp. 43–73. See

also Richard L. Morrill and Forrest R. Pitts: 'Marriage, Migration, and the Mean Information Field', *Annals Assn. of Amer. Geogrs.* 57 (1967), 401–22.

51 The Asby and Cleveland parameters are given by Duane F. Marble and John D. Nystuen: 'An Approach to the Direct Measurement of Community Mean Information Fields', *Papers Regional Science Assn.* 11 (1963), 99–109, reference on pp. 103–6; the parameter for small Midwestern cities is derived from Albig, 'The Mobility of Urban Population [see note 4], Table 6.

52 Op. cit. [see note 4 above], p. 161.

53 Caplow (op cit. [see note 4]), p. 415 (Table 2). Dewey (op cit. [see note 48], p. 120) claims to have observed the same phenomena on the outskirts of Milwaukee.

54 Green, op. cit. [see note 4], *Rept. No. 9*, p. 52, and *Rept. No. 11*, p. 54. Stouffer (op cit. [see note 4]), using the same data, found that directional variations and moves by ethnic group, distorted his explanatory model, which was based on housing opportunities.

55 [Homer Hoyt:] *The Structure and Growth of Residential Neighborhoods in American Cities* (Federal Housing Administration, Washington, D. C., 1939), pp. 114–18. Hoyt's conclusions are evaluated for Boston by Lloyd Rodwin: *Housing and Economic Progress* (Cambridge, Mass., 1961), Chap. 6.

56 Grigsby, op. cit. [see note 22], p. 79.

57 Lansing and Barth, op. cit. [see note 32], p. 21.

58 William Alonso: *Location and Land Use* (Cambridge, Mass., 1964); Lowdon Wingo, Jr.: *Transportation and Urban Land* (Resources for the Future, Washington, D. C., 1961); E. F. Brigham: *A Model of Residential Land Values* (Rand Corporation, Santa Monica, Calif., 1964); Richard F. Muth: 'The Variation of Population Density and Its Components in South Chicago', *Papers Regional Science Assn.* 15 (1965), 173–83; Warren R. Seyfried: 'The Centrality of Urban Land Values', *Land Economics*, 39 (1963), 275–84. See also John D. Herbert and Benjamin H. Stevens: 'A Model for the Distribution of Residential Activity in Urban Areas, *Journ. of Regional Science*, 2, No. 2 (1960), 21–36. Bernard J. Frieden discusses in detail the demand for access and the cost of access in *The Future of Old Neighborhoods* ([Cambridge, Mass., 1964], Chap. 3 and Appendix C).

59 Maurice H. Yeates: 'Some Factors Affecting the Spatial Distribution of Chicago Land Values, 1910–1960', *Econ. Geography*, 41 (1965), 57–70.

60 Lansing and Mueller (op. cit. [see note 45], p. 26) and Lansing (op. cit. [see note 45], p. 35) found three times as many people preferring to live further from the city centre than closer to it. Similar results were found by Theodore Caplow: 'Home Ownership and Location Preferences in a Minneapolis Sample', *Amer. Sociol. Rev.* 13 (1948), 725–30.

61 Janet Abu-Lughod: 'A Survey of Center-City Residents', in *Housing Choices and Housing Constraints* [see note 4], pp. 462–5; Michelson, op. cit. [see note 42], p. 193.

62 Rapkin and Grigsby (*Residential Renewal in the Urban Core* [see note 41], pp. 40–52) found that 50 per cent of residents in sample areas near the city centres gave access to social activities as the major factor in moving to the area. See also Lansing and Mueller, op. cit. [see note 45], p. 28.

63 Caplow, 'Incidence and Direction of Residential Mobility in a Minneapolis Sample' [see note 4], p. 416.

64 Green, op. cit. [see note 4], *Rept. No. 9*, p. 53, and *Rept. No. 11*, p. 54.

65 Ernest W. Burgess: 'The Growth of the City', in *The City* (Robert E. Park, Ernest W. Burgess, and Roderick D. McKenzie: Chicago, 1925), pp. 47–62.

66 Alonso, op. cit. [see note 58], pp. 107–9; John F. Kain: 'The Journey-to-Work as a Determinant of Residential Location', *Papers Regional Science Assn.* 9 (1962), 137–60.

67 Caplow, 'Incidence and Direction of Residential Mobility in a Minneapolis Sample' [see note 4], p. 416.

68 This hypothesis has been examined by Sidney Goldstein and Kurt B. Mayer ('The Impact of Migration on the Socio-Economic Structure of Cities and Suburbs', *Sociology and Social Research*, 50 (1965), 5–23, and 'Population Decline and the Social and Demographic Structure of an American City', *Amer. Sociol. Rev.* 29 (1964), 718–29) and by Karl E. Taeuber and Alma F. Taeuber: 'White Migration and Socio-Economic Differences between Cities and Suburbs', ibid. 29 (1964), 718–29.

69 Rodwin, op. cit. [see note 55], p. 103.

70 Willard B. Hansen: 'An Approach to the Analysis of Metropolitan Residential Expansion', *Journ. of Regional Science*, 3, No. 1 (1961), 37–55. T. R. Lakshmanan ('An Approach to the Analysis of Intraurban Location Applied to the Baltimore Region', *Econ. Geography*, 40 (1964), 348–70), obtained similar results.

[71] F. Stuart Chapin, Jr., and Shirley F. Weiss: *Factors Influencing Land Development* (Institute for Research in Social Science, Univ. of North Carolina, Chapel Hill, 1962), p. 17.

[72] Edward J. Kaiser: 'Locational Decision Factors in a Producer Model of Residential Development' (paper presented to the Regional Science Association, Philadelphia, 1965).

[73] Edward J. Taaffe, Barry J. Garner, and Maurice H. Yeates: *The Peripheral Journey to Work* (Evanston, Ill., 1963), p. 34, explain 46 per cent of variations in commuter location by a function of population and distance. See also Lapin, op. cit. [see note 39], pp. 123–40; Ira S. Lowry: 'Location Parameters in the Pittsburgh Model', *Papers Regional Science Assn.* 11 (1963), pp. 146–65; Beverly Duncan and Otis Dudley Duncan: 'The Measurement of Intra-City Locational and Residential Patterns', *Journ. of Regional Science*, 2, No. 2 (1960), 37–54; John R. Wolforth: *Residential Location and the Place of Work*, B. C. Geogr. Ser. No. 4, Vancouver, 1965; and J. R. Meyer, J. F. Kain, and M. Wohl: *The Urban Transportation Problem* (Cambridge, Mass., 1965), Chap. 6, 'The Interrelationship of Housing and Urban Transportation'. This last demonstrates the interaction of job location and type of housing structure in determining location.

[74] Lansing, op. cit. [see note 45], p. 74.

[75] Of the drivers, 53 per cent enjoyed the journey to work; 34 per cent did not care; and 13 per cent disliked it (ibid., p. 99).

[76] Goldstein and Mayer, *Residential Mobility, Migration and Community in Rhode Island* [see note 4], p. 24; Lapin, op. cit. [see note 42 above], p. 153; Beverly Duncan: 'Intra-Urban Population Movement', in Paul K. Hatt and Albert J. Reiss: *Cities and Sociology* (rev. ed.; New York, 1957), p. 307.

[77] Gladys L. Palmer: *Labor Mobility in Six Cities* (Social Science Research Council, New York, 1954).

[78] Lansing, op. cit. [see note 45], p. 90; Lapin, op. cit. [see note 39], p. 100: Lowry, op. cit. [see note 73], p. 150. See also Beverly Duncan: 'Factors in Work-Residence Separation: Wage and Salary Workers, Chicago, 1951', *Amer. Sociol. Rev.* 21 (1956), 48–56.

[79] The census has published data on intermetropolitan flows between SMSAs of more than 250,000 population (101^2 flow cells) ('Mobility for Metropolitan Areas', U. S. Census of Population, 1960; Subject Repts., *Final Rept. PC* (2), Part 2C, 1963, Table 2); and Berry has analysed a 43,000 × 4,300 matrix of commuter movements from census data (Brian J. L. Berry: *Metropolitan Area Definition: A Re-Evaluation of Concept and Statistical Practice* U. S. Bureau of the Census, Working Paper 28, 1968, p. 11. Long before electronic data processing Green (op. cit. [see note 4]) annually produced flow matrices among 321 census tracts (approximately 100,000 cells), using public-utilities data.

[80] See Sidney Goldstein: 'City Directories as Sources of Migration Data', *Amer. Journ. of Sociology*, 60 (1954–55), 169–76.

[81] Abu-Lughod and Foley, op. cit. [see note 4], Chap. 7, 'Consumer Preferences: The Dwelling'.

[82] William R. Ewald, Jr., edit.: *Environment for Man* (Bloomington, Ind., and London, 1967). This is the report of a symposium sponsored by the American Institute of Planners.

20. SOCIAL PROCESSES AND SPATIAL FORM: AN ANALYSIS OF THE CONCEPTUAL PROBLEMS OF URBAN PLANNING

D. Harvey

The city is manifestly a complicated thing. In part, the difficulty we experience in dealing with it can be attributed to this inherent complexity. But our problems can also be attributed to our failure to conceptualize the situation correctly. If our concepts are inadequate or inconsistent, we cannot hope to identify problems and formulate appropriate policy solutions. In this essay, therefore, I want to address myself to the conceptual problems only. I shall ignore the inherent complexity of the city itself and seek instead to expose some of the problems which we ourselves generate by our characteristic ways of looking at the city. One set of conceptual problems arises from the disciplinary specialization on certain aspects of city processes. Clearly, the city cannot be conceptualized in terms of our present disciplinary structures. Yet there is very little sign of an emerging interdisciplinary framework for thinking, let alone theorizing, about the city. Sociologists, economists, geographers, architects, city planners, and so on, all appear to plough lonely furrows and to live in their own confined conceptual worlds. Leven has thus recently remarked that much of the research which has been done in the recent past deals 'with problems in the city rather than of the city'.[1] Each discipline uses the city as a laboratory in which to test propositions and theories, yet no discipline has propositions and theories about the city itself. This is the primary problem to be overcome if we are ever to understand (let alone control) the complexity that is the city. If we are to do this, however, we must overcome some extraordinarily difficult methodological, philosophical, and conceptual problems.

The Geographical Versus the Sociological Imagination

Any general theory of the city must somehow relate the social processes that go on in the city to the spatial form which the city assumes. In disciplinary terms, this amounts to integrating two important research and educational traditions—I shall call it building a bridge between those possessed of the sociological imagination and those imbued with a spatial consciousness or a geographical imagination. Let me explain the meaning of this distinction.

Mills defines the 'sociological imagination' as something which: enables its possessor to understand the larger historical scene in terms of its meaning for the inner life and the external career of a variety of individuals. . . . The first fruit of this imagination . . . is the idea that the individual can understand his own experience and gauge his own fate only by locating himself within his period, that he can know his own chances in life only by becoming aware of those of all individuals in his circumstances. . . . The sociological imagination enables us to grasp history and biography and the relations between the two in society. . . . Back of its use there is always the urge to know the social and historical meaning of the individual in society and in the period in which he has his quality and his being.[2]

As Mills goes on to point out, this sociological imagination is not the sole possession of sociology, but it is the common bond of all disciplines in the social

From *Papers of the Regional Science Association*, 25 (1970) 47–69. Reprinted by permission of the Regional Science Association.

sciences (including economics, psychology, and anthropology) and is the central concern of history and social philosophy as well. The sociological imagination has an extraordinary powerful tradition behind it. From Plato through Rousseau to Marcuse, there has been a never-ending debate upon the relationship of the individual to society and the role of the individual in history. In the last half-century or so, the methodology associated with the social sciences has also become more rigorous and more scientific (some would say psuedo-scientific). The sociological imagination can now feed upon an enormous speculative literature, a plethora of survey research results, and a few well-articulated theories regarding certain aspects of the social process.

It is useful to contrast with this 'sociological imagination' a rather more diffuse quality which I shall call 'spatial consciousness' or the 'geographical imagination'. This imagination enables the individual to recognize the role of space and place in his own biography, to relate to the spaces he sees around him, and to recognize how transactions between individuals and between organizations are affected by the space that separates them. It allows him to recognize the relationship which exists between him and his neighbourhood, his territory, or, to use the language of the street gangs, his 'turf'. It allows him to judge the relevance of events in other places (on other peoples' 'turf')—to judge whether the march of communism in Vietnam, Thailand, and Laos is or is not relevant to him here in Santa Monica now. It allows him also to fashion and use space creatively and to appreciate the meaning of the spatial forms created by others. This 'spatial consciousness' or 'geographical imagination' is manifest in many disciplines. Architects, artists, designers, city planners, geographers, anthropologists, historians, and so on have all possessed it. But it has a far weaker academic tradition behind it, and its methodology still relies heavily upon pure intuition. The main seat of the spatial consciousness in western culture today still lies in the plastic arts.

This distinction between the geographical and the sociological imagination is artificial when we seek to relate to the problems of the city, but it is all too real when we examine the ways in which we think about the city. There are plenty of those possessed with a powerful sociological imagination (C. Wright Mills among them) who nevertheless seem to live and work in a spaceless world. There are also those, possessed of a powerful geographical imagination or spatial consciousness, who fail to recognize that the way in which space is fashioned can have a profound effect upon social processes—hence the numerous examples of beautiful but unlivable designs in modern living.

Into this interface between the sociological and the spatial approach to problems, a number of individuals and groups of individuals and even whole disciplines have crept. Many of those possessed of the sociological imagination have come to recognize the significance of the spatial dimension in the social process. Hallowell and Hall in anthropology (the latter proposing the new science of proxemics), Tinbergen and Lorenz in ethology, Sommer's studies of the role of personal 'psychological' space in influencing human reaction to environmental design, Piaget and Inhelder's studies of the growth of the spatial consciousness in children, philosophers such as Cassirer and Langer with their clear recognition of the affect of the spatial consciousness upon man's view of his relationship to the world around him, these are but a few examples.[3] We also find regional economists and regional scientists in this group. Others have moved into this interface from the other direction. Trained in a tradition of spatial consciousness, they have come to recognize how the fashioning of spatial form can influence the social process:

architects such as Lynch and Doxiadis (with his proposed new science of ekistics), city planners such as Howard and Abercrombie.[4] Straddling the interface, we also find the regional geographer who, in spite of his taboo-laden methodology and weak analytic tools, can still on occasion manage to convey some deep insights into the way in which regional consciousness, regional identity, and natural and man-made environment merge into one another over time to create a distinctive spatial structure to human organization. Recently, human geographers have been more active in exploring the relationships between social processes and spatial form.[5]

There is an enormous but widely scattered literature which relates to the interface. But it is difficult to pull it all together, to distil its message. Perhaps one of our first tasks in seeking to fashion a new conceptual framework for our understanding of the city will be to survey and synthesize this vast diffuse literature. Such a synthesis will probably reveal how difficult it is to work in this area without major conceptual adjustments. It is interesting to consider, for example, how long it has taken for the city planner and the regional scientist to adjust to each other in their attempt to understand city processes. The intricacies of spatial form problems seem to have escaped early workers in regional science. Space either generated a regional structure (by a process which was assumed rather than understood) to which could then be applied accounting frameworks devised for the national level (from which we have regional accounting and interregional input-output), or else space merely generated transport costs which could be substituted against other costs involved in the production process (from which we have most of location theory and the interregional equilibrium models). Space was simply another variable in a conceptual framework devised primarily for economic analysis. Regional scientists and regional economists still exhibit a predilection for understanding their economics and misunderstanding space. However, urban planning, dominated as it traditionally has been by a primary resort to drawing-board design and, in particular, by the process of designing from the map (a notorious instrument for self-deception if ever there was one), was completely immersed in the details of human spatial organization as expressed in land use. In making a planning decision about a particular parcel of land, the city planner had little or no use for the aggregated and not very well-substantiated generalizations of the regional scientist, the economist, or the sociologist. He coloured the parcel red or green on his planning map according to his own intuitive evaluation of the design of the spatial form and his rough assessment of economic and social factors as he conceived of them (provided, of course, that his decision was not solely determined by the balance of political pressures). Webber, who has been one of the strongest advocates on the spatial design side for pushing the planner into a greater awareness of the social process, thus comments on the vital necessity for the planner to disabuse himself 'of some deep-seated doctrine that seeks order in simple mappable patterns, when it is really hiding in extremely complex social organization, instead'.[6]

There are, therefore, signs of some pressure for bringing the sociological and geographical imaginations together in the context of the city. But it has been a struggle to do so. More often than not geographical and sociological approaches have been regarded as unrelated or, at best, as viable alternatives to the analysis of city problems. Some have sought, for example, to modify the spatial form of a city and thereby to mould the social process to achieve the necessary goals (this has typically been the approach of physical planners from Howard on). Others have sought to place institutional constraints on the social process and hope that this alone will be enough to achieve necessary social goals. These strategies are not alternatives. They should be regarded as complementary. The trouble is that the use of one sometimes conflicts with the use of the other. Any successful strategy must appreciate that spatial form and social process are different ways of thinking about the same thing. We must therefore harmonize our thinking about them both or else create contradictory strategies for dealing with city problems. Webber thus complains of the 'idealogical campaign to reconstruct the preconceived city forms that matched the social structures of past eras', and goes on to plead for the 'emergence of a pragmatic problem-solving approach in which the spatial aspects of the metropolis are viewed as continuous with and defined by the processes of urban society'.[7] Leven has similarly pleaded for 'some kind of theoretical framework within which we identify factors which are determinants of city form and which, in turn, produce some spatial form in an analytically predictable way. Then we search for some method of evaluating the resultant spatial performance which, in turn, probably would feed back upon the determinants of spatial form themselves.'[8]

I think by now that my general point should be clear. The only adequate conceptual framework for understanding the city is one which encompasses and builds upon both the sociological and the geographical imagination. We must relate social behaviour to the way in which the city assumes a certain geography, a certain spatial form. We must recognize that once a particular spatial form is created it tends to institutionalize and, in some respects, to determine the future development of the social process. We need, above all, to formulate concepts which will allow us to harmonize and integrate strategies to deal with the intricacies of the social process and the elements of the spatial form. And it is to this task that I now want to turn.

Towards a Philosophy of Social Space

It may seem strange to begin the quest to bridge the gap between the sociological and geographical imagination by giving detailed consideration to the situation on the geographical side of the fence. But it is useful to begin at this point because those imbued with a keen sense of space have, by and large, failed to articulate a view of space which is capable of analytic treatment and which can readily be understood by the analysts of the social process. If we attempt to understand more thoroughly what we mean by space, then I think that some of the problems which appear to lie in the way of our bridge-building effort will disappear.

There is, of course, a very substantial literature dealing with the philosophy of space. The trouble is that most of it is concerned with interpreting the meaning of space as it is conceptualized in modern physics. This is helpful in certain respects, but it is rather a special view of space, and I am not sure that it has any general validity for the examination of social activity. Other views need to be considered. In order to make this point clear, I shall need to develop some simple ideas regarding the modes of spatial experience, and the ways in which we can analyse that experience. Cassirer provides a useful starting-point here for he is one of the few philosophers who has taken a very general view of space. He differentiates between three basic categories of spatial experience.[9] The first *organic space*, refers to the kind of spatial experience which appears to be genetically transmitted and, hence, biologically determined. Much of the behaviour examined by ethologists (instinctive spatial orientation and migration, instinctive territoriality, and so on) fits into this category. The second, *perceptual space*, is far more complex. It involves the neurological synthesis of all kinds of sense experience—optical, tactual, accoustic, and kinesthetic. This synthesis amounts to a spatial experience in which the evidence of various senses is reconciled. An instantaneous schema or impression may be formed and memory may lead to the retention of that schema or impression over time. When memory and learning are involved, the schema may be subject to addition or subtraction by culturally learned modes of thought. Perceptual space is primarily experienced through the senses, but we do not yet know how far the performance of our senses is affected by cultural conditioning.[10] The third kind of spatial experience is entirely abstract; Cassirer calls this *symbolic space*. Here, we are experiencing space vicariously through the interpretation of symbolic representations which have no spatial dimension. I can conjure up an impression of a triangle without seeing one simply by looking at the word 'triangle'. I can gain experience of spatial form by learning mathematics and in particular, of course, geometry. Geometry provides a convenient symbolic language for discussing and learning about spatial form, but it is not the spatial form itself.

These three levels of spatial experience are not independent of each other. The abstract geometries which we construct require some interpretation at the perceptual level if they are to make intuitive rather than logical sense—hence, all the diagrams which a typical textbook in geometry provides. Our perceptual experience may be modified by things we learn from abstract analysis. The perceptual experience may be affected by organic experience. But, if we are to build an analytically tractable theory of spatial form, we must eventually resort to formal geometry. We need, therefore, to find some way of representing events as they occur on the perceptual or organic level by some abstract symbolic system which forms a geometry. Conversely, we may regard it as finding some interpretation on the organic or perceptual level for ideas developed purely at the abstract level.

I have discussed elsewhere some of the problems that arise in this process of transferring experience gained at one level to a mode of experience operating at another level.[11] The main thrust of the argument was that we need to demonstrate some structural isomorphism between the geometry used and the particular perceptual experience or set of experiences under analysis. Where such an isomorphism exists, we can 'map' the information derived from the perceptual plane into a geometry for analytic treatment. A successful mapping is one that allows us to transfer conclusions from the analytic geometry back into the realm of perceptual experience in such a way that we gain control or predictive power over the perceptual situation. On a flat plane surface, for example, I can predict physical distances between many objects from just a few key measurements, and I can do it by the use of Euclidean geometry and its derivative trigonometry. This example is an important one. Long experience of such mapping has taught us that Euclidean geometry is the relevant geometry for discussing the organization of objects in physical space—at least as far as earth-bound phenomena are concerned. Euclidean geometry is also the geometry in which the engineering process and the physical construction process find automatic expression, since it is the 'natural' geometry for working with physical laws as they operate on the earth's surface.

It might appear from this that all we require for an analytic treatment of spatial form is some development out of Euclidean geometry. We do not yet have such a development; we have not yet devised adequate methods for generalizing about shape, pattern, and form on such Euclidean surfaces, for example. But, even given this development, our problems would be far from over simply because social space is not isomorphic with physical space. Here, the history of physics has something very important to teach us. We cannot expect that the kind of geometry appropriate for discussing one kind of process will be adequate to deal with another process. The selection of an appropriate geometry is essentially an empirical problem, and we must demonstrate (either by successful application or by the study of structural isomorphisms) how particular kinds of perceptual experience can validly be mapped into a particular geometry.[12] In general, the philosophers of space tell us, we cannot select an appropriate geometry independent of some process, for it is the process which defines the nature of the co-ordinate system we must use for its analysis. This conclusion can, I believe, be transferred intact to the social sphere. Each form of social activity defines its space; there is no evidence that such spaces are Euclidean or even that they are remotely similar to each other. From this we have the geographer's concept of socio-economic space, the psychologist's and anthropologist's concept of 'personal space', and so on. A primary need, if we are to understand the spatial form of the city, therefore, is the articulation of an adequate philosophy of social space. In so far as we can only understand social space by reference to some social activity, we are forced to attempt an integration of the sociological and the geographical imagination.

The construction of a philosophy of social space will be difficult, for we need far more knowledge about the processes which go on in the perceptual realm of spatial experience. We know very little, for example, about the exact manner in which the artist or architect fashions space to transmit an aesthetic experience. We know that he often succeeds (or fails), but we scarcely know how. We know that the principles upon which an architect fashions space are very different from the principles employed by the engineer. Good architecture presumably incorporates two sets of principles of spatial organization—one set designed to prevent the structure created from violating physical constraints, and the other set designed to facilitate the transference of some aesthetic experience. The physical principles pose no problem—they are Euclidean and analytically tractable. The aesthetic principles are extremely difficult to deal with. Langer provides an interesting starting point for a theory of space in art.[13] She hypothesises that 'the space in which we live and act is not what is treated in art at all', for the space in which we have our physical being is a system of relationships whereas the space of art is a created space built out of forms, colours, and so on. Thus the visual space defined by a painting is essentially an illusion ... 'like the space "behind" the surface of a mirror, it is what the physicists call "virtual space"—an intangible image. This virtual space is the primary illusion of all plastic art.' In a later section, Langer goes on to extend this concept to architecture.[14] Architecture clearly has actual function, and it also defines and arranges spatial units in terms of actual spatial relationships which have meaning for us in terms of the space in which we live and move. But nevertheless, 'architecture is a plastic art, and its first achievement is always, unconsciously and inevitably, an illusion: something purely imaginary or conceptual translated into visual impression.'

What is this something which we translate into a visual impression? Architecture, suggests Langer, is an *ethnic domains*—'a physically present human environment that expresses the characteristic rhythmic functional patterns which constitute a culture'. In other words, the shaping of space which goes on in architecture and, therefore, in the city is a shaping which is symbolic of our culture, symbolic of the existing social order, symbolic of our aspirations, our needs, and our fears. If, therefore, we are to evaluate the spatial form of the city, we must, somehow or other, understand its creative meaning as well as its mere physical dimensions.

It has been an important principle in art and architecture that spatial form can be manipulated in various ways to yield various symbolic meanings. Until recently we have failed to study this process scientifically. There is a growing literature on the psychological aspects of art and a growing realization that we need some understanding of how the man-made environment takes on meaning for its inhabitants. The interiors of buildings, for example, often signify much about the nature of the social order and the nature of the social processes which are supposed to go on inside it. The design of a medieval church has much to say about the nature of the social hierarchy simply through the spatial relationship which some individual has to the central focal point. It is no accident that those in the choir somehow seemed closer to God (and hence more privileged) than those in the nave. Sommer has extended this principle and sought to show how different kinds of spatial design in a wide variety of contexts can affect human behaviour and activity systems.[15] This work is young, but it may not be too long before it yields some useful principles for understanding the role that spatial symbolism plays in affecting human behaviour. The same principles are perhaps applicable at a more general scale. Levi-Strauss has shown how the spatial layout of a whole village in a primitive culture may reflect in detail the mythology of the people and the social relationships which exist among various groups in the population.[16] The layout of a typical eighteenth-century village in England has much to say about the social order as it then existed with its dual sources of power in the Church and the nobility. Lowenthal and Prince have similarly noted how each age fashions its environment to reflect existing social norms.[17] The city as a whole, even the modern amorphous version of it, still possesses this symbolic quality. It is no accident that church and chapel spires dream over Oxford (a town created in the age of church power), whereas, in the age of monopoly capitalism, it is the Chrysler building and the Chase-Manhattan Bank building which brood over Manhattan Island. These are all crude examples, and the interactions between spatial form, symbolic meaning, and spatial behaviour are probably very complex. It is important that we understand these interactions if we are not (to quote Webber again) 'to reconstruct the preconceived city forms that matched the social structures of past eras'. The basic point I am trying to make is that, if we are to understand spatial form, we must first inquire into the symbolic qualities of that form. How can this be done?

I doubt very much whether we shall ever truly understand the intuitions which lead a creative artist to mould space to convey a message. But, I think we can go a long way to understanding the impact which that message has upon the people who receive it. In terms of the activity pattern of the total population, it is this reaction which we must learn to gauge. If the city contains all manner of signals and symbols, then we can try to understand the meaning which people give to them. We must seek to understand the message which people receive from their constructed environment. To do this we need a very general methodology for the measurement of spatial and environment symbolism. Here, the techniques of psycholinguistics and psychology have much to recommend them.[18] These techniques allow us to assess the significance of an object or event by examining the behavioural disposition to act with respect to it. We can tap this behavioural disposition in a number of ways. We can sample the mental state of the individual or of a group of individuals and discover their attitudes towards and their perceptions of the space which surrounds them. We can use a variety of techniques to do this from personal construct theory, semantic differential, through to more direct questionnaire techniques. The aim here is to try to evaluate the cognitive state of the individual with respect to his spatial environment. An alternative, favoured by behaviourists and operant psychologists, is simply to observe peoples' behaviour and, on the basis of this overt behaviour, gauge their reaction to objects and events. In this case, it is overt behaviour in space which provides us with the necessary clues to understand spatial significance. Practical considerations make it almost impossible to use anything other than overt behaviour when large aggregates of population are involved as, for example, in the study of journey-to-work and journey-to-shop phenomena as they occur at the total city scale of analysis.

A number of difficulties arise from using these techniques to measure the impact of the spatial symbolism that exists in the city. At the aggregative level, we have to rely upon the information provided by a generalized description of spatial activity in the city and this activity pattern may be a function of all kinds of things which have nothing to do with spatial form and spatial meaning. There is undoubtedly a substantial portion of the social process which operates independently of spatial form, and we need to know what portion of the activity is influenced by spatial form and which portion remains relatively independent. Even at the microlevel, we still face the problem that experimental controls over unwanted variables are difficult to institute. We can learn a lot from laboratory experiments on the reaction to various forms of spatially organized stimuli—reactions to complexity, depth perception, associations in meaning, pattern preferences, and so on, but it is extremely difficult to relate these findings to complex activity patterns as they unfold in the city.[19] Nevertheless, there is a growing (and very stimulating) literature on the behavioural responses to certain aspects of environmental design and on the way in which individuals react to and schematize various aspects of the spatial form that is the city.[20] I do not want to review these studies here, but I do want to try to identify the general philosophical framework for thinking which they point to.

This framework is one in which space only takes on meaning in terms of 'significant relationships', and a significant relationship cannot be determined independent of the cognitive state of some individual and the context in which that individual finds himself. Social space, therefore, is made up of a complex of individual feelings and images about and reactions towards the spatial symbolism which surrounds that individual. Each person, it seems, lives in his own personally constructed web of spatial relationships, contained, as it were, in his own geometric system. All this would make for a depressing picture from the analytic point of view, if it were not for the fact that groups of people appear to identify substantially similar images with respect to the space that surrounds them and also appear to develop similar ways of judging significance and behaving in space.[21] The evidence is far from being secure, but, at this stage, it seems reasonable to adopt as a working hypothesis the view that individuals possess some proportion (as yet undetermined) of 'common image' derived from some group norms (and probably certain norms in acting with respect to that image), and a proportion of 'unique image' which is highly idiosyncratic and unpredictable. It is the common part of the spatial image which we must first concern ourselves with, if we are to squeeze out some details of the real nature of social space.

I have already suggested that the material so far gathered on spatial images is very sparse. But it is very suggestive. Lynch, for example, indicates that individuals construct spatial schemas which hang together topologically—the typical Bostonian appears to move from one focal point (or node) to another along well-defined paths.[22] This leaves vast areas of the physical space which are not touched and are indeed unknown as far as the individual is concerned. The implication of this particular study is that we should think of city organization with the analytic tools of topology rather than with Euclidean geometry. Lynch also suggests that certain features in the physical environment create 'edges' beyond which the individual does not typically penetrate. Both Lee and Steinitz confirm his finding that boundaries can be identified for some areas in a city, and these areas seem to form distinctive neighbourhoods.[23] In some cases, these boundaries may be easily traversed, but, in other cases, they may act as barriers to movement in the city—ghetto avoidance behaviour on the part of middle-class whites and the strong prescriptive territoriality which can be found among certain ethnic and religious groups (as in Protestant-Catholic areas of Northern Ireland) are good examples. So we can expect strong discontinuities in socially measured spatial structures. At a more aggregated level (say the total journey-to-work pattern in a city), many of the individual differences in mental images may counteract each other and amount to some kind of random noise in a system which is capable of being tackled descriptively. But even at this level the evidence suggests that there is a good deal of inhomogeneity in spatial behaviour even when aggregated into very large groups for the purpose of developing gross interaction models of the city. There are distinctive group behaviours some but not all of which may be explicable in terms of the sociological characteristics of the group (age, occupation, income, etc.), and distinctive activity styles which suggest that rather different parts of the city have rather different attractive power. In these cases, we may be justified in generalizing to a more continuous geometry, but, even here, the work of geographers suggests that the space is far from being a simple Euclidean one.[24] At this point, we become involved in the question of the exact nature of the socio-economic surface we are dealing with and the problem of finding adequate transformations to permit the analysis of events on that surface.[25] In general, we have to conclude that social space is complex, nonhomogeneous, perhaps discontinuous, and almost certainly different from the physical space in which the engineer and the planner typically work.

The question then arises as to how these notions of personal space arise, how they are moulded by experience, and how stable they are in the face of a changing spatial form. Again, the evidence available to us is sparse. Much of the work of Piaget and Inhelder has to do with the way in which spatial consciousness develops in the young.[26] There seem to be distinctive evolutionary stages going from topology through projective relationships to Euclidean formulation of concepts of physical space. It appears, however, that children do not necessarily learn the same spatial ability in all cultures, particularly as far as schematizing spatial information is concerned.[27] The evidence suggests that cultural conditioning, group learning, and individual learning are involved in the formation of an individual's spatial schema. It is quite probable that different culture groups develop totally different styles of representing spatial relationships, and these styles may, in themselves, be directly related to social processes and norms. Different groups within a population may therefore have rather different spatial schematic abilities, and education undoubtedly plays an important role in determining spatial ability.[28] Certainly, there is a good deal of variance in any population as regards the ability to read maps, to maintain a sense of direction, and so on. There is also considerable variation in the way in which individuals or groups construct mental schemas. Perhaps the simplest is to remember relationships by rote learning (this appears to be characteristic of many primitive and poorly educated peoples). Others may have simple co-ordinate referencing systems developed to pigeon-hole experiences, and others may have far more complex (and perhaps even inconsistent) ways of schematizing spatial relationships. But much of the information which is built up on a spatial schema must be the result of individual experience, and the schema is likely to undergo continual change as more experience is had. The nature of that experience may be crucial to determining the symbolism—the area of a city you hate to go near because of unhappy memories; the area you always associate with good times. Experience continues to accrue, and that experience may modify or extend the nature of the mental map or the spatial form as recorded in the image. Memory itself may fade and parts of the spatial image which are not reinforced may very quickly disappear. Social space is not only variable from individual to individual and from group to group; *it is also variable over time.*

I have attempted to demonstrate in this section that space is not as simple as the physicists or the philosophers of science would have us believe. If we are to understand space, we must consider its symbolic meaning and its complex impact upon behaviour as it is mediated by the cognitive processes. One of the benefits of developing this view of space is that it is a view which seems capable of integrating the geographical and the sociological imaginations, for, without an adequate understanding of social processes in all their complexity, we cannot hope to understand social space in all its complexity.

Some Methodological Problems at the Interface

In the preceding section, I sought to show that an understanding of space in all of its complexity depends upon an appreciation of social processes. It would, I think, be possible to advance a similar argument with respect to social processes: that an understanding of the social process in all its complexity depends upon an appreciation of spatial form. Rather than attempt such an argument, however, I prefer to consider the methodological problems which lie at the interface between sociological and geographical work. This will demonstrate how difficult work at the interface is likely to be, and it will also provide some evidence for the importance of spatial form to study of the social process as it manifests itself in the city.

The bridge between the sociological and geographical imaginations can be built only if we possess adequate tools. These tools amount to a set of concepts and techniques which can be used to weld the two sides together. If the resultant construct is to be capable of analytic elaboration and susceptible to empirical testing, then mathematical and statistical methods will be needed. We must, therefore, identify the mathematical and statistical methods which will allow us to build the bridge. It seems likely that these methods will not be identifiable except in a given context. If, for example, we are interested in the interaction between spatial symbolism of the city, the mental maps of individuals, their states of stress, and their patterns of social and spatial behaviour, then we will require one set of tools. If we are interested in the gross aggregate changing form of the city and the gross social dynamics which are associated with that changing form, we shall require a different set. In the first case, we need a language which is capable of embracing the complexities of varying individual geometries and social activity systems. In the second case, we can afford to ignore the details of individual behaviour and content ourselves with examining the relationship between the spatial form of the city and overt aggregative behaviour in it. I cannot, therefore, set up any general methodological framework for working at the interface. I can, however, demonstrate the kinds of problem we face by examining the tools we possess for bridge-building in a certain context, namely, that of analysing the gross spatial form of a city and aggregate overt behaviour patterns within it. In this context, I want to concentrate upon the problem of inference and predictive control. I choose this particular focus because as Harris points out, planners are interested in making 'conditional predictions regarding function and development', and this does not differ from the interest of the social scientist who uses conditional prediction as a means for validating a theory.[29] Therefore, both prediction and theory formation as regards the city will depend upon the existence of a valid framework for setting up tests and making inferences. As I shall seek to show, such a framework does not exist at the present time. I have space to consider only selected aspects of this problem, and I choose to examine the problems of individuation, confounding, and statistical inference.

Individuation

It is generally agreed that an initial step in setting up a framework for inference is to define a set of individuals which make up a population. The process of defining an individual is termed 'individuation', and it is clearly very important. Logicians such as Wilson and Carnap have examined some general problems which arise in individuation.[30] One important distinction which they draw is that between individuation in *substance languages* and individuation in *space-time languages*. In the first kind of language, an individual may be defined by specifying a set of properties $(p_1, p_2, p_3, \ldots p_n)$ which the individual possesses—we may individuate a 'town' by stating the minimum size of the agglomeration, the nature of the employment structure, and so on. In the space-time language, however, the individuation depends upon specifying the location of an object within a co-ordinate structure which represents space and time (conventionally written as x, y, z, t). These two language systems have rather different properties, and it is therefore dangerous and difficult to mix them in the individuation process. The researcher on social processes characteristically uses a property language whereas the purely geographical approach makes use of the space-time language. Bridging the gap between the two involves making use of the two languages simultaneously or, preferably, writing some metalanguage which embraces the relevant character-istics of both languages. Such a metalanguage does not at present exist and some of the initial investigations into its properties indicate that its development will not be easy.[31] For our immediate purposes, therefore, we must remain content with using the two languages in the same context. The dangers in this procedure can best be demonstrated by examining the process of regionalization.

Consider the notion of 'equality' in the two languages. It is feasible in the substance language for two individuals to occupy the same position (two towns may have exactly the same population size, etc.) but such a condition is not possible in the space-time language (two towns cannot occupy exactly the same location). But individuals, once identified, can have many properties attached to them so that it is possible to identify many properties at a space-time location. One relevant property might be relative location (distances relative to other places). So space can be used to individuate objects, or it may be treated as a property of individuals defined in either a space-time or in a substance language. So, the two languages have different characteristics and space itself can enter into either language but in different ways.[32] It is scarcely surprising that this situation has generated a lot of philosophical and methodological confusion and that the regionalization problem is a controversial one. The controversy usually results from a failure to identify how and when the different languages are being used. Taylor has indicated that confusion arises because 'of a failure to appreciate that location occurs twice in the problem'.[33] We may use location as a discriminant variable (in which case we are treating spatial location as a property of individuals), or we may accept a given division of the space into locational units and use these space-time individuals (such as administrative areas) to collect information in a substance language. Regionalization may then be based on proximity in the substance language. We can also adopt various combinations or strategies, such as introducing contiguity constraints (i.e. using space as a property) in the grouping procedure, or searching for space-time individuals which are homogeneous with respect to certain property characteristics (this yields us uniform regions). Typically the urban planner accepts a set of locational units (usually census tracts), measures variables in each tract, and he may then group tracts according to similarity of properties while observing a contiguity constraint. I do not, however, want to discuss these strategies in detail for I have made my main point: the process of individuation at the interface between the sociological and geographical imagination requires a thorough understanding of two rather different languages and an adequate methodology to govern their combination. This may seem an obscure point in some respects, yet it is the basic methodological issue which lies behind the confusion of the planner when trying to combine ideas about physical neighbourhood (usually thought of in the space-time language) and social functioning (usually thought of in the substance language). The policy conclusions which a planner reaches may thus depend upon which language he regards as dominant and upon exactly how he combines the two languages into some framework for analysis.

Confounding

One of the trickiest problems to resolve at the interface is to control unwanted variables and to identify the role of each individual variable in complex interacting nonexperimental situations. Without an adequate experimental design procedure, it is all too easy to confound one variable with another, to confound causes with effects, to confound functional relationships with causal relationships, and to commit any number of first-order inferential sins. It is easy, of course, to be rather purist and negative about this, but, even if we attempt to be positive and do not insist upon a premature rigour, the problems still impinge upon us at every turn in research design. Consider the following simple example. The sociologist typically looks at the diffusion process as it operates between individuals, groups, social classes, cultures, and so on. The relevant variables in predicting the diffusion relate back to the personality characteristics of the individual. The geographer typically looks at the spatial aspect and regards locational proximity as the prime variable in determining the course of a diffusion process. Now, it so happens that people of the same class tend to live in proximity to one another. How, then, are we to distinguish how much the spatial variable contributes, and how much the personality variables contribute? In any situation, we must examine their joint effect, and, unfortunately, the two aspects are not independent of each other. We do not appear to possess adequate nonexperimental research designs to allow us to handle this sort of problem in any but the crudest fashion.

These problems of confounding, however, exist in work on the social process even when it is thought of as being independent of spatial form. It would thus seem as important for the sociologist working in his own sphere to try to eliminate spatial effects from his argument as it is for the geographer to eliminate the social effects from his. If these confounding effects are not eliminated in the research design, then it will be all too easy to get statistically significant but really spurious support for hypotheses. My own suspicion is that much of the work on social processes suffers because it fails to recognize the acute inferential problems which may arise from confounding spatial with sociological effects. Much of the work on the purely spatial side can similarly be criticized. Working at the interface does not, therefore, pose any new problems; it does shed light on the true nature of some of the old, and it also demonstrates that the social analyst and the spatial analyst cannot afford to work in ignorance of each other.

Statistical Inference

The problems of individuation and confounding lead to those of statistical inference. The problems involved are easy enough of explication but extraordinarily difficult of resolution. Ideally, we need a metalanguage in which we can discuss statistical significance in both a sociological and spatial sense simultaneously. Lacking such a metalanguage, we must resort to tests derived in the two separate languages and somehow combine them into a valid framework for statistical inference. The tests appropriate for validating hypotheses about a spaceless social process are well established. Under a given hypothesis, we can generate certain expectations and then seek to show that there is no significant difference between expectation and observation data. The lack of any significant difference is generally taken to mean that the hypothesis is confirmed, although this is only true under certain assumptions about the way in which the observed results are generated (e.g. eliminating all confounding variables), the way in which the hypothesis is set up, and so on. The tests appropriate for spatial distribution patterns are not so well established. We can generate certain spatial expectations and then compare these expectations with observed spatial distributions. Tests do exist to compare spatial arrangements of cell-type data.[34] The comparison of two surfaces, however, is not so easy, and we have no way of telling when an expected surface is significantly different from an observed surface. Similarly, we have no real understanding of the meaning of significant difference in point pattern arrangement. In general, therefore, there is no accepted definition of statistical significance in spatial inference and consequently there are serious problems inherent in the testing of hypotheses about spatial distributions. It seems that the only way in which we can formulate notions of significance is to make assumptions about the nature of the spatial distribution. Since we are often concerned to identify, rather than to assume away the spatial distribution, this approach is not always as helpful as it might seem. It appears, however, to be the only course open to us at the present time. For this reason, it is very easy to criticize the current methods of dealing with spatial data.[35]

The combination of social and spatial procedures into one framework for statistical inference might still seem feasible. Consider the following example in which we seek to predict the spread of some social characteristic over space—say the spread of nonwhite population over a series of census tracts located in a city. Under a hypothesis, we may generate certain expectations regarding the number of nonwhites in each cell. In order to test this hypothesis, we need to show that the hypothesis generates the correct number of people in each cell. We can test this by comparing the distribution of cells in frequency classes as they occur under the hypothesis and as they occur in reality. We may find there is or is not a significant difference at the 5 per cent level. But, we also need to show that the model predicts the correct spatial arrangement of the cell predictions. We can use a k-colour contiguity test to show that at the 5 per cent level there is or is not a significant difference between the spatial pattern generated under hypothesis and the spatial pattern observed in reality. If the two tests are totally independent of each other, we can join these two significance levels by the multiplication rule and say that the joint test operates at the 0·25 per cent level of significance. But, it is clear that the two tests are not independent of each other. In fact, joining the two tests in this manner may (and frequently does) involve us in a conflict in statistical logic. The social process tests rely upon independence in each item of data if their assumptions are not to be violated, yet the spatial statistics are explicitly concerned with measuring the degree of spatial dependence in the data. Automatically, therefore, we inject into the social process test the problem of autocorrelation, and this means that we violate the assumptions of the test unless we can somehow or other take evasive action (by filtering the data, and so on). This problem arises at almost every point in work at the interface. It is certainly unresolved, and often it passes unrecognized. It has always seemed strange to me, for example, that multivariate methods of regionalization rely upon correlation measures which, if they are to be judged significant indicators, require independence in the data observations, when the objective of the whole procedure is to group units into regions which have similar (and hence spatially autocorrelated) characteristics. The method and the objective in this case seem to be logically inconsistent or, at best, to generate a set of regions which cannot be judged significant in any meaningful sense. This seems to me to form an insuperable objection to the use of factor analysis in regionalization schemes. The problem of autocorrelation has, however, been extensively explored in the econometric literature with respect to the time dimension, and we can draw certain encouragement (and certain techniques) from that field. But, as Granger has observed, there are important differences between the time dimension which conveniently possesses direction and irreversibility and the spatial dimensions which do not possess either of these properties and which may also be characterized by complex nonstationarities and awkward discontinuities.[36] These problems lead Granger to doubt if the techniques evolved in econometrics to deal with time series can be generalized to spatial series except for certain classes of problem. The spatial autocorrelation problem looks like a difficult one to resolve satisfactorily, and a sound framework for statistical inference at the interface depends upon its resolution.

I am forced to conclude that we do not possess very sharp tools for dissecting the problems which arise when we seek to blend together sociological and geographical techniques to deal with urban problems. Consequently, we must anticipate difficulty in making conditional predictions and in validating theory. This may sound a depressing situation, but we cannot resolve difficulties by pretending they do not exist. Indeed, the proper identification of them is essential if we are to set about sharpening our tools for bridge-building at the interface. Meanwhile, it is important to be aware of the possible sources of error in spatial forecasting and in theory construction. Self-deception regarding these errors is no training for the social scientist, the geographer, or the planner faced with making difficult policy decisions. Each needs a thorough education in the methodological limitations which surround him while working at the interface.

Strategy at the Interface

We need an adequate analytic framework for coping with the complex problems at the interface between social and spatial analysis. I do not think that an adequate metalanguage will be forthcoming in the near future to integrate the two approaches. We must therefore devise temporary frameworks with which to construct a theory of the city. In making use of these, however, we must be careful, for the framework we select can affect our notions of social justice, our notions of the proper role of the planner, and our policy priorities. It is unfortunately all too easy for a 'logic in use' to become associated with an entrenched philosophical position. This problem can be demonstrated by a look at two rather different modes of approach to city problems.

It is possible to regard the spatial form of a city as a basic determinant of human behaviour. This 'spatial environmental determinism' is a working hypothesis of those physical planners who seek to promote a new social order by manipulating the spatial environment of the city.[37] It is also a convenient way to break into some of the complexities of the interaction between spatial form and social process for it sets up a simple causal framework in which spatial form affects social process. In some cases, this point of view appears to have become an entrenched philosophy, and, as such, it has come under attack of late. The democratic notion that what people want is important, together with some evidence (by no means conclusive) that altering the spatial environment may have little effect upon behaviour patterns, has led writers such as Gans, Jacobs, and Webber to attack the notion of spatial environmental determinism and to draw attention to an alternative working hypothesis in which a social process is viewed as possessing its own dynamic which, often in spite of the planner, will achieve its own appropriate spatial form.[38] Webber argues, for example, that a new spatial order is emerging as a response to changing technology and changing social norms. The planner cannot prevent this order. He can only delay its achievement or impair its efficiency. This working hypothesis, which reverses the cause relationship proposed in the first, seems to have become an entrenched philosophical position with some writers. The planner, according to this view, should be seen as a servant of the social process and not its master.

The differences between these two seemingly alternative approaches are a good deal more complicated than the argument of the preceding paragraph indicates. Undoubtedly, many of the early physical planners possessed a very naive kind of spatial environmental determinism in which a few rehousing projects, a few parks, and the like, were regarded as adequate cures for complex social ills. This approach is demonstrably untrue. But the modern environmental designers are very much more aware of the subtleties that exist in the relationship between an environment and a person's behaviour.[39] They recognize that there is little hard evidence upon which to base ideas about good city design, and they are concerned to provide it. Modern proponents of both approaches are also likely to acknowledge the role of feedback. The spatial environmentalist will know that if he alters the spatial structure of the transport network then the social process will probably generate quite substantial land-use changes. The social determinist will also recognize that if the social process is moving towards some dominant norm (say communication by automobile) then the creation of a spatial form suited for that norm can only reinforce it—most modern American cities are not built for walking in and, therefore, reinforce the need for car ownership and use. The differences between the two approaches are more subtle at the present time, but they are still important. Consider the following two quotations:

There is considerable evidence that the physical environment does not play as significant a role in people's lives as the planner believes. Although people reside, work and play in buildings, their behaviour is not determined by the buildings, but by the economic, cultural, and social relationships within them. Bad design can interfere with what goes on inside a building, of course, and good design can aid it, but design *per se* does not significantly shape human behaviour.[40]

Good design becomes meaningless tautology if we consider that man will be reshaped to fit whatever environment he creates. The long-range question is not so much what sort of environment we want, but what sort of man we want.[41]

At the present time, it does not seem to be relevant to debate the pros and cons of these approaches. The evidence is too slender, and the hypotheses are too ambiguous. It is perhaps more reasonable to regard the city as a complex dynamic system in which spatial form and social process are in continuous interaction with each other. If we are to understand the trajectory of the urban system, we must understand the functional relationships which exist within it, and the independent features in the social process and in the spatial form which can change the line of that trajectory. It is unnecessarily naive to think in terms of simple causal relationships between spatial form and social process (whichever way we choose to point the causal arrow). The system is much more complex than that. The two sides are inextricably interrelated. The two approaches should therefore be regarded as complementary rather than as mutually exclusive alternatives. Yet, it is often necessary to break into some complex interacting system, at some point, if any information is to be generated. Whether we choose to do so at the point of spatial form (and regard the social process as an output), at the point of the social process (and regard the spatial form as an output), or to devise some more complicated approach (with feedbacks and so on) should be a decision governed by convenience rather than by philosophy.

But all of these approaches are naive in the sense that they presuppose the existence of an adequate language to discuss spatial form and social process simultaneously. Such a language does not exist. We usually abstract from the complex system that is the city into a language to handle the social process or a language to handle the spatial form. Given this mode of abstraction, we cannot meaningfully talk about spatial form *causing* a social process (or vice versa) nor is it really correct to regard spatial form and social process as if they are variables which are somehow in continuous interaction with each other. What we are really trying to do is to translate results generated in one language (say a social process language) into another language (the spatial form language). These translations allow us to say something about the implications of one style of analysis for another style of analysis. It is rather like translating from a geometric result to an algebraic result (and vice versa) in that both languages amount to different ways of saying the same thing. The problem with the spatial form social process translation, however, is that there are no well-established rules for it. Under certain conditions, we can build frameworks to handle both dimensions simultaneously. Consider a simple programming problem in which we seek to optimize levels of activity at certain points in a network by minimizing transport costs. The solution is fairly simple all the time the network remains fixed. But, if we allow the network to alter, the number of activity points to change, as well as activity levels to vary, then we have a very complicated problem on our hands. The number of combinations quickly become astronomical, but very small problems of this type can be handled by combinatorial analysis. I suspect that certain simple problems which occur in city

planning or in environmental design can be treated in both dimensions simultaneously. But we are, for the most part, forced to keep either spatial form constant
(in which case we can solve quite complicated social process problems) or to keep
social process constant (in which case we can solve quite complicated spatial form
problems). In each case, we can only find a solution on one side by making fairly
strict assumptions about the conditions which exist on the other. This suggests that
one appropriate strategy for working at the interface is an iterative one in which we
move from spatial form manipulation (with social process held constant) to the
social process implications (with the new spatial form held constant). We can move
in either direction, and there is no reason why we should not manipulate both
spatial form and social process at different steps in an iterative sequence. This seems
to be the style that is developing in urban modelling. Several alternative spatial
designs are generated, and they are then evaluated in terms of some social process
(usually economic efficiency or cost-benefit), and evaluations compared to
determine the best design. In other cases, one part of the spatial design is altered,
and the impact upon other facets of the spatial design is then examined by way of a
spatial allocation model which makes strict assumptions about the nature of the
social process. This iterative approach is clearly very useful when taken in
combination with simulation techniques. But it does, of course, have some
important drawbacks, the most important of which is that it involves a translation
from one language to another when the rules of translation are assumed rather than
known. These assumed rules can have an important impact upon the results. This
can best be demonstrated by the problems that arise from the usual strategy
adopted in location theory.

The starting-point of location theory is that space can be translated into an
economic commodity by way of transport costs and that transport cost can then be
substituted into a social process model designed to find equilibrium production
conditions for each industry or firm. Once these equilibrium conditions have been
specified, the results are then translated back into spatial form results by making
certain assumptions about the nature of the conditions which exist on some surface
(equal transport facilities, flat plane surfaces, and so on). It is generally held,
however, that these assumptions are mere conveniences and that they do not in any
way interfere with the equilibrium conditions defined in the process model. This
supposition can be criticized on a number of grounds. In the first place the problem
of feedback has to be overcome. In the Löschian case, for example, the population
change which must result from an achievement of equilibrium must disturb the
nature of the spatial form conditions which allow that equilibrium to be spatially
specified.[42] The urban system presumably develops some trajectory and there is no
guarantee that any real equilibrium can be reached in the social process because the
spatial form is constantly changing. The system may, therefore, be an explosive one
which does not stabilize. In the spatial sense, the main trend is towards
agglomeration, therefore, it might be more appropriate to call the system an
implosive one. A second major citicism, however, is that the geometric assumptions
themselves have an impact upon the specification of equilibrium. If we assume a
beach of finite length, the social activity of three ice-cream sellers becomes
theoretically indeterminate, and it is no accident that most of location theory
assumes infinite plane surfaces, for, without this assumption, the social process
equilibrium point often cannot be determined. In general, the spatial form
assumptions injected into location theory are more than mere conveniences—they
are fundamental to the results. Let me make clear that I am not attacking the

location theorist or the urban analyst for making assumptions about spatial form. In practice, I believe we have little choice but to use assumptions of that sort. But it is important to recognize that these are frail bridges with which to cross a huge gulf of a problem. We cannot possibly use them to discuss the kinds of complexity indicated earlier in which space itself is seen as multidimensional, nonhomogeneous, perhaps discontinuous, highly personalized, and meaningful in different ways in different social activity contexts. The location approach is operational, but we buy this operationalism at a cost. We ought therefore to be aware of how much we are paying in terms of realism when we adopt certain strategies, and in what ways the assumptions involved in a particular strategy are fundamental to the results of any analysis. We cannot avoid such questions in seeking to construct a genuine theory of the city. Ultimately, we may be able to transcend the problems inherent in our way of conceptualizing social processes and spatial form. Until that time, however, all we can do is to attempt some kind of evaluation of their implications and adapt our research strategies and our policy making accordingly. It is, after all, a major tenet of scientific thought that errors can only be estimated and combated if we have an understanding of the sources from which they arise.

NOTES AND REFERENCES

[1] C. Leven, 'Towards a Theory of the City', in G. Hemmens, ed., *Urban Development Models* (Washington: National Academy of Sciences, Highway Research Board Special Report 97, 1968).

[2] C. Wright Mills, *The Sociological Imagination* (New York: The Oxford University Press, 1959), p. 5.

[3] E. T. Hall, *The Hidden Dimension* (Garden City, New York: Doubleday & Company, Inc., 1966); A. I. Hallowell, *Culture and Experience* (Philadelphia: University of Pennsylvania Press, 1955); K. Lorenz, *On Aggression* (New York: Harcourt, Brace and Company, 1966); N. Tinbergen, *Social Behaviour in Animals* (London: Methuen & Co., Ltd., 1953); R. Sommer, *Personal Space: the Behavioral Basis of Design* (Englewood Cliffs, New Jersey: Prentice-Hall, Inc., 1969); J. Piaget and B. Inhelder, *The Child's Conception of Space* (London: Routledge and Kegan Paul Ltd., 1956); E. Cassirer, *An Essay on Man* (New Haven: Yale University Press, 1944) and *The Philosophy of Symbolic Form* (New Haven: Yale University Press, I, II, 1955, 1957); and S. K. Langer, *Feeling and Form: a Theory of Art* (New York: Charles Scribner's Sons, 1953).

[4] K. Lynch, *The Image of the City* (Cambridge: The M.I.T. Press, 1960); C. A. Doxiadis, *Ekistics* (New York: The Oxford University Press, 1968).

[5] See D. Harvey, *Explanation in Geography* (London: Edward Arnold, 1969) and A. Buttimer (Sister Mary Annette, O.P.), 'Interdisciplinary Perspective on Social Space,' *Geographical Review,* LIX, 1969 [also reproduced as Chapter 8 in the present work].

[6] M. Webber, 'Order in Diversity: Community without Propinquity', in L. Wingo, ed., *Cities and Space: the Future Use of Urban Land* (Baltimore: Md: The Johns Hopkins Press, 1963), p. 54.

[7] *Ibid.*

[8] Leven, op. cit., p. 108.

[9] Cassirer, *An Essay on Man,* op. cit., pp. 42–7.

[10] M. H. Segall, D. T. Campbell, and M. J. Herskovits, *The Influence of Culture on Visual Perception* (Indianapolis: The Bobbs-Merrill Company, 1966).

[11] Harvey, op. cit., Chap. 14.

[12] H. Reichenbach, *The Philosophy of Space and Time* (New York: Dover Publications, Inc., 1958), p. 6.

[13] Langer, op. cit., p. 72.

[14] Ibid., p. 93.

[15] Sommer, op. cit.

[16] C. Levi-Strauss, *Structural Anthropology* (English edition; New York: Basic Books, Inc., 1963).

17D. Lowenthal and H. Prince, 'The English Landscape', *Geographical Review*, 54 (1964), 304—46.

18I have reviewed some of these in D. Harvey, 'Conceptual and Measurement Problems in the Cognitive-Behavioral Approach to Location Theory', in K. R. Cox and R. G. Golledge, eds., *Behavioral Problems in Geography: a Symposium* (Evanston: Northwestern University, Northwestern Studies in Geography, No. 17, 1969).

19J. Hogg, ed., *Psychology and the Visual Arts* (Harmondsworth, England: Penguin Books Ltd., 1969).

20K. Craik, 'Human Responsiveness to Landscape: an Environmental Psychological Perspective', and A. Rapoport, 'Some Aspects of the Organization of Urban Space', in G. J. Coates and K. Moffett, eds., *Response to Environment* (Raleigh: North Carolina State University, School of Design, 1968).

21See for example, Chombart de Lauwe, *Paris et L'Agglomeration Parisienne* (Paris: CNRS 1952); S. Keller, *The Urban Neighborhood: a Sociological Perspective* (New York: Random House, (1969)); T. R. Lee, 'Urban Neighborhood as a Socio-Spatial Schema', *Human Relations*, November, 1968, pp. 241—67; Steinitz, C., 1968, 'Meaning and Congruence of Urban Form and Activity', *Journal of the American Institute of Planners*, 34 (1968), 233—48.

22Lynch, op. cit.

23Lee, op. cit.; Steinitz, op. cit.

24W. Tobler, 'Geographic Area and Map Projections', *Geographical Review*, 53 (1963), 59—78; W. Warntz, 'Global Science and the Tyranny of Space', *Papers of the Regional Science Association*, 19 (1967), 7—19.

25See Harvey, *Explanation in Geography*, op. cit., Chap. 14.

26Piaget and Inhelder, op. cit.

27F. E. Dart and L. Pradhan, 'Cross-Cultural Teaching of Science', *Science*, 155 (1967), 649—56.

28I. D. McFarlane Smith, *Spatial Ability* (New York: John Wiley & Sons, Inc., 1964).

29B. Harris, 'Quantitative Models of Urban Development: Their Role in Metropolitan Policy Making', in H. Perloff and L. Wingo, eds., *Issues in Urban Economics* (Baltimore: Md.: The Johns Hopkins Press, 1968), p. 363.

30R. Carnap, *An Introduction to Symbolic Logic*, (New York: Dover Publications, Inc., 1958); N. L. Wilson, 'Space, Time, and Individuals', *Journal of Philosophy*, 52 (1955), 589—98, I have summarized their argument in Harvey, *Explanation in Geography*, pp. 212—17.

31M. F. Dacey, 'Some Observations on a Two-Dimensional Language', Technical Report, No. 7, ONR Task No. 389—142 (Evanston: Northwestern University, Department of Geography, 1965).

32One of the best statements in philosophy is contained in G. Bergmann, *Logic and Reality* (Madison: University of Wisconsin Press, 1964), pp. 272—301.

33P. J. Taylor, 'The Location Variable in Taxonomy', *Geographical Analysis*, I (1969), 181—95.

34A. Cliff and K. Ord, 'The Problem of Spatial Autocorrelation', in A. Scott, ed., *Studies in Regional Science* (London: Pion 1969); M. F. Dacey, 'A Review on Measures of Contiguity for Two- and K-Colour Maps', in B. J. L. Berry and D. Marble, eds, *Spatial Analysis* (Englewood Cliffs, N.J.: Prentice-Hall Inc., 1968).

35C. W. Granger, 'Spatial Data and Time-Series Analysis', in A. Scott, ed., *Studies in Regional Science* (London: Pion, 1969).

36Ibid.

37Webber, op. cit., p. 32.

38Ibid.; H. J. Gans, 'Planning for People, not Buildings', *Environment and Planning*, I (1969), 33—46; J. Jacobs, *The Death and Life of Great American Cities* (New York: Random House, 1961).

39Sommer, op. cit.

40Gans, op. cit., pp. 37—8.

41Sommer, op. cit., p. 172.

42W. Isard, *Location and Space Economy* (New York: John Wiley & Sons, Inc., 1956), pp. 271—2.

21. DISPERSAL AND CHOICE: TOWARDS A STRATEGY FOR ETHNIC MINORITIES IN BRITAIN

N. Deakin and B. G. Cohen

In a situation in which clear guide-lines for policy are often almost impossible to discern, the notion of dispersal of immigrants stands out as a clear-cut policy goal to which assent has been given at one time or another by almost all those concerned with policy in the field of race relations.

The core of the argument for dispersal is that residential dispersal of minorities, by reducing the strain on social services in city-centre areas and by allowing encounters between black and white to take place in a context free from the frictions endemic in such areas, will greatly accelerate the dispersal in education and thereby slow down the growing trend towards 'ghetto schools'. In default of such dispersal, recourse has been had to clumsy expedients like the bussing of children, recommended by the Department of Education and Science in 1965 on the ground that: 'it is inevitable that, as the proportion of immigrant children in a school or class increases, the problems will become more difficult to resolve and the chances of assimilation more remote.' Hence, the introduction of dispersal should be seriously considered 'since it is to everybody's disadvantage if the problems within a school become so great that they cause a decline in the general standards of education provided'. (Department of Education and Science, 1965.) It is only recently that this orthodoxy has come to be challenged. The notion that there might be some virtue in the concentration of minorities has been inhibited by the poor material condition and deprived environment in the areas of settlement. However, as individual communities have taken root, some of the compensating advantages of concentrations have come to be appreciated. Their supportive value for newcomers, the basis they provide for communal institutions and services, and their function as a base for penetration of the political institutions of the majority society by minority group leaders are among these advantages. And, as always, the American example has been influential. The black militants' view of the ghetto, as a colony in which the oppressed minority must seize the levers of political and economic power and manipulate them to their own advantage, has gained ground rapidly (for instance, Carmichael and Hamilton, 1968), and has been accepted in part by the Administration, at least to the extent that the 'enrichment' strategy (injecting additional resources into the ghetto) rather than the integration strategy has now become the more fashionable policy.

The first serious attempt in Britain by a body directly involved with the evolution of official policy to deal with these new concepts of the countervailing disadvantages of dispersal has been made by a subcommittee of the Central Housing Advisory Committee under the chairmanship of Professor J. B. Cullingworth. In their report (Cullingworth, 1969) the Committee devotes a whole section (paragraphs 397—413) to the question of the dispersal of minorities. The conclusion was that in a situation where too little was known about the viability of a dispersal policy and its consequences for those most directly affected by it 'any

From *Environment and Planning*, 2 (1970), 193—201. Reprinted by permission of the authors and Pion Ltd.

policy of dispersal in the field of housing must be implemented with great sensitivity, with no element of compulsion or direction, and can proceed only at the pace of the needs and wishes of the people involved' (Cullingworth, 1969, paragraph 409). Basing themselves in part on evidence given by the Institute of Race Relations (paragraph 406), the Committee was inclined to think that there might be some differences between the needs and wishes of West Indians and of Asians: sufficient, at least, to impel them to underline the necessity for housing managers to ensure that they had made every effort to understand the wishes of different minority groups and not imposed a solution at the cost of breaking up stable and contented communities.

The Cullingworth Committee's important report goes some way towards clarifying the basic issues. But in view of the shortage of evidence on dispersal in the British context—which the committee rightly laments—the significance of the far better-documented American experience has continued to dominate discussion. Yet it is debatable whether this experience is relevant to an understanding of the implications of dispersal for a society in which ghettos, properly understood, do not exist and in which the cultural diversity of immigrant groups undermines all generalizations made about them. It is true that the coloured immigrant population is unevenly distributed within Britain with some major concentrations, especially in the conurbations. At the time of the 1966 Census, 59 per cent of those born in the three major areas of emigration (the Caribbean, India, and Pakistan) were found in just two of the conurbations—Greater London and the West Midlands (Deakin *et al.*, 1970). But on closer examination these concentrations prove to be comparatively thin and scattered. The highest concentration of coloured immigrants in any local authority area was 7·4 per cent in the London Borough of Brent. Nowhere outside London was there a local authority area at the time of the Census with 5 per cent of its population born in the three major areas of emigration. Doherty (1969) in his analysis of 1966 Census data for Greater London shows that there was no ward with a majority born in the New Commonwealth. The highest single concentration was in Northcote ward, Ealing, where just over 30 per cent of the population were born in the New Commonwealth (24 per cent of them in Asia). The proportion of those born in the West Indies—whom Doherty described as 'the most segregated of the immigrant groups, at least in residential terms'—barely topped 20 per cent in two wards in London. At the other end of the scale, only 9 per cent of the West Indian population of Greater London, compared to 60 per cent of the total G.L.C. population, lived in wards where West Indians comprised less than 1 per cent of the population. However, nearly half (43 per cent) the West Indian population of London live in wards where they comprise less than 5 per cent of the population. Earlier evidence from the 1961 Census showed a very similar pattern of concentration and dispersal, in Birmingham as well as London (Peach, 1968). Concentration, and areas where coloured immigrants are almost totally absent, are both common features of the residential pattern of the main conurbations. But it is clear that the situation has not yet reached a stage where direct parallels with the American predicament are justified. Even allowing for the under-enumeration of the coloured population and the fact that the figures quoted above exclude children born in this country, nothing approaching the all-coloured district yet exists.

Nevertheless, there are arguments for suggesting that the very fact that the situation has not yet reached the stage of *de facto* segregation underlines the importance of considering the possibilities for dispersal, at a stage when it can still be achieved without major social and economic upheaval. At the same time it is imperative to examine the alternative strategies implicit in Roy Jenkins's definition of integration as 'equal opportunity, accompanied by cultural diversity in an atmosphere of mutual tolerance'.* The difficulty is to strike a balance between the benefits which would undoubtedly flow from a measure of voluntary dispersal by minorities and the countervailing advantages of communal solidarity. That some guidance on this point is essential has been demonstrated by the experience of the Cullingworth Committee. Local authorities, who occupy a key position in this debate by virtue of their central position in the local housing market—another factor differentiating our situation from that of the United States—showed themselves in giving evidence both to be divided and uncertain about the legitimate aims of policy in this field, and to be anxious for a clear lead.

The first essential, if such a lead is to be provided, is to agree on what is meant by dispersal. Some of the more enthusiastic advocates of such a policy for this country have in mind a systematic programme analogous to that adopted by the Dutch Government to deal with Indonesian repatriates. It cannot be said too often that such a policy is no longer a practical possibility, whatever arguments there might have been in its favour fifteen years ago. The compulsory dispersal of newcomers, which, however humanely administered, should make democrats a shade queasy, can only be undertaken successfully if it is adopted from the beginning of a migration. Stop-gap measures of control by restricting the issue of employment vouchers in areas where concentrations of immigrants have built up will only be effective if supplemented by a measure of control through time over the employment of newcomers. Such control is open to all the objections urged against similar control when operated against aliens. Moreover, it could only be contemplated in the case of those newly admitted for employment—and such small numbers are now involved (less than 5,000 per annum) that such measures could have only marginal consequences for dispersal.

It should therefore be clear that what is under discussion is voluntary dispersal by minorities. Policies directed to this end could be divided into two categories—the elimination of obstacles and the provision of inducements. Both are related to the exercise of choice by the individual, and may influence the decisions he takes by providing him with additional information or incentives.

The obvious example in the first category is anti-discrimination legislation. During the passage of the Race Relations Act of 1968, the importance of those sections of the Act that relate to housing, in permitting the ambitious to escape from the poor conditions of the inner city and obtain better-quality housing in suburban districts free from the stresses characteristic of central areas, was repeatedly underlined. And there is no doubt that there will be those who will take advantage of this new opportunity. But such legislation opens up a potentiality: it does not provide the positive incentive that would help to set such a process in motion on a substantial scale.

Such momentum could be provided by new inducements offered to minorities. These could range from a stress on the improved educational opportunities available outside zones of concentration—and it is clear that the prospect of better school facilities is a powerful attraction to a group deeply concerned with the possibilities for advancement through the educational system—to the provision of better job opportunities.

* Address given by the Home Secretary, the Rt. Hon. Roy Jenkins, M.P., on 23 May 1966 to a meeting of Voluntary Liaison Committees (London N.C.C.I.).

At its broadest, this might mean no more than the Government, as part of the process by which it currently exercises influence over the location and development of industry, making available employment of a kind which might be attractive to immigrant workers outside the areas in which they are now concentrated. A concrete example often quoted in this context is that of the new towns. A paradox exists at present in the fact that the new towns are one of the few areas in the South-East which, although providing new job opportunities on a substantial scale, have not attracted immigrant labour in any numbers. In part, their failure to establish themselves in these areas can be ascribed to the operation of the Industrial Selection Scheme (see, for example, Cullingworth, 1969, paragraph 431). But given the high proportion of skilled and semi-skilled workers in the immigrant labour force, it is difficult to resist the conclusion that we should also look for explanations in the priorities adopted by Development Corporations. There are now signs that these attitudes are in the process of changing: an attempt to persuade coloured minorities, both through the usual media of communication and by making direct contact with organizations within the various immigrant communities and exploring the theme of the potentialities of new towns, might well have constructive consequences.

Finally, inducements to disperse can be seen at an altogether different level. It can be argued that, for the coloured individual, the move out of the area of concentration is the only step at present open to him as an individual that provides any real prospect of establishing himself in the broader setting of British society. It is arguable that this experience can be a painful one for those not prepared for the suspicion—and, occasionally, downright rejection—that they may encounter when first penetrating an all-white neighbourhood. None the less, the findings from a wide range of studies conducted in the United States by sociologists and social psychologists show that it is in the contacts between individuals of equivalent social status in an atmosphere free from competition and stress that the chief hope of reducing the incidence of prejudice lies. In a review of the literature in his important treatment of this theme, Pettigrew (1969) points to a whole range of studies confirming this finding in situations as varied as public housing estates, the merchant marine, a police force, an army platoon, department stores, and university campuses. The benefits of such contact are not confined to those members of the majority who learn to shed their prejudices. There is evidence to show that integrated schools tended to reinforce this effect by producing pupils, both black and white, who are more likely to live in an inter-racial neighbourhood and hold more positive racial attitudes, than comparable adults who have known only segregated schools (US Commission on Civil Rights, 1967). More than this, these schools tended to be the most effective in terms of educational performance (US Department of Health, Education, and Welfare, 1966). From this point of view, integration is not a symbolic gesture or a luxury only to be afforded by an ambitious black or brown bourgeoisie but a source of solid practical benefit.

Yet, even if it could be shown that the beneficial effects of education in an inter-racial environment devoid of stress did extend to schools in this country, and that this information was generally available to West Indian and Asian parents, it seems likely that at this stage in the evolution of race relations what Professor Pettigrew calls the 'comfortable solution'—the proximity of familiar faces and circumstances—will continue to prove more attractive to all but a minority within the minority. A majority will prefer, at least during the earlier stages of their adaptation to the new circumstances brought about by migration, to remain in the company of other members of the same ethnic group—especially at a time when hostility on the part of the majority is on the increase.

The evidence at present available suggests that while there is some general reinforcement of concentration, a degree of dispersal by individual members of minority groups to areas of low concentration is also occurring. The reinforcement of concentrations is a function of the growth in numbers due to natural increase and continuing migration. As the coloured population is generally younger than the white, and therefore has a higher birthrate, a tendency for there to be areas with growing concentrations of minority group members is to be expected. With continuing additions through migration, further reinforcement occurs but this is usually less than would be expected, as the new migrants often differ considerably from the existing population. Thus new entrants on employment vouchers include a very high proportion of professionals whose distribution is not necessarily similar to that of the coloured population as a whole. The main flow into the concentrations has come from the dependants of earlier migrants, who are distributed (as one would expect) very much in accordance with the existing pattern of settlement. However, there are some signs of dispersal. An illustration of this is shown in Table 1, which is derived from a reanalysis of 1966 Census data for the Greater London conurbation area. If two groups in the West Indian born population in London are compared—those living in boroughs of high concentration (defined as those containing more than 5,000 West Indians) and those in boroughs of low concentration (defined as those containing less than 2,500 West Indians)—differences emerge.* As can be seen from Table 1, over a quarter of the

TABLE 1

Proportion of West Indians living in selected London boroughs, 1966 sample Census, by previous residence one year earlier.

Residence one year before

Present residence	Same address	Same bor- ough	Another borough in rest of GLC	Rest of the South- East	Rest of England and Wales	Rest of UK	Others including abroad and not stated
Boroughs of high concentration[a]	74·2	14·9	6·8	0·2	0·4	—	3·4
Boroughs of low concentration[b]	71·3	6·2	16·9	1·5	0·7	—	3·4

[a] Boroughs of high concentration are defined as those containing more than 5,000 persons born in the West Indies—Brent, Hackney, Hammersmith, Haringey, Islington, Lambeth, Lewisham, Newham, Southwark, Wandsworth, Westminster.
[b] Boroughs of low concentration are defined as those containing less than 2,500 persons born in the West Indies—Barking, Barnet, Bexley, Bromley, Enfield, Greenwich, Harrow, Havering, Hillingdon, Hounslow, Kingston upon Thames, Merton, Redbridge, Richmond upon Thames, Sutton.

Sources: special tabulations by the Research and Intelligence Unit, GLC, of 1966 Census.

* As data for Asians in London are extremely unreliable, we have confined this comparison to West Indians. The West Indians are the largest coloured minority group in Britain, and well over half (57%) live in the GLC area. Thus, while the evidence here relates only to one minority group in one conurbation, it would seem to us to be of considerable basic importance in its own right, apart from any more general validity it might possess.

West Indians in boroughs of both high and low concentration had moved in the year previous to the Census. The significant difference was the proportion which had moved from another borough in the GLC area—17 per cent in 'dispersed' boroughs. As the bulk of the West Indian population of London (78 per cent) lived in the 'concentrated' boroughs and only 7 per cent lived in the 'dispersed' boroughs, it seems fair to assume that the majority of those who had moved into 'dispersed' boroughs from other boroughs had come from boroughs of high concentration. This flow into the dispersed boroughs, while considerable in terms of the West Indian population of the 'dispersed' boroughs, constituted only 1·1 per cent of the total West Indian population of London. But our definition of dispersal and concentrations is rather arbitrary and some dispersal may also be occurring within 'concentrated' boroughs.

Further examination of the profiles for West Indians who live in 'dispersed' and 'concentrated' boroughs shows that the housing situation of those in 'dispersed' areas is better. Thus, as can be seen in Table 2, West Indian households live at lower densities (persons per room) in dispersed boroughs and when one considers extremes of over-crowding—over 1·5 persons per room—the difference is very considerable. As far as tenure is concerned, West Indian households in the 'dispersed' areas are likelier to be owner-occupiers (54 per cent to 30 per cent in 'concentrated' areas) and are less likely (21·3 per cent to 43·1 per cent) to be in furnished accommodation. In 'dispersed' boroughs only 28 per cent of persons in West Indian households are sharing compared to 69 per cent in the 'concentrated' boroughs. Finally, if we look at their employment status, the individuals concerned tend to be drawn to a great extent from non-manual occupations; 19 per cent of men in 'dispersed' boroughs as opposed to 7 per cent in 'concentrated' boroughs fall into this category. The disparity is even more striking for women—60 per cent as opposed to 26 per cent.

TABLE 2

Proportion of households where head was born in the West Indies living at different densities (persons per room).

Persons per room	Concentrated boroughs	Dispersed boroughs
under 0·5	4	15
0·5	15	23
0·75—0·99	8	14
1·00	27	22
1·01—1·50	20	16
over 1·50	26	10

Notes and Sources: as for Table 1.

There are at least two reasons for challenging the common view that the situation should be allowed to work itself out. The first is that the identification in the minds of the white majority between colour, poor housing conditions, and a squalid environment, is constantly reinforced as long as concentration, in the inner city, persists and even increases. If it were the case that viable coloured quarters could be created without those attendant circumstances—a brown Golders Green, for the sake of argument—then such concentrations are cause for no more than mild concern. But the reinforcement of aversion created by this identification on the part of the majority will make it progressively more difficult for those who wish to leave to do so. The situation is therefore not a static one.

Moreover, decisions about dispersal will inevitably appear on the agenda of local authorities, whether they like it or not, as long as the tendency persists for residential accommodation in the city centre to come into public ownership by one route or another. Whenever local authorities are presented—as they are in the present system—with the task of clearing areas with substantial immigrant settlement, rehabilitating houses in immigrant occupation, and rehousing black applicants from the housing list—and there are signs of an increasing tendency, at least, on the part of West Indians to try for Council accommodation (see, for example, Daniel, 1968)—housing authorities will need to have a clear idea of what line to take on the question of dispersal.

In the past, the tendency has been to break up existing homogeneous communities and substitute a discreet degree of dispersal, without benefit of records. As the County Councils Association puts it, in their evidence to the Cullingworth Committee 'immigrant families should not be encouraged to congregate in "pockets", but councils should recognise that they will not wish to be completely isolated from their own community.' This policy (if it can be so described) has been tempered in some cases by a caution about the allocation of too many units in high-status post-war council accommodation to highly visible newcomers; the risks attached to provoking a hostile response from present or potential white council tenants have been very much in the minds of such authorities (Burney, 1968).

An opposite tendency has been detectable in other spheres of local authority activity. For example, it has been suggested that the public health powers available to authorities, particularly those relating to multi-occupation, have been used in an attempt to confine disadvantaged minorities to certain restricted areas (Rex and Moore, 1967). In the allocation of mortgage funds some local authorities are also prone to the view (held as an article of faith by most estate agents) that certain areas are 'suitable' for coloured settlement and others are not. Such authorities tend to be in some difficulty when assistance is sought for Housing Associations, which now exist in most areas of substantial immigrant settlement, and do not necessarily accept these criteria.

This uncertainty—sometimes amounting to downright contradiction—in the approach to the problem adopted by local authorities is of vital significance, coming as it does from those who occupy a central position in the operation of what Elizabeth Burney calls 'the clumsy strings of the housing market' (Burney, 1968).

As the Cullingworth Committee acknowledged, there is still insufficient information on which to give advice which will apply to all the wide variety of circumstances that are likely to arise in this country in the immediately foreseeable future. Nor is it yet necessary to contemplate the kind of drastic steps that Anthony Downs recommends in his searching examination of the policy options open to American society (Downs, 1968). Downs argues that if present policies are not significantly amended there is a strong possibility of a catastrophe which the United States could not survive in any recognizable form. After reviewing the alternative strategies open to the Administration—a choice between concentration and dispersal in broad terms, together with supplementary choices between an option for integration or segregation within smaller communal units, and between enrichment and non-enrichment in the provision of services—Downs opts for dispersal, coupled with a degree of separatism in small units, and underpinned by enrichment. He concludes that such a policy of dispersal into suburban areas could only become viable if it were promoted by means of inducements to communities prepared to accept the movement of minorities into their area, as well as to the minorities themselves. A large-scale injection of Federal funds into such communities, and preferential treatment in the allocation of new resources (for example, Federal installations providing additional employment), are the chief inducements contemplated. It does not need much imagination to forecast the kind of objections, from vested interest of all kinds, that such proposals would evoke.

Yet without resorting to this kind of extreme measure, there is none the less a case for re-examining, as Downs has done, the range of alternatives open to central government and the means available for achieving them. Such re-examination would require substantial original research, but in approaching these alternatives, there is some coherent advice that can be given. First, that the case for dispersal is not merely official rhetoric, but involves practical benefits both for individuals (in terms of both their life-chances and those of their children) and for the minorities as a whole. Equally, the supportive value of concentration seems clear, especially for those groups with problems of communication—social and linguistic problems in particular. The fact that areas of concentration still tend to be multi-class areas, providing a range of skills and potential leaders not found in one-class districts, is also a factor to be weighed in their favour. The virtues of the coloured quarter as a power base for political activity, in the style recommended by Stokely Carmichael and Charles V. Hamilton (Carmichael and Hamilton, 1968), are more dubious—especially while geographical concentrations of coloured minorities in Britain continue to be relatively low. Nor is it clear that the consequences of liberating the coloured quarters, if that could be achieved, and seizing the levers of power, would necessarily rebound to the long-term benefit of the minorities concerned. All the evidence suggests that the factor of colour—blackness, if you prefer—is not in itself yet a sufficient basis for creating variable separate communities. The creation of a 'half-way' house situation permitting entry into the majority society on terms that will not constitute a lasting handicap seems to be the realistic maximum that can be achieved from this approach.

The key to the situation lies in the factor of choice. While minorities desire special facilities which can only be provided in areas of high concentration, those facilities should as far as possible be made available. But equally it is essential to ensure that those benefits of diversity provided by dispersal and integration are simultaneously open to those who want them. A separation that closes the options is to be avoided at all costs. For ultimately the issue resolves itself into the question of whether integration (pluralistic integration, in the Jenkins definition, not the confused notion of assimilation that still swims at the back of many politicians' minds) is still a feasible goal. The acid test of whether it can be achieved is whether it is wanted, by minority and majority alike. And despite a good deal of windy talk on both sides of the colour line, the best evidence is that integration is still desired. That being so, all of those concerned with policy in this field have a responsibility to try and determine how it can best be achieved. This paper is not intended to provide any final answers to the immensely complex questions involved but rather to raise the issues in a form that may stimulate further discussion.

ACKNOWLEDGEMENTS

The basic data for the Tables are derived from the special tabulations of 1966 Census data by the Greater London Council, Research and Intelligence Unit. The authors wish to acknowledge the making of these data available to them, and wish to state that the responsibility for any interpretation is theirs, and not that of the GLC. They also acknowledge the help of Trevor Williams and Alan Marsh in processing these Tables.

REFERENCES

Burney, Elizabeth, 1968, *Housing on Trial* (Oxford University Press for the Institute of Race Relations, London).

Carmichael, S., Hamilton, C. V., 1968, *Black Power* (Penguin, London).

Cullingworth, J. B. (Chairman), 1969, *Council Housing: Purposes, Procedures and Priorities.* The Ninth report of the Housing Management Sub-Committee of the Central Housing Advisory Committee, Ministry and Local Government (HMSO, London).

Daniel, W. W., 1968, *Racial Discrimination in England* (Penguin, London).

Deakin, N., with Cohen, B. and McNeal, J., 1970, *Colour, Citizenship and British Society* (Panther, London).

Department of Education and Science, 1965, 'The education of immigrants', Circular 7/65, June (D.E.S., London).

Doherty, J., 1969, 'The distribution and concentration of immigrants in London', *Race Today,* 1, No. 8 (December), 227–32.

Downs, A., 1968, 'Alternative futures for the American ghetto', *Daedalus,* 97, No. 4 (Fall), 1331–78.

Peach, C., 1968, *West Indian Migration to Britain* (Oxford University Press for the Institute of Race Relations, London).

Pettigrew, T. F., 1969, 'Racially separated or together', *Journal of Social Issues,* 25, No. 1. 43–69.

Rex, J., Moore, R., 1967, *Race, Community and Conflict* (Oxford University Press for the Institute of Race Relations, London).

US Commission on Civil Rights, 1967, 'Racial isolation in the public schools' (Washington, DC).

US Department of Health, Education and Welfare, 1966. The Coleman report: 'Equality of educational opportunity' (Washington, DC).

22.   OPPORTUNITY AND AFFLUENCE

E. M. Rawstron and B. E. Coates

Prospects for Employment[1]

Just as a child's education prospects vary from one district to another, so also do his prospects for type of employment and size of income when he leaves school. If he is willing to move and knows where to go, his opportunities increase. If he is reluctant to move, then they are circumscribed by the place in which he lives. Some places are good, some bad, and some indifferent, for there is in the United Kingdom a range from high incomes and high diversity of employment in some districts to low incomes and low diversity in others. But income is not always related to degree of diversity, and low earned incomes are not by any means a sure sign of local economic specialization. Nevertheless, places characterized by specialization are less secure and more restricted environments in which to begin working life than are diversified places.

In the United Kingdom about 7 per cent of the working population is employed by primary industries such as agriculture, mining, fishing, and forestry; about 36 per cent are in secondary industries comprising the manufacturing and processing sector; 57 per cent are in tertiary industries including transport, the utilities, wholesale and retail distribution, construction, finance, the professions, and public administration.

Opportunity for employment varies considerably over the country from a high degree of limited and narrow specialization in a declining group of industries in some places to highly diverse employment in flourishing manufacturing and service industries, notably in South East England. Lack of varied opportunity for employment restricts the local social environment, and it can also lead to the suppression of many talents, which may remain for ever latent and wasted.

If a school-leaver decides to stay and work in any of the following places—and there are many more like them—it means that he is severely limiting his employment opportunities: Bradford, where 31 per cent of employment is in textiles, mainly wool; Sheffield (30 per cent in metal trades); Stoke-on-Trent (34 per cent in ceramics); Kettering—Wellingborough—Rushden (36 per cent in clothing, mainly footwear); Luton and Dunstable (32 per cent in vehicles); Holland, Lincolnshire (32 per cent in agriculture); Dundee (21 per cent in textiles, mainly jute), or Barrow (40 per cent in shipbuilding and marine engineering).

These are not necessarily bad places in an absolute sense. Their restricted opportunities may provide reasonable security, tolerable prospects, and adequate income. But they are bad in a comparative sense, and because they cater inefficiently for the wide range of potential talents of their inhabitants. As a class of town, they are likelier to lose population to areas with better opportunities and to attract population only on a selective basis. Thus Bradford would attract those seeking employment in wool if the industry were expanding, and Luton does attract workers to its motor industry which is a growing and prosperous trade.

[1] This article first appeared in the *Guardian,* 26 July 1965.
From *Geography*, 51 (1966), 1–15. Reprinted by permission of the authors and The Geographical Association.

In contrast, because opportunities are excellent, there is no general incentive on grounds of employment to leave Greater London, though other centrifugal forces do operate in a small way. London offers the best opportunities for many reasons. Employment in manufacturing approximates to the national average and is extremely diverse, and this diversity contains a higher proportion of expanding trades than elsewhere. The most rapidly expanding sector of all in the national economy is the service or tertiary sector, and of this London has more than its fair share. Moreover, a great deal of employment classed as manufacturing in London is office employment which in effect augments the expanding tertiary sector. Finally, security is high and incomes are above the national average in the Civil Service whose better-paid jobs are concentrated in London.

The employment structure makes people want to remain in London and induces others to seek work there. Thus people with a wide range of aptitudes and skills are drawn from the rest of the United Kingdom and from abroad. London's pre-eminence is bad for the country since it saps the strength of many other districts, causes the partial neglect of their resources, and lacks the benefit of the healthy competition of a rival within the United Kingdom. New York has several rivals within the United States of America; Tokio does not dominate Japan; West Germany has no London at all; Rome is not the only major centre in Italy; and Paris, which certainly dominates France, now faces competition from other centres in the Common Market.

Between the supposed good of London and the supposed bad of Londonderry or Dundee lie degrees of indifference. The West Midland Conurbation and the cities of Leicester and Nottingham present the best employment structures and opportunities outside London. They are diversified, though less so than London, and the major elements in their diversity flourish. They lack London's wealth of opportunity for service employment but provide an ample range of good jobs for those who wish to work on the shop-floor.

The national employment magnet thus has two poles, of which the south is the more powerful and concentrated. The weaker and more diffuse north pole functions between the Chilterns and the Trent, but more selectively with regard to employment and its ability strongly to attract population than does the south pole. Birmingham is a workshop, not a metropolis, more like a Pittsburgh or a Detroit than a Chicago or a Los Angeles.

Leeds is similar to Birmingham in its wide diversity and is better as a centre of service employment; but neighbouring towns in West Yorkshire fret under a blanket of wool. There is no rapid decline, but little advance. The industry is profitable for its owners and provides a reasonable living for its workers. There are few incentives to greater effort and the local range of opportunity is poor. But if London or the Midlands are out of reach, commuting to Leeds serves fairly well instead.

Glasgow and Clydeside have great diversity and yet the employment structure must be deemed very indifferent indeed; for, unlike Birmingham, their diversity has the appearance of a remnant sale, full of discontinued lines. New lines are introduced from time to time, but not at the required rate. This area is indifferent to bad in the opportunity it offers.

Manchester and its satellites are simply indifferent. Cotton has declined but is steadily and fairly adequately replaced. Diversity increases, and Manchester has more service employment (62 per cent) than Birmingham (43 per cent), but well-paid jobs are generally less plentiful in the Manchester region.

Other parts of the United Kingdom could be similarly classified according to the

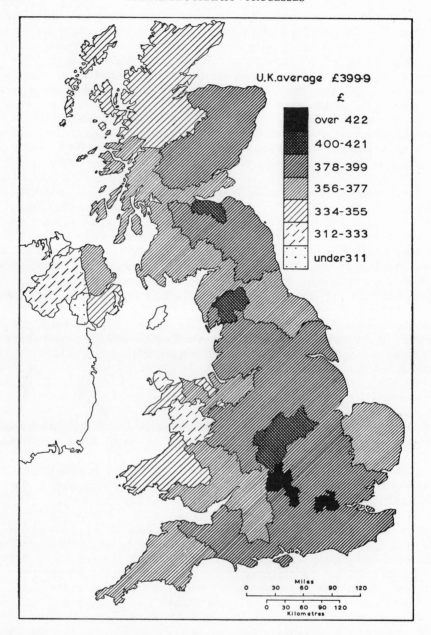

U.K.average £399·9

£

over 422
400-421
378-399
356-377
334-355
312-333
under 311

Miles
0   30   60   90   120

0   30   60   90 120
Kilometres

Figs. 1 and 2. *Affluence on the Move:* the distribution of total net incomes (before deduction of tax)—earned and unearned—in 1949–50 *(left)* compared with 1959–60 *(right)*. On each map the two top categories represent incomes above the national average. The relative prosperity of Northern Ireland, most of Scotland, and

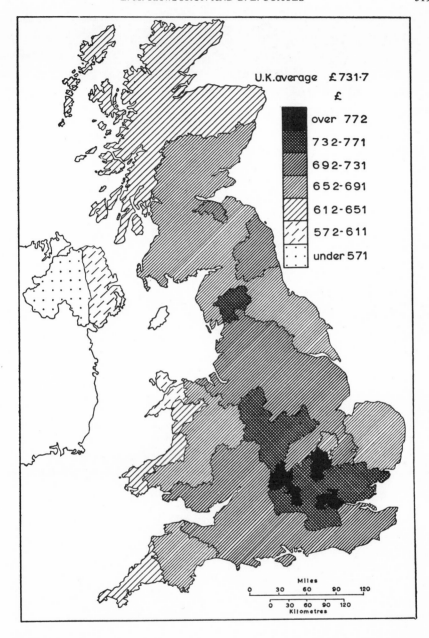

Caernarvonshire and Cornwall, among other counties, declined. South Wales, Staffordshire and South-east England were among the areas which improved their relative positions. (Data refer to place of work.)

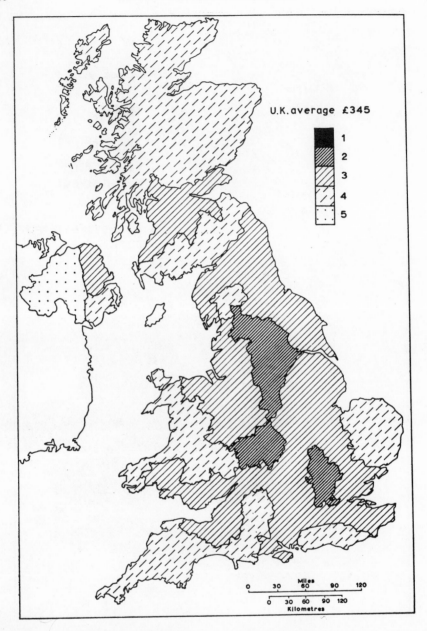

Figs. 3 and 4. *The Shifting Power to Earn:* the distribution of wages and salaries (Schedule 'E') incomes in 1949–50 *(left)* and in 1959–60*(right)*. Wage-earners in the West Riding, Worcester, Shropshire and Perth, for example, were relatively worse off in 1959–60; those in Flint, Glamorgan, Monmouth, Stafford, Leicester and the South-east were relatively better off. National average schedule 'E' income

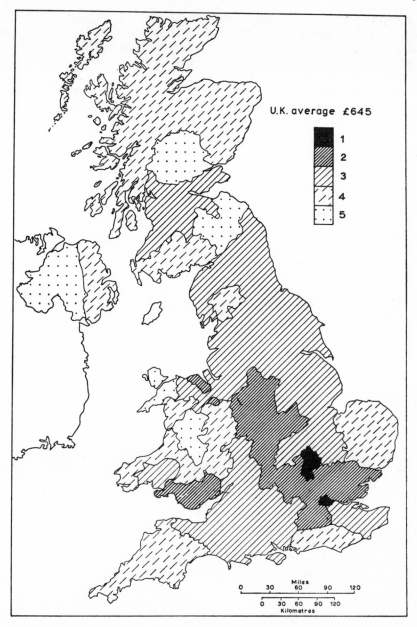

U.K. average £645

was £345 in 1949–50 and £645 in 1959–60. Key: (1) more than 10 per cent above national average; (2) up to 10 per cent above national average; (3) 0–10 per cent below national average; (4) 10–20 per cent below national average; (5) more than 20 per cent below national average. (Data refer to place of work.)

opportunities they offer for employment. But the main point must already stand out that the best area at present lies between London and the Trent, and that the quality of opportunity declines outwards from this 'magnetic' area. At least two hopeful signs for improvement can be discerned. One is the success achieved during the past 15 years in replacing cotton by other enterprises in Lancashire. The other, which perhaps gives even more cause for optimism, is the quiet revolution that has occurred in South Wales, converting a very narrowly specialized economy in extraordinarily difficult natural and social conditions into one that is diverse beyond the hopes of the greatest optimist of 30 years ago.

Variations in Income[2]

Prospects for a good income vary from district to district as do those of employment. Although the available information from annual reports of the Commissioners for Inland Revenue is less detailed than for employment, the patterns of income are striking and correspond in large measure to many of the facts known about the distribution of employment.

The mean income of those who were subject to deduction of tax in the United Kingdom in 1959–60—the latest detailed information shown on Fig. 2—was £732. This had risen by 1962–3 to £853, but no county data are available for that year.

The range was from £524 in Armagh, £645 in Argyll and Bute, £579 in Anglesey, and £642 in Cornwall to £787 in Bedfordshire, £784 in Middlesex, £874 in the old County of London, and £1158 in the City of London itself. Counties with a mean above that for the United Kingdom were concentrated, apart from Westmorland, in a belt from Surrey and Essex north-westwards to Staffordshire and Leicestershire. The anomaly of Westmorland is explained by the unusually high proportion of Schedule 'D' (profits and professional earnings) and investment income returned there. Otherwise, incomes declined consistently away from the South East and Midlands except for Northumberland and Midlothian. When it is borne in mind that these county statistics exclude civil servants and pensioners of the Crown, whose combined average income of £840 was well above the national mean, the dominance of the South East and London in particular is even stronger.

Between 1950 and 1960 Northern Ireland and much of Scotland showed a marked relative decline, whereas there were increases in several parts of Wales (compare Fig. 2 with Fig. 1). The striking change in England was the building up of the area of high average incomes between London and the Midlands. It is not surprising that, as incomes have grown in this area, few people have been induced to leave it, and many have moved in from less prosperous districts.

Most people depend mainly upon Schedule 'E' earnings. They pay as they earn and have few investments or other income than a wage or a salary. The pattern of Schedule 'E' earnings (Fig. 4) and the changes that have occurred since 1949 (compare Fig. 3 with Fig. 4) are of greater general and social interest than data for personal incomes from all sources. Categories 1 and 2 on both maps indicate areas where average wages and salaries exceeded the national averages of £645 in 1959–60 and £345 in 1949–50.

Once more it is clear that there has been a shift during the decade towards a concentration of high average earnings along the London-Birmingham axis. But the significance of the upgrading of South Wales should not be overlooked. As with employment, there is hope also in South Wales for incomes. What has been achieved there should be feasible elsewhere.

There is no doubt, however, that the best opportunities for high wages and salaries are now to be found in the large area extending from Derbyshire, Leicestershire, and the West Midlands to Essex and Surrey.

Just over 15 per cent of taxable incomes exceeded £1,000 in the United Kingdom in 1959–60; but London had 23 per cent while the City of London had 34 per cent. The City had more personal incomes over £1,000 than the whole of Wales, and almost as many over £5,000 as Wales and Scotland added together. Yet there were only 353,000 taxpayers in the City compared with 2,762,000 in Scotland and Wales. There were 56,000 personal incomes over £1,500 in the City compared with £48,000 in the whole of the West Riding.

These are extreme examples which serve only to highlight the contrasts that exist over the United Kingdom. A more realistic index is the fact that the continuous area (marked 'very high' on Fig. 5) of London, Middlesex, Surrey, Berkshire, Buckinghamshire, and Oxfordshire exceeds the national proportion of incomes over £1,000 according to place of work. The extra purchasing power thus created is spread over the more well-to-do residential areas of South East England.

Adjacent to the 'very high' area are two groups of counties—Essex, Hertfordshire, Bedfordshire; and Warwickshire, Staffordshire, Leicestershire, and Worcestershire—with an excess of incomes between £800 and £1,500. These seven counties are areas where manufacturing flourishes and work on the shop-floor brings a high return. Taken together with the 'very high' group of counties including London, they form the magnet for opportunities for both income and employment in Britain.

The remaining areas, apart from Flintshire, have an excess of 'medium', 'low', or 'very low' incomes. Particularly notable is the 'low' category for central Scotland which does not match up to the industrial regions of England and Wales. The greatest excess of very low incomes occurs in Northern Ireland where Armagh, Fermanagh, Londonderry, and Tyrone have more than 70 per cent of personal incomes under £600 compared with a national figure of 48 per cent. Indeed, Fermanagh has 77 per cent.

Among the poorer parts of the United Kingdom there were, however, some indications of wealth apart from that brought in by commuters who worked in neighbouring counties. Sussex, Cambridge, Gloucester, Hereford, Dorset, and Somerset returned more than the national proportion of incomes over £1,500, as did certain counties of mid-Wales. In Scotland the same could be said of Perthshire, the Border Counties, and Midlothian. Westmorland was unique in having excessive numbers of incomes at the extremes, namely, over £1,500 and under £400.

But there are no such redeeming features in Northern Ireland, North and south-west Wales, Cornwall and Devon, the East and North Ridings, Norfolk, Suffolk, and the parts of Scotland not mentioned in the preceding paragraph. Without doubt Northern Ireland as a whole has least of all to offer in opportunity for income and employment.

One final point must be made about affluence. Since 1961–2 relief has been given for the lower ranges of surtax on earned income. A far greater proportion of this bonus must have become available for spending in the London area than elsewhere. Thus has the effective affluence of South East England been appreciably increased by a stroke of a Chancellor's pen, even since the 1959–60 survey of personal incomes.

London Against the Regions

Opportunities for a wide range of employment and high incomes largely coincide

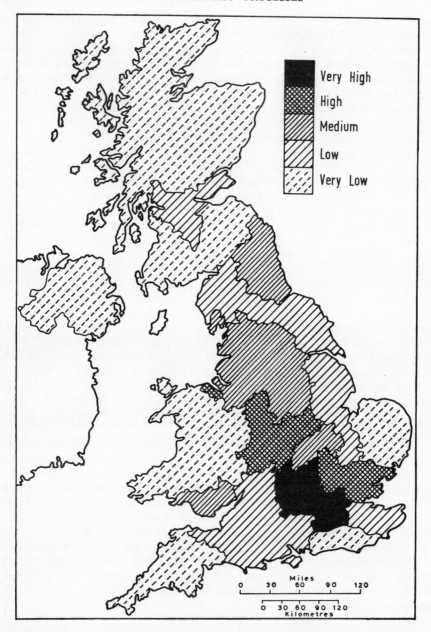

Fig. 5. *The Affluent Places*, 1959–60: regional grades of affluence, ranging from a proportional excess of 'very high' incomes in one area to an excess of 'very low' incomes in seven areas. Northern Ireland has the largest proportion of 'very low' incomes. Lancashire and the West Riding, for example, have a slight excess of 'medium' incomes. London has a large excess of 'very high' incomes. (Data refer to place of work.)

regionally within the United Kingdom. The magnet of employment, polarized between London and the Trent, is also the magnet of income. No kind of national plan can be socially or even economically sound unless adequate account is taken of these facts, especially when they are linked to the renewed upward trend in the rate of population increase, the persistence of inflation and the underuse of parts of the nation's resources.

The magnetism and internal problems of the area of greatest opportunity for employment and incomes in Britain sap the strength of the country quite unnecessarily, and this adverse effect seems likely to intensify. The social injustice so clearly portrayed by the Schedule 'E' map for 1959–60 is in itself a sufficient case for policies aimed at a more even spread of wealth, and for action to resuscitate run-down environments in those districts where the legacies of nineteenth-century development and economic specialization dominate the social scene. But there are other, and perhaps stronger arguments.

First, there is the suppression and draining-off of talents resulting from differential environmental influences. The alternative for potentially able people in poor environments is either to leave them for better, or to take jobs locally that do not give full scope to ability. The former is an inefficient selective process, but it is effective enough to skim off some of the cream. The latter alternative is simply wasteful.

Secondly, the magnetism of the affluent area imposes a harmful geographical distortion upon the national economy. The trend towards proportionately more and more people with higher and higher incomes in metropolitan England reinforces the accepted inflationary factors that do not so strikingly differentiate between areas. The harmful effects of the affluent area are twofold. There is a tendency to augment the forces that put up the price of labour, both throughout the country, for which London is the pace-setter for many basic wage and salary agreements, and locally through extra payments made necessary because of competition between employers for labour. There is also a tendency to raise the prices of those goods and services that are produced in London and that have high labour or high land components, because of the large geographical distortion that London creates in costs of labour and land. Furthermore, the comparative affluence of the huge market in the London area gives greater scope to pricing policies based on the ability and willingness of the customer to pay; in short, to careless expenditure. For 'postalized' items, for which the same price is charged throughout the country, this factor may well be relevant to general price increases in these commodities.

There are forces operating to mitigate these ill effects and to justify higher wages and salaries in London. For example, the incentive to save labour is stronger and the feasibility of achieving economies of scale is greater. The cost of living is higher. But none of these is adequate to justify a *laissez-faire* attitude. And, in relation to the pattern of incomes, the cost-of-living argument is probably overrated. Apart from obvious items such as housing, land, commuting, and second-hand cars, all of which cost more in London, there are many items in the ordinary weekly budget that are probably dearer outside London, and many are the same wherever they are purchased in Britain. Sound evidence on geographical variations in the prices of consumer goods is, however, lacking. Moreover, incomes are high between the Chilterns and the Trent where the cost-of-living argument could not be used in justification.

The strength of the foregoing argument depends on the quality and quantity of available data. More refined information not only on employment and incomes but on geographical variations in the cost of living, profits and costs of individual industries, productivity of labour, and the economy in general, is needed to permit sounder measurements and conclusions to be made about variations from place to place within the United Kingdom. Otherwise regional and national economic planning will be undertaken blindly, and the prices and incomes policy, as well as the national plan, will miscarry. The authors are aware of a number of defects in the information that they have been obliged to use. It is the best that they and probably the Government have available; for in Britain, where planning has long been attempted, far fewer local and regional statistics are collected and published than in the free-enterprise United States of America.

Proposals

The metropolitan region has been turned into the inflation-leader for the country. Just as the supermarket runs loss-leaders to attract trade, so the United Kingdom is running a localized and powerful inflation-leader which raises prices, costs, and incomes generally throughout the country. A prices, incomes, and productivity policy for the national economy is an alternative to periodic devaluation and balance-of-payments crises. It is an attempt to give us an edge over our overseas competitors and the ability to pay our way in the world. But as a broad-spectrum antibiotic to cure many ills throughout the national system, it will prove specifically ineffective against London as a primary source of infection for the general inflationary disease. One has also the feeling that many in London are beset by the apathy of affluence, and that London's monopoly of leadership infects the whole country with this disease.

Metropolitan Centres

Thus a national plan is needed not only to stabilize prices and incomes and to increase productivity, but also to diminish the inflationary and complacent ill effects of the affluent area of metropolitan England and, at the same time, to cope with the expected increase in the population of the United Kingdom. The necessary cure is to make a start on two new and well-planned Londons elsewhere as quickly as possible. If, as seems likely, room for the equivalent for some 15 additional towns the size of Birmingham has to be found by the turn of the century, surely two new metropolitan centres could be created during this period to reduce the magnetism of London; to increase the spread of wealth and opportunity, and to restore the competition which existed at least between Manchester and London during the second half of the nineteenth century. Each of these metropolitan centres might aim at populations of at least 3 millions and each should have its own 'City', West End, theatreland, etc.[3] Osaka was once called the Manchester of Japan; the converse is now required. We need at least one Osaka in Britain, more than 150 miles from London. By these means the pressure will also be removed from London, and the problems of planning the capital itself will be eased.

Several locations are feasible for new Londons, including a refurbished Manchester and Glasgow, a greatly expanded Edinburgh, Metropolitan Humberside or Tyneside. Even 'Rhubarb-land' in West Yorkshire would serve. Whatever the choice, it is certain that all the old nineteenth-century towns will have to be gutted and rebuilt before A.D. 2000. To choose two of the outlying conurbations for conversion to metropolitan status during this process would be quite feasible given a determined lead from the central Government.

The physical reconstruction is a small task in comparison with the social, economic, and political difficulties that will arise in convincing those involved that a drastic rearrangement within the United Kingdom is necessary. But without such a rearrangement, inflation and apathy will continue until the ill effects of present trends in the affluent area bring on a persistent depression, marking the transition to national senile decay.

New Londons will not be enough. The creation of new and expanded towns will also be needed, as far away from London as can reasonably be contrived. Plymouth and somewhere in Cornwall, Pembroke and Cardiganshire, the Welsh Marches, and even Lleyn, Solway and south-western Scotland, Inverness, and Northern Ireland could all receive a quota. *Rapprochement* and agreement with Southern Ireland would be of great mutual benefit, for there is no larger wastage of resources and potential amenities in the British Isles than has been contrived by history in Ireland.

Practical Difficulties

It may be argued that to set up new metropolitan centres and to enlarge many towns as growth points is all very well in theory, but it will not work in practice for three main reasons. First, most of us like to be left undisturbed. We prefer the routine, the devils we know, and the security of the present to promises for the future. Secondly, most of the top decision-takers and top people prefer either to live in South East England, in or fairly near London, or to seek seclusion in some area like the Scottish Borders where they may remain undisturbed. Thirdly, management wishes to work no harder than it need and have ready access to what it deems are the good things of life.

The first preserves our 'Coronation Streets'. The second either augments the effect of the third, for top managers are top people, or indicates withdrawal from the unequal struggle. The third is crucial, for it is management which takes locational decisions for the rest of us to follow. Notwithstanding the restrictions of Industrial Development Certificates, the belated embargo on office building in Greater London and the normal planning procedures applicable to any economic enterprise, management has had a pretty clear run. Yet isolated locations are considered irksome. Distance from London is deemed a nuisance for both economic and social reasons, while distance from Birmingham is viewed as a nuisance simply from the supposed economic standpoint.

This inconvenience or nuisance factor makes for managerial errors, and thus diseconomies, and for harder work. It encourages the acceptance of the *status quo*; for moving to a location outside the magnet of employment and income involves changes in the work pattern, because more intricate forward planning of both supplies of materials and deliveries of product to market has to be arranged at a distant location than in a great commercial agglomeration like London. Personal contact, except by telephone, cannot be so easily maintained.

Swings and Roundabouts

Greater costs arising from a changed location would for most enterprises be offset by advantages accruing from the change, for what they might lose on the roundabout of transport they would more than gain on the swings of lower wages, reduced pressure for increases, cheaper land and buildings, space, lack of congestion, and readier access in many parts of the United Kingdom to open country that is far more plentiful and more attractive than almost anything in South East England or the Midlands.

Given new metropolitan centres within reach, pleasing architecture in the town chosen for the new location, and good transport and communications to other parts, there is no sizeable obstacle to a policy for redistributing secondary and much of tertiary industry, apart from the urgent need to convince managements of the benefits to be gained thereby.

The 'Coronation Street' mentality plays its part in the lives of management as well as labour, and only the Government can act effectively on the scale required and in the time available to dispel it before the damage is too great. The measure of the will of past Governments to act is seen in Lytham St. Annes, Newcastle, Cardiff, Chesterfield, and other places to which Departments have been sent. Far better than remodelling Whitehall would be the total removal of the central Government to locations outside London—the core to Windsor, and routine departments right outside the present magnet.

Equality of opportunity has been a conventionally accepted goal towards which we have long been moving by degrees. Unless the pace is stepped up and the emphasis changed from individual equality to geographical equality, we shall be in sorrier straits long before the century is out. To achieve a more equitable spread of opportunity, it is necessary for the Government and all sections of industry to shift their emphasis from the individual as a person irrespective of where he lives and works to the individual in his geographical and, in the widest sense, environmental setting. Inequality of opportunity is a sufficient evil in itself to warrant vigorous action. When, additionally, it imperils the welfare of all sectors of the community, even of the sector that is more equal than others, it reflects not only the ineptitude of past Governments, but short-sighted selfishness among leaders of commerce and industry.